WALKING IN GRACE

2023

Formerly *Daily Guideposts*
New name…same inspiration

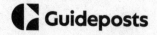

Acknowledgments

Every attempt has been made to credit the sources of copyrighted material used in this book. If any such acknowledgment has been inadvertently omitted or miscredited, receipt of such information would be appreciated.

Scripture quotations marked (CEB) are taken from the *Common English Bible*. Copyright © 2011 by Common English Bible.

Scripture quotations marked (CEV) are taken from *Holy Bible: Contemporary English Version*. Copyright © 1995 American Bible Society.

Scripture quotations marked (CSB) are taken from *The Christian Standard Bible*. Copyright © 2017 by Holman Bible Publishers. Used by permission.

Scripture quotations marked (ESV) are taken from the *Holy Bible, English Standard Version*. Copyright © 2001 by Crossway Bibles, a division of Good News Publishers. Used by permission. All rights reserved.

Scripture quotations marked (GNT) are taken from the *Holy Bible, Good News Translation*. Copyright © 1992 by American Bible Society.

Scripture quotations marked (GW) are taken from *GOD'S WORD Translation*. Copyright © 1995 by God's Word to the Nations. Used by permission of Baker Publishing Group.

Scripture quotations marked (ICB) are taken from *The Holy Bible, International Children's Bible®*. Copyright © 1986, 1988, 1999, 2015 by Tommy Nelson™, a division of Thomas Nelson. Used by permission.

Scripture quotations marked (ISV) are taken from *The International Standard Version of the Bible*. Copyright © 1995–2014 by ISV Foundation. All rights reserved internationally. Used by permission of Davidson Press, LLC.

Scripture quotations marked (JPS) are taken from *Tanakh: A New Translation of the Holy Scriptures according to the Traditional Hebrew Text*. Copyright © 1985 by the Jewish Publication Society. All rights reserved.

Scripture quotations marked (KJV) are taken from the *King James Version of the Bible*.

Scripture quotations marked (MSG) are taken from *The Message*. Copyright © 1993, 1994, 1995, 1996, 2000, 2001, 2002 by Eugene H. Peterson.

Scripture quotations marked (NASB and NASB1995) are taken from the *New American Standard Bible*. Copyright © 1960, 1962, 1963, 1968, 1971, 1972, 1973, 1975, 1977, 1995 by The Lockman Foundation, La Habra, California. Used by permission.

Scripture quotations marked (NCV) are taken from *The Holy Bible, New Century Version*. Copyright © 2005 by Thomas Nelson.

Scripture quotations marked (NIV) are taken from *The Holy Bible, New International Version*. Copyright © 1973, 1978, 1984, 2011 by Biblica, Inc. Used by permission of Zondervan. All rights reserved worldwide. zondervan.com

Scripture quotations marked (NKJV) are taken from *The Holy Bible, New King James Version*. Copyright © 1982 by Thomas Nelson.

Scripture quotations marked (NLT) are taken from the *Holy Bible, New Living Translation*. Copyright © 1996, 2004, 2007 by Tyndale House Foundation. Used by permission of Tyndale House Publishers Inc., Carol Stream, Illinois. All rights reserved.

Scripture quotations marked (NLV) are from the *New Life Bible*. Copyright © 1969 by Christian Literature International. Used by permission. All rights reserved.

Scripture quotations marked (NRSV) are taken from the *New Revised Standard Version Bible*. Copyright © 1989 by the Division of Christian Education of the National Council of the Churches of Christ in the United States of America. Used by permission. All rights reserved.

Scripture quotations marked (TLB) are taken from *The Living Bible*. Copyright © 1971 by Tyndale House Publishers, Inc., Carol Stream, Illinois. All rights reserved.

Cover and interior design by Müllerhaus
Cover photo by Shutterstock.
Monthly page opener photos by iStockPhoto (pp. 135, 303, 337, 370) and Pixabay (pp. 1, 35, 66, 100, 169, 202, 237, 270)
Indexed by Kelly White
Typeset by Aptara

Printed and bound in the United States of America
10 9 8 7 6 5 4 3 2 1

Dear Friends,

Welcome to *Walking in Grace 2023*, formerly *Daily Guideposts*—the same authors and inspirational content that our long-time fans have always enjoyed, now with a new title. We are so happy to welcome long-time and new readers to a year filled with inspiring reflections and praise to God. *Walking in Grace 2023* is filled with 365 all-new devotions designed to inspire you to live your everyday life closer to God's heart, encouraged and joyful, as you are surrounded by a faithful community of writers and readers who are united in their love of and belief in God.

The theme for *Walking in Grace* this year is "Filled with Praise," based on Psalm 95:1–2, "Come, let us sing for joy to the LORD; let us shout aloud to the Rock of our salvation. Let us come before him with thanksgiving and extol him with music and song." Whether we endured hardship or basked in blessings this year, we found ourselves focusing on God's goodness, making a joyful noise to the Lord, thanking and praising Him.

In an uncertain world, God's Word and love for His children remain steadfast and unchanging. Our fifty-one writers turned to Him this year—to His peace, wisdom, joy, and love.

Edward Grinnan shares how God uses his golden retriever, Gracie, to teach him to wait upon the Lord during uncertain times; Erin Janoso tells us how she was able to use anger to fuel graceful, Spirit-led work in her community; Rick Hamlin remembers a time his nephew inspired his family to be still before the Lord and listen to Him during a hike through the Appalachian Trail; Roberta Messner thanks God for the time a funny footwear malfunction turned into an opportunity to share her faith; Julia Attaway shares about a daily walk she takes through the Cloisters Museum, saying thank you to God for beauty she knows is there even when she cannot see it; Marci Alborghetti delights with a story about God working through her when she (and her husband) least expected it; God uses a funny technology mishap at church to bring joy and mirth to Daniel Schantz; and many more.

We have seven special series for you this year. Penney Schwab shares the story of the passing of her late husband, Don, and her grief journey in "A Lifetime of Love." Ashley Kappel reflects upon the blessing and work of caregiving in "Building Cathedrals." Pam Kidd recalls time after time—through finding her way home in a foreign city to inspiring acts of service her friends perform—that God has used different people and circumstances to point the way back to Himself in her inspired series "The Pink House." We join Marilyn Turk in her poignant series as she experiences a new life transition, "Letting Go" of her grandson Logan as he moves out of her home. Stephanie Thompson shares a personal and fascinating series entitled "Hymns of Praise" that includes the backstory of many well-known and beloved hymns. We are blessed to have Patricia Lorenz guide us through Holy Week this year in her series "Resurrection Joy." Erin MacPherson shares from the heart in her uplifting series for Advent, "A Simple Christmas."

This year, we are pleased to welcome two new writers into the fold: J. Brent Bill and Gabrielle Meyer. We are delighted they are joining us. We also want to say a fond and happy "Welcome back!" to Bill Giovannetti, who has returned this year.

We pray God's blessings upon you as you begin this new year, filled up with praise for all He is doing and all He will do.

Faithfully yours,
The Editors of Guideposts

P.S. We love hearing from you! We read every letter we receive. Let us know what *Walking in Grace* means to you by emailing <u>WIGEditors@guideposts.org</u> or writing to Guideposts Books & Inspirational Media, 100 Reserve Road, Suite E200, Danbury, CT 06810. You can also keep up with your *Walking in Grace* friends on facebook.com/DailyDevofromGP.

Going Digital? Especially for You!

Get one-year instant access to the digital edition of *Walking in Grace* delivered straight to your email. You'll be able to enjoy its daily inspiration and Scripture anytime, anywhere, on your computer, phone, or tablet. Visit WalkinginGrace.org/WIG2023 and enter this code: **praise**.

JANUARY

*The LORD is my strength and
my shield; my heart trusts in
him, and he helps me. My heart
leaps for joy, and with my song
I praise him.*

—Psalm 28:7 (NIV)

New Year's Day, Sunday, January 1

Wash me, and I shall be whiter than snow. —Psalm 51:7 (KJV)

Day One of 365 . . . New Year's morning always feels like turning the first page of a new chapter in a much-loved book. I love that feeling. With a caffeine-enhanced skip of joy in my step, I opened the front door to shake out the welcome mat in anticipation of the friends who'd soon be arriving for brunch. I did a double take. An unexpected blanket of snow covered my walkway. I looked up. The Colorado sky was a cloudless, azure blue. Snow hadn't been mentioned on last night's weather forecast for last night or today. Beyond my walkway, which was currently under the protective shadow of the eaves, there was not a hint of snowy white in sight. I phoned my son, who lives five minutes away, and he confirmed that his neighborhood was entirely flake-free.

Weird, I thought. *Even for the Rockies.* I picked up my broom, but my snow-covered walkway was so perfect, so pristine and untouched, that I hesitated to sweep away the beauty of the freshly fallen flakes. It felt like a God-given picture of my year ahead. A clean slate. No missteps. No wandering in circles. No veering off the path God set before me. So far, anyway. But it was only Day One.

No matter how lovely and perfect that untouched path seemed, I knew life couldn't be lived standing still. I had to move forward, loving and learning my way through the days ahead. I prayed the footprints I left behind me this year would be ones I'd be proud for my grandchildren to follow in. Then I stepped across the threshold and swept away the snow, welcoming in whatever lay ahead.

Father, thank You for forgiving what lies behind me and guiding me forward onto a path of grace and growth.
—Vicki Kuyper

Digging Deeper: Proverbs 3:5–6; Isaiah 1:18; 1 John 1:9

"The kingdom of heaven is like a grain of mustard seed that a man took and sowed in his field. It is the smallest of all seeds, but when it has grown it is larger than all the garden plants and becomes a tree . . ."
—Matthew 13:31–32 (ESV)

A urora, run and grab me some kindling, please," my husband, Jim, said to my daughter as he carried an armload of firewood over to our woodstove.

"But there's already such a big pile of wood in here, Papa!" she answered.

Jim laughed. "All the big wood in the world won't do me a bit of good without the small stuff to get it started," he replied.

Kinda like love, I thought to myself as I listened to their exchange. I looked down at the letter I was holding in my hands. It was from my childhood band teacher. It had been a delightful surprise in the mail that day. I was so touched that this person from my past would take the time to write and send me something.

And Aurora had brought my coffee to me that morning in bed. What a wonderful little gesture to wake up to.

And here was Jim, cheerfully bringing in firewood so we could stay warm on this wintry Alaskan afternoon. Earlier, my mom had messaged me, saying Jim had called her out of the blue, just to check on her and chat. "It made my day," she'd told me. And hearing that had made mine.

Grand gestures of love, like big trips to faraway places and expensive gifts, can be amazing and exciting. *But,* I thought with a smile, *it's these little things, love's kindling, that really allows its fire to blaze.*

Thank You, Lord, for the countless little things in my life that all add up to the biggest thing of all: I am loved by You.
—Erin Janoso

Digging Deeper: Luke 16:10; John 6:9

Tuesday, January 3

"Be still, and know that I am God . . ." —Psalm 46:10 (NIV)

Gracie, my golden, is curled up sleeping on the couch while I work. Outside the wind sways the trees, causing the winter sunlight slanting through the west window to ripple across her. We just got back from a cold, snowy hike in the hills of western Massachusetts. She plowed through drifts and vaulted over fallen trees. Plunged her snout into snowbanks, seeking out some scent I could only guess at. At the summit, she sat and leaned into me, staring out past the tree line at the distant, snow-covered, checkerboard farm fields, fences half-buried.

I can't help but stare at her now. She is so peaceful, so serenely relaxed. I doubt I have ever achieved such a state of complete rest. My mind is too restless, as if my brain paces even when I am sitting. I envy this dog and her gift of tranquility.

Deep, slow breaths rise and fall in her chest in a hypnotic rhythm. I try to mirror her, syncing my breathing with hers. As the minutes pass, I feel a peace come over me, as if I am tapping into her serenity. I relax, internally and externally, body and soul. I experience something like spiritual equilibrium rippling through me.

Not everyone has a dog. Not everyone has loved one. For most of my life, I have. For us dog lovers, they teach us to live intentionally, to live with gratitude and optimism (is there a creature more optimistic than a dog?), to find peace in the stillness of the moment.

In a minute, my mind will turn itself back on and I will go back to work. For now, I want to breathe with Gracie, to achieve that state of being completely present, at peace in the moment.

Almighty God, You are pure spirit. Help me to meet You in the moment, to breathe in Your spirit, to close my eyes and find You within.
      —Edward Grinnan

Digging Deeper: Isaiah 26:3; Philippians 4:6–7

Again Jesus spoke to them, saying, "I am the light of the world. Whoever follows me will not walk in darkness, but will have the light of life."
—John 8:12 (ESV)

It's cold out. I don't mean a little coolish. I mean cold. Like zero Fahrenheit. The kind of cold where going outside to refill the bird feeders is a hurried task. As I hustle along, the wood on the deck floor pops like small firecrackers as it contracts in the freezing temperatures.

The sun is out though, which adds the illusion of warmth. Outdoors it is only an illusion, but indoors the sunlight actually adds to the warmth.

That's because we designed our house to take advantage of passive solar energy—windows are situated so as to flood winter floors with sunlight and warm them up. My writing office is tiny, but its two small windows help heat the room. My desk is right beside them. The rays coming through them fall on my arms and shoulders. It feels good and healing on days like this.

The radiant heat those windows let in reminds me that I need to bask in God's light more often. Yes, I need the divine light to see my way, especially in the dark days of metaphorical winter—no matter what season the calendar says it is. I welcome and depend on that light for my journey.

Some days, though, I just need the warmth with which God's light imbues me. I long to rest easy in it. I hunger to relax and soak up its spiritual warmth and feel it deep in my soul. To let it kindle anew the fire in my bones, as Jeremiah called it.

The light warming my little room and body reminds me to always look toward the light and relax in the divine love it brings.

Loving Eternal Light, warm and illumine me as I seek Your way. Amen.
—J. Brent Bill

Digging Deeper: Psalm 36:8–10; John 1:1–9

Thursday, January 5

And as you say, older men like me are wise. They understand. But true wisdom and power are God's. He alone knows what we should do; he understands. —Job 12:12–13 (TLB)

The electric stove in my condo was put in when the building was built in 1969, so this year marks my stove's fifty-fourth birthday. Numerous friends and family members have encouraged me to get a new one. But why? The oven and every burner still work fine; one burner is even designed to heat up extremely fast and it still does.

A few years ago, I won honorable mention in my county for having the second-oldest still-working hot water heater. It was forty-eight years old at the time. That year, I did give in to the pressure from my loved ones and replaced it—only to notice that the new one was only guaranteed to last eight years.

Why fix things that aren't broken just because they're old, I ask. Faith is old. Prayer is old. Love is old. Kindness is old. I'm old! I had a great-uncle who lived to be 104, so I'm patterning myself after Uncle Collie and hope to live at least another twenty-five years. My point is that it all still works. I'm not going to stop swimming, biking, hiking, dancing, laughing, and flirting just because I'm old.

The thing I love most that's old is faith. Generations after generations after generations have relied on faith to get them through the tough times. And believe me, once you hit your mid-to-late seventies like me, you have seen your share of tough times. But why worry? We have our faith. We have love. We have kindness. We have Jesus and each other. I think that's all we need. That and a good, solid stove.

Lord, You taught us the basics of life. Everything we need is rooted in You and Your message.
—Patricia Lorenz

Digging Deeper: Genesis 15:5–6; Proverbs 16:31

". . . the rising sun will come to us from heaven . . . to guide our feet into the path of peace."—Luke 1:78–79 (NIV)

It's a stretch for my imagination—the Epiphany story of a heavenly light leading wise seekers to a specific destination. But I ponder it today, in one of the rainiest winters on record. Nothing but gray skies overhead. I haven't ventured out as much as usual, but I've kept in touch with friends and family.

Most mornings, a neighborhood teen calls to check in before starting her school day. Our chat is usually lightweight and lighthearted. What did you have for breakfast—or dinner last night? Is today a gym day or a chorus day? Yesterday morning, despite a day's reprieve in the weather, she seemed subdued. Or was it I—not accustomed to sunshine—getting comfortable with ennui? I made a suggestion. "Let's both look out the window. You there. Me here. Have you noticed? No rain. No storm clouds. Look, there's *light*!"

Perking up, she broke into song—a refrain by the Nashville Nine that she'd learned at Young Life, a faith-based club for teens: "Let there be light—shining in the shadows . . ." The declaration inspired me throughout the bright day. The sky remained clear till dusk—and beyond, as I discovered when I went outside at 10 p.m. to see if I could see the month's showcased "supermoon." Yes! There it shone—a full-faced orb reflecting the sun-star that would soon enough rise at dawn.

As I headed inside, along the sidewalk and up the outside stairs, I remembered the last line of the teen's morning song. It steadied my step: our God—"He is the light that leads us home."

Jesus, Light of the world, shine on us today. Guide us from dark shadows to Your perfect light.
—Evelyn Bence

Digging Deeper: Matthew 2:7–11; Revelation 21:22–22:5

Saturday, January 7

"Again, truly I tell you that if two of you on earth agree about anything they ask for, it will be done for them by my Father in heaven."
—Matthew 18:19 (NIV)

A friend was standing outside my log cabin, and I was mortified. I'd been delivered from years of pain and dependence on prescription opioids, but lack of money and wherewithal had wreaked havoc on my home as well. There was peeling paint, logs that needed restaining, a warped screen door barely hanging on its hinges, a forest of overgrown trees and shrubs. That was just the outside.

There was nothing to do but face her. "This place is a shambles, Stephanie," I said, hanging my head. "Used to be a showplace. Folks took their Christmas card photos here. Probably sending pictures to the authorities now."

"What do you need *this minute,* Roberta?" she asked. Her voice was warm and kind.

"A respite," I said. "To sit by the fire and talk to God. Simple beauty and peace. I sure don't need any showplace!"

"Glad you cleared that one up," she said. She stretched her head toward the heavens and threw up her hands in joyous laughter. "The Bible says when we pray, we need to *agree* on these things. One of us can't be asking for a showplace and the other for a respite. That'll get 'em all confused."

The thought took me aback, but Stephanie did have a point. Every day we both prayed for that dear desire of my heart. I'm telling you all about it right now from the snug wing chair by my cozy fire.

> *You said it first, Lord. Heaven hears when we agree to agree!*
> —Roberta Messner

Digging Deeper: Matthew 18:20; John 14:14; Acts 1:14

Do not forget to show hospitality to strangers, for by so doing some people have shown hospitality to angels without knowing it. —Hebrews 13:2 (NIV)

It was a normal, busy Sunday morning. My husband had left for worship practice, and I was rushing to get dressed for church. But a normal morning soon turned my world upside down. I had felt a lump in the shower.

As the week unfolded and I endured several tests, I was forced to go about my life as usual, working, caring for my family, and running errands. But as I walked around the grocery store, meeting the gazes of strangers, I started wondering to myself: How many of them are waiting for a biopsy result? A financial breakthrough? A relationship to heal? How many are fighting hardships we cannot see?

The answer: all of them. Everyone is fighting a hard battle in quiet desperation.

When my doctor finally called with the results, I heard the words: benign. Noncancerous. Nothing to be concerned about. I celebrated and praised God—yet, I realized, not everyone gets a good result. Sometimes a doctor's call means continuing down a road of unknowns, fear, procedures, and more.

I decided then and there that I didn't want my journey to end with the phone call I received. The good news became a catalyst to push me down a new path of caring for others. This path allows me to see the quiet desperation in the faces of the strangers I meet each day. The simple act of smiling, stepping aside, putting others before myself, hoping that if they are fighting a battle I cannot see, I will be a ray of light in their dark world—and not another stumbling block for them to climb over.

Lord, help me to see the people around me with Your eyes, putting their needs before mine, whether they are a friend or a stranger.
—Gabrielle Meyer

Digging Deeper: Matthew 25:34–39; Colossians 3:23–24;
Hebrews 13:16

Monday, January 9

Amazement seized all of them, and they glorified God and were filled with awe . . . —Luke 5:26 (NRSV)

Running in snow. Not the ideal circumstances for a morning jog. When it's first coming down, it's okay. You can still get secure footing. You might even see your footsteps as you gaze behind. As long as it's just a few inches—not feet—and there is no ice underneath.

True confessions: Running itself is not always my idea of fun. I seem to get slower at it every year, and there's always an ache here or there to contend with. I remind myself of the pluses. The exercise is good for me. There are some nice views in the park—my usual loop taking me around the Cloisters Museum, a superb collection of medieval art in a building that, in fact, does look like a monastery, with parts of it coming from real churches and monasteries with Gothic arches and stained-glass windows.

That Monday, after a recent snowfall, I headed out a little cautiously. Some of the snow had melted. I ran along a cleared path. What I really wanted to do, though, was simply stop and gaze at the wonder of the snow-dusted landscape. Wouldn't that be cheating?

Just then I came to a spot on the path where the snow hadn't been cleared. I slowed down, stopped, treaded very carefully, and, as I did, marveled at how beautiful everything looked, clean and fresh and white. I gazed across the Hudson to the cliffs along the river. I turned around and could see the tower of the Cloisters above me, like an arrow pointing heavenward.

"God," I thought, "You must have orchestrated this." Giving me a blessed opportunity to stop and see and wonder with awe. Before I headed on my way, huffing and puffing up the hill.

Thank You, Lord, for every pause You give me in a day. Let me use it wisely. Giving it back to You in wonder.
—Rick Hamlin

Digging Deeper: Exodus 15:11; Psalm 33:8

And the King will say, "I tell you the truth, when you did it to one of the least of these my brothers and sisters, you were doing it to me!"
—Matthew 25:40 (NLT)

*L*ord, *please use me today* has got to be the most disruptive prayer ever answered. Moments after my pious petition, inspired by this morning's devotional reading, I heard my phone ring—from the last person on earth I wanted to talk to. Recently, this person had made me mad enough to spit nails. I grabbed the phone, but before I could say something I would have regretted, I heard: "I need help. My dog is hurt. He needs a vet and I can't take him now." My anger vanished. I interrupted with, "I'll be there in twenty minutes."

Time spent awaiting the vet's diagnosis flew by as I meditated on the lesson of Jesus asking His disciples to serve the "least of these" and the "undeserving." I was convicted: it wasn't that the dog's owner was undeserving because of our argument; instead, it was that God had called me when I was at my least deserving—clinging to bitterness—and He transformed my sin of anger into compassion.

That evening, I returned the dog, who had miraculously suffered only a sprain and not a broken bone. Leave it to God to ask an undeserving heart like mine to show His love where it's needed most.

Sweet Jesus, thank You for forgiving me, even when I'm not quick to forgive. Thank You for using me, "the least of these," to serve others with the best of You. Lord, I honestly ask You again: Please use me today.
—Erika Bentsen

Digging Deeper: Matthew 25:31–46; Ephesians 6:7

Wednesday, January 11

Let brotherly love continue. —Hebrews 13:1 (CSB)

You got the package?" Matt asked. His voice was slightly distorted, but it was good to see his face over video chat.

I lifted a brown parcel in confirmation.

"Open it!" he said.

I began stripping away packaging tape.

Matt and I had been friends since college. We hadn't seen each other in person for years, but he was one of my closest friends. I had been overjoyed last month when he announced his engagement.

I unfolded box flaps. On top of the foam packaging was a note that read, "Would you be one of my groomsmen?"

I grinned. "Matt, I would be honored."

Matt waved his hand. "Yeah, yeah, yeah. Now comes the good part—there's a gift in there."

I reached into the packaging until I found something solid, then pulled it out. It was a pocketknife with a dark wooden handle. I flipped it open. It felt made for my hand. "Matt, it's . . ."

"It's totally you, isn't it?" he said. "I picked that handle because it looks classic."

I closed the blade and turned the knife over, admiring the wood grain. I was at a loss for words. The knife was exactly what I would have chosen for myself. Matt's gift made me feel known.

My friendship with Matt ran deep. Matt didn't just know things about me. He knows how I think, how I feel, and who I am. And to be truly known is one of the greatest gifts in the world.

"Matt, I just . . ." I trailed off.

"No need to say anything," he said. "I get it."

And I believed he did.

> *Lord, thank You for the gift of being known.*
> —Logan Eliasen

Digging Deeper: Psalm 139:13; Jeremiah 1:5

"When you are praying, do not heap up empty phrases as the Gentiles do; for they think that they will be heard because of their many words. Do not be like them, for your Father knows what you need before you ask him." —Matthew 6:7–8 (NRSV)

A friend was describing the anguish of dealing with a loved one's addiction. She and her family had tried everything. They'd held an intervention, gathering family members and friends to caringly confront the person with the pain the addiction was causing, only to have their effort angrily rejected. They tried tough love, letting the person live with the consequences of the addictive behavior, but the illness had such a grip that nothing worked, including several stints in rehab centers.

My friend looked at me in despair. "The only thing we can do now is pray."

I offered some comforting words and promised to join their prayers. But later I wondered why it is that we wait to turn to God. Why is God ever our last resort? I can't count the times I've said something like it myself: "In the end, all I can do is pray."

Both my friend and I know that God is all-powerful and can do everything and anything for those who have faith. Yet, it's one thing to know this ultimate truth and another, it seems, to feel it. I find it hard to accept that I have so little control over the events and, yes, the people in my life. I need to ask God's help with my need for control. *Before* I try to fix it.

> *God, All-in-All, help me to make it my practice to turn to You first. And again. And again.*
> —Marci Alborghetti

Digging Deeper: Psalm 21:1–4; Jeremiah 16:19–20

Friday, January 13

And God is able to make all grace abound toward you; that ye, always having all sufficiency in all things, may abound to every good work.
—2 Corinthians 9:8 (KJV)

My mom lives right next door, and every night I go to her house for a cup of tea and to catch up on the day's events. Sometimes we do a puzzle that stays on her kitchen table. The more challenging the puzzle, the longer it takes. Right now, we are piecing together the Mona Lisa; with many dark and similar pieces, it's taking us much longer than we hoped. We are averaging two pieces each, each hour.

"Sabra," Mom leaned in, "we have these two young bucks that come. Their antlers are just about the size of my hand. They were sparring today."

"If you ever find a shed antler, I would love it."

"I've never found one," Mom said. "But I'll keep an eye out."

We worked more on the puzzle, barely making progress, and I walked home to make dinner. The next night when I went to Mom's house, a young buck's shed antler was on the table in front of the puzzle, in front of my chair.

"You'll never believe it," Mom said. "Strangest thing, I walked outside this morning and there it was. Living here all these years and never seen one before today. Right on the ground, right in front of me. For you."

I held the antler in my hands—it was smooth like sanded wood— only it held the beauty of the deer and the amazing glory of God, who gives gracious blessings that show He is listening. He hears.

Heavenly Father, thank You for the precious gifts You give that masterfully come together like pieces in a puzzle.
—Sabra Ciancanelli

Digging Deeper: John 1:2–4; Ephesians 1:3

In their hearts humans plan their course, but the LORD establishes their steps. —Proverbs 16:9 (NIV)

If you were driving on Route 65 near Pittsburgh last Saturday, my apologies. I was the guy waving frantically, urging you to move over, away from my stalled Toyota in the right lane. (Yes, I should have used my flares, but they were safely stored in my wife Sandee's car.)

It was quite a scene—me windmilling my arms while calling AAA. I looked like an amped-up mime, wildly gesticulating, screaming "wake up!" to the guy in the Mustang who nearly clipped my kneecaps.

Eventually AAA arrived, and I hitched a ride with the driver. As fate would have it, the tow-truck driver (with my now-dead Toyota on his flatbed) had to maneuver around another derelict vehicle on Route 65. Turns out, it takes time and skill to avoid a sudden new obstacle ahead of you, especially at forty-five miles an hour.

It took a while for the lesson to sink in: One person's emergency is another person's nuisance. First we sit stuck, waiting for help, halfway onto the berm, watching the thoughtless drivers whizzing past us and never stopping. Then we're towed away, rescued, crisis averted, join the other drivers, and quickly become annoyed and irritated at the cars stuck in the slow lane, halfway onto the berm. You'd think we'd recognize the irony, but we do not. Thankfully we can rely on Someone who sees our missing flares, who hears our desperate prayers.

Lord, save us—not only from the breakdown lane but also from the pride that blinds us from seeing ourselves in the eyes of those who need a tow, some flares, or maybe just a helping hand.
—Mark Collins

Digging Deeper: Proverbs 19:21; Micah 6:9

Sunday, January 15

"Where, O death, is your sting?"—1 Corinthians 15:55 (NIV)

Pete passed away last night."

The words in the text message this morning should not surprise me. We knew the end of his cancer journey was near. Yet the stark reality of those words still stunned me. Pete had been a good friend in a circle of four families that gathered regularly through the years. Our kids grew up celebrating New Year's Eves and annual summer outings together in the mountains. We toasted at family weddings. We created many memories.

Now Pete was the first to leave that circle.

His earthly journey ended yesterday, and I know I should be celebrating the beginning of his new life with the Lord, but right now, I confess, I am grief-stricken. "Where, O death, is your sting?" is a question asked at funerals. I've always had my own quick answer. The sting is with those of us grieving here, in spite of the celebration for his new life there.

Pete's wife and kids and grandkids are beginning to navigate a new reality without him, surely comforted by many good memories, but missing his hugs and laugh and words. We all will live in the hole of his absence, which is largest for his immediate family. We will feel the sting.

I know God has prepared a place for Pete and he's been welcomed there. Surely I will think of that more in the days to come. But for this moment, I'm absorbing the reality of death and the layers of grief that brings. I'm feeling the sting.

O death, where is thy sting? I know, Lord, that death does not sting the one who leaves us and enters a new life with You. For that we celebrate, and know You walk with us in our grief.
—Carol Kuykendall

Digging Deeper: John 5:24; 2 Timothy 4:7

Martin Luther King Jr. Day, Monday, January 16

"Then will I purify the speech of all people, so that everyone can worship the LORD together." —Zephaniah 3:9 (NLT)

One look at any of my elementary class photos and I can easily recall stories of my childhood school days. In a class of over thirty students, I was usually the only minority, perhaps one of two if the cards fell differently. Of course, there were the obvious differences between me and my classmates—our skin tone or the texture of our hair—but that rarely affected our friendships. We bonded over the things we had in common: Our love for show-and-tell, ice cream Fridays, and field trips. We felt the same dislike for pop quizzes in math and the monthly fluoride rinse with an aftertaste that lasted for hours.

Yet every once in a while a situation would remind me that I wasn't always judged by the content of my character. I remember receiving a birthday invitation to a sleepover along with the rest of the girls in my class. My excitement was still bubbling over when I received a call the next day, my classmate rescinding the invitation. "My mom said you can't come to my birthday party because you're Black." I don't recall exactly how her words made me feel, but I do remember wondering about who all would show up. What would I miss?

Dr. Martin Luther King Jr. said, "We must learn to live together as brothers or we will perish together as fools."

My friend and I still played together. We shared classes from elementary through high school, and we treated each other with mutual respect. From the experience, I learned not to judge a person based on another's actions or beliefs, no matter if they were a parent, teacher, or friend.

Dear Lord, help me to see others through Your eyes. There is no racial divide that can't be healed with the love of Christ.
—Tia McCollors

Digging Deeper: Psalm 72:17; Ephesians 2:14–16, 4:32

Tuesday, January 17

"For the LORD your God is bringing you into a good land . . ."
—Deuteronomy 8:7 (NKJV)

The first things I do every morning are to turn up the thermostat, turn on the kitchen lights, and pour a glass of cold water. These represent three things I appreciate profoundly.

My earliest memories are of the 1940s, living in a rural Ohio parsonage. Our house was heated with coal, delivered by truck. I loved watching the big, black rocks sliding down the chute into our coal bin, but the temperature of our house was never quite right—always too hot or too cold. A film of coal ash covered everything: furniture, walls, clothes, houseplants.

Although we had electric lighting in our parsonage, some of the farmhouses we visited used kerosene lamps. I thought the lamps were clever, but the houses were depressingly dark, and it was hard to read or write unless you were sitting very close to a lamp. In contrast, our house today has seventy bright lightbulbs.

Our parsonage used a well and a cistern. I remember my mother cranking a hand pump in the kitchen sink. Sometimes it would pump out an earthworm, and she would let out a shriek. Our bathroom was an outhouse, a smelly outdoor closet with cold wooden seats and lots of visitors: spiders, centipedes, wasps, birds, bats, even black snakes. Once I got trapped in the outhouse during a terrible thunderstorm, when the door jammed shut. I sat there, crying and begging God not to let me die in this awful place.

So, every night, when I pour a glass of bedside water, turn down the thermostat, and turn off the lights, I say to God:

Thank You, Father, that I live in the land of everyday wonders.
—Daniel Schantz

Digging Deeper: Deuteronomy 8:10; Psalm 92:1

You did not choose me, but I chose you and appointed you so that you might go and bear fruit . . . —John 15:16 (NIV)

A t loose ends, I stared out the window at the rain. Christmas was over, New Year's Day two weeks gone, and here in the Deep South, we were experiencing our signature string of dismal January days. Considering all the needy souls out there, had I not been chosen to do more than watch the weather?

I sat down to the twenty-third chapter of Genesis, instantly engaging with the life of Sarah. Indisputably called by God, Abraham's wife had birthed the heir of a nation, the miracle of her ninety-year-old body setting the stage for the Lamb of God to be sacrificed for my sin. Now *that* was action. That was chosen-ness.

But Sarah, too, suffered her January days where she might have questioned her usefulness in the Master's hands. Not only was she complicit in her husband's lies to save his own skin, but she also willfully sent him into the arms of another woman. And when she heard she had been chosen to bear a son, she laughed at the plan of God!

What pierced the fog of my thoughts was a no-brainer: chosen-ness neither begins nor ends with life's highs and lows. Sarah was chosen even when she didn't feel like it—or believe it. The juxtaposition of imperfection and calling lightened me, sparking thanksgiving for a new day—dreariness and all.

I am chosen! And while salvation as a gift never ceases to amaze me, its mystery is equaled by God's constant willingness to replace my laughs of doubt with the opportunity to bear fruit for eternity, just as He did for Sarah.

> *Dear Lord, neither I nor this day is perfect, but we both bear*
> *Your indelible stamp—enough to make me abandon my*
> *empty stare, get up, and rejoice.*
> —Jacqueline F. Wheelock

Digging Deeper: Genesis 12–15, 17:15; 1 Peter 1:2

Thursday, January 19

So I say, let the Holy Spirit guide your lives. —Galatians 5:16 (NLT)

I yawned. It was late. *Just one more search.* After signing on to a Facebook page for German shepherd enthusiasts I scrolled, looking for puppies. Sunrise, my thirteen-year-old golden retriever, wasn't able to go on hikes and horseback rides anymore. Those ventures into the woods by myself were my coveted times with God, but I didn't feel safe going alone. It was already January. *God, You know that if I'm going to meet You in the mountains this summer, I need to get a pup soon.*

For the past year, I'd been praying and looking seriously for a pup. I'd compiled a list of what I was looking for. But it seemed like every time I got close, the pups were sold or a warning flag popped up.

As I scrolled down, a new video caught my eye. It showed a German shepherd that retrieved blunt arrows out of a target. The dog even knew how to get a soda out of the refrigerator! I chuckled when I discovered the name of the kennel where it was bred—"Valhalla," an old Norse word meaning "heaven." And it was only an hour south of me.

The next morning, I made the call. Yes, the breeder "just happened" to have a new litter on the ground. That afternoon, I met the dogs and left a deposit. Driving home, I marveled at how, after searching throughout the western United States for a year, the Holy Spirit led me to a pup that was born in my valley at a kennel named "Heaven." Oh, and I just happened to buy her on my birthday and pick her up six weeks later on my brother's birthday.

> *Lord, it amazes me how, when I ask for direction, You weave*
> *my life together in such a special way. Amen.*
> —Rebecca Ondov

Digging Deeper: Proverbs 3:6; John 16:13

A good man leaves an inheritance to his children's children . . .
—Proverbs 13:22 (NKJV)

T hank you, Sweet."
 I love it when my husband calls me "Sweet." He picked it up from me after hearing me say it to the children. I picked it up from my Big Daddy, who died when I was sixteen but who always referred to me as "Sweet."

It warms me to think about my grandfather influencing people he never met. It's like a rock tossed into water—it disappears quickly, but its ripples reach far, long after the rock itself can no longer be seen. I love knowing that Big Daddy's gentleness reaches through time, an echo of a life well lived.

I also love knowing that an inheritance can be so much more than material things.

Big Daddy was a cutup, always making jokes and being silly. My dad, his only child, is just like him. Whenever my daughters do something that makes me laugh, I tell them they "come by it honest," this legacy of bringing joy.

My grandfather returns to me in those moments, just as he returns whenever I smell sawdust, taking me back to when I was a little girl in his big workshop, watching him make furniture, each piece bearing some special flourish that only he would create. I still have some of his old tools, and sometimes I just like to touch them and remember that he once held them in his hands.

I've spent far more years on this earth without my grandfather than I spent with him. But one day, thanks to Jesus, I'll see him again, and we'll have all of eternity to catch up.

> *Lord, because of You, love continues forever.*
> —Ginger Rue

Digging Deeper: Philippians 4:9; 2 Timothy 1:3–7

Saturday, January 21

Yes, even if I walk through the valley of the shadow of death, I will not be afraid of anything, because You are with me. —Psalm 23:4 (NLV)

I know this Wisconsin lake very well. We bought a cabin here eighteen months ago.

I love to walk on the ice in the winter. One early day last January, I was watching my nine-year-old ice-skate with my wife.

We'd walked onto the ice for the third or fourth time since it had frozen to sufficient thickness in late December. It was about a half-mile on the lake to the place that was plowed and prepared for ice-skating.

An hour later, as the sun shone brightly, we retraced our steps on the lake, back toward our cabin. We were within one hundred years of it when the ice cracked and—BAM!—I fell through. It happened without warning.

My wife, who was beside me, fell partially through the opening I created. She was one leg in. On another lake, a teenager had fallen through the ice just a week earlier and had died. We'd heard about him on the car radio earlier that day.

My daughter began to scream. As my wife pulled herself out, I flailed and broke more ice. Our daughter ran for help.

I was able to get out of the icy water, thank God. But I don't know how to actually thank God for my safety, when others are less fortunate. It is difficult to accept that God saved me when others die. I am grateful. But I am humbled. And I recognize, more than ever, the responsibility I have to care for people around me, to help those in need—people in my family and strangers, too. Everyone "falls through the cracks" at one time or another.

With thanks to You, I will do something real and concrete today, Lord, to help people in my community who are in need.
—Jon M. Sweeney

Digging Deeper: Psalm 27:1

Every man according as he purposeth in his heart, so let him give;
not grudgingly, or of necessity: for God loveth a cheerful giver.
—2 Corinthians 9:7 (KJV)

Growing up, we never missed church. My father was the minister, so attending was just like eating breakfast or going to school. So was tithing. I remember mowing the grass when I was ten years old and my dad paying me four crisp one-dollar bills. The smell of the cash was even better than the fresh-cut grass as I calculated the ten percent I'd be giving to God.

My family had a wonderful way of encouraging me along. From my grandmother Bebe, who often said, "Brock, you can't outgive the Lord," to my mother, who would gently push me toward thinking about the offering plate. "Your dad and I don't have a lot of money, but we always manage. We believe God takes care of us. So why wouldn't we give our first ten percent to Him?!"

Not long ago, I was stunned to read that a recently conducted poll found that for the first time ever, church membership had fallen below fifty percent.

I guess that makes sense, considering the ways of the world, I said to myself. *But what a sad statistic.*

Church is where children learn how to treat others in the ways that Jesus taught. And it's at church where we are taught how to give.

In his 2008 book *Gross National Happiness*, Arthur C. Brooks wrote, ". . . happiness CAN be bought. It comes from giving to charity and making a difference in the lives of others."

How very true, I think as I touch the stewardship card from my childhood church. As I fill it out, the joy of my grandmother's words come to mind again, and my world is set right.

> *Father, lead us on a new path. One where Your children*
> *learn the joy of giving.*
> —Brock Kidd

Digging Deeper: Leviticus 27:30–32; Malachi 3:10

Monday, January 23

In my Father's house are many mansions: if it were not so, I would have told you. I go to prepare a place for you. —John 14:2 (KJV)

In a radio interview the other day, Paul McCartney mentioned a fir tree given to him by fellow Beatle George Harrison that grows by his gate. Whenever he notices it, he sees George, who died back in 2001. "George has sort of entered that tree for me," McCartney said, laughing.

Is "fir" British for "pine" or a different tree? I wondered as I listened. I wanted to see that fir and started Googling. Every hit was about another tree, though: a pine planted in Harrison's memory in Los Angeles that got infested with beetles and had to be replaced.

After my failed search for McCartney's fir tree, I turned to start a resolution I make every New Year: reducing the 2,500-plus emails in my inbox to keep it from being shut down. I tell myself that as part of this gargantuan business of sorting and deleting, I will automatically delete each day's emails at midnight.

I never do it, though. There are messages from dead people in my inbox: twenty-plus years of friends, family members, colleagues, and students who've died over the years. I rarely think about them until I begin deleting. In one email, a friend reports asking God to cure her morning sullenness and subsequently always waking with hymns in her head. In another, a student's annoyance at our class's ignorance of her African homeland becomes inspired prose.

As I read, the email writers return from death in my mind, as alive as McCartney's fir tree, surviving in an existence I believe in, though I've never been there. Their surviving emails speak to my hope in things unseen, the substance of my faith.

Let my memories of those who went before me, Father, reinforce my
confidence in Your plans for those who love You.
—Patty Kirk

Digging Deeper: Hebrews 11–12:3

A LIFETIME OF LOVE: Saying Goodbye

But Stephen, full of the Holy Spirit, looked up into heaven and saw the glory of God, and Jesus standing at the right hand of God. —Acts 7:55 (NIV)

My husband, Don, lost thirty pounds, had an irregular heartbeat, and became too short of breath to walk upstairs, but extensive medical tests failed to pinpoint the problem. Then two months later, his heart rate soared. He was flown to urban hospitals twice for surgeries, but his damaged heart couldn't be repaired, so we brought him home. With help from home healthcare workers, hospice, and our family doctor, Don enjoyed five weeks of visiting with family and friends.

The day before Don died was surely arranged by God. Pastor Doug, Don's sister, Karen, and friends Susan and Dixie visited. Just before supper, our neighbor, Phil, drove up. "It's a beautiful evening," he told Don. "Let's look over your farm and watch the sunset." Phil helped Don get to a chair on the front porch, where all had front-row seats for a magnificent display of God's glory.

Don slept most of the next day. Our children and daughter-in-law, Patricia, were there, plus grandson, Mark; my brother, Mike; his wife, Connie; and our friend Glenda.

Late in the afternoon, Don's breathing slowed. We held him and each other. My brother read scriptures and those who could sang "It Is Well with my Soul." I could only cling to Don and cry. Then Don's eyes opened wide and he stared into the distance. "Can you see something I can't?" I asked. He smiled, nodded, and squeezed my hand.

At 6:33 p.m., his spirit left his body. My son, Michael, read Matthew 6:33: "But seek ye first the kingdom of God . . ." It was the perfect benediction for a life well lived.

> *Lord, I thank You for all the days of Don's life and for the glimpses of heaven at his death.*
> —Penney Schwab

Digging Deeper: Psalm 19:1; Ecclesiastes 3:11; 1 Corinthians 15:54–57

Wednesday, January 25

Moreover, I will give you a new heart and put a new spirit within you; and I will remove the heart of stone from your flesh and give you a heart of flesh. —Ezekiel 36:26 (NASB)

The huge stone fireplace was the focal point of the renovation project. They just didn't make them like this anymore. It would be the first thing to catch a potential buyer's eye. But decades of grime and smoke had left the white quartz dull and gray.

We went at it with scrub brushes, bleach, and barrels of elbow grease. Nothing seemed to work. Finally, a heavy-duty grinder with a stiff wire wheel began to make slow progress, which became a long process. Plenty of time for contemplation.

We've all heard about hearts like stone. I wondered as I worked—my arms aching more with every passing minute—is this what God feels like as he chips away at a lifetime of stubborn blindness in my own life? My hard heart, the focal point of *His* renovation project.

I prayed as I worked. "I'm sorry, Lord, Your arms must be exhausted."

And after that prayer, I felt His love. It overwhelmed me, got me in a headlock, took me to the mat. I felt like a layer had been sandblasted off my heart, leaving it bare and new.

Do you ever marvel at God's infinite patience? I thought about giving up on that rock more than once. But, even at my most obstinate, He has never, ever given up on me. He is the definition of unwavering perseverance.

In the end, arms shaking, I stepped back and looked at that beautiful quartz shining brilliant white in the light of the setting sun. Pure and fresh as new snow, as if all those years had never even happened.

Can you imagine? He sees us the same way.

Dear God, thank You for softening my stone-hard heart.
Thank You for bringing out the power tools!
—Buck Storm

Digging Deeper: 1 Samuel 16:7; Psalm 51:10; Jeremiah 17:9–10

"For You are my help, and in the shadow of Your wings I shout for joy."
—Psalm 63:8 (JPS)

I didn't see the ice on the ramp from the kitchen to my backyard, but I knew it was there the moment my foot suddenly shot out from under me. Instinctively, I threw my falling body forward ("Whatever else you do, do NOT fall on your back!" sounded in my head). I bounced off the ramp and landed somehow on my left shoulder, then my right knee, and found myself with my nose in the wet grass.

After about ten seconds of being stunned, I struggled to my feet and limped back into the house, avoiding the spot that had ambushed me on the way down. At my age, falling and not appearing to have broken anything could only be counted as good news. After I reached what I thought of as safety, I took Tylenol and remained satisfied by my ability to remain independent. *Thank God I can take care of myself,* I thought.

But, as it turned out, my satisfaction was short-lived. The bruising from the fall made me unable to go up or down stairs or drive the car. I had to accept help from friends and neighbors. I tried to do it with gratitude, rather than reluctance, and the more I tried, the more I thought about what it all meant.

Slowly, I remembered that, when I was at Penn State more than fifty years earlier, I was required to take a sport. Not being a sporting person by nature, I had chosen ice-skating. And the first thing they teach you is how to fall. "Remember this," the instructor had said. "You may fall any number of times and not just here." I realized, quite late in life, that my being independent was built on the contributions of other people and that I could thank God for sending them into my life.

> *You know what's good for me when I don't, Lord. Help me*
> *to recognize that more often.*
> —Rhoda Blecker

Digging Deeper: Psalm 146:5; Isaiah 41:13

Friday, January 27

Jesus Christ is the same yesterday and today and forever.
—Hebrews 13:8 (ESV)

A new day dawned, but the anxiety that was my companion yesterday still pressed on my chest. Only months before, I would awake looking forward to the day ahead. Now I struggled to get out of bed, fearing what the day held.

In those recent months, I'd lost two loved ones, experienced a separate trauma that caused post-traumatic stress disorder, and then weathered stressful career instability. Many aspects of my happy life had changed, and not for the better.

I'm known in my family as the one who dislikes change. The truth is that I welcome positive change. But unpleasant, negative change? That, I dread. Just the thought of some changes that may lie ahead—more loss, pain, and danger—is enough to overwhelm me with fear.

Because of the series of hard changes I experienced in those months, I was caught in a cycle of fear and couldn't find a way out. Where was hope in light of the grim reality that everything good seems doomed to change?

Searching for comfort, I turned to Scripture. And there I found this amazing promise: Jesus never changes. He's the same today as He has been for all eternity. He will be the same tomorrow and forever. There isn't even a shadow of change in Him.

As the truth filled my soul, my anxiety lifted, allowing me to breathe again. Something good will never change. That something—Someone—is Jesus, who promises to never leave me or forsake me. When I experience unpleasant change or await future changes, I want to remember that Jesus is always with me, always good, and always in control of every change that comes my way.

> *Father, help me to rest in You and the knowledge that*
> *You will never change.*
> —Jerusha Agen

Digging Deeper: Numbers 23:19; Hebrews 13:5; James 1:17

Teach me Your way, LORD; I will walk in Your truth; Unite my heart to fear Your name. —Psalm 86:11 (NASB)

It snowed last night!" I said to my husband, Kevin, as I looked out the back window of our cabin. A fresh, unstained carpet waited to be explored under the whitened boughs of ponderosa pines in northern Arizona.

Our dog, Mollie, pounced in the nearest snowdrift as we pulled on hats and mitts, zipping up jackets in the twenty-five-degree morning. Nose to the ground, she followed a trail of rabbit tracks, easily identified by the leapfrogging trail left in the snow made by their long back feet landing slightly ahead of their front. Under the chatter of a mountain chickadee, Mollie sniffed out a mouse trail next.

"What is this?" I wondered, bending closer to examine a path of four-toed prints much smaller than Mollie's. With tiny claw marks visible on some of the tracks, I figured they were canine.

"Looks like a fox," Kevin said. "There's been a pair in the area."

Back at the cabin, I checked my email—still no results from a recent mammogram. Even as a fourteen-year breast cancer survivor, I still struggled with "scanxiety" and jumping to worst-case scenarios.

"Give me Your peace," I breathed in prayer, closing my laptop.

Later we went exploring again. The slight breeze and sunlight had distorted the fox tracks, so they appeared much larger than before. If we had not seen the footprints at the beginning of the day, we could easily have thought a wolf had moved into the neighborhood, lurking in the deep shadows while we slept.

I took a deep breath and thanked God for the lesson of the fox tracks and for keeping me from jumping to all kinds of worst-case scenarios.

Jesus, while I wait in the long season of winter, guard my heart from distorting realities into something bigger than they are.
—Lynne Hartke

Digging Deeper: Psalm 25:12; 3 John 1:3–4

Sunday, January 29

Do not conform to the pattern of this world, but be transformed by the renewing of your mind. . . . —Romans 12:2 (NIV)

I couldn't believe it was real! After two years of incorporating my art into hobby baking, I was on a nationally televised cookie competition.

As the time ticked away, my nerves were shot. There was flour on the floor and icing on my shoe, and I kept misplacing one thing after another. Thankfully, my cookies were not as disastrous, and the judges gave me rave reviews.

Yet once we lined up for eliminations, I was the first to go. "We loved the artistry of your cookies," they said, "but it was more a painting of a Christmas mug than an actual Christmas mug cookie."

Because my cookies did not fit the criteria, my "tea time" was up. I smiled and thanked them, but I walked away in shock. I had purposefully stayed away from the mug cookie cutter, knowing everyone else would use them. I chose rectangular cookies; on one, I piped my mug inside, using the extra space to display milk pouring out, and on the other, I piped a mug holding candy canes, paintbrushes, and pencils.

Why didn't you just use the mug cutter! It would have been easier and you could have won. I scolded myself as I touched up my make-up for my exit interview. But the answer was plain, and there was no use being hard on myself over this.

"I will always think outside the cookie cutter," I said to the camera in my last interview, "because that's who I am. And if I'm eliminated for daring to be different, then thank you for the compliment."

> *Lord, in a world that constantly expects us to conform, thank You for Your Word that tells us we don't have to.*
> —Karen Valentin

Digging Deeper: Psalm 139:13–14; 1 Peter 4:10

But make sure that you don't get so absorbed and exhausted in taking care of all your day-by-day obligations that you lose track of the time and doze off, oblivious to God. . . . Get out of bed and get dressed! Don't loiter and linger, waiting until the very last minute. Dress yourselves in Christ, and be up and about! —Romans 13:11–14 (MSG)

One day while indulging in my favorite fast-food meal, I watched a young mother do the same with her toddler twins as they sat at the table across from me. The little girls enjoyed their food, and the evidence was everywhere—mustard on faces, ketchup on shirts, French fries in their laps and on the floor. But their mom came prepared with cleaning wipes and two extra tops, and the next few minutes provided entertainment for the rest of us. The toddlers preferred their dirty clothes and refused to wear the clean ones. No amount of reasoning or bribing could change their minds.

This devoted mother and her ketchup-loving twins came to mind when I read these verses in Romans 13 the following morning during my quiet time. In many ways, I resembled the twins. How many times had I preferred my comfort zone and ignored God calling me to something new? How many mornings did I spend more time selecting clothes to wear on my body than with the One who promised to live inside me forever? And like the twins' caring mother wanting the best for her children, God dresses me, His child, in the love and power of His Son—the perfect outfit for every day and occasion. Because of Jesus, I'm always clean in my Heavenly Father's eyes.

Lord, thank You for Your saving grace. Give me the wisdom and strength to reflect and share the love and mercy of Your Son Jesus Christ everywhere I go.
—Jenny Lynn Keller

Digging Deeper: Isaiah 61:10; Luke 24:45–49; Galatians 3:26–27

Tuesday, January 31

The student is not above the teacher, but everyone who is fully trained will be like their teacher. —Luke 6:40 (NIV)

During a workshop examining child welfare, our presenter spoke of the impact of caring adults in a child's life. Personalizing the point, she asked us to share the name of a teacher who positively influenced our childhood years. I immediately recalled two teachers—Mr. Neal and Mrs. Simms. Mr. Neal, a blond, gray-eyed man in specs reminiscent of John Lennon, taught second grade at my tiny Lutheran elementary school. Mrs. Simms, a woman with the aura of Michelle Obama, donned pencil skirts and black slingbacks while teaching honors English to upperclassmen at my all-girls public high school.

These teachers couldn't be more different from one another. And yet they had two things in common: First, a love for literature that spilled out of their hearts and poured into their students. Second, they ignited my love for learning, fed my appetite for great books, and encouraged me to not only read ravenously but also pursue the writing life. Mr. Neal loaned his personal books to me, opening my mind to the amazing worlds of *The Lion, the Witch and the Wardrobe; Gulliver's Travels;* and *A Wrinkle in Time.* Mrs. Simms further challenged me with the depths of Zora Neale Hurston's *Their Eyes Were Watching God,* Maya Angelou's *I Know Why the Caged Bird Sings,* and Toni Morrison's *The Bluest Eye.*

I hadn't thought about these teachers in many years, but the presenter's exercise had transported me back to my young aspiring-writer self. Truly, a caring, passionate teacher can make all the difference in the life of a child. Mr. Neal and Mrs. Simms definitely did in mine.

Lord, may I inspire young people in my life with wisdom and love,
as others have inspired me.
—Carla Hendricks

Digging Deeper: Proverbs 22:6; Romans 12:5–8; 1 Peter 4:10

LET US SING FOR JOY

1 _____

2 _____

3 _____

4 _____

5 _____

6 _____

7 _____

8 _____

9 _____

10 _____

11 _____

12 _____

13 _____

14 _____

15 _____

January

16 _____

17 _____

18 _____

19 _____

20 _____

21 _____

22 _____

23 _____

24 _____

25 _____

26 _____

27 _____

28 _____

29 _____

30 _____

31 _____

FEBRUARY

LORD, you are my God; I will exalt
you and praise your name, for in
perfect faithfulness you have done
wonderful things, things planned
long ago.

—Isaiah 25:1 (NIV)

Wednesday, February 1

Sing to the LORD a new song; sing to the LORD, all the earth.
—Psalm 96:1 (NIV)

The first time I heard "Lift Every Voice and Sing," I was captivated. I loved the marching beat that drove the lyrics—by turns haunting ("the days when hope unborn had died"), tragic ("treading our path through the blood of the slaughtered"), and faithful ("God of our silent tears").

Pastor Jevon, a pastor in my current church, called it the Black National Anthem. He had sung it nearly every Sunday growing up. I'd missed out on that, growing up in a white church.

My parents worked for civil rights in the 1960s. They fully expected that we'd have racial equality by now. Fifty years later, when my church celebrated the anniversary of the March in Selma, I sang "We Shall Overcome," held hands across the aisle, and cried. I began my own march toward equal rights for my sisters and brothers of color.

The Black National Anthem would be my marching song! I found it in our Methodist hymnal and began memorizing the words.

On February 1, my daughter sent me a list called "28 Ways to Celebrate Black History Month." Number 24 leaped off the page: "Learn the full version of 'Lift Every Voice and Sing'!"

As long as I can remember, I've sung and prayed hymns throughout my day. *How had I learned all those hymns?* I remembered the story Pastor Jevon had told us: As a child, surrounded by his church family, he had sung that hymn every Sunday. Just like my own childhood.

I found a beautiful recording on YouTube: the Abyssinian Baptist Church Choir singing "Lift Every Voice and Sing," most of them without a hymnal. I joined them online every day. By the end of February, I was singing my new favorite hymn by heart.

Dear Lord, I pray with Your hymn, "Let us march on 'til victory is won."
—Leanne Jackson

Digging Deeper: Psalm 26:12; Colossians 3:16; Hebrews 13:1–2

For God so loved the world . . . —John 3:16 (NIV)

Navigating the streets of Old Delhi is not for the faint of heart. Skirting open manholes, dodging honking motorbikes, and squeezing my way through narrow alleyways congested with market stalls and throngs of people left me feeling frenetic and overwhelmed.

Even breathing felt like a risky proposition. The hot, dust-filled air was pungently perfumed with the smell of exhaust, spices, flowers, and the crush of humanity. Thankfully, my guide led me into a darkened archway and up a crumbling flight of cement stairs, leaving the claustrophobic city street behind.

We emerged onto a quiet rooftop overlooking a jumble of mismatched tenement buildings. The scene looked like an artistic tableau of Indian life. Laundry-covered balconies, off-kilter patios, and rooftop workshops revealed snapshots of a few of Old Delhi's inhabitants. A woman wove bamboo strips into mats. A young Islamic boy unrolled carpets, preparing for noontime prayer. Two men, dressed in long pants and button-down shirts, lay side by side on a tattered sheet of cardboard, catching a quick pre-lunch nap.

This momentary God's-eye view was a perspective-changing gift. I knew Old Delhi was one of the most densely populated cities in the world. But in my mind, thirty thousand people per square mile was simply a statistic. On this rooftop, God reminded me that each of those numbers had a name. Each possessed his or her own unique story, dreams, and spiritual journey. How I long to be able to truly see the world through God's eyes—one beloved, irreplaceable person at a time.

Father, please help my heart become more like Yours. Help me really see the individuals I cross paths with today. Remind me how much each one means to You.
—Vicki Kuyper

Digging Deeper: 2 Chronicles 16:19; Job 31:4; Luke 12:6–7

Friday, February 3

Be completely humble and gentle; be patient, bearing with one another in love. —Ephesians 4:2 (NIV)

The snowman is still here," I said to my husband, Kevin, as we unpacked the car for a weekend stay at our cabin in northern Arizona. Standing at eighteen inches tall—with his coffee-bean face and miniature carrot nose—the snowman was more of a snowboy. I glanced at the calming woods surrounding him and welcomed the chance to relax from an overloaded week that still weighed heavy on my shoulders.

The next morning, with the winter sun warming the ponderosa pines and cedar trees, the coffee beans slid off the snowboy's melting face. We scattered birdseed around the snow-covered base, an invitation for dark-eyed juncos, chipping sparrows, and mountain chickadees to visit the frozen friend. The allure proved too much for a gray squirrel, who promptly took off with the carrot nose. As icicles dripped from the roof, the snowboy's head bent closer and closer to the ground, amazing us when he didn't break into pieces.

"He lost his eyes and mouth, which explains his humbled position," our son texted when we sent him a photo of the leaning snowboy.

Humility. Bending. Not my usual stance, but maybe I needed to submit my stress-filled calendar to His light. At the thought, some of the tension thawed inside me.

Over bowls of steaming tomato soup, we watched a pair of stellar jays swoop in for a birdseed snack. With a cozy fire burning in our stone fireplace, peering outside the window became our favorite spectator sport as we observed nature's response to the whimsical addition to their neighborhood.

Night fell as winter snows still covered the landscape with white familiarity. Our snowboy bowed low to the finale of the day.

Jesus, may I bend to the melting work of Your presence
of all that is frozen in me.
—Lynne Hartke

Digging Deeper: Romans 12:16; Colossians 3:12; James 4:10

BUILDING CATHEDRALS: Growing through It

Whoever would foster love covers over an offense, but whoever repeats the matter separates close friends. —Proverbs 17:9 (NIV)

There's an old saying that motherhood is like building cathedrals; you do the hard work for a finished product that you may only truly see decades from now, if you're lucky enough to see it at all. I remind myself of this often as I recall that I'm not tasked with parenting tiny people; I'm charged with raising godly, kind, and considerate adults.

One day, I was venting by text message to my girlfriends about a playground bully situation, mentioning how we were trying to help our kindergartener handle the conflict. "I'm sorry that he's having to grow through that," my friend wrote back. "I'm glad you're there to help him."

Her words gave me pause. Was that a typo? I was certainly helping him *go* through the experience, but was I helping him *grow* through it?

That night, instead of rehashing what happened that day and how we would approach the next, we sat down and prayed for our playground frenemy. For his heart, for his family, for his peace, and for our own hearts, families, and peace.

"You know," I told my kiddo as I tucked him in, "you are going to encounter bossy kids and bullies your whole life. I'm sorry you're having to experience this, but I'm glad that you're doing it when Mom can sit and hold your hand through it."

Lord, whatever I'm growing through today, remind me that You are constantly by my side—loving, caring, and enduring.
—Ashley Kappel

Digging Deeper: Luke 6:31; John 15:12–14; Romans 12:10

Sunday, February 5

Charm is deceptive, and beauty is fleeting; but a woman who fears the LORD is to be praised. —Proverbs 31:30 (NIV)

On a cold February afternoon, I connected with Mary, a longtime *Daily Guideposts/Walking in Grace* reader visiting her daughter and son-in-law nearby. Her daughter, Beth, served a delicious lunch at a table arranged to perfection. Yet it wasn't the food or decorative accents I remember most.

It was the words of her son-in-law. Jeff had joined us in the dining room after finishing up a project in his carpentry shop. The second he found a seat, he gazed across the table at Mary. "I have the best mother-in-law in this world, Roberta," he told me. "She has the most personal, intimate relationship with Jesus of any person I've ever known. When she talks about Him, I fully expect Him to walk into the room."

Because Jeff is a pastor and encounters all manner of faith-filled folks, his comment startled me. Until my mind reflected on Mary, that is. Twenty-five years before, I'd spoken at a retreat she attended. Hearing about my never-ending pain, Mary vowed to talk to Jesus about it every day until I was healed. Four years later, when my mother passed away, Mary, who lived in another state, somehow learned of it. At Mom's request, there was a family-only graveside service. Mary climbed that steep cemetery hill, kissed my hand, and said, "*I'm family,* Roberta."

I began to grasp the depth of Jeff's words. As Mary talked about Jesus that afternoon, He *had* walked into the room. In the presence of adoring, caring, and serving Mary, heaven had touched earth. Jesus had stayed with us the whole time.

Our family of Daily Guideposts/Walking in Grace *readers, Lord, is a priceless blessing. Thank you.*
—Roberta Messner

Digging Deeper: Psalm 46:5; Proverbs 31:10; 1 Peter 3:3–4

Are not two sparrows sold for a penny? Yet not one of them will fall to the ground apart from your Father. And even the hairs of your head are all counted. So do not be afraid; you are of more value than many sparrows.
—Matthew 10:29–31 (NRSV)

The forecast promised an entire week of frigid weather, including a two-day-long snowstorm followed by subzero temperatures, and then, to add insult to injury, two days of rain. I groaned. It had already been a severe winter in Connecticut, including a blizzard in early December, and now the first part of February looked worse.

Obsession with the weather runs in my family. My father raised my sister and me to study every meteorological sign, watch the sky, chart the seasons according to rainfall and temperature swings. I took this all very seriously, and, like my dad, am deeply affected by the weather. I've been trying to change that tendency, focusing on Jesus's many reminders that we are in the Father's hands and trying to control what He controls doesn't make sense.

Still, when my husband, Charlie, asked what was wrong, I couldn't stop myself. "There's a monster storm coming, and then it's going to freeze, and *then*, pouring rain. This winter is endless!"

Charlie, who does not share my weather worries—or any other worries for that matter—asked hopefully, "Doesn't that mean daffodils will be out soon?"

From anyone else, that would have been a joke. Not Charlie. An eternal optimist, he really believed that February snowstorms would result in daffodils. The Lord gave me a moment of grace, because in the second it took me to bite back an exasperated response, I realized Charlie was right. Spring would come after the storm. All in God's time.

Loving Creator, help me to live peacefully, joyfully, within
Your divine plan.
—Marci Alborghetti

Digging Deeper: Job 26:7–13

Tuesday, February 7

And Simon answering said unto him, Master, we have toiled all the night, and have taken nothing: nevertheless at thy word I will let down the net. —Luke 5:5 (KJV)

An aggravating physical symptom had stolen my sleep, and I knew I had entered one of my infamous worry loops. I followed my ritual toward my coffeemaker, then began my morning devotion, only to be directed to a scripture that appeared to nudge me into further unsettledness. If the Son had made me free, it said, I was "free indeed." As I nursed my cup of coffee, it occurred to me that last night's nagging concern, along with its attendant anxiety, was a glaring display of freedom compromised.

Compromised? But wasn't I trying to walk with Him faithfully every day? Hadn't I offered prayers throughout the night?

Still, worry had found ways to sneak back in.

Too sleep-deprived to take on that spiritual conundrum, I set down the mug in dismay. Unbidden, another scripture claimed my thoughts: "Master, we have toiled [fished] all the night, and have taken nothing: nevertheless at thy word I will let down the net."

Suddenly I knew it was time to give it another go. Having "fished" all night for peace, at my Savior's bidding, I was willing to pray again. It was clear that unlike the crowd in Luke 5:1 that "pressed upon him to *hear* [emphasis mine] the word of God," I'd been too worried to listen. The Holy Spirit in His perfect timing now pressed the Word upon my ear: fish again. Fearful anticipation was vanquished, prompting me toward peace.

Whether our "all-the-night" battle is an eight-hour sprint or a quarter-of-a-century journey, we are constantly called to pray again. Hope again. Love again.

Father, thank You for Your Word—and for Your Spirit, who knows just when to apply it.
—Jacqueline F. Wheelock

Digging Deeper: Psalm 34:4, 119:105; John 8:36

But the fruit of the Spirit is love, joy, peace, forbearance, kindness, goodness, faithfulness, gentleness and self-control. Against such things there is no law. —Galatians 5:22–23 (NIV)

When I awoke this morning, I beheld a fluffy white blanket covering the farm. It had started snowing just after noon the day before and continued long after I had retired for the night. Nine inches had fallen. As I look out the window, an unbroken expanse of snow greeted me. It was beautiful. Pristine. Unsullied.

Then the birds started flocking to the feeders and gathering beneath them looking for dropped morsels. The farm cats wandered around, adding their tracks. A squirrel bounded through the deep snow. Soon deer tracks, farm-boot tracks, and huge plow tracks down the long driveway would join them.

But for now, a white scroll, unmarked, unfolded, as far as my eye could see.

As I looked at it in the early morning light, I thought how much my day, at this moment, was like that. Not a mark on it. The cares of yesterday had not yet left their tracks. Neither had today's to-do list. Soon enough they would, along with things expected and unexpected. But for now, I was content to contemplate freshness—both of the snow and the day before me that was a gift from God.

I considered what tracks I would put on this scroll. The choice was mine. I decided that I should endeavor, with Divine assistance, to leave a trail of love, kindness, gentleness, and the like as I moved through this day. So that whoever might follow or look at my tracks would see the goodness of God in them. But most of all, so I could see the working of the Spirit in me.

God of all good things, nudge me please to walk daily with You and learn the ways I might manifest the fruits of the Spirit. Amen.
—J. Brent Bill

Digging Deeper: Psalm 51:7; Lamentations 3:22–24

Thursday, February 9

Finally, brothers and sisters, rejoice! Strive for full restoration, encourage one another, be of one mind, live in peace. And the God of love and peace will be with you. —2 Corinthians 13:11 (NIV)

I became a motherless daughter at age twenty-two.

My beloved mom, who, along with my grandmother and father, had been the center of my life, died as a result of lung cancer.

It was initially difficult to navigate my young adult life without Mom, but since then, I have been blessed to have a few self-selected "God-mothers"—women who serve as my spiritual guiders, who are always eager to hold out a helping hand to lift me up. They also lovingly lead me back to the Lord when I may forget my way.

I met Sister Tonnie when my family and I joined our current church home nearly twenty-two years ago. Tonnie already had sons, daughters-in-law, and grandchildren of her own, but she loved on me and warmly welcomed my family into hers.

Tonnie possesses a wonderful gift of hospitality, which she readily shares with others. I've been the grateful recipient of many of her special meals, and she freely shares her cooking tips with me. I even joined our church's hospitality ministry for a time because it allowed me to spend more time with her, soaking up her love and attention and snacking on her delicious quiches.

But what inspires me most is Tonnie's commitment to her faith. She has experienced life's highs and lows, including travails with racism as a young Black woman in the southern United States. But above all, she praises God and always reminds me to lift my concerns to the Lord. Her leadership inspires me to press forward and to leave a legacy for the next generation.

Father, I thank You for "God-mothers." Their gracious sharing of themselves is a greater influence than they may even realize.
—Gayle T. Williams

Digging Deeper: Romans 15:2; 1 Thessalonians 5:11

And the King will answer them, "Truly, I say to you, as you did it to one of the least of these my brothers, you did it to me." —Matthew 25:40 (ESV)

It is a strange thing to admit, but I am a huge fan of the Wiggles, an Australian music group for children, whose tunes are a staple in my home. I try to take my children, JoElla and Jacques, to see them in concert whenever their tour comes to a city near us. Nashville, here we come!

The concert was magical as always, and I experienced such joy with my children. We were thrilled to hear our favorites, "Hot Potato" and "Fruit Salad." Toward the end of the performance, I was reminded why I am a fan when Anthony, the Blue Wiggle, calls up the group's biggest fan from the audience, a young man with special needs. The joy in this young man's face while sharing the stage and singing with his favorite band led me to tears. I hold this memory close to my heart, not just because I am a Wiggles fan, but because the Christian tenet of "love your neighbor" was front and center in the auditorium that day.

On the drive home from the concert, I was frustrated with closed lanes and road work. My instinct was to protect my place in traffic—to not let anyone in. But my heart drifted toward the Wiggles concert, and I knew that small gestures of love and kindness would have a profound impact on others. I knew that the Lord was calling me to bring joy, light, and peace to others.

I yielded and allowed cars to go ahead of me from the merging lane.

Lord God, help me to bring Your light each and every day to those I meet. Help me to be mindful of my actions. May they always show kindness and love. I ask this in Your holy name. Amen.
—Jolynda Strandberg

Digging Deeper: John 13:34–35; Ephesians 4:1–3; 1 Peter 4:7–9

And yet other seed fell into the good soil, and grew up, and produced a crop a hundred times as much. —Luke 8:8 (NASB)

Our eight-year-old grandson, Isaac, hustled snow-shoveling jobs in his neighborhood, accepting whatever payment was offered. With his earnings, he bought thoughtful Christmas presents for nearly a dozen family members. But not his mother—as she was the one driving him around shopping.

Isaac stayed overnight with us at the end of February. He wanted to finally buy his mom a gift—but he was broke. It hadn't snowed much since Christmas.

The next day, we had a good snowfall. With the (generous!) money he earned helping me shovel, he went to the hardware store with his grandpa. He found a useful kitchen gadget for his mom.

The hardware store had a toy aisle. He had money left over. But the store also sold garden seeds. Isaac had recently planted an apple seed in a pot in his room and proudly shown me its sprout. He told me that, as he stood in the store, he thought to himself, "Toys/seeds. Toys/seeds." He came home with radish and lettuce and corn and watermelon and carrot seeds.

He told me he could have fun watching them "grow up." Is it any surprise that Isaac wants to be a farmer? He might be just eight, but Isaac is living out the teachings of Jesus—perseverance, generosity, and selflessness—and is making choices that multiply a yield.

Jesus opened His arms to children, saying, ". . . the kingdom of God belongs to such as these."

Although Isaac might not understand, to his grandma he's a "kingdom messenger."

> *Lord, Your messengers come in all kinds of "packages."*
> *Keep me ready to receive.*
> —Carol Knapp

Digging Deeper: Matthew 19:13–15; Luke 8:4–15; Galatians 6:9–10

One person gives freely, yet gains even more; another withholds unduly, but comes to poverty. A generous person will prosper; whoever refreshes others will be refreshed. —Proverbs 11:24–25 (NIV)

I have a confession to make. I'm a hoarder. Thankfully, I only hoard one thing. Yarn. There's yarn stored in nearly every room of my home, in addition to an entire room dedicated to yarn. The truth is, I own more yarn than some yarn stores. One of my favorite things to do is sit in my yarn room and sort through the bins, flip through knitting patterns, and dream of all the possibilities represented there. So much yarn. So little time.

To tell you how bad it is, a woman wrote me about her group who knit for charity. She heard about my legendary yarn stash and asked if I'd be willing to donate yarn to her and her group. I assured her I would. My heavens, I couldn't knit up all my collection in two lifetimes. And yet when I went through my stash, I found myself unable to give up a single skein. I went to a local hobby store and purchased yarn to give her. That's how serious my addiction is.

Gradually, the Lord is showing me that I don't need to be so tightfisted when it comes to letting go of the very things I love. So little by little, I'm surrendering my yarn to charitable organizations, letting go of that selfish part of myself. And when I do, God speaks to my heart and reminds me there is plenty of yarn in heaven, waiting for me.

You know how precious my yarn stash is to me, Father, and how hard it is to release a single skein. Thank You for the assurance that there is plenty of the very best possible collection awaiting me once I join You.
—Debbie Macomber

Digging Deeper: Matthew 6:20; 2 Corinthians 9:11

Monday, February 13

"But ask the beasts, and they will teach you . . ."—Job 12:7 (ESV)

I hoisted the last of the grocery bags into my arms and slammed the car door, feeling the weight of my load shift dangerously. *It probably would've been smarter to make two trips,* I thought. But it was too cold for all that. The snow squeaked like Styrofoam under my feet as I walked, and my breath fogged in clouds around my face. The frigid air felt sharp.

Suddenly, a loud, agitated chatter sounded from above. My presence had offended our resident red squirrel. This happened often, but today, I felt a pang of pity for it. It was so exceptionally cold. *Poor thing,* I thought. I sure was glad I didn't have to be stuck outside in this weather.

No sooner had the thought formed in my mind than the squirrel scampered into view, stopping in front of the steps to our deck. Sitting up on its haunches, it seemed to focus on me as it nibbled on something gripped in its teeth. After a few seconds, its fixed gaze started to make me feel downright self-conscious. I noticed its plump, well-fed little body. Thick, glossy fur. Unlike me, it didn't seem to be growing increasingly anxious over its freezing fingertips and ears. Indeed, that squirrel seemed at ease . . . comfortable in its element.

Eventually, the squirrel darted back up into the trees, and I continued toward the welcome warmth of the house. But my pity had vanished. It had been replaced with wonder at God's creation. And with respect for that small, loud squirrel, whose survival skills in this harsh subarctic environment were a thousand times what mine could ever be.

Thank You, Lord, for this lesson in humility and for the reminder that the right way to approach the natural world is not with condescension, but with the respect and awe Your creation deserves.
—Erin Janoso

Digging Deeper: Job 39:26; Psalm 107:24; Matthew 6:26

Love bears all things, believes all things, hopes all things, endures all things. —1 Corinthians 13:7 (ESV)

My daughter, Charlotte, worked remotely while her husband, Reuben, did an online internship. To save money until Reuben was employed, they stayed with my husband, Kris, and me for three months this winter. It was exciting getting to know our new son-in-law, reacquainting ourselves with our daughter as a grown-up, and watching their beagle, Milo—an indoor dog—join our family of Oklahoma farm dogs.

We soon had a routine. Kris and I cooked on weeknights, and the kids cooked on weekends. Everyone followed my New Year's resolution to "eat what's in the freezer." We divvied up the cleaning.

By day, Kris disappeared to his office, Reuben to the upstairs study, Charlotte to her laptop at the kitchen table, and me to my computer in the living room. Evenings, Reuben and I beat Kris and Charlotte at cards, while Milo vacillated between being out in the cold with our two dogs, celebrating the thrill of cattle and passing trains, or in the warmth with us, waiting for delightful tidbits to fall from the table.

Describing it sounds more idyllic than it was, though. I'm accustomed to my solitude—a prerequisite to writing—and the coziness often rankled. We disagreed frequently on political topics. Discussions of household matters often felt like critiques.

On Valentine's Day, I read an article about a submarine commander who offered this advice about sharing tight quarters: Assume good intentions. Love, I decided, does not suspect ill will but trusts in others' best.

> *Lord, help me love those around me better by trusting their motives and believing they mean what they say.*
> —Patty Kirk

Digging Deeper: Ephesians 4:1–7

Wednesday, February 15

But when you are praying, first forgive anyone you are holding a grudge against, so that your Father in heaven will forgive you your sins too.
—Mark 11:25 (TLB)

Shortly before her fiftieth birthday, my daughter said something that really hurt my feelings. Her almost-daily phone calls stopped, and for weeks I was so hurt that I did nothing to try to repair the relationship.

During that time, our assistant pastor, Father Rob, told a story during one of his sermons that felt like a bucket of water over my head. He said that when he was a sophomore in high school, he had an overdeveloped sense of adventure. One day he felt that he needed some attention, so he drove his pickup truck up the steps of his high school gymnasium and parked it right there at the door, got out, and went to class. Father Rob said he knew his dad would approach him that night with a punishment. And he did. His dad said, "That was cool, but you're not driving the truck for two weeks."

Father Rob went on to say, "What my dad was really saying to me was, 'I know you. I love you. I forgive you.' My dad didn't criticize me. He simply gave me a reinforcement of his love for his son."

That night, I texted my daughter. She texted back. I kept texting, and each time she responded until eventually we were on the phone chatting again like old times. In my heart, I remembered Father Rob's experience with his dad. I learned that there are many ways to let someone know that you know them, love them, and forgive them.

Father, You have no idea how much I depend on the fact that You know me better than anyone. You love me. You forgive me. You are amazing.
—Patricia Lorenz

Digging Deeper: Luke 17:1–4; Ephesians 4:31–32

From the breath of God ice is made, And the expanse of the waters is frozen. —Job 37:10 (NASB)

I woke up to the clattering sound of an ice storm. Lying in bed, I went over all the things to get done—a fast-approaching deadline at work, groceries I needed to buy, and laundry waiting and getting wrinkly in the dryer.

I poured myself a cup of coffee and looked out the window. The sun was coming up and the sleet was still coming down. My dog, Soda, waited at the door, needing to go out, so I grumbled a little and bundled up. Putting on his halter and leash, then my mittens, and lastly my hat, we headed out the door.

Outside, details of every living thing and every other thing glistened in the rising sun. Soda pulled a little on the leash, and we started on the trail that my husband snowplowed for us to walk on—only now everything had turned to ice. "Slow, slow," I said. I took tiny careful steps and waited in between. The deer-netting barricade around last year's garden had become amazing art, a cascading series of twinkles and flashes; the old elm on the property line sparkled.

"It's beautiful, Soda," I said. "Just beautiful."

We made our way to the driveway, which I realized almost too late had become a treacherous slide, so we circled back, inching our way slowly and carefully, discovering the gifts of the storm—ephemeral blessings—that I was thankful to see.

Lord, this morning I woke feeling overwhelmed with everything I had to do, but now I'm ready to take on the day, slow enough to see the dazzling details that Your hand has so wonderfully crafted.
—Sabra Ciancanelli

Digging Deeper: Isaiah 33:17; Lamentations 3:25

Friday, February 17

You, Lord, hear the desire of the afflicted; you encourage them, and you listen to their cry. —Psalm 10:17 (NIV)

The third Friday in February is National Caregivers Day in honor of all those workers on the front lines of caregiving. These dedicated professionals, often overworked and underpaid, deserve our applause, our gratitude, and our prayers.

Yet who isn't involved in some form of caregiving these days, whether it's for a spouse, a parent, a child, a friend, a neighbor, even a pet? We devote our time and our hearts to the health of those we love. Even with all the love we bring to our efforts, the stress can be overwhelming.

My mother died of Alzheimer's, the same disease both her older sisters and one of her three brothers succumbed to, as did their father, my pop-pop. My sister and my brother and his wife took on the day-to-day duties for Mom. I lived in New York, some six hundred miles from my family in Michigan. When I got a call that they found her wandering through her neighborhood in the middle of the night, telling the cops who found her that she was late for church, it tore me apart that I wasn't there.

Given my family history, a day rarely goes by that I don't question my memory and brain health. More than anything, I worry a lot about the care I could someday require and whether I will be a burden on a loved one.

But what is my faith if not complete dependence on the Lord? Is He not the great caregiver? It is not possible to be a burden on Him for His love is infinite and often His love is expressed through the love of others for us. When and if that day comes for me, I will remember whose care I am always in.

Lord, let Your blessings rain down on all caregivers, professional and otherwise, on this third Friday in February.
—Edward Grinnan

Digging Deeper: Joshua 1:9; 2 Corinthians 1:3–4

Your enthusiasm by now has spread to most of them.
—2 Corinthians 9:2 (MSG)

I reached into a cabinet and pulled out a stack of books from my kids'
childhood. "Let's read this one!" my three-year-old granddaughter,
Harper, exclaimed, extracting a book with sound buttons to press. But
pushing them produced no sound. "Dead batteries," I said. We sighed
and moved on to another book.

Later that day, Harper stood at the top of our stairs, sound book in
hand. "Grandad found new batteries!" she announced as if it was the
most wonderful news of the year. "Let's read it!" Another day, Harper
raced into where I was sitting and breathlessly informed me, "We're
making lemonade!" By her tone of voice, you'd have thought it was
Christmas morning.

Harper's excitement in these and many other instances opened my eyes
to how blah and subdued so many of my communications are throughout the day. So I decided to try turning some of my blah into bouncy.

Instead of my usual mumbled "morning" to my husband, I grinned,
gave him a hug, and said, "Good morning, my handsome husband!" I
think that woke us both up. When he asked if I wanted to ride with
him to the store, instead of a quiet "okay," I gave an enthusiastic "Sure,
I'd love to!" As I continued turning my apathetic into animated, I
noticed an increase both in my enjoyment and in my husband's appar-
ent enjoyment of me.

While I can't realistically utter every sentence as if I'd just won the
lottery, Harper's enthusiasm has made me at least try to put more gusto
into my daily conversation. I feel certain Jesus approves.

> *Lord, may the tone in which I speak reflect the joy I so often*
> *feel but don't make the effort to express.*
> —Kim Taylor Henry

Digging Deeper: Psalm 66:1–5

Sunday, February 19

A LIFETIME OF LOVE: Caring for Don

When the Sabbath was over, Mary Magdalene, Mary the mother of James, and Salome bought spices so that they might go to anoint Jesus' body. —Mark 16:1 (NIV)

The hospice nurse arrived an hour after Don died. She confirmed the time of death, notified our family doctor to certify the death, and made the official call to the funeral home. When she'd finished those tasks, she turned to me. "Would you like to help bathe Don?" she asked. I nodded, although I wasn't sure I could actually do it.

While family members visited outdoors, I brought a basin of warm water, a soft cloth, towel, and a comb. The nurse helped me gently remove Don's clothing, carefully preserving his dignity. While we washed him, she reminded me that death is not the end for believers, but the beginning of a new life with Christ. Although I knew that to be true, it was comforting to hear her words and her prayer for peace that followed. We dried and dressed Don, then I parted his hair on the right side, just the way he liked it. When the funeral director arrived to take his body, I was able to let him go.

Not everyone would have the opportunity or be comfortable with washing a loved one's body. For me, it was the last act of service I would ever do for Don—a husband, father, grandfather, and friend, who throughout his life placed the needs of others first. That act—and the memory of it, which I returned to often—was the beginning of my healing from the grief of his loss.

Gentle Jesus, after Your death, those who loved You longed to anoint Your body. Thank You for the precious opportunity to care for my husband of fifty-eight years one last time.
—Penney Schwab

Digging Deeper: Psalm 16:9–11; Luke 23:50–56; John 14:1–4

"[Love] takes pleasure in the flowering of truth." —1 Corinthians 13:6 (MSG)

Whether during a bracing, still, seven-degree winter morning, spring's explosion of green, or the late fall exposure of bare branches, I'm invigorated by views of the 1,339-foot-high Storm King Mountain from our front porch.

I imagine General George Washington eyeing the same range while riding on horseback from the Revolutionary War Military Cantonment at New Windsor, some four miles to the north, to West Point, five miles to our southeast. The massive red oak tree in our neighbor's yard could have been a sapling in Washington's time.

The close proximity of terrain familiar to the "Father of our Country" brings his person near. I aspire to embody his tempered, thoughtful, wise, and true leadership.

Then, memories of one of our favorite Washington, DC, locations—the National Cathedral—recall our sixteenth president, Abraham Lincoln. The northwest corner of the Cathedral nave contains a larger-than-life bronze statue of the "Illinois Rail Splitter."

To think of "Honest Abe" is to be inspired by someone tempered by difficulties; who fashioned suffering into a record that gives direction and lasting inspiration to us to this day.

The sincerity, integrity, and honorable strength of character possessed by these presidents inspire me. Truthfulness, candor, and care with speech are lasting attributes of a people who "out of the many, aspire to be one."

To You, ever-creating God, we give thanks and raise anthems of praise. In the words of the Psalmist of old, and in accord with the presidents we honor today, may we "walk straight, act right, and tell the truth" this day and always. Amen.
—Ken Sampson

Digging Deeper: Judges 5:31; Psalm 15:1–4; Ephesians 6:14

Tuesday, February 21

Let us draw near with a true heart in full assurance of faith . . .
—Hebrews 10:22 (KJV)

I pray the Holy Spirit gives me the right words to say," I said to my brother, Aaron, as we discussed a Bible study project I was working on. "I don't want to lead anyone astray. If I do, it isn't intentional."

"Don't stress about it," Aaron replied. "When the Spirit is guiding you, you'll have no doubt." He spoke of feeling the Spirit enter him when the opportunity arose for him to witness to a woman at work. She had ridiculed Aaron for years, calling him "that churchy guy." When hard times came into her life, she came to him to ask about his faith, admitting she could see how he faced life with more peace. Seeing she was genuine, he breathed a quick prayer for guidance.

"Suddenly, love for this woman washed over me," he said. "Up until now I didn't even like her, but warmth and compassion filled me completely. I told her about Jesus's love for us and His intent that we find rest in Him." She left the company soon after, and Aaron still has no idea if his witness had any effect on the woman. "All we can do is plant the seed," he said. "But I still feel warmth from that encounter, and I seek out every opportunity to experience it again."

"Lord," I prayed as I began my project with new confidence, "in this, and in all things I do, please fill me with You."

Father God, fill me with You until there is no more room for me.
—Erika Bentsen

Digging Deeper: 2 Corinthians 1:4; 1 Thessalonians 5:15;
2 Thessalonians 3:3

". . . you are dust, and to dust you shall return."—Genesis 3:19 (NRSV)

Ash Wednesday takes me back to Palm Sunday and an ancient ritual our church practices. Stick with me. Let's start with Palm Sunday, some nine or ten months earlier.

I'm not that dexterous, but one thing I love to do on Palm Sunday is to take the palms we've been given at church and weave them into little crosses. Sitting there in the choir loft, I'm reminded of how the events of Holy Week start with this joyous crescendo and then catapult into the Last Supper, the Crucifixion, and finally the Resurrection.

Those crosses sit on my desk for months, the green turning to brown, my attempts at basket weaving drying up on the edge of a pencil holder or letter box. If I'm ever tempted to throw them away, I remind myself of how their purpose will come soon enough, just as the Christ story resonates with us throughout the year.

On Shrove Tuesday, when our church hall smells of pancakes and sausages, those old palms are gathered and burned in the night air. On Ash Wednesday, they will become the ashes our ministers mark us with, the reminders of our own mortality.

I'll stand in line and the minister will say, "You are dust, and to dust you shall return," marking me with those ashes.

"Gosh, it seems so dreary," I might say to myself, this marking of death. Then I think of where those ashes came from and how they are part of the story. We held up those palms, rejoicing, seeing how death wasn't the end but the beginning, how our salvation came through Jesus's one life, lived heroically, sacrificially, showing us mortals the way to eternal transformation.

The cross we're marked with has changed our lives forever.

As Lent begins, let me give up what gets in the way of following Your Way.
—Rick Hamlin

Digging Deeper: Mark 1:15; Luke 9:23

Thursday, February 23

A person's discretion makes him slow to anger, And it is his glory to overlook an offense. —Proverbs 19:11 (NASB)

I stood in the garage on the phone in early January in disbelief. Terry and I needed a vehicle with fewer miles than our present one—one we could trust. Especially if we were going to pull the vintage travel trailer we'd purchased the summer before.

For tax purposes, we would withdraw from a retirement account by the end of the year half the amount we anticipated spending for the SUV and the remainder at the start of the new year. We met with our financial advisor in December to arrange the transfers.

Now, after the new year had already started, I heard him say, "I dropped the ball. I didn't get the money out at year's end."

He'd forgotten! From somewhere in my heart I summoned, "Don't worry. Either we aren't meant to get something now, or there will be another way to pay for it."

The call ended. Terry's "fix-it" projects spread out around me. I wondered how God was going to "fix" this. At the same time, joy flooded me. Instead of blaming, I'd responded with compassion. *Is this how God feels when He extends mercy to me?*

A month later, searching online, Terry found a vehicle that seemed right. A rarity—an older model in good condition with lower mileage. He and a friend traveled sixty miles to check it out. And Terry drove it home.

The most astonishing thing? We did not need the money the financial advisor had forgotten to withdraw! The price was just the amount we had agreed to withdraw in the new year.

> *Father in heaven, thank You for the "mercy fixes"*
> *You show me time and time again.*
> —Carol Knapp

Digging Deeper: Exodus 34:6; Matthew 5:7; Hebrews 4:16

The LORD replied, "My Presence will go with you, and I will give you rest." —Exodus 33:14 (NIV)

A tube in a truck," I said. "I can't do this."

My husband, Lonny, and I sat in our car. I have a history of back issues, and a disk had slipped again. Because the pain was debilitating, my doctor had gotten me the first available MRI appointment. Which meant a mobile unit parked outside a rural clinic.

"You have to," Lonny said.

Years before, our son had been trapped in an underground cave for twenty-one hours. I'd been claustrophobic since.

My heart hammered as Lonny pushed my wheelchair toward the clinic. A few minutes later, a young radiology technician helped me to a table that would slide into the machine. I hadn't been able to stand for days, yet I struggled to think of going into that small space.

"Knock on the walls if you need help," the tech said. "I'll get you out."

The table moved into the cylinder and panic moved over my soul. I banged on the walls until I was removed.

"Let me get your husband?" the compassionate young man asked. "Maybe that will help."

Lonny soon held me tight. "Can I touch her shoulder?" he asked the technician. "When you do the MRI?"

I wept as I moved back into the machine with my husband's hand firmly on my shoulder. Next, I could feel only his fingertips. But that gentle pressure reminded me that I wasn't alone. Lonny was with me, and the Lord was, too. The more I recognized His powerful presence, the less confined I felt. I could breathe. My fists uncurled. The tears stopped and I stayed still until the MRI was complete.

In my place of panic, God's presence brought rest.

Lord, because You are with me, there's no room for fear. Amen.
—Shawnelle Eliasen

Digging Deeper: Psalm 139:7; 2 Corinthians 3:17

Saturday, February 25

"The ear that hears, the eye that sees—the Lord made them both."
—Proverbs 20:12 (JPS)

I had been feeling fragile after the deaths of two friends, both younger than I was. I relied on my antianxiety medications more than usual.

About a month after I had stopped looking for comfort, I noticed that a large leaf had fallen onto the two thornbushes in the tubs on my deck. I'd chosen thornbushes because everything else I planted in the tubs had fallen prey to the squirrels, even the plants they weren't supposed to want to eat. The thornbushes had been unmolested for several years. The leaf seemed to be resting lightly on a couple of thorny twigs. I kept thinking I should lift it off, but I never did it. I continued to be depressed, and I told myself that if God wanted me to snap out of it, He would let me know.

This year's huge winter windstorms did the usual damage—knocking branches from the deciduous trees and evergreens surrounding the house, filling the gutters with enough leaves and debris to make me glad I had not hired anyone to clean them out at the end of the summer, and tossing enough limbs onto the roof of the house to startle me with every thud and bang.

After the first such storm, I noticed that the leaf had not been blown away. It still clung to the thornbush twigs but looked very precarious. I figured it would be gone after the next high wind. I was wrong.

We had two more increasingly violent storms, and after each I expected the leaf to have vanished, but it was still there when spring arrived. And then I realized that just as the leaf had weathered the storms, so could I. I was finally paying attention to what God was telling me.

Sometimes it takes me quite a while, God, but with Your help,
I get there in the end.
—Rhoda Blecker

Digging Deeper: Job 13:1; Jeremiah 28:7

Tell it to your children, and let your children tell it to their children, and their children to the next generation. —Joel 1:3 (NIV)

When you're a child, and maybe even when you're all grown up, you're afraid of things that go bump in the night. And in my childhood parsonage home, I was also afraid of a somber, moody painting of a woman looking straight at me. She hung there, immovable, day and night, at the top of the stairs.

But my bedtime journey was soothed by my mother's musical enticement. At the bottom of the stairs, oldest to youngest, we siblings lined up behind her and climbed to the second floor while singing, "We're marching upward to Zion, the beautiful city of God." Even as youngsters, on some level we understood the metaphor. There was nothing celestial about our upstairs bedrooms, but the song's otherworldly dimensions set our pace, settled our spirits, and identified our ultimate destination.

I hadn't heard the lyrics in years, and then on a recent Sunday overcast with foreboding storm clouds—real and metaphorical—I listened to the Washington National Cathedral worship service. The recessional featured a vibrant rendition of the classic Isaac Watts hymn "Come We That Love the Lord," with its familiar gospel refrain: "We're marching to Zion." Hearing the chorus, I set my sights on the promise of a less ominous world.

I shared the Internet link with my out-of-town family, who later tuned in. One sibling responded, "Good night, all." I was surprised to learn that the song now inspires a third—or is it fourth?—generation. "Mom sang it to me to get me to bed," my niece says. "And now it works for my boys." The power of music transports hearts to a higher plane.

> *Lord, remind me today of some tradition that draws my attention upward, to You.*
> —Evelyn Bence

Digging Deeper: Psalm 95:1–7; Isaiah 65:23

The desert and the parched land will be glad; the wilderness will rejoice and blossom. —Isaiah 35:1 (NIV)

New England winter has dragged on far too long. The gray skies, the residue of dirty snow and ice, and the dead-looking grass and trees make Lent especially bleak. God seems particularly distant in this empty season. I empathize with Jesus in the wilderness. It's the end of February and I am only now packing away the last of the Christmas decorations. I dust and return a few photos and knickknacks to their customary places, then pause as I move my desert rose from an obscure corner to the top of my low bookshelf.

My son and his wife had gifted me with this sandy-looking object years ago upon return from their honeymoon in Tunisia. Also known as a Sahara rose or sand rose, this unusual rock formation occurs when selenite gypsum crystalizes in the Sahara Desert following contact with moisture. The wafer-thin crystals form arrays of "petals" like a flower; some are single "blooms," while others, like mine, have many clusters. Now I hold it in my hand and regard it more thoughtfully.

A rose in the desert, something exquisitely lovely, enduring—and unexpected—has emerged from what otherwise seems an arid waste-land. What other mysteries might emerge from a desiccated landscape? From a bleak Lenten season? From my heavy heart?

I turn my desert rose this way and that in my hands, marveling at its exquisiteness. Out of vast, scorched sands God has created something of beauty that I am privileged to see. I begin to reconsider the mysteries—and potential beauties—in my own desert spaces.

> *Creator God, may I always discern the tiny wonders that*
> *show You are near.*
> —Gail Thorell Schilling

Digging Deeper: Deuteronomy 32:10; Isaiah 40:3–5; Mark 1:12–13

Let all bitterness and wrath and anger and clamor and slander be put away from you, along with all malice. —Ephesians 4:31 (ESV)

"H ow dare you!" "An outrage!"
There are two groups of monks, one Greek Orthodox, the other Armenian Apostolic, who are custodians of one of the holiest churches in Christendom: Church of the Holy Sepulchre, on the spot where Jesus was crucified, in the Old City of Jerusalem.

At least twice in the last fifteen years, brawls have broken out between them over what each has determined to be insults perpetrated by the other.

And it isn't just these two groups who occasionally fight. Other Christians claim responsibility for the Church of the Holy Sepulchre as well. Once, in 1970, when a few Coptic (Egyptian) Christians left their rooftop post for a few minutes, some Ethiopian Christians took over that spot and changed the locks.

"This was the point when the concept of 'love thy neighbor' went out the window," said one television commentator when one of the fracases hit the news. What an embarrassment this is to Christians everywhere!

But how common it is. Each group believes they are better prepared, or more entitled, to safeguard the cross of Christ. We fight over turf and authority, and we believe we will be rewarded for our faithfulness.

I do it, too. There was the time, recently, when I took issue with a church friend's "take" on a political issue on social media. It turned sour quickly. We haven't spoken since.

I felt, at the time, "righteous." I was wrong. I'm going to find him soon and apologize.

God, expose my own arrogance today. Show me when I assume that I am better than others. Give me the courage to make amends.
—Jon M. Sweeney

Digging Deeper: Galatians 5:16–25

LET US SING FOR JOY

1 _____

2 _____

3 _____

4 _____

5 _____

6 _____

7 _____

8 _____

9 _____

10 _____

11 _____

12 _____

13 _____

14 _____

15 _____

16 _____

17 _____

18 _____

19 _____

20 _____

21 _____

22 _____

23 _____

24 _____

25 _____

26 _____

27 _____

28 _____

MARCH

*Let the word of Christ dwell in you richly, teaching
and admonishing one another in all wisdom,
singing psalms and hymns and spiritual songs,
with thankfulness in your hearts to God.*

—Colossians 3:16 (ESV)

Be joyful in hope, patient in affliction, faithful in prayer.
—Romans 12:12 (NIV)

Early evening, my brother drove my parents from his home to their city apartment. As Mom was getting out of his car, she fell and broke her hip.

The next morning, I called the hospital and talked with my mother. She told me that it was the worst pain she ever experienced. Two days later, she had surgery. The hip surgery went well. But things got complicated due to her heart condition. She was moved to the ICU while she stabilized and to have her heart monitored.

I thought she would be out of ICU in a few days. But the days turned into weeks. Every time I could get a chance, we would talk on the phone or FaceTime. After several weeks in the hospital, she was moved to a rehabilitation center for physical therapy to get her back on her feet. Throughout this time I kept praying, but I was sad and concerned. *How is she going to get through this time, especially with her heart issues?* I worried.

While I worried and prayed, Mom was at peace. She remained calm and grateful, especially because she was one step closer to getting home. I reflected on my mom's life. She's been through a lot: In high school, she got rheumatic fever and spent a year at a hospital in recovery. In her fifties, she had open-heart surgery. Now she was dealing with another health issue but trusting God for comfort in her affliction.

Her faith and trust in God make us stronger as a family.

Eternal God, fill us with peace and calmness in the midst of adversity.
—Pablo Diaz

Digging Deeper: Psalm 18:2; Isaiah 26:3

Thursday, March 2

"I said to you, 'Have no dread or fear.'" —Deuteronomy 1:29 (JPS)

L.E. had always been Keith's cat. After Keith died, she eventually warmed up to me, but it took a long time, and I treasured her company.

The day finally came when she stopped eating even the little, cookie-like biscuits that were her evening treat, and I knew it was time to call the vet. But I balked at the idea of stuffing her into the cat carrier that she hated, taking her out of the home she had been so happy in, and making her necessary death frightening to her. However, I didn't want her to suffer from the inoperable mass in her abdomen that had been diagnosed only a few weeks before.

I shared my hesitation with my friend Dawn, who knew well what I was feeling, having been a dog and cat owner for many years. "What would you do?" I asked her.

Dawn said, "I use the mobile vet. She comes to your house to do exams and euthanasia, and she just got a new van so that she can do surgery, too. She's very good. I can call her for you, if you want."

Several hours later, a vet I had never met showed up at my door. I sat on my couch, cradling and murmuring to my cat, while the unfamiliar vet talked me through helping L.E. die without fear or discomfort. I had expected I would cry, but instead I felt a sense of wonderment that this all seemed so right to me.

After the vet left, Dawn and I had some tea. "I don't know why I'm not sadder," I said to her.

"Keep thinking about it," she said.

That's when I realized what I was really feeling. "She's Keith's cat again," I said, smiling. "I think they're both happy about that."

> *God of compassion, may the death of everyone I love be as*
> *easy and hopeful as L.E.'s was.*
> —Rhoda Blecker

Digging Deeper: Psalm 68:21; Song of Songs 8:6

Moreover, when God gives someone wealth and possessions, and the ability to enjoy them, to accept their lot and be happy in their toil—this is a gift of God. —Ecclesiastes 5:19 (NIV)

I make tables out of used toboggans. I find them in classified ads where people list their old sleds for sale. Mostly these transactions are uneventful, but some take a strange turn.

One elderly woman hung on to the sled, gently rubbing the worn wood. "This is from my childhood," she said wistfully. "My sisters and I would ride on it—then, later, my own children would sled down that hill over there. I hope *your* kids enjoy it as much as I have."

A smart buyer would've said, "Sure!" I am not a smart buyer. "Ma'am, my daughters are grown and gone," I confessed. "I'm going to cut up this toboggan to make a table. If you'd rather sell this sled to someone who will keep it intact, I understand."

She looked crestfallen at first, and then she said, "No. It's yours now. Do what you want. I have my memories."

Which is all any of us have, really. She could still recall the thrilling rides with her siblings, then repeating the experience with her own children. For more than half a century, the toboggan had carried its joyful cargo; its work was done. The memories would remain.

The toboggan now sits in my workshop, ready to be transformed. But now I'm the one who's hesitating—wondering if I have the skill, the courage, to make this memory into a new memory, wondering if I, too, am worthy enough to be transformed.

> *Lord, Your father on this Earth was a carpenter. Let the toil of my hands reflect what You see in us: as works who are worthy enough to be redeemed.*
> —Mark Collins

Digging Deeper: Psalm 19:14; 1 Corinthians 15:58

Saturday, March 4

Do not repay evil with evil or insult with insult. On the contrary, repay evil with blessing, because to this you were called so that you may inherit a blessing. —1 Peter 3:9 (NIV)

Do you still love your grandkids, even though they're Black?"

My mother looked at her neighbor in shock at her question.

"Of course," she answered, "I love my grandkids no matter what color they are."

We were visiting my parents in Florida for a few weeks, and now I understood why the widow downstairs never let my children pet her dog.

The next day, we came back from the grocery store and passed her patio where she was sitting. My father, who did not know about the exchange, lovingly petted the little dog my kids were forbidden to touch. I glared at her as I walked by without a word, but my mother stopped with my father and spoke kindly to the woman.

I didn't say anything that day, but I was annoyed with my mom. *How could she show such kindness to a woman who hated my kids, simply because of the color of their skin?* That evening, I watched my mom fill their plates with homemade food, kiss their curly heads as they ate, surprise them with ice cream for dessert, and snuggle with them on the couch as they watched television.

Her expressions of love were beautiful to watch, and I couldn't stay mad. She doesn't know how to be hateful, even to repay hate. There's likely nothing my mother can do to change a hateful heart, but she can simply be an example of what love and humanity should be.

> *Lord, thank You for the example of those who love their enemies. Help me to do the same.*
> —Karen Valentin

Digging Deeper: Matthew 5:44; Ephesians 4:32

BUILDING CATHEDRALS: Glory in the Ordinary

. . . You are not your own; you were bought at a price. Therefore honor God with your bodies. —1 Corinthians 6:19–20 (NIV)

When I contemplated motherhood, I had no idea how much of my time would be spent prepping and serving food and cleaning up in the kitchen. It turns out, if you have tiny people, you have to feed them. Like, a lot. Daily.

Our go-to winter fruit, the humble pear, never disappoints. We buy them in bulk and rotate them so that we always have a little bowl of perfectly ripe ones, ready for the grabbing. But after the kids watched me cut soft spots from strawberries, they wondered why we still ate the "yucky" parts of the pear, the browned, bruised spots.

"Well," I said, "I have a little secret to tell you. The brown parts on the pear are the sweetest." I sliced the pear into quarters, letting them taste for themselves. I explained the process of bruising—lots of oxidizing enzymes and phenols I won't bore you with—and at the end of the taste test, we agreed—the bruised parts were sweeter!

As they munched, I took the chance to remind them that just as they found flavor and joy in their not-so-perfect pears, Jesus loved them exactly as they were, bumps, bruises, and all. And that sometimes, God uses our bruises to make us even sweeter. We talked about how family challenges had made us emerge stronger. A hard moment on the playground reminded us how to treat others. A missing party invitation brought out our empathy for future guest lists. In all things, God works good for his glory and turns our bruises into badges.

Lord, remind me that while You never long to see me suffer, You have promised to bring good from all things.
—Ashley Kappel

Digging Deeper: Philippians 3:21; James 1:12; Revelation 21:5

Monday, March 6

Therefore, if anyone is in Christ, he is a new creation. The old has passed away; behold, the new has come. —2 Corinthians 5:17 (ESV)

April showers bring May flowers, they say. But what does March bring?

Mud.

Especially here in the Berkshires, where we had a lot of snow accompanied by a lot of cold that kept the ground covered for most of the year until a brash March heatwave swept the hills and melted everything, seemingly at once. Suddenly our Currier and Ives landscape was transformed into something like a mudflat.

I'm sorry to go on about this, but the mud gets into everything. I spend half the day wiping my feet and the other half wiping our dog Gracie's paws. Gracie *loves* the mud. I watch her like a hawk and never take her off leash on our hikes. She can't be trusted. Rolling in mud is her specialty. Sometimes I think she does it to mock my dislike of mud season. I've given her two baths this week already.

It hasn't escaped my attention that mud season coincides with Lent. If there is a spiritual lesson in the muddy misery I suffer every year, it is that pristine winter doesn't just morph into plush spring. There is this transitional, colorless subseason where we await the resurrection of the earth. As a boy, I always felt like we awaited Easter in a kind of gloom, too. I remember serving Mass during Holy Week in a dim, candlelit church suffused with incense and burning wax, statues of the saints shrouded until Easter morning when they would be revealed, flanked by extravagant arrangements of lilies. The sanctuary seemed to burst with light.

So I will take this lesson from mud season: Its very misery portends rebirth. And, well, if my dog wants to roll in the mud to celebrate, then so be it.

Lord, You defeated death so that we may all live redeemed. Lead me from the darkness to the light of Your resurrection.
—Edward Grinnan

Digging Deeper: Romans 12:2; Colossians 3:10

Seek the LORD and his strength; seek his presence continually!
—1 Chronicles 16:11 (ESV)

I t's my birthday. I wake and walk to the kitchen. There's much to be grateful for. A son made coffee. Summer sun presses through the front-door window. My husband will be home from work early. Later, a couple of our boys will bake a cake and another will come home from out of town.

Yet there's a longing. One son couldn't make it home. His seat will be empty.

I go about my morning, driving kids to clubs and camps, and I reason this out. Grant works in a hospital. He tried to make it work, but no one could cover his shifts. The drive is long, too long for one day.

Sensible. But I'll miss him still.

By afternoon, there's clatter in the kitchen and the sweet scent of barbecue from the backyard. I can hear my boys, voices that have changed pitch from boys to men. My arms are full of folded towels as I walk past the front door.

And there is Grant. On the other side of the glass.

He sets his bag down and comes in. His eyes, like my grandfather's, sparkle bright blue.

"Hi, Mom," he says. "Happy birthday."

I don't know how his schedule changed, but Grant is here. Towels go to the table and my arms go to his neck. I would've understood his absence. I would've given grace. But Grant's presence speaks. *I value you. Our time together is important. Our relationship is worth a sacrifice. I want to be with you.*

When we gather around the table, every seat is full. I never doubted my son's love for me. But I'm so very glad he's here.

Lord, give me passion to seek You—to spend time with You. Time to know Your Word. To listen for Your voice. To hear Your heart. Amen.
—Shawnelle Eliasen

Digging Deeper: Psalm 5:3; Luke 6:12

Wednesday, March 8

Yet the LORD longs to be gracious to you; therefore he will rise up to show you compassion. For the LORD is a God of justice. Blessed are all who wait for him! —Isaiah 30:18 (NIV)

Sometimes God reaches out to me in the most unlikely places. Earlier this year, the pressures of life and work were really getting to me. I'd been going through a season of extra-heavy responsibilities in the church I pastor. Some of them were simple growing pains, but others involved tough conversations with people I cared about. My anxieties were getting me down.

My wife, Margi, saw it happening. She came to me one afternoon and gently said I'd been crabby and she could see it. "What's going on?" she said. "How can I help?" We had a great conversation, and I realized I needed to adjust my attitude. No excuses.

I prayed. I asked God to remind me that the pressures I faced were never greater than the grace He supplied.

Later that week, my prayer was answered—God spoke to me from a humble bag of frozen French fries. I mean that literally. Once again, I was super busy and feeling overwhelmed but needed to make a quick stop at my local grocery store on the way home.

I stood, holding a bag of fries in the frozen food aisle of my grocery store. But God had turned it into a sanctuary. There, printed on the same bag of fries I had purchased countless times before, was something I'd never noticed. A Bible verse. The manufacturer of this brand actually prints Isaiah 30:18 on the back of its bag. God met me in a special way right then, right there. The noise of the store faded away as God gave me just the reminder I needed. No matter how great my anxiety, he longs to be gracious to me and rises to show compassion to me.

> *Gracious Father, remind me again and again that Your*
> *grace always exceeds my need.*
> —Bill Giovannetti

Digging Deeper: Philippians 4:19

The LORD is nigh unto all them that call upon him . . .
—Psalm 145:18 (KJV)

Okay, I admit it. I like golf.

If you don't play, it might look easy, hitting a ball around a lush green field. But golf is an incredibly difficult sport. One that I'm not really good at but enjoy all the same.

Even as a novice golfer, I know that the spring Masters Tournament at the beautiful Augusta National Golf Club is the height of a golfer's success. So when a friend had the opportunity to attend the Masters, I looked forward to hearing a firsthand report of his experience.

"Brock," he said over lunch, "it was amazing. Standing on that hallowed course, watching the best golfers in the world!" He continued, "The grounds were immaculate, the crowd had this incredible energy, and the tournament was so well organized that it rolled along like a well-oiled machine!"

Sure, I'd heard other descriptions of Augusta, but as he continued, his words took on a wider meaning. "But to me," he said, "the thing that stood out was how the players practiced continuously—on the driving range, on the practice greens, on the chipping area. One of my favorite players hit balls out of the sand trap for over an hour!"

I mulled over the word "practice" as my thoughts moved to my ongoing struggle with faith. Imagine what might happen if I practiced following the words of Jesus the way I practice golf. Imagine how much better my life would be if I laser-focused on prayer and kindness and forgiveness in the same way I focus on my swing.

Golf didn't seem so important now, as I imagined myself out in the great green expanse of life, practicing living a life of good, with Him.

Father, be my Partner in this great game of life. I can think of
no better practice than being with You.
—Brock Kidd

Digging Deeper: Jeremiah 33:3; John 16:24

Friday, March 10

"In your anger do not sin . . ." —Ephesians 4:26 (NIV)

Only three minutes left, the treadmill's workout timer said. A moment ago, my lungs had been burning, and my legs were tired. But then the memory of a local governance meeting I'd attended the night before started churning through my mind. I'd been horrified by what I'd heard. Officials charged with empowering the vulnerable within our community were instead using their authority to cause harm. The more I thought about it, the more my anger flashed, its energy flooding my tired muscles. My weariness was gone. I felt I could run another five miles, no problem.

And so I did. I ran and ran, unsettled by the power of the feeling that gripped me. Its potential seemed volatile and dangerous. But also fierce and strong and real. *Help me, Lord,* I called out. *Give me some wisdom.* Was it wrong to feel this way? What was I supposed to *do* with all this angry energy? I didn't know, so I just kept going until my body's physical exhaustion tempered what I was feeling inside.

By the time I got home from the gym, an idea had formed, an answer to prayer. I pulled out my laptop and started writing. "This Letter to the Editor is in response to . . ." I began. Emails followed to and from community members and leaders. There were things that needed to happen in response to that meeting, and I felt like my fingers couldn't type fast enough.

"Anger is energy with a message" someone had said to me once, and suddenly I understood. With my destructive rage spent on the treadmill, what was left—focused in this careful, prayerful way—didn't feel wrong at all. In fact, it felt like God-given fuel for work that had been waiting for me all along.

> *Anger is confusing, God. Yet, it's an emotion even Jesus felt.*
> *Help me, always, turn from my rage toward You and the*
> *righteousness You desire. Thank You.*
> —Erin Janoso

Digging Deeper: Nehemiah 5:6; Psalm 4:4, 37:8; James 1:19–20

Surely goodness and mercy shall follow me All the days of my life; And I will dwell in the house of the LORD Forever. —Psalm 23:6 (NKJV)

My friend Mary Starr trains sheepdogs, or herding dogs. Some are trained to perform competitively. Others are actually used by sheep ranchers and farmers who raise livestock in New Mexico, Colorado, and Montana. On more than one occasion, while driving through the Western states, I've seen shepherds leading their flocks to greener pastures. Twice I've had to stop my car on a rural road so a man and his bleating flock could cross from one side to the other. The shepherd is always out front while his dog brings up the rear or runs beside the flock, making sure all the sheep stay together. The dog barks, using aggressive behavior to make the sheep obey its "orders." The dog makes sure none of the sheep stray, that they follow in the footsteps of the shepherd.

Recently in my Bible study group, I learned that the Hebrew word *follow* as used in Psalm 23 is really a much stronger verb that means *pursue* or *chase*. Mary Starr's trained working dogs immediately came to mind. I easily imagined the Lord's goodness and mercy bounding alongside David the psalmist like twin sheepdogs, actively urging him to follow the path of righteousness. Don't you love that image? It has changed forever how I will read Psalm 23, for I know the Lord's goodwill and loving-kindness are guiding me too, pursuing me along the trail that leads to eternal life where I will dwell in the house of the Lord forever.

Heavenly Father, You are indeed the Good Shepherd. I thank You for Your goodness and mercy toward me.
—Shirley Raye Redmond

Digging Deeper: Psalm 23; Hebrews 4:16; 1 Peter 1:3

Sunday, March 12

How good and pleasant it is when God's people live together in unity!
—Psalm 133:1 (NIV)

From fourth grade onward, my best girlfriends came from diverse religious traditions: Greek Orthodox, Congregationalist, and Jewish. In high school, I added a close Catholic friend. We were always friends first; our faith traditions and their differences did not define us. We enjoyed sharing our faith stories, yet never considered one's faith better than the other, any more than our eye color. During the 1960s, a time of intense ecumenicalism and outreach, when our church youth group visited other houses of worship, I first visited a synagogue. The Torah fascinated me, especially when kids I knew could read it.

I again visited a synagogue few years ago, when I attended "Instructional Sabbath" here in town. During this, the rabbi paused to explain each part of the beautiful service to a congregation composed of Christians and the curious. Words of the unfamiliar songs and prayers especially inspired me as they expressed a desire to be close to God. And our church has reciprocated.

At least once a year, our Episcopal ministry study group invites the local rabbi to be a guest speaker. Most recently, Rabbi Robin spoke about Sabbath: origins of the traditions, interpretations within Judaism, memories from her childhood, and her own deep feelings for this sacred celebration. Invariably I learned more about my own faith in the light of new knowledge and reaffirmed that God loves me and all His children very much.

Lord of all, may I see Your face in each person I meet. Amen.
—Gail Thorell Schilling

Digging Deeper: John 13:34; Romans 14:19;
2 Corinthians 13:11; Hebrews 13:1

Teach us to number our days, that we may gain a heart of wisdom.
—Psalm 90:12 (NIV)

Our British Lab, Darby, had always been a quiet observer in our chaotic household. Gentle and meek by nature, she didn't demand a lot of attention. She had been a constant companion for eleven years, playing with the children, greeting us at the front door, and cuddling up beside anyone who took a moment to rest.

But something was wrong. I took her to the vet and our fears were confirmed: Darby was sick, though we would have to wait a few days for the test results.

As my family grappled with the news, I couldn't help but wonder if we were going to have to say goodbye. I wasn't ready and neither were my husband and children. I felt guilty. For the past eleven years, I had been busy raising children and I had taken Darby for granted. Why hadn't I spent more time with her?

On Monday morning, the vet called. Darby had diabetes, and, if we were willing, we could give her an inexpensive insulin injection every day. We discussed it with the children, and everyone committed to helping. Six months later, Darby is alive and doing well, though we know each additional day is a gift from God.

I learned a valuable lesson during Darby's illness, one I have applied to watching my children grow up and my parents age. We will never have enough time with the ones we love, even if we have a lifetime with them. There is no place for guilt or what-ifs and maybes that plague us. Instead, I've learned to use that energy to appreciate each day and devote myself to not taking it—or the people and dog I love—for granted any longer.

Lord, when I am feeling overwhelmed by the passage of time and missed opportunities, help me to focus on the gift of today.
—Gabrielle Meyer

Digging Deeper: Ecclesiastes 3:1–2; James 4:13–14

Tuesday, March 14

"Now be pleased to bless the house of your servant, that it may continue forever in your sight; for you, Sovereign LORD, have spoken, and with your blessing the house of your servant will be blessed forever."
—2 Samuel 7:29 (NIV)

I'd only agreed to temporarily bring the fourteen-year-old couch into our new home because I couldn't decide on new furniture. In my perfect world, every room would have been outfitted and every window draped before the last moving box was unpacked. Yet, most of the rooms were empty. I'd perused numerous furniture stores and décor shops with one of my good friends in hopes of being inspired and pinpointing the perfect look for our space. I felt overwhelmed with making decisions instead of gratefulness for the blessing of a new home.

The brown leather couch that had seen better days welcomed me home every time I plopped down on it at the end of the day. But that wasn't what I'd envisioned. I wanted guests to enter our home and gasp at the perfection of my interior design—all worthy of a magazine spread. I wanted to create a home of beauty that my children could feel proud about and enjoy.

My husband didn't seem to be disturbed by the hodgepodge of furniture scattered haphazardly about the room, but he sensed my growing frustration. "Stop rushing. Enjoy the process, and things will work out in time."

He was right. Our new home wasn't about decorating it with the finest furniture or following the latest trends. It was about creating a home that brought us joy, welcomed the presence of God, and was filled with the greatest thing—love. A house isn't a home without it. And my house still has the old brown couch that welcomes me home.

Lord, may Your love abide in our home as we follow You and invite others in to tell them of Your peace, goodness, and faithfulness.
—Tia McCollors

Digging Deeper: 1 Samuel 25:6; Proverbs 24:3–4

Point your kids in the right direction—when they're old they won't be lost. —Proverbs 22:6 (MSG)

Y ou have to clean your room!" I repeated almost daily when my daughter Kendall was growing up. Her messy room became a familiar battleground. She is the youngest of our three children and always had the messiest room. I feared she would grow up to live in a messy house, creating chaos for her own family, all because I was a bad mom.

As the years went on, I began to lighten up, maybe because parents often lighten up with the youngest over time. But more importantly, I realized her room was the only space in our house that was truly hers, and I should let her live in that space as she chose. I celebrated my changed attitude when I discovered a small, framed message at a gift shop. I purchased it. The next day, while Kendall was at school, I climbed over the stuff on her bedroom floor to hang it on her wall as if to anoint her space with this message:

"I'd rather be messy and creative than neat and boring."

Kendall is now a busy wife and mother of three young children but still manages to paint and even sells some of her paintings; she creates beautifully framed calligraphy messages and rearranges rooms of furniture for friends because she has an instinct for comfort and décor. And surprise! She lives in an organized, clean home. Except for her youngest daughter's bedroom. It's usually a total mess, which makes me smile.

> *Lord, thank You for growing me up while I was trying to grow my child up.*
> —Carol Kuykendall

Digging Deeper: Ephesians 6:1–4; 2 Timothy 4:2

Thursday, March 16

So with you: Now is your time of grief, but I will see you again and you will rejoice, and no one will take away your joy. —John 16:22 (NIV)

My bedroom window looks out across a field and onto my mom's house. At night when I close my curtain and get ready for bed, her house is dark, but in her front yard, every night of the year—winter, spring, summer, and fall—a string of Christmas lights sparkles in the darkness like a constellation.

Turning on the lights year-round began the night my oldest sister died in her sleep on St. Patrick's Day. The bulbs were still strung on Mom's trellis from the holidays, so that life-changing evening, overcome with shock and grief, Mom plugged them in to bring a little light into the world. At least that's what I thought.

It wasn't until months later, when I was leaving Mom's house, that she said, "Sabra, on your way out, plug in the lights, okay? So your sister can find the house from heaven."

That walk home, I looked up at the sky, thinking how love is so beautiful, infinite, and pure, outstretching, outlasting anything and everything. My heart ached yet soared, witnessing the ties that bind us to one another and the promise that connects us to heaven and to the grace of God.

> *Lord, tonight, thirteen years later, the lights still glow,*
> *a reminder of Your everlasting love.*
> —Sabra Ciancanelli

Digging Deeper: Psalm 34:18; Romans 8:18

St. Patrick's Day, Friday, March 17

The LORD is my light and my salvation; whom shall I fear? The LORD is the stronghold of my life; of whom shall I be afraid? —Psalm 27:1–2 (NRSV)

With a name like Sweeney, you can be almost certain that generations ago, my grandparents came over on a ship from Londonderry to Boston. Leaving behind everything they knew for an uncertain future in a potentially hostile place was their fate, yet also their reason for hope.

On those ships, to sit below deck in a shared cabin was a good way to make anyone claustrophobic. To be above deck was to face ominously dark nights and, often, sheets of cold rain and winds that made it impossible to stand up.

I can only imagine how frightening the journey must have been.

Then, when they arrived, unless they remained in the Irish neighborhoods of Boston or New York, they quickly faced signs that read, "No Irish" and "Irish need not apply."

The courage of my Irish immigrant ancestors inspires me. Even more important, they were people of abiding faith. The Lord was truly their strength. The Lord was really their light, despite what felt dark in the world before them.

I take their experience with me today, on this special day for Irish and would-be Irish everywhere. You don't have to have had Irish grandparents to share in the joy of this day. That's what is so fun about it.

St. Patrick's Day is for all of us, and for all of us with God, there is no need to be afraid.

> *Your light shines before me, Lord.*
> —Jon M. Sweeney

Digging Deeper: Psalm 91

Saturday, March 18

Give, and it shall be given unto you . . . —Luke 6:38 (KJV)

Driving and shopping wear me out fast, so when my wife, Sharon, said, "Let's drive down to Boonville and do some shopping," I suddenly felt sleepy but went anyway.

When we bridged the Missouri River into Boonville, I noticed a middle-aged woman trudging along the berm. She was wearing a ruffled white blouse, a long blue skirt, and sandals. "Not exactly walking clothes," I said to myself, "and much too warm for a July day."

After a day of shopping, I was exhausted and anxious to get home, but my wife pointed across the street. "Look, there's that woman we saw on the other side of town, when we arrived this morning. She's limping!"

I pulled alongside the woman, and Sharon rolled down her window. "Ma'am, are you okay? Do you need help?"

The woman explained that her car had died in the morning and that she had no way to get home except to walk. "I live that way," she said, pointing further south. "About twelve miles." Her clothes were soaked in sweat.

I cringed at the thought of adding twenty-four miles to our day, but I could see that this woman was on the verge of collapse. "Get in!" I urged her, reaching for the door handle.

The twelve miles flew by. I helped the lady out of the car and up the rickety steps to her aged trailer home. Her eyes were moist with gratitude.

Soon we were winging our way north, bound for home, when I noticed—for the first time all day—that I was not tired. I was, in fact, exhilarated, with the energy that comes from being used by God.

> *When I give mercy, Lord, You give me wings.*
> —Daniel Schantz

Digging Deeper: Proverbs 3:3; Hosea 6:6

He will carry the lambs in his arms, holding them close to his heart.
—Isaiah 40:11 (NLT)

A light breeze skittered some leaves across the trail behind Sunrise, my golden retriever. I sighed. It had been an "off" day. Even my prayer time this morning had seemed disconnected. In a few feet, Sunrise stopped and glanced over her shoulder, her white face revealing her age. She seemed to squint and cock her head as she looked toward me, then she trotted off. *That was strange.*

Normally we'd walk a loop on the vacant land, but today I'd planned to detour a bit and check the mail. When we got to the place where I wanted to clip on her leash, I called, "Sunrise." No response. *The breeze must be playing tricks with her ancient ears.* I yelled. Her head came up and she stared straight at me. I yelled louder, "Sunrise, c'mon." Her head snapped away from me, as if she thought I was in front of her. Then she took off running full speed—in the wrong direction. I hustled down the trail. I knew her eyesight and hearing were fading but not this badly. *Lord, I don't need another thing to go awry today. Keep her safe.*

Ten minutes later, she bounded over the hill, coming straight for me, her nose locked on my scent. She wiggled like a puppy when she stopped in front of me. I clipped on the leash. "You've got to stay close to be safe." *Stay close to be safe.* Instantly the verse about God holding the lambs came to mind. The lambs were so close they could hear His heartbeat. *That's where I need to be.*

> *Lord, when I start my day, help me to press in—and wait—until*
> *I become so close to You that I hear Your heartbeat. Then I*
> *want Your presence to stay with me all day. Amen.*
> —Rebecca Ondov

Digging Deeper: Psalm 92; John 15:5

Monday, March 20

Let us hold fast the confession of our hope without wavering, for he who promised is faithful. —Hebrews 10:23 (ESV)

I start making dinner around five o'clock each evening because my husband, Dwight, is home by six. The kids usually wander into the kitchen sometime in between and ask, "What's for supper?" It's been our daily routine for so many years now that I take it for granted. But one day recently, I stopped to think about how extraordinary it all is.

Why do I cook at a certain time? Why do the kids ask what we are having?

It's because, over time, we've all built up certain expectations of one another. We've done the same things for so long that we don't wonder whether or not they will happen; instead, we fully expect that they will.

We've developed faithfulness.

Dwight is faithful to go to work and come home each day. I'm faithful to prepare a meal each evening. Our solid track record gives us every reason to think that our patterns will continue.

It's the same with God. I don't have any worry about whether God will be there for me when I have a problem or whether He really has prepared a place for me in heaven. I know I can trust Him because He is faithful. Because He has always taken care of me, I have every confidence that He will continue to do so.

I can't imagine my children suddenly wondering whether they're going to have supper or not. I can't imagine Dwight one day deciding not to come home. And I can't imagine God not fulfilling all His promises to me. He has shown me time after time that I can trust Him. He is faithful.

Father, great is Your faithfulness!
—Ginger Rue

Digging Deeper: Deuteronomy 7:9; Isaiah 25:1

So then, just as you received Christ Jesus as Lord, continue to live your lives in him, rooted and built up in him, strengthened in the faith as you were taught, and overflowing with thankfulness. —Colossians 2:6–7 (NIV)

Whenever my family and I break bread together, we begin by saying a blessing over our meal, followed by what we call "Thankful." It's a time when we each offer a short description of one thing that we're grateful for that day.

It allows us to reflect on our day and creates a chance for each of us to discuss the high and low points. It's also a reminder that no matter what occurred that day, the Lord remains on the throne, and we will band together to help each other through whatever comes our way.

Our "Thankful" statements commend large and small events: good grades, a good health report, or the ability to enjoy a long walk. On other days, we're simply grateful for the obvious blessings that we sometimes take for granted, such as food, shelter, and warmth. When we're tired, hungry, or aggravated, the statement may just be "I'm glad this day is nearly over."

But even on stressful days, there are things that I am genuinely thankful for: peace in my home, continued employment, love and respect from my husband and sons, a supportive work team, a great conversation with my mother-in-law, or the love of my caring and honest friends.

I pray that I keep my eyes open to these small things that have monumental value and take nothing for granted. Christ's love is viewable in all ways, at all levels, and for that, I am truly "thankful."

Lord, I can't thank You enough for all the blessings You have bestowed upon me. Let me always be aware of Your grace.
—Gayle T. Williams

Digging Deeper: Psalm 118:1; Colossians 3:15; Hebrews 12:28

Wednesday, March 22

And Moses said, I will now turn aside, and see this great sight, why the bush is not burnt. —Exodus 3:3 (KJV)

During the antebellum South, African American slaves knew the printed word was precious. Repeatedly, they defied their forced routines, risking their lives to learn to read. So I found it disturbing when, well into the latter half of the twentieth century, the thousands of volumes I oversaw as a school librarian were largely ignored. Students passed by the library each day without so much as a backward look, never pushing past those double doors except by mandate.

Granted, turning aside can require grit. When Moses saw the curiosity of a burning yet unconsumed bush, he could have allowed fear to keep him from investigating. Or, like some modern-day students, he might have reasoned, "This is not my assignment; I don't *have* to do this." By turning aside to see the strangely illuminated bush, Moses helped to advance the trajectory of the Almighty Himself, and while Moses's encounter with God was a promising harbinger of the future, taking time to turn aside can also help us savor God's blessings both present and past.

An intentional change in direction to reflect upon His great compassion can help us to clearly see this truth: Escaping our routines to gaze upon what God has *already* performed—a loved one's healing, a missed car accident, a restored relationship—can make today's concerns much less daunting. While the students of my librarian years might have missed a life-changing experience, believers have a never-ending opportunity to take a moment and glorify God.

Though it demands deliberateness, if we take time to indulge in God's faithfulness, His endless gifts can stir us toward praise. And quite often that praise flavors our days with the priceless sweetness of peace.

> *Gracious Father, I so desire to pause daily and appreciate*
> *Your manifold blessings.*
> —Jacqueline F. Wheelock

Digging Deeper: Psalm 103:1–5, 107:8–9

The world and its desires pass away, but whoever does the will of God lives forever. —1 John 2:17 (NIV)

The folder of tax documents sat by my reading chair. I glanced at it at least twice a day. My to-do list was long and free time was short, and a walk in the spring air seemed far more appealing. Also, I kind of wished that for once my husband would do the tax prep. I knew for certain that would be a really bad idea, but some wishes die hard.

My normal rule of thumb for a task I dislike is twofold. If it will take less than five minutes, I do it immediately to get it off my list. If it will take a longer amount of time, I break the task into bite-size chunks. Trust me, this is not due to virtue: I simply dislike the weight of having things hanging over me more than I dislike doing them.

But the taxes did not get done. I reminded myself it wasn't going to be all that hard to do. Nor was it going to take me all that long. God would be with me, every step of the way. Yet somehow this year it simply felt impossible. By mid-March, the W-2s were almost shouting at me, and the 1099s giggled wickedly. Finally, in frustration, I asked myself point-blank, "*Why* aren't you doing this?"

The reply was straightforward: "I don't wanna!" I laughed out loud. Even well into middle age, my inner three-year-old was alive and kicking. I took a deep breath and said a prayer to the God who loves me and is with me always, even during tax season. Then I pulled out the file and got to work.

Lord, remind me that "I can't" is often code for "I don't wanna!"
—Julia Attaway

Digging Deeper: Acts 5:29; Hebrews 10:36

Friday, March 24

For he will command his angels concerning you to guard you in all your ways. —Psalm 91:11 (NIV)

My community had experienced devastating flooding. That included the storage facility where I'd rented a unit. By the time I pulled my U-Haul into the gravel lot to check on my treasures, it was absolute bedlam. Vehicles were wedged everywhere, and folks were frantic with worry.

One lady had housed the sum total of her worldly goods there. Another toted a water-logged box containing family photos. A man swam for a tabletop Christmas tree from his boyhood.

A lean guy in a dark denim jacket and baseball cap appeared at my U-Haul window. "Water's rising fast, ma'am," he said calmly. "It'll submerge your axle and your wheels won't move. Stay right here."

I turned my head, and the denim-jacketed guy was nowhere to be seen. But he had such a knowing, concerned way, I followed his advice and didn't move.

All day long, I asked others about him. "You mean the walking owner's manual for every vehicle ever invented? He was here, then—*poof!*—he was gone."

When the water receded, I returned to the facility to retrieve my belongings. I spotted that dark denim jacket. "We've been looking all over for you," I said. "We decided you were an angel."

"Nah!" he said. "I'm a mere mortal mechanic. Everyone else was doing something important. All I knew was to keep the vehicles running."

No matter what you called him, he'd been heaven-sent. Not a single vehicle had broken down, been swept away, or gotten mired in the muck.

Just an everyday person doing what he does best, Lord.
Help me to do the same.
—Roberta Messner

Digging Deeper: Psalm 78:25, 103:20; Colossians 1:16

They are like trees planted by streams of water, which yield their fruit in its season . . . —Psalm 1:3 (NRSV)

I headed out for a Saturday afternoon walk. I'd been reading a book about prayer, and the writer pointed out that taking a prayer walk and reflecting on the beauty of what you were seeing every step of the way might connect you to the Creator.

Hmmmm, I thought. I was not totally convinced. I generally close my eyes when I pray. How would I pray while walking?

At any rate, I figured I'd try. I set out, ambling along the sidewalk where normally I'm running in the mornings, my earplugs tuned in to some podcast. I realized that . . . well, yes, you did notice more things when you were walking and not listening to some commentator. That curious crack among the rocks, the sound of a bird flapping its wings, the buds pushing up beneath the trees. *Green shoots already?* I thought, wondering, *God, are you here?* Or more exactly, *God, what are you telling me? That I need to slow down a bit? Stop and smell the roses, as they say?*

I came to an overlook and *stared* at a grove of trees. Spindly right now, no leaves on their branches. That bird's nest, though—wasn't it amazing? It looked like it had been constructed of pieces of cotton. And that one looming oak tree amidst them all. Could have been there for at least a hundred years. Twisting where the wind had blown it, still pushing up.

Then it came to me: Be like that oak. Raise your gaze. Weather life's storms. Spread your arms out to shield those you love. Offer shelter and shade to others.

Wow, I'd never identified with an oak tree before. I stood a little taller, happier, braver. And walked on.

> *Blessed Creator, may I always be listening and learning*
> *and hearing what You have to say.*
> —Rick Hamlin

Digging Deeper: 1 Chronicles 16:33; Hebrews 11:3

Sunday, March 26

The LORD is good to all, And His tender mercies are over all His works.
—Psalm 145:9 (NKJV)

My library includes a hundred-year-old volume valued by my pastor dad. *Forty Thousand Quotations* provided a lifetime of inspirational lines to bolster his Sunday bulletins. In the tome, I've found a William Wilberforce sentiment: that roses are "the smiles of God's goodness."

My dad agreed, and his love of roses is part of my emotional inheritance. Every time we moved to a new parsonage, he planted and tended some ten bushes. For a decade of Sundays, a florist's fresh rose graced the church pulpit. We placed lavish sprays on my parents' coffins.

A few weeks ago, knowing I needed some cheer, my sister sent me a dozen roses—yellow, red, pink, and white. They immediately set my world aright. On the first day, I carried them upstairs or down as my locus shifted. Later I divided the bouquet among smaller vases displayed in different rooms.

Then, as the blossoms faded and drooped, my spirits fell. As I drained the water, I sighed and accepted reality: Nature's blooms are short-lived. But before I discarded the stems, I plucked off petals of various colors to add to a decorative bowl I'd set aside.

This morning, when I noticed the rose potpourri on a dining room shelf, I smiled—with gratitude for the goodness of God, evident in this temporal world.

Lord, thank You for graciously sending us signs of Your goodness.
—Evelyn Bence

Digging Deeper: Psalm 145

A LIFETIME OF LOVE: Celebrating Don's Legacy

He makes clouds rise from the ends of the earth; he sends lightning with the rain and brings out the wind from his storehouses. —Psalm 135:7 (NIV)

Four memories from my husband Don's graveside service stand out. First, my grandson Mark created a moving video of photos that spanned Don's eighty-one years. We watched it before and after the service.

Second, our pastor read a tribute that my grandson Caleb sent minutes before Don died: "I can't stop thinking about how blessed Grandpa's life is and how his devotion to God brought so many blessings to his life and his family. So it's a blessing that he is at the home he built, on the land he farmed, surrounded by the family he helped create and loves. He's surrounded by his legacy right now. I don't think he would have it any other way, and I don't think God would either. It's really beautiful."

The third memory was the flag ceremony. Don was a veteran, so the casket was covered with the American flag. My grandson David and my brother Mike, active and retired Marines, folded the flag and presented it to me before "Taps" was played to end the service.

The last memory was the gusty south wind that came up just after the service began, toppling flowers, rattling the awning, and making the microphones squawk. "Don farmed outdoors in the Kansas wind," I said when the funeral director apologized for the havoc. "He would have loved this. In fact, I can almost hear him laughing."

It was beautiful. Really beautiful.

God of all creation, thank You for the legacy of a life lived with humor, appreciation for nature, and deep love.
—Penney Schwab

Digging Deeper: Psalm 126, 128; Luke 6:21

Tuesday, March 28

And God said: "This is the sign of the covenant which I make between Me and you, and every living creature that is with you, for perpetual generations: I set My rainbow in the cloud, and it shall be for the sign of the covenant between Me and the earth. —Genesis 9:12–13 (NKJV)

For the last six weeks, Georgia has been deluged with cold winter rain. The March skies swirl sludge gray, and the world is dim and depressing. Late last night as I turned off my reading light and settled back into darkness, I heard raindrops tap on our bedroom windows and wind rustle our old pecan tree. I escaped into the ether of sleep, longing for an elusive spring.

Exhausted, I slept later than usual the next morning. When my eyes did flicker open and I peered out the window, my heart instantly danced and sang. The sky was brilliant blue without a cloud in the sky. I sensed I was glimpsing a timeless view back into Eden and receiving the good news that life is bright and beautiful. I felt spontaneous hope and happiness that is above and beyond reason. I heard the promise of God to Noah that the storms of life will not destroy or prevail against the loving will of God.

Symbols are important in our lives. And God often speaks through symbols in ways that only our spiritual eyes can see.

Dear God, I praise You for eternal symbols that remind me of Your goodness and love. I am grateful for blue sky at morning. Amen.
—Scott Walker

Digging Deeper: John 1:43–50; Ephesians 2:4–7

My sheep hear my voice . . . —John 10:27 (KJV)

My daughter and boats don't get along.

I was proud of her when she handled the passage from Kauai to the smaller Hawaiian island of Ni'ihau. But when the trip back got rough, I could see her struggling.

The captain's voice came through the speakers. "It's getting choppy out here, folks. A little advice—stay on deck and keep your eyes on the horizon."

I sighed as a dozen lime-green tourists ignored this good advice and headed below to find a bench to lie on.

"What should I do?" my daughter asked.

I put my arm around her. "Exactly what the captain said. Also, put your fingers in your ears."

"Will that help me feel better?"

"Trust me."

She did—just in time to block out the inevitable and horrible sounds coming from the bunch inside.

Are you like me? Ridden a squall or two in this life? And we know what to do—*listen to the Captain.* It's easy for me to shake my head at clueless tourists who didn't listen to the captain, yet how many times have I ignored *my* Captain's voice and found myself miserable and suffering on some self-imposed bunk?

My daughter made it back to port in fine shape. As for me, I came away with a nice, heavenly reminder. I'll be keeping my face to the wind and my eyes on the horizon. And if I put my fingers in my ears, it'll only be *after* the Captain speaks.

> *Praise You, God, You alone are my Captain. You are the*
> *Master of the Waves.*
> —Buck Storm

Digging Deeper: Job 33:31; Isaiah 28:23; Romans 10:17

Thursday, March 30

As iron sharpens iron, so a friend sharpens a friend. —Proverbs 27:17 (NLT)

My friend Susan and I went out for coffee one day and sat in my car discussing our struggles, as we typically do when we're together. Mine was that my daughter and son-in-law, who'd been living with my husband and me for months, had suggested they might live with us several more months; I was desperate for my solitude and routine.

"I keep wondering what God is trying to teach me through this," I whined piously.

Susan, though usually mild-mannered and supportive, was suddenly critical. "God's not trying to teach you anything," she said sternly. "If you say that, you're saying God makes bad things happen in our lives to teach us lessons. People are always saying stuff like that. But they're wrong. God's not like that."

She stared down at her coffee. When she looked up, her lashes were wet, and I guessed she was thinking about the death of her son, Samuel, some years ago.

I felt bad. Susan was right. God had caused neither Susan's loss nor my petty struggles. My words belied impious attitudes about this life's sorrows—and about God—that I didn't even realize I had.

Ever kindhearted and forgiving, as only the best friends are, Susan immediately smoothed over my embarrassment and the pain I had caused her. "You just need to say it differently," she counseled. "Say, 'What does God want me to learn from this?'"

I love how God, in his ever-redemptive spirit, uses all the goodness of his creation—companionship, the diversity and complexities of language, our children, the fruits of coffee trees—to redeem our worst errors and make us more like Him.

Father, use my friends, my family, and my many other blessings
to make me more like You.
—Patty Kirk

Digging Deeper: Genesis 1–2; Romans 12

A wife of noble character who can find? She is worth far more than rubies. . . . She is clothed in fine linen and purple. —Proverbs 31:10, 22 (NIV)

It was a few days before Easter, and my favorite morning show had turned its focus to Easter egg hunts, floral dresses, and recipes for glazed ham and sweet potatoes. My ears perked when they turned the spotlight on a retired school principal whose "church-lady hats" had gone viral on social media. A slideshow displayed her collection of elaborately designed hats. I felt a connection to this lady I'd never met, drawn to her warm smile, smooth brown skin, and those gorgeous hats.

She reminded me of my mother. My mom had dressed impeccably, especially on Sundays. She would often proclaim, "We dress our best for work or for a Broadway show. Shouldn't we give God our best, too?"

After my mother's passing, friends and family often reminisced over her fashion sense. I would smile and nod but preferred to focus on her inner qualities—her intelligence, leadership abilities, and impact as an educator. Yet watching the hat lady on the morning show reminded me that my mom's outer beauty and adornment had been a joy for others as well.

Hours after the feature on the "hat lady," my daughter, Joelle, watching a show from the '90s, asked me what a tennis bracelet was. I shared a description and mentioned that my mom had loved tennis bracelets. Joelle smiled and replied, "And Grand-mommy loved her hats."

I couldn't believe it. Twice in the same day, I'd been reminded of my mom and her hats. I laughed and thanked God for a mom who had left a beautiful mark on the world.

Father, may we embrace our uniqueness and discover creative ways to add beauty to the world.
—Carla Hendricks

Digging Deeper: Proverbs 31:25–31; Matthew 5:16

LET US SING FOR JOY

1 _____

2 _____

3 _____

4 _____

5 _____

6 _____

7 _____

8 _____

9 _____

10 _____

11 _____

12 _____

13 _____

14 _____

15 _____

16 _____

17 _____

18 _____

19 _____

20 _____

21 _____

22 _____

23 _____

24 _____

25 _____

26 _____

27 _____

28 _____

29 _____

30 _____

31 _____

APRIL

*Now may the God of hope fill you
with all joy and peace in believing,
that you may abound in hope by
the power of the Holy Spirit.*

—Romans 15:13 (NKJV)

Now if God so clothes the grass of the field, which today is, and tomorrow is thrown into the oven, will He not much more clothe you, O you of little faith? —Matthew 6:30 (NKJV)

I'm always ready to brave the early spring chill for a chance to glimpse the first flowers of the season. I walk daily through several neighborhoods in New London, Connecticut, and after twenty years, I know where to find the best gardens.

I detour into Mitchell College to drink in cherry blossoms and pass Pequot Avenue's waterfront mansions to see pastel hyacinths. A side street by the old Lighthouse Inn offers the delicate pink and yellow of early tulips. A cul-de-sac with private driveways and spacious yards boasts masses of azaleas in every shade from white to magenta. One large stucco home has almost a quarter acre of vibrant daffodils.

But those aren't my favorite displays. The route from these majestic properties back to our apartment downtown takes me by a soup kitchen; public housing; and small, squat apartment buildings. The "gardens" here are more precious to me because they are not carefully cultivated or pruned. Pale crocuses shiver in weeds around a makeshift basketball court. A spray of forget-me-nots nestles against a cracked foundation. A gnarled magnolia tree showers pink-streaked petals onto a patch of trampled grass by a parking lot.

And while I seldom see anyone but landscape workers at the other homes, these properties are lively with kids shooting hoops, others skipping on hopscotch grids chalked onto uneven sidewalks, and older folks wrapped in sweaters on plastic lawn chairs. It's as if they know that their Creator has decorated their spring with the bright hope that no human hand ever could. And they mean to appreciate it.

> *Thoughtful Father, thank You for revealing signs of Your love
> and mercy to all Your children.*
> —Marci Alborghetti

Digging Deeper: Psalm 113:1–8; Matthew 5:1–5

Palm Sunday, April 2

RESURRECTION JOY: My Friend Jesus

The next day, the news that Jesus was on the way to Jerusalem swept through the city, and a huge crowd of Passover visitors took palm branches and went down the road to meet him, shouting, "The Savior! God bless the King of Israel! Hail to God's Ambassador! —John 12:12–13 (TLB)

When I was younger, Palm Sunday was my least favorite church service because the priest always read the entire Passion of our Lord Jesus as the Gospel reading for that day and it seemed to take forever.

Then one Palm Sunday, each member of our congregation was asked to pick up a long palm frond in the gathering space and process with all the members of our church outside, around the parking lot, past the prayer garden, around the bell tower, and back into church. I was suddenly part of the crowd that waved to Jesus as he entered Jerusalem on a donkey. During that procession, I imagined that Jesus came up behind me, and as He passed, He looked directly into my eyes, smiled, nodded, and said, "Hello, Patricia."

My heart started pounding. *Wow, Jesus spoke to me! He knows me personally!* I smiled, waved my palm to acknowledge our friendship, and whispered, "Thank You, Jesus."

My heart was overflowing. Later, during the reading of the Passion, my heart ached for what Jesus, my friend, was about to experience.

Now that I have experienced many Palm Sundays since that time of the outdoor procession, I look forward to the Palm Sunday Gospel. Every word feels like a powerful course in Christianity with such detailed descriptions of how much Jesus loves me that I am touched to the core.

Heavenly Father, thank You for the gift of Your Son, who knows me personally and who has my back no matter what struggles happen in my life.
—Patricia Lorenz

Digging Deeper: John 12; Luke 13:22–25

Your word is a lamp to my feet and a light to my path.
—Psalm 119:105 (NRSV)

We didn't know quite what to do with it. The immense old Bible had been in Carol's family for generations. From the inscription in front, it seems to have been her great-great-great-grandmother's. "This book belongs to Rebecca Moon," faded-ink writing proclaims. The pages are yellow, the leather cover fragile, the words in an ancient font. The woodcut illustrations are fetching, but the commentary is woefully out of date, and the whole thing is too heavy to put in your lap.

It's hard to tell if anybody ever did pore over its pages. You don't see any underlining or check marks on favorite passages, no dog-eared pages. But then you wouldn't really want to mess with a book like this. Too grand, too precious. I confess that we did what others have probably done with the old book for generations: Put it on a shelf and let it gather dust.

Until the other day when I was working from home and was looking for something to stack under my computer so that I could type standing up. *Hmmm, I wonder if that old Bible will do.* I took it down, dusted it off, put it upright, and rested my laptop on top. Perfect. Sturdy as a rock and just the right height.

I had to smile to myself. We talk about leaning on Scripture. Here I was—quite literally—writing on top of it. It made me think that the ease with which we can access Scripture is something we take entirely too much for granted. Struggling for a verse, I can find it on my phone, my Kindle, or any one of several copies on my desk. Maybe we'd treasure it more if it were just like this, too precious for words.

May I always be guided by knowledge of Your Word.
—Rick Hamlin

Digging Deeper: Isaiah 40:8; Matthew 24:35; 2 Timothy 3:16

Tuesday, April 4

"Seven days you shall eat unleavened bread." —Exodus 12:15 (JPS)

It's not easy to find kosher food in Bellingham. Most of the year that isn't a problem because I don't keep kosher all the time; I do what we call "kosher-style" food during ordinary times. I am, however, scrupulous about following all the special food rules during Passover. I didn't have to think twice about finding "kosher for Passover (KFP)" matzoh (held to a stricter standard than regular matzoh) or kosher chicken in Los Angeles because there were delis every few blocks and special Jewish markets that made sure their products conformed to the rules. Where I live now, the Jewish food on the shelves is generally not for Passover use, and the stores don't seem to be aware there's a difference.

When we first moved here, the nearest place to shop for Passover food was Seattle, and it was a full day's excursion down I-5 to the city. That kind of shopping trip lost its luster after Keith got ill, and I never went back to it. One year, I was reduced to eating mostly eggs, canned tuna fish, and potatoes for the eight days, though I bought a box of KFP matzoh from a friend who had bought a five-box pack and only needed four.

This year, a friend mentioned that her daughter, who lives in New York, was sending her a box of "the real stuff" from a market in that city, and I heard myself think *Duh!* I went to the computer, found a deli in New York City that delivered anywhere in the United States, and had a wonderful time shopping for some kinds of Passover food that I hadn't eaten since we left Los Angeles. Every meal was special.

Thank You, God of my ancestors, for finally showing me how to get what I needed to obey Your rules. And for overlooking any complaints because of my own ignorance.
—Rhoda Blecker

Digging Deeper: Deuteronomy 16:4; Leviticus 11:3

My Father's house has many rooms; if that were not so, would I have told you that I am going there to prepare a place for you? —John 14:2 (NIV)

Our family has always had pets. From the time the kids were old enough to be responsible, we've had cats and dogs, guinea pigs, fish, ducks, chickens, and goats. Peterkins was our family dog for over seventeen years. Although he was Wayne's dog, I was the one who chose him out of the litter, trained him, took him to the vet, fed him, and cared for him.

Bogie came into our lives as empty nesters, and he was my dog. His mother was killed in a freak accident shortly after he was born. He needed a mama, and he chose me. Bogie was my comfort dog when our son Dale died. When I said, "Word of the Lord," Bogie would go to my prayer desk and sit at my side, and when I said, "Work," Bogie raced into my office. He'd patiently wait there until it was time for our afternoon walk. In the evenings, he sat at my side while I knitted, read, or watched television. He thought Wayne was an okay guy, but he preferred my company. I deeply loved that dog.

Bogie died last week, and we buried him by the seawall where he liked to run, ears back, facing the wind. I can't imagine heaven without my Bogie. This precious little dog showed me so beautifully what it is to be loved unconditionally, a living example of how our heavenly Father feels toward each one of us.

*Through my tears, I thank You for the eleven wonderful years we had
Bogie, for showing me what unconditional love is so that
I am able to understand Your great love for me.*
—Debbie Macomber

Digging Deeper: Proverbs 3:3; Ephesians 3:17–18

Maundy Thursday, April 6

RESURRECTION JOY: Our Humble Servant

So he got up from the supper table, took off his robe, wrapped a towel around his loins, poured water into a basin, and began to wash the disciples' feet and to wipe them with the towel he had around him.
—John 13:4–5 (TLB)

A few days before my husband, Jack, died, just five days after Ash Wednesday, I fed him, gave him his meds, readjusted his bed, gave him a sponge bath, then rubbed cream into his dry, rough, cracked feet. Jack wasn't talking much those days, but I think he appreciated the foot rub, although, to be honest, it was not the most pleasant thing I'd ever done.

Later, during Easter week, I felt bad that Jack did not live to experience Easter that year because it was his favorite church celebration.

During Easter week that year, I thought about how Jesus washed the feet of his twelve disciples before the Last Supper, which reminded me of the time I'd rubbed cream into Jack's calloused feet as I stood at the foot of his bed. Imagine, Jesus, the King of the Jews, the Son of God, the ruler most supreme, getting down on his hands and knees on the floor to wash the dirty feet of his followers. That has always been the defining act of humility and selflessness in my mind.

Imagine the queen of England or the president of the United States or any ruler doing such a thing. Jesus simply sat on the ground and gently washed the feet of those people he loved the most, the men who had all changed their lives drastically to follow him and preach his word.

Now, every Maundy Thursday, when I recall the memory of washing and rubbing Jack's feet, I'm reminded that no sacrifice is too great for someone I love. Once again, Jesus taught by example.

Jesus, thank You for the foot-washing reminder that to be more like You I need to be a lot more accepting, gentle, humble, and selfless.
—Patricia Lorenz

Digging Deeper: Genesis 18:3–5; John 13:6–17

RESURRECTION JOY: The Promise of Life Eternal

He replied, "You of little faith, why are you so afraid?" Then he got up and rebuked the winds and the waves, and it was completely calm.
—Matthew 8:26 (NIV)

There are many days when I have been afraid. When I had to spend the entire day and all night alone in the airport in Malaysia. The day I had a double knee replacement. All the days my youngest son, Andrew, has been hospitalized. The days, weeks, and months that my husband, Jack, was hospitalized before he died. All of us have fearful days, right?

But imagine how afraid Jesus was on this day, Friday, the day He was going to die a slow, painful death. He went through a mockery of a trial, was spat upon, flogged, and laughed at, and then nails were pounded into His hands and feet so His body could hang on a wooden cross for all to see as He died slowly from asphyxiation. But the good that came from His horrible death cannot be described.

I've learned firsthand that fear can strangle me into doing nothing. Or I can choose to accept what is before me, knowing that a much greater good is about to become a reality. I'll always remember my adventure in Malaysia and the kind family I talked to at the airport gate area. My two new knees have given me many painless miles. Andrew's faith has grown during his illness. And I'm learning to live life with grit, gusto, and grace after Jack's death.

Jesus chose to die a painful, horrific death because He knew what came next. Surely I can choose to see what's ahead—the greater good—and look fear in the face knowing the healing resurrection of Jesus brings us smack-dab into life eternal with God Himself.

Oh Jesus, what a blessing that what You suffered on Good Friday was not the end of the story.
—Patricia Lorenz

Digging Deeper: Matthew 27:45–53; Hebrews 2:14–18

Holy Saturday, April 8

RESURRECTION JOY: Hold on to Hope

This will be their line of argument: "So Jesus promised to come back, did he? Then where is he? He'll never come!" —2 Peter 3:4 (TLB)

Holy Saturday is a strange day. I can picture the apostles wandering around sad and fearful, going from house to house talking to each other, asking all sorts of questions. "Could it really have happened? Did they really kill our leader? Was it all a mistake? What if Jesus wasn't the real Messiah? What if all that pain on the cross was for nothing? How could something so awful actually have anything to do with a loving and just God? Jesus is dead! Now what? How can our new leader be dead at age thirty-three after just a few years of preaching and teaching us a whole new way of life? What's the point? Do we even know enough to go out and try to spread this new Christian way of life?"

As I ponder how I think the apostles struggled on that very strange day, I remember days when I've asked myself big, scary questions. "Should I marry this man? What if it doesn't work? Should I have this surgery? What if something goes wrong? What if my daughter doesn't speak to me again after that last phone conversation where we both said things we regret? What if I take this new job? What if something happens on that long trip I'm supposed to take? What if I end the friendship with my toxic friend? Then what?"

I consider Holy Saturday doubting day. Wait until tomorrow and you'll see what happens. It's going to be amazing. Tomorrow, Easter Sunday, will help me answer all my "what-ifs." I just know it.

Jesus, You taught me how to survive turmoil, fear, pain, and angst.
Never let me forget what's next in Your beautiful plan.
—Patricia Lorenz

Digging Deeper: Matthew 14:25–33; John 20:19–21

RESURRECTION JOY: He Lives

These men of faith I have mentioned died without ever receiving all that God had promised them; but they saw it all awaiting them on ahead and were glad, for they agreed that this earth was not their real home but that they were just strangers visiting down here. And quite obviously when they talked like that, they were looking forward to their real home in heaven. —Hebrews 11:13–14 (TLB)

Before he died at age ninety-eight, my dad would question his nephew Jerry, a Monsignor in the Catholic church, about his faith. "If God is so good and loves everyone that He created, why would He create a hell? How could Jesus actually die on the cross and then be alive again days later?"

Like my dad, I often ask myself questions about my faith. *What actually happens when we die? How do we know for sure that it's not just the end of everything for us?*

And then, every year, something wonderful happens. Easter Sunday. Suddenly the answers are there. Simply, joyfully, and intellectually, the resurrection of Jesus Christ answers all my questions. He died and two days later ascended into heaven. Real people saw it happen. Real people witnessed Jesus paving a way for all of us, even the questioning ones, to enter heaven with Him.

Imagine the questions Mary Magdalene had when she found Jesus's tomb empty. Imagine what Matthew thought on Easter Sunday morning when he actually saw Jesus walking around, alive. He'd seen Jesus die and saw His body put inside the tomb two days earlier. How on earth could Jesus now be walking around alive?

Mary Magdalene and Matthew saw it with their own eyes. Jesus came back alive after being dead. He rose, He walked, He lives, He saves our doubting hearts. He does.

Jesus, thank You for the joy of Easter and for calming my questioning nature. Never let my faith falter.
—Patricia Lorenz

Digging Deeper: Matthew 21:21–22; Luke 17:5–10; Romans 1:16–17

Easter Monday, April 10

RESURRECTION JOY: A New Beginning

"With water I baptize those who repent of their sins; but someone else is coming, far greater than I am, so great that I am not worthy to carry his shoes!" —Matthew 3:11 (TLB)

Perhaps because I was baptized as an infant, raised by two devout Catholic Christian parents, and attended Catholic schools for fourteen years, including my first two years of college, I have always taken my faith for granted. Sometimes that's not always good. I attend Mass nearly every weekend and volunteer at church every now and then, but in my heart, I've never really measured up to what I think the good Lord expects of me.

But somehow Easter helps me rally every year. It's a faith booster of the best kind. Christianity coming into being is a miracle, pure and simple, a miracle that was created for every single human being on the face of this big earth.

Jesus died on Friday, walked out of the tomb on Saturday, and entered heaven on Sunday. So much excitement and drama. After a joyous Easter Sunday, I find Easter Monday can be a letdown, especially after the Easter dinner dishes are cleaned up, the good china is put away, the guests have gone home, and the pink marshmallow Peeps are starting to dry out.

But Easter Monday should definitely be one of the best days of the year because it's the first day of the rest of our spiritual lives. This is the day we get to begin living the new life that Jesus gave us by dying on the cross for us. This is the greatest day because now that Holy Week is over, we can put everything we learned into motion. Today we get to start walking the walk and talking the talk.

Heavenly Father, today on Easter Monday, help me to get down to the business of living and sharing my faith so that Your miracle lives on.
—Patricia Lorenz

Digging Deeper: 1 Kings 12:4; Proverbs 10:28–32;
Philippians 1:12–18

Taking the five loaves and the two fish, he looked up to heaven, and
blessed and broke the loaves, and gave them to the disciples . . .
—Matthew 14:19 (NRSV)

This morning, I deboned my holiday ham—a boiled and then baked smoked picnic. Navy beans nestling among bones now simmer in broth. My mom's recipe for potatoes scalloped with onions, carrots, and ham is next on my list.

As I set aside jars of extra broth for a few soup makers, I fondly remember an Easter Saturday several years ago when my friends Charley and Lynn invited me to attend the annual blessing of the Easter baskets at their Catholic church.

Children hoping for hefty hauls at the later egg hunt arrived with empty baskets. But adults, most of Polish descent like Lynn, brought in the ingredients of their Easter dinners, setting their delicacies along the altar rail. I came prepared to participate. I internalized the priest's blessing as he sprinkled holy water on my own fixings: ham, raw potatoes, and decorated eggs. After the service, I complimented Lynn's elaborate basket display. "The butter—it's molded into a lamb!"

"Yes," she said. "It represents the Lamb of God. And everything here has a symbolic meaning. The eggs—life and resurrection. The bread—Christ. The meat—joy and abundance . . ."

Earlier this year, Lynn passed away. Despite my sadness, the memory of her bountiful basket increases my Easter joy. And my appreciation of the season's abundant blessings overflows now, having just returned from delivering ham stock and scraps to a few creative cooks.

Lord, on this ordinary day in Eastertide, I thank You for and ask You to
bless the food I eat and serve.
—Evelyn Bence

Digging Deeper: Exodus 23:25; Luke 9:13–17

Wednesday, April 12

Be joyful in hope, patient in affliction, faithful in prayer.
—Romans 12:12 (NIV)

Our family loves coloring Easter eggs. This past year, we had so much fun decorating eggs that we boiled way too many. After we'd had all we could eat, I decided to give an egg to our dog, Cookie. Just as I was about to peel it for her, I thought of how much she enjoys gnawing on something new, so I did a quick internet search to see if dogs could eat eggshells. Turns out, one eggshell a week is actually good for a dog's bones.

Cookie took the egg in her mouth and trotted outside with it. I watched from the window to see what she'd do.

Cookie was puzzled by this odd new item. Was it food? It smelled like food. Was it a toy? It had an interesting texture. What was she supposed to do with it?

I watched as she kept trying to find the correct angle to bite down on the egg. Each time she tried, the egg would roll away. I felt sort of bad for my pup and came close to going out and cracking the egg for her. But eventually, she figured out how to hold the egg with her paws and bite it with the side of her mouth. That was the ticket! After that, I could see how proud of herself she was and how much more she enjoyed the egg because of her effort.

Many times, I want God to make things easy for me, but I know He understands that sometimes the real reward is in the struggle. I'm going to remember to thank Him for that today.

Lord, I don't usually thank You for hard times, but help me to see that You're teaching me something through them.
—Ginger Rue

Digging Deeper: Galatians 6:9; Colossians 3:23–24

. . . even there your hand will guide me, and your strength will support me. —Psalm 139:10 (NLT)

Mud splatters both sides of the pickup. Winter rain has turned the gravel road to soup. A cardboard box on the seat beside me fills the cab with the aroma of Chinese food I'm delivering to surprise my friend Heidi, who had broken her arm. I didn't have the exact address, but I'd been sent to this general location and told to "look for her rig." I put the pickup in four-wheel drive as the road climbs steeply uphill through the pines. The road branches. Rows of mailboxes speak of the many homes that are hidden in the trees. *Lord, I am so lost.*

Far behind me, a delivery truck churns up the same muddy ruts. It has followed me since I'd left pavement, but it neither gains on me nor stops at any house. *Oh well, it's probably against company policy to ask him for directions.* I turn right. Around the corner, I spot what I think is Heidi's horse. I turn into the nearest driveway, but there aren't any rigs for me to recognize. *Was her doctor's appointment today?* I step out and head for the door. Dogs erupt into frenzied barking—thankfully from inside the house. It's obvious no one is home. My phone has no signal here. *How do I know if this is right, Lord?*

Tires crunch in the gravel behind me. It's the delivery truck. A man leaps from the cab, shoves a box in my hand, and says, "Package for Heidi." He gets in his truck just as fast and is gone before I can say anything or explain why I'm laughing. I didn't know my guardian angel wore a uniform.

Blessed Lord, You rescue me. You comfort me. You protect me. You are at work in the minor details and the major storms. Praise Your name!
—Erika Bentsen

Digging Deeper: 2 Samuel 22:48–49; Psalm 18:35, 32:7

Friday, April 14

. . . you must not harvest all the way to the edge of your field; and don't gather every remaining bit of your harvest. Leave these items for the poor and the immigrant . . . —Leviticus 23:22 (CEB)

The rabbits are eating the birdseed!" My granddaughters called me over to my living room window, which overlooks the stunted evergreen where I'd hung several birdfeeders. Sure enough, three large rabbits were chowing down on the seed that had fallen to the ground from the feeders above. I explained to Lula and Shea how happy I was that food that looked like it was going to waste was actually keeping the bunnies that lived behind my home fat and happy.

Immediately I thought of the book of Ruth. Thanks to the Old Testament practice of allowing those in need to glean from the excess grain left behind after harvest, Ruth and her mother-in-law not only secured food to eat but also a place in the family tree of Christ. Although the closest I get to harvesting a field is picking up produce at my local market, King Soopers, the biblical concept remains valid.

To allow others to glean from the abundance God has afforded me, I try to leave margin in my budget. When money is "left over" at the end of the month, it's easier for me to respond generously when I see someone in need. When something I own no longer fits into my life, I give it away. Instead of trying to make more money by selling it (that I would probably use to buy more stuff!), I donate it to charities that help the "poor and the immigrant." If the animals God created can glean from one another, certainly I can learn to do the same.

Father, open my eyes and heart to the need of those around me. Help me better reflect Your generosity by sharing freely with others.
—Vicki Kuyper

Digging Deeper: Deuteronomy 24:19–21; Ruth 1–4; Proverbs 19:17; 2 Corinthians 9:7; James 2:15–16

. . . be content with such things as you have. —Hebrews 13:5 (NKJV)

I was feeling blue, praying about some big bills coming due. My wife, Sharon, was shopping at a fabric store, so I decided to take a walk, to calm myself. Alas, the neighborhood was not inspiring: old, rundown houses surrounded by junked cars and trash.

Some children were playing softball on a vacant lot, and I was drawn to their cheering. There were nine children, four on each team; one boy stood off to the side, pretending to be a sportscaster. "It's a high fly into center field," he shouted.

The batter was using a tree limb for a bat. Flattened cardboard boxes served as bases. There were no ball gloves, uniforms, helmets, or a scoreboard.

I had been watching the game for five minutes before I realized that they didn't even have a softball! I was dumbfounded. Apparently they couldn't afford a ball, but it didn't stop them from having fun. So well did they pretend that I could almost *see* a ball at times.

I thought of an old Nat King Cole song that goes, "Pretend you're happy when you're blue . . . it isn't very hard to do . . . and you'll find happiness without an end . . . whenever you pretend."*

As we drove home from the fabric store, I pretended to be happy, humming along with radio tunes and rehearsing my blessings instead of my bills.

And when we pulled into our driveway, I no longer had to pretend that I was happy, because I was.

Thank You, Father, for our smallest teachers, who show us how to make a lot out of a little.
—Daniel Schantz

Digging Deeper: Ecclesiastes 4:6; Philippians 4:12–13

---

*"Pretend," copyright 1952, Music Sales Corp., written by Cliff Parman, Frank LaVere, Dan Belloc, and Lew Douglas.

Sunday, April 16

What they trust in is fragile; what they rely on is a spider's web.
—Job 8:14 (NIV)

I was watching the morning news and a bit worried about the world when I first saw it outside my living room window. I reached for my remote, turned off the TV, and went to the front porch to get a better look.

A spider had built a stunning web between our two rocking chairs on my front porch. I'm not a fan of spiders, and it was quite large, its body as big as a dime. But its web was a glorious spectacle glowing in the rising sun.

The wind gently blew, and the chairs rocked back and forth. The spider stayed still and centered. Throughout the day, I found myself checking on it. A few times the web was bare and I feared the worst, but then I would spot one of its many legs curled around the spindle of the chair and I'd sigh with relief.

Life is fragile yet resilient, I thought. *Just like this spider in the web, you are stronger than you think. Hold on, be still—everything will be okay.*

For a week, I kept tabs on the spider, checking on it when I woke and turning on the porch light and looking once again before I went to bed. Then one afternoon it had simply moved on, leaving behind the web. Amazingly, it stayed that way for a few more days, comforting me and reminding me to have faith and be still, to see the delicate beauty of life that endures.

Dear Lord, thank You for creating such mystical and magical creatures that help me stay centered when the world seems out of control.
—Sabra Ciancanelli

Digging Deeper: Psalm 9:10; Hebrews 13:8

I appeal to you . . . to present your bodies as a living sacrifice, holy and acceptable to God, which is your spiritual worship. —Romans 12:1 (ESV)

A couple of kittens were a great help to me last year, which was a difficult year in many ways. It seemed as if my world was filled with drama and problems, but we adopted two kittens in the spring and delighted in playing with them and watching them grow.

I always woke up first, before the sun rises—and the kittens would surround me with purring and love.

No, let me correct that. They often climbed on my back or lay heavy on my legs, in bed, "encouraging" me to wake up before the sun, so that they could then surround me with love and attention. Either way, I was grateful.

I sit quietly and pray most early mornings, just me and the cats. They even seem to pay attention.

Then the sun comes up, and I feed them. And just as quickly, their stomachs now full, they leave my side and retreat to a couch or a comfy chair and go back to sleep. There's a lesson in there somewhere.

When I'm lonely and hungry, I look for God's company and help. And when I feel good, my need for God suddenly decreases.

It is good to be hungry from time to time. I don't wish food insecurity upon anyone, and I don't suffer from it. Neither do I fast as I should, to remind me that I should hunger and thirst for the God of my salvation all the time.

And I am grateful for even a gift as simple as adorable cats asleep nearby to remind me of my need for God.

I need You, Lord, now and always.
—Jon M. Sweeney

Digging Deeper: Psalm 38:9

Tuesday, April 18

The hearing ear and the seeing eye, the LORD has made them both.
—Proverbs 20:12 (ESV)

*H*ow do you make a kaleidoscope? Why do volcanoes explode? What do
you call that bug? When he was younger, our grandson, Micah, was
a fountain of endless questions. I had struggled to know how to connect
with this fact-loving boy, so I was glad when he asked for binoculars for his
seventh birthday. As an amateur bird watcher, I hoped this would give us
a common interest.

Before wrapping the gift, I tested out the binoculars to make sure they
were as awesome as advertised. I focused the lenses to view the regular
attenders at my three feeders: Inca doves, finches, and house sparrows. A
newbie—a brownish-gray bird—scratched for seeds under the orange tree.

A female cardinal? I focused the binoculars. *Nope. No tufted or crested
head.* I stepped closer. *A thrasher? No, too small.* The little fellow turned,
displaying its black mask, the distinctive characteristic needed to identify him. *An Abert's towhee.*

Micah loved his present and immediately began counting all the birds
attracted to their property near a desert wash. In the months that followed, Micah sent me pictures of birds or feathers, asking for help with
identification. We participated in the Great Backyard Bird Count, sharing our lists with each other. Gifts of birdseed and bird books followed.

"Grandma," Micah asked me, several years after he had received the
binoculars, "what's a brown bird with a black mask called?"

"An Abert's towhee," I said, showing him a picture, as Micah added
the bird to his list. He grabbed his binoculars and headed outside,
while I gave thanks for a child-sized gift that allowed me to see not only
the birds but also the heart of my grandson.

*Jesus, open my eyes to see the everyday gifts You have for me
to open, as You give wings to my prayers.*
—Lynne Hartke

Digging Deeper: Matthew 20:32–34; Ephesians 1:18–21

Be kind and compassionate to one another; forgiving each other, just as in Christ God forgave you. —Ephesians 4:32 (NIV)

If looks could kill, I'd have been dead twice over.

I'd taken Gracie to one of her favorite places—Tractor Supply Company. Gracie has trained the cashiers there to give her treats, planting her big paws on the counter. Smart girl. But I had a secret agenda, and when Gracie perceived my nefarious plan, I got the look.

A bath.

At the rear of the store is a little doggie spa with tubs, shampoo, towels, blow dryers, combs, everything you need to bathe your dog.

I've never understood how a dog who loves to roll in mud finds a bath so objectionable. I talk softly to her and ply her with treats, and she still acts as if she's been led to the gallows.

At home, she retires to one of her several beds and shows me her back. Turning their backs is a way dogs sometimes demonstrate that they are upset with you. Today she was particularly adamant in her affect. Even when I brought her a peace offering—a bit of string cheese, her favorite, she snatched it from me without making eye contact.

So, I settled in to watch the Yankees drop another game to the Rays. I was nodding off when I felt a cold nudge on my hand. Gracie. She looked up at me as if to say, "All is forgiven. Let's be friends again."

Forgiveness is difficult. I'm not always as magnanimous as my dog. I can cling to a grudge. Maybe I derive satisfaction in nursing a sense of injustice. Yet I know that forgiveness is a necessary ingredient in a strong faith. Jesus came to earth to forgive our sins. We are expected to forgive.

I scratched behind Gracie's ears, and she laid her head on my knee. It was nice to be friends again.

Lord, You know I have trouble forgiving a wrong. Today help me let go of a resentment and take a closer step toward You.
—Edward Grinnan

Digging Deeper: Galatians 6:1; Colossians 3:13

Thursday, April 20

Now faith is the assurance of things hoped for, the conviction of things not seen. —Hebrews 11:1 (NRSV)

Though I've been Christian for decades and studied Scripture, biblical history, and theology, I still feel mystified by the "resurrection" promised by Jesus. Rising from the dead defies my feeble mortal logic. I cannot begin to fathom how this transformation can occur, much less how it will look or feel.

Yes, I can believe that Jesus rose again—He's divine, after all—but me? I can't even understand how my wireless printer works. Or how monarch butterflies know the way to Mexico. Or how a human being can compose a symphony.

But do I need to understand mere mechanics to believe that something is so? To appreciate what seems impossible and be amazed? Like the father of the epileptic boy, I pray, "Lord, I believe; help my unbelief" (Mark 9:24 [NKJV]). And I think of Jesus's parable of the mustard seed and His insistence that a tiny bit of faith is enough.

I garden a lot, so seeds are something I can relate to, even though I don't know exactly how they transform, either. Nonetheless, I'm fascinated that specks like sand grains can become carrots, that tiny black seeds can turn into green lettuce, and that a brown lump of bulb can shoot up to transform into the green foliage and spectacular blooms of a scarlet amaryllis. Even indoors in winter. Dead-looking seeds, bulbs, husks, and tubers offer no hint of the splendor to come.

And though I don't quite understand how seeds "work," I continue to plant them because I know they do. I believe the pictures on the packets. I believe in resurrection. Perhaps each miracle will help me to better grasp the other.

> *Dear God, grant me the faith to believe Your promises. Amen.*
> —Gail Thorell Schilling

Digging Deeper: Matthew 17:20; Mark 9:24; John 11:25–27

Carefully guard your thoughts because they are the source of true life.
—Proverbs 4:23 (CEV)

Horrified, I stared at the screen as I read the article. Over the past months, I'd fed on news of wickedness and violence that threatened to tear our nation apart and to pit us as Americans against each other. Anger and irritation had become my constant companions. My golden retriever, Sunrise, nudged me and whined, asking me to wrap up the day. I rubbed her side. "You're getting round. We've got a new puppy that we take on walks several times a day. Shouldn't you be losing weight?"

Sunrise went to the puppy pen to visit Willow, our new German shepherd, while I headed into the kitchen to make dinner. I shook my head in agitation. *God, I feel so helpless and angry that I haven't gotten more involved.* The sound of Willow pushing her food bowl across the pen caught my attention. The bowl clanged against the bars. *Her bowl must be empty.* But it wasn't. Instead, Willow was playing hockey with her food bowl. And as soon as she pushed it against the side, Sunrise stretched her tongue through the bars and lapped up the kibbles.

"Sunrise!" Innocently, her large brown eyes glanced at me. I moved the bowl to the center of the pen. "Time to push back from the food bowl." And as I said that, I knew that I needed to do the same thing. I'd been feasting on the negative news so much that it had infected my whole life. It was time to diet; time to create a balance of being informed and to become a part of the solution.

Lord, help me limit the amount of time I focus on the world's view of life. Show me how I can make a difference. Amen.
—Rebecca Ondov

Digging Deeper: Psalm 19:14, 51:10

Saturday, April 22

Cast all your anxiety on him because he cares for you. —1 Peter 5:7 (NIV)

I have a fear of heights. High bridges and scenic overlooks on winding mountain roads terrify me. The view from tall buildings, such as Seattle's Space Needle, causes my heart to pound and my hands to perspire. An aunt told me I fell out of a tree in her backyard when I was two years old. Perhaps that's why I'm afraid of heights. I've lived with the fear for as long as I can remember.

So, when my husband announced he'd been offered a hot-air balloon ride, I surprised him by declaring, "I want to come, too!" I even surprised myself, but my desire to soar like a bird was stronger than my fear. When the pilot agreed to take us both along, I made up my mind to enjoy the adventure. Did I really believe the Lord offered a greater safety and a deeper security than my long-held fears? Could I rest in Jesus, trust Him completely? Taking a deep breath, I decided this was an opportunity to test my grit *and* my faith.

The first thing I did that sunny Saturday morning was to pray. Even before I climbed into the basket attached to the bottom of the balloon, Jesus quieted my nerves as only He can do. I discovered I was filled with anticipation rather than fear. My heart pounded with excitement, not anxiety. The flight over Albuquerque proved to be exhilarating, one of the most memorable adventures of my life. Afterward, I thanked the pilot for the flight, and I thanked the Lord for his loving kindness, which had sent my spirit soaring even higher than that balloon.

Dearest Heavenly Father, You are Lord of the heavens and the earth, the high places and the low. You are my strength and my shield.
—Shirley Raye Redmond

Digging Deeper: Joshua 1:9; John 16:24; James 4:10

They are planted in the house of the LORD; they flourish in the courts of our God. —Psalm 92:13 (NRSV)

When Charlie and I are in Concord, New Hampshire, we visit Christ the King Church. Originally, the congregation had been divided into three parishes, and combining them had been bittersweet, especially for those who'd attended one of the other churches. But the pastor had been patient and compassionate through the process, and they'd formed a strong, united parish family.

So we were surprised when we pulled into the parking lot and saw construction frames and barricades around the majestic church edifice. To the side, on a ragged patch of ground, was a large plastic tent enclosing seats, lighting, and a makeshift altar with a large crucifix as the centerpiece. It turned out that long-needed work on the outside and improvements on the inside had been underway for months. For several weeks, we joined parishioners slogging through the muddy path into the tent during the rainy season. One evening, the wind and rain were so harsh, the tent shook and lights flickered.

On our last weekend in Concord, Christ the King opened its doors. We arrived early and sat in the back, watching longtime parishioners file slowly into their home. Eyes widened with excitement, oohing and aahing softly, pointing to new tiles, fixed cracks, and the beautiful, brilliantly lit altar. People gazed around in awe and deep pleasure. I thought about how long the Israelites lived in tents in the harsh wilderness; this must have been how they felt when they finally reached the Promised Land, their place, their home. This is how it feels to find the place where we belong, with God.

Lord, be it tent or palace, help me to remember that
You are everywhere I look for You.
—Marci Alborghetti

Digging Deeper: Isaiah 2:2–3; Luke 2:46–50

Monday, April 24

And the cares of this world, and the deceitfulness of riches, and the lusts of other things entering in, choke the word, and it becometh unfruitful.
—Mark 4:19 (KJV)

I stare . . .

Without fail, our yearly garage clean-out boggles my brain. Somewhere in the world, I imagine some physicist has a formula all worked out regarding available space / material collected = trips to Goodwill, but let me tell you, that particular brand of mathematical brilliance is *way* over my head.

Where does it all come from? I can't figure. The world spins and things just pile. It's amazing how fast it happens. It's funny; I'm sure every single thing in here seemed important at the time. Now I can hardly remember where any of it came from.

The thing is, when I step back and take a hard look at my life, I'm convinced my mind and spirit are a whole lot like my garage. So much baggage I've picked up (or been handed) along the way. And so much I still carry whether I realize it or not. All of it felt so important back then. If I'm honest, some even consumed me for a while. If I'm *brutally* honest, more than a few of them wedged themselves between myself and God for longer than I care to admit. Do I need all the baggage? Of course not. In fact, the destination I'm headed for requires no suitcase at all.

And so, I stand here in the center of my self-imposed garage chaos and scratch my head.

Truckloads, man, truckloads.

Yeah, it's high time to let things go.

You know what? I'm glad God's truck is bigger than mine.

I open my hands, Lord. I let go. Clear my mind and heal my heart.
Strip me of everything until only You remain!
—Buck Storm

Digging Deeper: Ecclesiastes 3:6; Luke 9:62; Hebrews 12:1

"Trust in the LORD with all your heart, and do not lean on your own understanding. In all your ways acknowledge him, and he will make straight your paths." —Proverbs 3:5–6 (ESV)

My family adopted Snow Mist, our nineteen-year-old horse, almost a year ago, committing to give her a home full of love. Soon after we brought her home, I realized she did not reciprocate our affection. She didn't trust us at first; she was unsure about our intent.

My first indication was Snow Mist's insistence on shifting her 1,200 pounds into me when I tried to clean her hooves, ensuring I knew her feelings. She then refused any treats except carrots, and we felt deflated. Adding salt to the wound, my heart shattered the time she turned and nipped me. Snow Mist was indifferent, or annoyed, by our presence in her life, and we were head over heels for her.

We didn't know if Snow Mist's behavior was permanent or would change, but we were undeterred. And determined to faithfully care for her. One day after many months, we tried to give her a new treat, and, much to our surprise, she took it. She now places her head lower for scratches. Little by little, she finds her way to us.

Like Snow Mist, my own trust in God takes time. I find it difficult sometimes to surrender; I like knowing and being in control. Thankfully, the Lord is head over heels for me and undeterred, just as He is for each of us. Although I still struggle to let go, I trust Someone will walk with me no matter what the future holds.

Father, open my heart to You in all ways and in all times. May my trust in You bring Your love to those around me.
—Jolynda Strandberg

Digging Deeper: Psalm 4:5–6; Jeremiah 17:7–8; 2 Corinthians 5:6–10

Wednesday, April 26

"I, Jesus, . . . am the root and the descendant of David, the bright morning star."—Revelation 22:16 (NASB)

I was reading 2 Timothy 4 when a phrase popped out. The Apostle Paul wanted Timothy to join him in his work as "Demas, having loved this present world" (4:10), had deserted him. Intrigued by the thought of Bible people captured in phrases, I began searching out others.

In the Third Letter of John, I discovered "Diotrephes, who loves to be first . . ." (1:9). Paul, in Romans, sends a greeting from "Gaius, host to me and the whole church" (16:23). He greets "Mary, who has worked hard for you" (16:6) and "Rufus, a choice man in the Lord" (16:13).

I found in Acts "Apollos . . . an eloquent man . . ." (18:24) and "Lydia . . . a seller of purple fabrics, a worshiper of God . . ." (16:14). Genesis tells of Abraham, "an old man and satisfied with life . . ." (25:8). And God calls David "a man after My heart . . ." (Acts 13:22).

As I got to "know" these people by their phrases, I wondered what phrases would fit me. Ones I—or others—might choose. Maybe Carol, "song of joy"—the meaning of my name. Carol, "who talks more than she listens." Or "who genuinely cares for others." Carol, "explorer of nature" and "full of wonder."

My thoughts jumped to God. What phrases might He use to explain me? The Bible tells me over and over I am Carol, "child of God," "a woman forgiven," "strong in the Lord," "gifted by His Spirit," "loved with an everlasting love."

Phrases might be only small collections of words—but they say big things.

Jesus . . . Son of God, light of life, faithful Savior, bread from heaven . . .
let my life's phrasing be found in You.
  —Carol Knapp

Digging Deeper: Luke 9:47; John 13:1; Revelation 4:8

A LIFETIME OF LOVE: Surrounded by Community

Bless the LORD, O my soul: and all that is within me, bless his holy name. Bless the LORD, O my soul, and forget not all his benefits. —Psalm 103:1–2 (KJV)

My husband, Don, taught me a lot about farm management during his last weeks. A local farmer does the planting, harvesting, and everything in between, but I faced dozens of decisions. The first was selling the corn. Despite studying markets, I sold too soon and didn't get top prices. I honored a contract to drill a new irrigation well, but my hands shook as I wrote out the largest check of my life. Changing accounts to my name only was easy at some businesses but required legal assistance at others.

Then there was upkeep on the house and surrounding five acres. Don maintained extensive flower beds. He mowed the yard and the weeds around the barn and outbuildings. I'm not a gardener, and mowing gives me hay fever. Don did the household repairs. We trapped a mouse and small snake in the basement because I didn't remember that cracks at the base of the house need sealing each fall.

But there were blessings. The well hit good water. My sons mowed and sprayed weeds. My daughter-in-law Patricia came every Tuesday to care for the flower beds and also helped me apply sealant. The basement is now mouse- and snake-free, but we ruined our clothes and I had to cut a goop-filled chunk out of my hair. My daughter Rebecca and grandson Mark did odd jobs, and friends and neighbors pitched in as needed. With their help and God's, I'm learning what I can do by myself and when to ask for help.

> *God of life and learning, thank You that Your blessings*
> *far outweigh my problems.*
> —Penney Schwab

Digging Deeper: Luke 10:29–37; 1 Timothy 6:18–19

Friday, April 28

The desert and the parched land will be glad; the wilderness will rejoice and blossom. Like the crocus, it will burst into bloom . . .
—Isaiah 35:1–2 (NIV)

It's spring, that miraculous time of year when the natural world that appeared winter-dead seems to almost overnight leap to life. I am amazed as I see trees and bushes that just yesterday looked bald and skeletal now burgeoning with greenery and colorful blossoms. I am in wonder as I view what looked like bare soil, now erupting with stems and flowers. *How does it happen so fast? How can all this vibrant and colorful life suddenly burst forth from seemingly nothing?*

It did not happen overnight, I remind myself. The preparations have been happening for a long time. Throughout the cold and desolate winter, there was growth going on that was hidden from my eyes. All I saw were the lifeless forms, seemingly barren soil. But, beneath the surface, there was much happening that I could not see.

I think of multiple times in my life when things have looked bleak and hopeless, and then, suddenly, the sun has broken through and flowers of joy have burst forth. Disparate occurrences that had made no sense have congealed to bring good. All that time, God had been working, preparing the good to come. I just had not, could not have, seen it.

As I gaze up at a magnificent cherry tree, exploding with pink blooms, I realize that trust is the key to all. Just as I trust that winter's lifeless forms are, beneath the surface, generating springtime bouquets, I must trust that God is working unseen in the winters of my life, to bring about springtimes of good.

> *Lord, deepen my trust; help me to know that even when I can't see it, You are working all things together for good.*
> —Kim Taylor Henry

Digging Deeper: Song of Songs 2:11–13, 7:12;
Habakkuk 2:3; Romans 8:28

And my God will supply every need of yours according to his riches in glory in Christ Jesus. —Philippians 4:19 (ESV)

Eleven-year-old Isaiah carries a tray across the backyard. The tray holds brown paper pots. The pots hold seedlings—tiny leaves holding tight to faint-green stems thin as threads.

We're planting a garden. The sun spills over this new yard like gold. Isaiah and his daddy built three boxed beds, then filled them with dirt made rich by the river.

"Time to get these in the ground, Mom," Isaiah says. He's longed for a garden, and his face shines like the day.

We kneel down and run our hands through the warm earth. Isaiah takes a trowel and opens the ground. With care, he settles the seedling. His hands push and pat the dirt and then offer water from a copper can.

The seedling looks weak and small in the empty bed.

Inside, I feel like that seedling. After home teaching five sons over twenty-two years, the next school year may be my last. My head swirls with thoughts of what my new life will look like. It's starting over. Where there was confidence and comfort, there's an empty unknown. I feel weak and wobbly. Spindly and undeveloped, like these strands of spring green.

But that little plant has everything it needs to thrive. And so do I.

God's Word is rich with promise. He walks beside me. He goes before me and after me. He lights my path, and because of His goodness, I'm surefooted.

My insides quake, but the Lord's nourishment is real and true.

Isaiah finishes the watering. Then, like he has a window to my soul, my son speaks to his seedling. "There you go, little one. You're going to be okay."

Lord, when I feel weak and uncertain, I will trust in You. Amen.
—Shawnelle Eliasen

Digging Deeper: Psalm 18:33, 139:5

The righteous will flourish like a palm tree, they will grow like a cedar of Lebanon; planted in the house of the LORD, they will flourish in the courts of our God. —Psalm 92:12–13 (NIV)

I sat with my mom on her back porch. A breeze drifted through the screens.

"It's been good to have you home for a few days," my mom said.

Being at my parents' house was relaxing. It was a break from the day-to-day obligations of life and lawyering. For months, I had felt caught in a constant cycle of drafting briefs, teaching Bible study, and working out at the gym.

"Look at the willow tree," my mom said, motioning toward the yard. The willow's thin leaves fluttered in the wind. Its enormous boughs swayed.

"How old is that tree now?" I asked.

"Three years," she said.

I was fresh out of law school when we selected the willow at the nursery. We had combed through rows of trees until we found the perfect one.

I wished I could slip back to that day, when obligations of school were behind me and the stress of post-grad life was still ahead.

"Can you believe that tree once fit in our van?" my mom asked.

I looked at the willow, nearly a story tall. It hardly seemed the same spindly tree that had lain between the seats of the minivan.

"It has really grown," I said.

So had I. In the last three years, I had become a better leader and a better writer. I was stronger and more confident.

As nice as it would be to return to the past, that was a place where I no longer fit.

I watched the sprawling willow continue to move with the wind. And I thanked God for the opportunity to continue to grow and change.

Father, thank You for continually growing and changing me.
—Logan Eliasen

Digging Deeper: 1 Samuel 2:26; Luke 2:52

LET US SING FOR JOY

1 _____

2 _____

3 _____

4 _____

5 _____

6 _____

7 _____

8 _____

9 _____

10 _____

11 _____

12 _____

13 _____

14 _____

15 _____

April

16 _____

17 _____

18 _____

19 _____

20 _____

21 _____

22 _____

23 _____

24 _____

25 _____

26 _____

27 _____

28 _____

29 _____

30 _____

MAY

*Great is the LORD, and greatly
to be praised, and his greatness
is unsearchable.*

—Psalm 145:3 (ESV)

Monday, May 1

For I am the LORD your God who takes hold of your right hand and says to you, Do not fear; I will help you. —Isaiah 41:13 (NIV)

This is a transitional time for me. I recently celebrated my seventieth birthday, and I will retire from Mercer University in a few weeks. While I will continue to teach one class per semester and interact with students, I am officially entering a stage of life I have not experienced before. Amidst the rejoicing and the celebration of retirement, there is also the anxiety of the unknown.

Early this morning, I picked up my Bible and simply opened it at random. I found that the page I was staring at was from the prophecy of Isaiah. My eyes focused on a verse I had underlined in faint pencil years before: "Do not fear, for I am with you; do not anxiously look about you, for I am your God. I will strengthen you, surely I will help you, surely I will uphold you with My righteous right hand" (Isaiah 41:10 [NASB1995]). I instantly knew that God was speaking to me.

Every transition in life is characterized by risk. But it is also filled with so much possibility and joy. God makes the same promise to each of us that He made thousands of years ago to Isaiah. Today I am going to accept again this assurance from God that "I will strengthen you, help you, and uphold you."

> *Father, thank You for Your promises that I must rediscover*
> *many times in my life. Amen.*
> —Scott Walker

Digging Deeper: Psalm 23:4, 27:1, 34:4–5;
Matthew 8:25–27; Luke 14:27

"Do not withhold good from one who deserves it when you have the power to do it." —Proverbs 3:27 (JPS)

When my greyhound, Anjin, died, I needed another dog immediately, and Halle came to live with me the very next day. The death of L.E., my cat, did not affect me in the same way. I missed her, but it was more than a week before I began thinking about getting another cat. I reflected on the difference and decided that I had needed a dog, but I wanted a cat who needed me.

I mentioned this to a friend who told me at once that she knew of a shelter in the next county that had cats. The shelter was near my local family, so they went over and picked out a cat for me.

ZZ was a Manx, six years old, and likely would not have been adopted at a time when everyone really wanted kittens. I was doubtful when she came out of the cat carrier in my living room. I was accustomed to slender, graceful cats, and ZZ was round, a little butterball with a stub of a tail and spatulate feet that resembled snowshoes. I'd never seen a Manx in the flesh before, so it was startling. I found myself thinking, *Is that really the cat for me? Why couldn't God have given me a pretty one?*

But if I was dubious, ZZ seemed to know instantly that she was home and safe. Before the evening was over, she'd climbed up on the arm of the couch—L.E.'s nightly perch—pressed her body against my shoulder, and purred in my ear. She was so confident and comfortable from the beginning that it was as if she'd put in an order for a place to belong and got mine. Once again, I'd been reassured that God knew what He was doing.

When I think I know best, God, You always find a way to gently remind
me I might be wrong about that.
—Rhoda Blecker

Digging Deeper: Psalm 16:9, 55:9

Wednesday, May 3

Who of you by worrying can add a single hour to your life? Since you cannot do this very little thing, why do you worry about the rest?
—Luke 12:25–26 (NIV)

Just like that, the digital rug was pulled out from under me. Right in the middle of a Zoom meeting, my internet connection went kaput! I immediately called my provider, trying to keep the hysteria out of my voice. Mysteriously, the technician connected me to a series of technical screens while he guided me through a complicated systems check. I discovered several interesting things, including the name of the satellite that handles my communications.

After a good forty-five minutes, he said, "I'm sorry, but we'll have to schedule the dreaded service call." He didn't actually say *dreaded* but that's what I heard.

I hung up in a state of despair. How could I survive without email, websites, social media? "How will I be able to check the weather?"

"Well, you can always just go outside," my wife, Julee, suggested.

Eventually it dawned on me that the loss of the internet left me with time on my hands. A little more time to think and reflect, to pray and meditate, to read and write, to cook a meal from scratch, to watch a movie with Julee, to hike with my dog, Gracie.

So, I vowed not to stand at the window all day waiting for the tech to arrive. I accepted that the world still turns, God is in His heaven, and life goes on without the internet.

Until the tech arrives.

Lord, You've blessed the world with many ways to stay connected. Yet sometimes I am too connected. Help me remember that life is not a URL. But don't forget to keep an eye on satellite EchoStar-17 orbiting somewhere up there in outer space.
—Edward Grinnan

Digging Deeper: Psalm 112:7; Colossians 3:2

Cheerfully share your home with those who need a meal or a place to stay. —1 Peter 4:9 (NLT)

I removed my three candles from the corner table and set them in a storage bin. I dusted off the table surface before unpacking the boxes of plants. A miniature Madagascar palm. An arrangement of young succulents in a teacup. A prickly cactus. I arranged and rearranged my daughter's plants in the morning sunlight coming through the eastern window.

"At least we have the plants in place," I joked with a friend on the phone as I detailed my concern of doubling the number of people under our roof and tripling the number of pets when our daughter, Aleah; her spouse, Todd; and their two-year-old daughter, Juniper, moved in later that day. They would stay with us for several months while their new home was being built. I wondered how our ten-year-old dog, Mollie, would respond to the upheaval of her quiet existence after Herriot and Penelope, their two rambunctious pups, arrived.

"Life is all about finding room," my friend responded when I joked about having extra adults in the kitchen.

When Aleah and family arrived with their stacks of boxes and suitcases, I couldn't help but remember how, thirty-five years earlier, my parents had made room for us—me, my husband, and baby son—in our own transitional season. Mom and Dad had welcomed us despite the noisy interruption to their empty-nest lives. They found room.

The first thing Aleah and Todd unpacked was Juniper's crib so their displaced toddler could have a much-needed nap after waking up at 4:30 a.m. She had sensed her world was about to change. Juniper settled into her familiar bed in an unfamiliar space, surrounded by her lovies and blankets. Within minutes, she was sound asleep in her new room.

> *Lord, help me to always choose to find room to welcome others into my space, my schedule, and my home.*
> —Lynne Hartke

Digging Deeper: Isaiah 58:6–10; Romans 12:13–16

Friday, May 5

There are things about God that people cannot see—his eternal power and all the things that make him God . . . They are made clear by what God has made. —Romans 1:20 (ICB)

"Mimsy, do you have flowers in your backyard?" my four-year-old grandson asked, his brown eyes wide with wonder, marveling at the blossoms blooming in the yard of his new home.

The California neighborhood my daughter and her family had moved into was filled with trails, trees, and lots of gloriously growing greenery that a non-gardener like me couldn't possibly name. My grandson, Xander, was enamored with every verdant square inch.

I explained to him that my home in Colorado, which Xander hadn't had the opportunity to visit yet, had a very short time when flowers could bloom. Also, I didn't really have a backyard. A small, walled cement patio was my only outdoor space. I told Xander that I didn't have any soil where flowers could grow, but I did have a chair and a little table where I could sit and read during the brief summer months.

"Well, when I come for a visit," Xander said, "I'm going to bring you a flower from our yard because everyone needs a flower. They're beautiful."

I guess even a four-year-old can recognize that beauty isn't just a nicety but a necessity. If God didn't think beauty was important, I don't believe He'd have woven it so tightly into the fabric of the universe. Perhaps I do need a flower on my little back porch, every petal a visual hymn of praise reaching up toward its Creator, reminding me to take the time to do the same.

Father, thank You for filling this world with such beauty and diversity. Thank You for how it fills my heart with awe and draws my thoughts toward You.
—Vicki Kuyper

Digging Deeper: Psalm 24:1; Isaiah 55:12; Luke 12:27, 19:37–40

BUILDING CATHEDRALS: Sisters in Faith
But he knows the way that I take; when he has tested me, I will come forth as gold. —Job 23:10 (NIV)

We're no strangers to tornadoes in Alabama. Living in Tornado Alley means we're never far from the touchdown sites, and this last one was no exception, marking a path of destruction only eight miles from us.

The next day, the sun came up and we could see the needs growing. Suddenly, the idea came to me: diapers. I live in a young neighborhood where almost everyone has kids, so having an extra pack of diapers around is the standard. I hustled to our group page and asked, "Would anyone like to put any out on their porch, or send me cash to buy them at the store?"

Two days later, I found myself with over $500 and a map dotted with pickup locations. Over and over, people thanked me for allowing them to feel useful, to help in such a hard time. In turn, I thanked them for allowing me to be the hands and feet gathering their goods. I ended up going to the store five times. Each time I would go and spend the donations plus some money of my own, I would get home to find that more money had been dropped off. Back to the store I went!

In the end, our little neighborhood gave almost 1,300 diapers, enough to cover plenty of bottoms for several weeks until parents could get back on their feet. And while we gave a lot, the feeling of community gave us all that we needed that day.

Lord, never let me forget the feeling of being Your hands and feet on this earth. Help me to take care of those for whom You care endlessly.
—Ashley Kappel

Digging Deeper: Acts 14:22; Hebrews 12:1; Revelation 2:10

Sunday, May 7

Above all, maintain a constant love for one another, for love covers a multitude of sins. —1 Peter 4:8 (NRSV)

As grown kids, we used to tease Mom about some of the things she told us when we were growing up, maxims she issued with great authority, like "It's a good thing none of you are too good-looking because that way you develop your personality." For years, that one echoed in my head until I was maybe fifty and looked at a picture of us. What was Mom talking about? We were good-looking kids.

Ever since Mom died—swiftly at age ninety-three—I find myself thinking of her not only with love but also with deep admiration. Has that ever happened to you? That as you reconsider the life of a parent, you rediscover them. I think of how Mom delighted in us, listening intently to all our stories, posting a picture we made on a refrigerator door, saving our essays in files. Of course, she lost her temper at times, but then it was all over and done. One thing I never doubted is that we were loved. It never would have crossed our minds.

Mom wasn't especially vocal about her faith. She taught Sunday school, she served on church boards, and she had this very book of daily devotionals by her bedside (I didn't check to see if any pages were marked, but she would comment at times about something I wrote or somebody else wrote). The way she mirrored God's love, which clearly she felt, was by passing it on. Loving unconditionally. God willing, I have done as much with my kids and my wife.

"Thanks, Mom," I'll say to her memory, over and over again. "I'm still developing my personality, with you as my model."

> *Dear Lord, we are grateful for the examples and models of Your love that we see in the world and get to follow.*
> —Rick Hamlin

Digging Deeper: Isaiah 49:15; 1 Corinthians 13:13

". . . as the sky soars high above earth, so the way I work surpasses the way you work, and the way I think is beyond the way you think."
—Isaiah 55:9 (MSG)

I live in a neighborhood of Milwaukee that has tree-lined streets and is nicely wedged between a bike path on one side and Lake Michigan on the other.

I was walking my dog, Max, the other day when I looked over and saw a neighbor gesticulating from behind his living room window. He was also tapping loudly on the glass.

Waving his arms in the air, my neighbor—whose name I don't even know—was opening and closing his mouth as if to scream something, but I couldn't hear him. I paused. Again, he pointed, and this time I could tell that he was pointing behind me.

So I turned around. And I suddenly saw that, not even twenty feet behind me, on the sidewalk, stood a coyote.

It didn't flinch. It just looked right back at me.

Then Max turned around, and when Max saw his distant but much scarier cousin, he uttered a growl like one I'd never heard before. It was a guttural *AWRRRR* that sent the coyote running in the other direction. We stood and watched it turn the next corner and disappear into an alley.

I don't know what to make of the coyote yet, except I'm told they are becoming common in cities across the United States. Perhaps it was a lesson in paying attention. Even everyday routines, like walking my dog, should not become mindless habits.

Today, I am appreciating my surroundings more, both while walking Max and while walking alone. I'm looking and listening. I'm paying attention.

You should, too, before God uses a coyote to shake you awake.

I'm here, Lord, ready and waiting.
—Jon M. Sweeney

Digging Deeper: 1 Samuel 3:11

Tuesday, May 9

. . . he created all the nations throughout the whole earth. —Acts 17:26 (NLT)

I still remember the look the gal at the bank gave me when she asked me my occupation and I proudly said, "I run cows."

Her nose wrinkled and she held my application away from her immaculate suit with manicured, mile-long fingernails. "Why?" she blurted. "It's so dirty!"

That memory from my college days jumped to the foreground recently as I helped sort calves on foot in the corral after a thorough rain. The mud was almost knee deep. The calves had the advantage as they weren't worried about losing their boots with each step. But we got the job done and kept our socks fairly clean in the process. Everything else got splattered, and the grit in my teeth wasn't tasty, either.

I wondered about that banker gal. Which of us chose a better career? I cannot say. Even today, working in a bank sounds as inviting to me as prison—indoors, around folks all day, and in town. And I'm confident Ms. Banker still wouldn't trade with me.

Isn't it precious how God has created each of us—bankers, ranchers, people of all colors—in His image? We are all His children. We are all loved. We each fill a unique role that is vital to one another in society. How boring it would be if we were all the same! We wouldn't have banks if everyone were like me, and there would be no food if we were all like my banker gal. What a wondrous array of hopes and dreams, gorgeous skin colors, and fascinating cultures, all beautifully knit together by God's own hand.

Thank You for city people, country people, and every walk of life You have placed in Your creation. Remind us today how much we need one another, almost as much as we need You.
—Erika Bentsen

Digging Deeper: Genesis 1:27; Acts 17:26–27

The king was distressed, but because of his oaths and his dinner guests, he ordered that her request be granted. —Matthew 14:9 (NIV)

I'm strong, Grand!"

My granddaughter, when she's not a princess complete with a pink gown and a dazzling tiara, stands, showing off her would-be muscles as she struggles to lift her daddy's kettlebell. In the midst of my over-cheering, it occurs to me that we live in a culture where weakness is near anathema. Whether weightlifting or triumphantly smiling through our tears, dispelling the appearance of weakness is more and more sought after, while an open sob is often shunned.

Matthew 14 suggests it has ever been that way. Though claiming the royal oath demanded the head of John the Baptist, it was also his need for a show of power before his friends that made the king act so radically.

As a Christian, I, too, find myself admiring strength, equating the ability to push through anything dry-eyed as a mark of unswerving faith. But then Apostle Paul reminds me to "be strong in the Lord, and in the power of his might"—not in my facade of stoicism but in the strength of God! "When I am weak," Paul says, "then I am strong." The Lord's strength can be depended upon during our times of vulnerability. To quote my pastor: "You pour out the tears; God pours in the strength."

Showing off human strength isn't limited to little ones like my granddaughter. The attempt to conquer weakness—gilded with pride—ranges from peasants to kings. What cry for help, like the one in Matthew 14:9, might we be hiding from God today because of the "dinner guests" in our lives? What part of our need to release is being thwarted by someone we are trying to please?

Lord, when my soul needs a good cleansing, give me the grace to cry.
—Jacqueline F. Wheelock

Digging Deeper: 2 Corinthians 12:8–10; Ephesians 6:10

Thursday, May 11

So you too, outwardly appear righteous to people, but inwardly you are full of hypocrisy . . . —Matthew 23:28 (NASB)

It came to me suddenly—the gentle chiding of the Holy Spirit. "You're acting just like that cougar." That stopped me in my tracks.

A cougar had been roaming our mountain for several days. I never saw it, but I could hear its *kee, kee, kee* hiss as it staked its perimeter.

My husband, Terry, and I had resided for seven years with our "roomies," friends who owned the mountain property and gladly shared it—each with our own living space.

Then these friends sold five acres to close relatives of ours who lived in an urban setting sixty miles away. And now those relatives were putting up a prefab shed an outfield's throw from our kitchen window and converting it to a cabin getaway.

We loved spending time with them—visiting them in their urban setting and inviting them the sixty miles to our home.

So, what was wrong with me? The hissing cougar was the clue. I was being territorial. The mountain was my sanctuary. Selfishly, I didn't want to add anyone else.

God called me on my hypocrisy. Our entire time in this beautiful setting was because this couple—now octogenarians—had generously opened their home and shared their place with us! Jesus demonstrated an expansive heart. One of His most beloved teachings is, "Treat people the same way you want them to treat you" (Luke 6:31 [NASB]).

I had an opportunity to live the Golden Rule and widen the mountain welcome. Jesus was asking me to stretch my heart.

Jesus, You demonstrated that making room in my life for others is how I make room for You.
—Carol Knapp

Digging Deeper: Matthew 25:35–40; Luke 6:42;
Romans 12:9–11, 15:7

May the God of hope fill you with all joy and peace as you trust in him,
so that you may overflow with hope by the power of the Holy Spirit.
—Romans 15:13 (NIV)

Many years ago, we sat in the auditorium, watching my son's high school band performance. "Ashokan Farewell," a mournful song with a beautiful violin lead, began. About a minute in, a senior student stopped playing, rose from his chair, put down his instrument, and left the stage. Followed by another, and then another, and another. Slowly, one by one, as the song progressed, all the seniors walked off the stage as the band played on.

I was overcome with emotion, my throat tight, tears in my eyes. I remember being relieved that this heartfelt moment was years away for me, for us, for my son. I wondered, *How will I feel when he is grown—when he is a senior and moving on to college? How will I feel when it is Solomon's turn to put down his instrument and leave the stage?*

During Solomon's senior year, for unavoidable reasons, the concert was canceled. When I got the email letting us know there wasn't going to be an "Ashokan Farewell" moment, I cried. I went for a long walk and pictured the concert in my mind. I listened to the song on my phone, both sorrowful and hopeful. I imagined Solomon getting up and leaving the stage, and I smiled and cried, thinking how amazing it is that grief and hope can live together within me right at the same time—and I thank God for that.

> *Dear Lord, when disappointment comes, You lead me*
> *through the sadness to hope.*
> —Sabra Ciancanelli

Digging Deeper: Jeremiah 29:11; Hebrews 11:1; 1 Peter 5:10

Saturday, May 13

The LORD your God is with you, the Mighty Warrior who saves. He will take great delight in you; in his love he will no longer rebuke you, but will rejoice over you with singing. —Zephaniah 3:17 (NIV)

Warming myself at a cozy campfire in the middle of the woods was a peaceful way to spend a cool evening—until the sounds of "Here Comes the Bride" drifted through the trees and surrounded me with music. My husband and I leaped from our chairs like we expected a woman wearing a wedding gown to emerge from the dark forest and walk toward us. As the song concluded, we still had no idea if someone was playing a joke on us or if a wedding was taking place somewhere in the vicinity.

Several days later, we learned the answer. A nearby bed-and-breakfast recently built a chapel on the highest point of its property and now specialized in weddings. Since sound carries farther over water than land, we would be serenaded frequently. Why? Because the chapel gained instant popularity, and our firepit is in the backyard of our hilltop house across the river from the inn.

Do we mind the free concerts? Not at all. Weddings celebrate a joyous life event, and a string quartet plays most of the songs. The night a harpist joined the musicians delighted everyone on our side of the river when heavenly melodies floated our way. I imagine the only revelry with a sweeter sound comes from above when God sings over us, although I suspect His angels rejoicing is a close second.

God, help me to have faith in Your strength, seek calm in Your unfailing love, and listen for Your sweet song of delight when I trust in You.
—Jenny Lynn Keller

Digging Deeper: Luke 2:8–14, 15:7; Revelation 5:11–12

Then God opened her eyes, and she saw a well of water. And she went and filled the skin with water and gave the boy a drink. —Genesis 21:19 (ESV)

My son hands me a card crafted from the page of an old music book. A picture of birds from a days-gone-by wall calendar adorns the front. The script is short and sweet: *Mom, thank you for taking care of us. Thanks for what we don't see.*

The rest of my boys, gathered around our table to celebrate Mother's Day with my husband, my parents, and me, uphold tradition with homemade cards, too. But as we share lunch, the message in that first card returns like an echo.

What we don't see.

Not far from our table is our wool rug. I've taught my boys to dance over it, but I've also been facedown in prayer. Our creaky wooden rocker sits close. I've rocked babes and begged blessing. Now as my own mama rises to serve cake, I think about how she carries my worries in her own chest. I wonder what battles bound her, as she smiled, sang, braided our hair, or turned pages of books. Last week, I met with a mama who wept but brushed away tears when her littles woke. Another friend's husband is in heaven. She raises her boys alone.

Mamas.

We can feel like Hagar in the desert. Hardships sting our souls like hot sand. But Hagar had an intimate encounter with the Lord (twice), and she called Him El Roi because He saw her. He not only saw, but He also provided.

He provides for us, too. He brings quiet glory to our hushed and hidden battles.

We finish our cake and the boys clear the clutter. I place the cards on the piano for all to see. But mostly I'm glad for the God Who sees.

Lord, You see secret places. And You provide.
—Shawnelle Eliasen

Digging Deeper: Genesis 16:13; Psalm 33:18

Monday, May 15

I will walk among you and be your God, and you shall be My people.
—Leviticus 26:12 (NKJV)

It's mid-afternoon and I need to take stuff down to the compost pile. As I come out the porch door onto the deck, the farm cats that happen to be close to home, lazing around instead of out exploring, come trotting to see if I'm bringing food. Seeing no bag or can, they look away. Until, that is, I start down the hill. Then they follow. It's been that way for many years now. When I stop at the compost pile, they look up as if to say, "Is that it? Aren't we going on a walk?"

So we do. Down the grassy hill. Onto the trails I've made and mowed. Through the woods. Me and the cats. Sometimes they're a short distance back or ahead. Sometimes, especially Gracie or Ebony, they wind between my feet as I stride. If I stop, they want me to pick them up and give them some attention. They walk with me until . . . until they don't, their attention diverted by sighting a mouse or chipmunk or other prey. Then they're off.

I'd be disappointed, except I know it will happen almost every time we walk.

I wonder if that's how God deals with my following in this way—wishing I'd stick closer but knowing that I'm prone to wander. Yes, sometimes I'm right there, walking alongside the Great Lover of my soul and listening and learning. Other times, though, I'm at a distance, distracted by some new sparkly thing or another. Occasionally, I just want to be left alone to ramble—but still know that I'm being watched over. And, because God loves me, I am.

Thank You, God, for Your patience with me as I follow You in my erratic way. Thank You, too, for always keeping me in sight—whether I lag behind or run too far ahead. Amen.
—J. Brent Bill

Digging Deeper: Psalm 128:1–2; Luke 24:13–32

Cast thy bread upon the waters: for thou shalt find it after many days.
—Ecclesiastes 11:1 (KJV)

I was shopping at Target when an elderly lady approached me. "I'd know that sweet little twang anywhere," she said in a tiny voice. "You're Roberta from the Veterans hospital! You were on duty the night my boy died."

Her Sammy had passed away on May 16, 1978. I was in my early twenties, in my second month as a VA nurse. I'd telephoned to tell her he'd taken a turn for the worse. She lived way out in the country, but she'd set out on that West Virginia mountain road alone.

"It's been over forty years," I said. "I can't believe you remember me." What I didn't say was that I'd retired a while back. I doubted anyone remembered much of anything about me.

"As I walked to Sammy's room, I didn't know what I was in for," she said. "I watched from the doorway as you washed his face and hands, then combed his thick, coal-black hair. The way the light over his bed hit the stripe on your cap, it looked like a halo. 'Someone real special is on her way to see you, Sammy,' you were telling him. 'Your *mama*.'

"Don't guess you ever knew I heard that," she went on. "When I go back to that time, I don't think how sick he was or the way he suffered. Just how you said that word *mama*. And how purty he looked when he went to see Jesus."

> *Oh, Lord Jesus, what we do really does matter. Don't let me squander a single second.*
> —Roberta Messner

Digging Deeper: Proverbs 3:3; Philippians 1:6; Colossians 3:17

Wednesday, May 17

HYMNS OF PRAISE: Holy, Holy, Holy! Lord God Almighty

And one called to another and said: "Holy, holy, holy is the LORD of hosts; the whole earth is full of his glory!" —Isaiah 6:3 (ESV)

A few years ago, I received my Bible Study Fellowship (BSF) assignment—volunteer co-leader for the young toddler class. Our children's program made it convenient for mothers of preschoolers to attend, but our class was more than childcare, with a curriculum that included singing specific hymns eight times during the year.

My instinct was to sing catchier, more age-appropriate songs to these fifteen-month-old babies. It seemed pointless, but I reluctantly followed the program that BSF headquarters had set in place. I plopped on the floor and sang, "Holy, Holy, Holy." The class sat circled around me and stared without comprehension.

First written as a poem by Reginald Heber, bishop of Calcutta, more than two hundred years ago, Heber's widow found the verse among her husband's papers after he passed. Thirty-five years later, a music publisher rediscovered the four-stanza poem, put it to a melody, and in 1861 created the popular Christian hymn.

Holy, holy, holy! Lord God Almighty!
Early in the morning our song shall rise to thee.
Holy, holy, holy! Merciful and mighty,
God in three persons, blessed Trinity!

Months into the BSF year, a young mother lingered in our doorway after class. She shared how while running errands, a toddler's voice sang, "Holy, holy, holy, Lord God all mine be," from the back seat.

I smiled. That antiquated hymn was still relevant today—even for toddlers.

Dear God, I may not understand Your ways, but help me walk in them.
                    —Stephanie Thompson

Digging Deeper: Exodus 15:11; Psalm 96:9; Revelation 4:8

. . . the Holy Spirit, whom the Father will send in my name, will teach you all things and will remind you of everything I have said to you.
—John 14:26 (NIV)

I sat in the front row in our crowded church, trying to control a grow-ing panic as I waited my turn to give a eulogy for my friend Leslie. I'd worked hard to create a message to honor her memory, and those words were written on a piece of paper in my clammy hand, but I could hardly see them. My contact lenses were suddenly fogging over. When this happens, I have to take them out, carefully rinse them with a solution, and put them back in. There was no chance of that now. Our pastor was speaking, and I was next.

I took some deep breaths as the pastor walked away from the podium. I stood up on jelly legs, blinking hard, hoping my eyelids might act as windshield wipers on my contacts. I placed my paper on the podium and miraculously, I could see a few words. I remember little about getting through my message, and when I got back to my seat, I felt like I'd had an out-of-body experience.

Later, when people commented on things I'd said, I realized I'd included most of my message and felt humbled by the level of fear I'd felt. Especially as I remembered assuring Leslie, when she felt fearful about the next steps of her journey, that God would give her what she needed *when* she needed it, and trusting that promise would give her strength. I could imagine Leslie smiling and asking God to remind me that He gave me what I needed *when* I got up to speak, not when I sat in the front row in a panic.

Lord, when I tell others about Your promises, I need to
humbly believe those promises for myself.
—Carol Kuykendall

Digging Deeper: Psalm 119:105; Jeremiah 29:11; John 15:7

Friday, May 19

Where there is no guidance the people fall, But in an abundance of counselors there is victory. —Proverbs 11:14 (NASB)

My fifteen-year-old daughter had finally earned a spot in our community's summer musical. But after the first practice, she came home with a heavy heart. The play didn't honor her faith or her convictions, and the other cast members were unknowingly mocking her beliefs.

For two weeks, she battled whether she should continue with the show. She had been taught to honor her commitments and she understood the consequences of walking away, but each day she came home more upset. My husband and I spent hours discussing her options, but she still didn't feel settled. One night, as she shared her heart, she asked, "Mom, do you mind if I ask Emily and Erin for advice?"

Emily and Erin are two of my dear friends. Both are wise and godly women with teenagers of their own. When my daughter asked if she could seek their counsel, my internal response was why? Hadn't I already given her all her options? What more could my friends add to the discussion? But then I realized that my daughter was exhibiting a maturity beyond her years and I needed to step out of her way. It took courage to ask for advice and wisdom to know where to look. As she ages and moves on with her life, I won't always be there to guide her. It's a relief to know that she recognizes the need for an abundance of godly counselors.

After receiving the advice she needed, my daughter made the choice to bow out of the play gracefully. And in the process, she gained a wealth of wisdom from adults she trusted.

Lord, I ask that You give me the wisdom and grace to step aside and allow others to minister into the lives of my loved ones when the need arises.
—Gabrielle Meyer

Digging Deeper: Proverbs 12:15; 2 Timothy 3:16–17

For which of you, desiring to build a tower, does not first sit down and count the cost, whether he has enough to complete it? —Luke 14:28 (ESV)

It was a rare hour in the park for a neighbor girl and me. She had permission to be out. I had energy and vision, even finding someone who could pump air into her softened basketball. When we arrived, she ran to the empty court. Wearing my classic leather loafers, I lagged behind. From the far sidelines, I watched her dribble and shoot—and miss the very first basket. Neither of us was fast enough to catch the ball before it rolled down a rocky bank and into a gently rolling run—otherwise known as a creek. "Miss Evelyn!"

I heard panic and warned, "Stay back. I'll get it." After a few downward steps, I hesitated, afraid *I'd* be the one to lose my footing on the boulders. "Lord, keep me steady," I prayed as I considered risks: What if I fell on my way down the bank? What if I waded barefoot into the water and stepped on broken glass? What if I protected my feet and ruined the shoes I hoped would last me ten more years?

The ball floated southward. I didn't have much time. I stopped. And turned around. Like a biblical—or contemporary—manager, I counted the cost. "We have to let it go," I said decisively. "I'll buy you a new ball."

We went to a store. She claimed a brick-red Wilson and dribbled it across the parking lot. I drove home, thanking God for sturdy shoes, dry feet, and a sensible plan. I hoped someone downstream might be able to retrieve the lost ball.

> *Lord, when it's time for me to make decisions, give me*
> *presence of mind, and help me "keep my head."*
> —Evelyn Bence

Digging Deeper: James 1:5, 17–27

Sunday, May 21

Why, my soul, are you downcast? Why so disturbed within me? Put your hope in God, for I will yet praise him, my Savior and my God.
—Psalm 42:11 (NIV)

Several years ago, on the first Sunday after my dear friend Jean had suddenly passed away, my husband practically dragged me to church. I didn't want to go. I was bereft and could not stop crying. I didn't want to be around anyone beyond my immediate kinfolk. But my husband encouraged me to join, so I went.

We arrived just as the church was in the middle of a lively praise and worship song, tambourines jingling and drums pulsing.

Although I wanted to simply slink into a seat in one of the rear pews, some kind soul made room for us in the second row from the front and gestured for us to join him there. Folks were standing, singing praises to our God, and all I wanted to do was hide. I began to cry again and sat with my head in my hands, as everyone else around me stood, sang, danced, and worshipped.

After a few minutes, afraid that people would wonder what was wrong with me and wanting to feel some of this goodness that was permeating the congregation, I forced myself to stand up.

And while I was unable to sing a note or speak a word, I found that I could lift my hands. It didn't seem like much praise, I suppose, but it was huge for me: I realized that even through this difficult and painful moment, I could still worship God. I may not have been able to speak my worship, but my pained heart began to be calmed by the Lord's peace.

Thank You, Father, for giving me the ability to glorify You, even in the smallest ways and in my darkest moments.
—Gayle T. Williams

Digging Deeper: 2 Samuel 22:50; Psalm 9:2; Micah 7:7

Be not quick in your spirit to become angry, for anger lodges in the heart of fools. —Ecclesiastes 7:9 (ESV)

I try to avoid arguments, but one neighbor of mine seems to live for them. Recently, he began making wild accusations against me. The more I tried to convince him that he was mistaken and must have misunderstood something, the angrier and more belligerent he became. Finally, I just gave up and ended the conversation—or so I thought. He made sure to get in the last word.

Years ago, I'm not sure I could have stood for this. I'm pretty quick on my feet, and I'm relatively certain that I could've come up with something sharp to say back to this rude fellow. But strangely enough, I felt a peace about letting it lie, and I'm convinced that this was God's handiwork in my heart. My only thought was, *If it makes him feel better to have the last word, then let him have the last word.*

When I was a teenager, a lady at church told me that there's only one thing in the Bible that we're guaranteed to receive if we ask for it and that's wisdom (James 1:5). I've been praying for it ever since, so Lord willing, as I get older, perhaps it's slowly kicking in.

Situations may call for me to stand up for myself, the ones I love, or simply what is right, but I'm learning that some arguments just aren't worth getting in the ring over.

After my neighbor got his coveted last word, I focused my energy into a new project and had one of the most productive days I'd had all week.

> *Father, please grant me wisdom and let Your Spirit grow*
> *in me the fruit of self-control.*
> —Ginger Rue

Digging Deeper: Galatians 5:22–23; Ephesians 4:31

Tuesday, May 23

The humble He guides in justice, And the humble He teaches His way.
—Psalm 25:9 (NKJV)

When I retired from college teaching, I figured I would write the Great American Textbook, travel the world, and speak at conventions. Somehow that never worked out.

Recently, I had just left the house when my wife, Sharon, came running after me. "Danny! Come quick, there's a bird in the house!"

Somehow a sparrow had flown inside the house and was frantically darting from window to window, seeking the sky. For a while, I chased him with a broom toward an open door but with no success. Then I had an idea. I closed the blinds on all windows and doors, except for the front door, which I left wide open. Sure enough, in just seconds the little aviator found his way out.

As I look back on my retirement, I can see that God quietly pulled the blinds on some things I thought were important back then. My Great American Textbook was crowded out by things like correspondence with former students, who needed the kind of help not found in books. Most of our travel has been short trips, which are actually more fun than sleeping on airport floors. Rarely do I speak at conventions, but almost every Sunday I help out in some little area church, where I feel truly needed and appreciated.

My retirement may lack drama, but it is permeated with peace and hums with happiness. Isn't that what retirement is supposed to be all about?

> *I'm no eagle, Lord, just a sparrow, who is thankful for Your*
> *help in finding the right doors of service.*
> —Daniel Schantz

Digging Deeper: Acts 16:6–10, 32:8–9

HYMNS OF PRAISE: It Is Well with My Soul

You will keep him in perfect peace, Whose mind is stayed on You, Because he trusts in You. —Isaiah 26:3 (NKJV)

The balance between God's sovereignty and my heartbreak—betrayal of trusted friends, job losses, untimely death of loved ones—has always mystified me. Since God is in charge of all, why does He allow tragedy?

My twenty-first-century problems pale compared with what Horatio Spafford, a Chicago lawyer and real estate investor, faced. Father of five, his young son died in 1871. That same year, much of his business was destroyed in the great Chicago fire. Back on his feet two years later, the family set sail for a European vacation, but business demands kept Spafford behind.

Days later, he received a telegram from his wife: "Saved Alone, what shall I do?" A shipwreck claimed the lives of 226 of the 313 passengers, including all four of his daughters. Stafford boarded an ocean liner to bring his wife home. On the voyage, the captain showed him where the other vessel sank. There on the ship, Stafford penned the lyrics:

When peace like a river attendeth my way
When sorrows like sea billows roll
Whatever my lot, Thou hast taught me to say
It is well, it is well with my soul

Spafford's strong faith told him his daughters were not in that watery grave but in heaven with their Lord. Oh, to have an eternal perspective like Horatio Spafford did! The hope of heaven helps me reconcile God's sovereignty with worldly suffering. Thanks to this hymn, I'm inspired to lean closer to God, trust Him, and claim the peace that "it is well with my soul" no matter what trial I face.

> *Loving Father, may I cling to You in all of life's storms*
> *and remember this world is not my home.*
> —Stephanie Thompson

Digging Deeper: Psalm 147:3; Isaiah 62:3; John 14:27; Philippians 4:7

Thursday, May 25

He has showered his kindness on us, along with all wisdom and understanding. —Ephesians 1:8 (NLT)

I gripped the steering wheel and shook my head as I drove to the humane society. *I can't believe I'm going to do this!*

Years ago, after I buried Tasha and Ruby, I'd made the decision to not have any more cats. But a couple evenings ago, I'd trekked down to the barn to spiff up the tack room. When I opened the door and flipped on the lights, at least fifty mice covered the floor. *Gross!* Somehow one had found a way in and discovered a bag of grain. That mouse must have announced the smorgasbord to the whole mouse kingdom. The worst part was, when I entered, not one of them moved; they just kept feasting like I wasn't there.

I shut off the light, closed the door, and tried to figure out how to get rid of mice—without getting a cat. After whining to God about not wanting an indoor cat, His response shocked me. "Go to the Humane Society and get the *yellow* cat."

Gravel crunched under my tires as I pulled into the parking lot. The staff ushered me into one of the cat rooms, in which at least thirty cats sprawled all over carpeted towers and beds. I pointed to the *one* yellow cat, which perched looking out the window. "What do you know about that cat?"

"Oh, that's what he does all day. He wants to live outside." The gal was shocked when I told her I'd take him.

I'd never thought of it before, but it was as if God cared about what the cat wanted, too. In His kindness, He gifted us to each other.

> *Lord, help me to know and understand the depth of*
> *Your kindness in a new way. Amen.*
> —Rebecca Ondov

Digging Deeper: Psalm 23:6, 33:18

But he wanted to justify himself, so he asked Jesus, "And who is my neighbor?" —Luke 10:29 (NIV)

My young daughter is obsessed with the dump. She and her dad love to go there to scavenge for treasures. At first, the thought of my little girl rummaging through other people's discards made me uncomfortable. I tried explaining that the dump is where you go to throw things away, not accumulate them. But Aurora disagrees. In her opinion, it's where she finds things of great value that others have foolishly cast aside.

And I can't argue with the results. Aside from the toys, which are always Aurora's favorite finds, they've brought back an elliptical machine, jewelry, and dozens of nearly new tools. Seriously—who throws this stuff away?

Recently, as I watched Aurora unload another armload of dump prizes, I found myself thinking about Jesus and the lepers, tax collectors, prostitutes, Gentiles, and other castoffs He welcomed into relationship, despite the mutterings of others. Not even the ancient rift between Jews and Samaritans was safe. Imagine the surprise of the Jewish law expert in Luke 10:29 when, after pressing Jesus about who must be loved, Jesus centered a Samaritan as the hero of his answering parable. Weren't Samaritans justifiably despised? Not in Jesus's eyes.

In my experience, it's disturbingly easy to participate in groupthink that either intentionally excludes or blindly walks past people not considered "acceptable." Jesus pushes back on this human tendency time and again, refusing His followers their comfortable status quo by making His position unmistakably clear: Within the Body of Christ, there's no such thing as throwaway people.

Lord Jesus, when faced with outcasts, You always acted with mercy, justice, and inclusion. In short: with love. Please grant me the courage to "go and do likewise."
—Erin Janoso

Digging Deeper: Micah 6:8; Acts 10:28; Galatians 3:28

Saturday, May 27

All things were made through him, and without him was not any thing made that was made. —John 1:3 (ESV)

Hold on a second, Mom," I said.

I set down the phone and picked up Sport's empty food dish. Seeing the promise of breakfast, the Labrador pup dashed back and forth across the kitchen.

I filled the dish with kibble, then bent to set it on the floor. Before I could, a wild rush of puppy collided with me. Kibble scattered across the floor. I groaned, then picked up the phone.

"I'm guessing Sport is awake," my mom said.

"Yes. And he's just winding up for the day."

I had brought Sport home a month earlier. He was a distant cousin of my parents' Lab, Rugby. As a puppy, Rugby had spent his days playing gently and sleeping on laps. Sport—not so much. He was constantly making messes and loud noises.

"He's just a puppy," my mom said.

"He's not the kind of puppy I wanted."

There. I'd said it. Weeks of frustration had finally spilled out.

"Maybe not," my mom said. "But he's the puppy God gave you."

My face burned with embarrassment. I hadn't thought about God creating Sport's personality. Sport's energy and excitement weren't bad qualities—they were just different from what I expected.

Maybe Sport wasn't the one who needed to change.

"Can I call you back, Mom?" I asked.

"Do you have a mess to clean up?" she asked.

"No," I said, watching Sport joyfully chase his dish. "I have a wild puppy to play with."

> *Father, help me to appreciate the goodness in all of Your creations.*
> —Logan Eliasen

Digging Deeper: Genesis 1:25; Colossians 1:16

*And God is able to make all grace abound to you, so that having all
sufficiency in all things at all times, you may abound in every good work.*
—2 Corinthians 9:8 (ESV)

Navigating life with a horse has been an adventure-filled blessing.
That blessing seemed tempered when the barn where we boarded
Snow Mist informed us we needed to find a new facility for her. She
was naughty; Snow Mist had once broken her halter off, quickly followed by a dismounting fall by JoElla. Although it seemed abrupt to us,
the facility would no longer keep her since she had become a liability.
JoElla, my eleven-year-old daughter, felt especially hurt and unfairly
treated. At the time, we prayed the Lord would lead us to the right barn.

My heart ached to see JoElla so hurt. Nevertheless, we had decisions
to make. We visited places and talked with trainers. When Sarah, the
trainer at Rose Clover Farm, sincerely said, "I think I can help you
guys," JoElla and I knew this barn was where the Lord led us.

Sarah provided consistency in care and training for JoElla and Snow
Mist. Since the move to the new barn, Snow Mist is gaining needed
weight, looks immaculate, and takes great care of JoElla when she is riding.
Sarah also helps to shape JoElla into a great little rider. The barn and Sarah
are the perfect fit for us, and it is more than we ever dreamed possible.

After being settled with Snow Mist for some time, we glance back
to see God, in all His wisdom, placing us in the best situation, even
though it hurt when He moved us. As a parent, I want JoElla to know
the messy situations we sometimes live through bring us to blessings
we could never have imagined. The Lord's faithfulness leads us to blessings in unexpected twists and turns; our landing at Rose Clover Farm
is proof!

*Omniscient Father, may I always look back to see Your blessings through-
out times of my life that may be unexpected and difficult. Amen.*
—Jolynda Strandberg

Digging Deeper: Psalm 84:11–12; Matthew 6:30–33; Luke 12:22–26

Memorial Day, Monday, May 29

Blessed are the people who know the passwords of praise . . .
—Psalm 89:15 (MSG)

Notification came through the Past Conflict Repatriations Branch, Ft. Knox, Kentucky. Would I be willing to give a DNA swab to help identify unknown World War II prisoner-of-war soldiers who died in the Philippine Islands?

My mom's brother, Henry Noska, was a Bataan Death March survivor who died of dysentery and malaria on August 15, 1942. His DNA is known. Through a process of reverse identification, hopefully my DNA could help identify unknown comrades of his, now recently found.

With hesitation (was this some sort of scam call?), I reluctantly agreed to provide a sample. The DNA swab packet I received, however, also included photocopies of documents relating to Uncle Henry.

One of the declassified forms, dated August 27, 1946, charted the personal effects carried by Uncle Henry. "Photos," a "billfold (no money)," and "books" were checked. Then, on an additional remarks page, in the first listing under "Damages," was written "Prayer Book is badly damaged by moisture—stained."

Oh, was my heart encouraged to read those words. They were a tangible affirmation to me that even in the most distressing times imaginable, our God would never desert His precious people (Psalm 94:12). I imagined Corporal Noska—even in the most draining, difficult times—raising "passwords of praise" to our compassion-filled God. And, in the process, I receive strength for the journey as well.

Wonder-working God, enliven our spirits today, inspired by Your Spirit working within servants of the past. We thank You for our Armed Forces members serving globally this day. Amen.
—Ken Sampson

Digging Deeper: Psalm 91:8; Isaiah 55:11; 2 Timothy 1:14

Let us not become weary in doing good, for at the proper time we will reap a harvest if we do not give up. —Galatians 6:9 (NIV)

When I was in labor over ten years ago, I let everyone in the house sleep. My previous labor had lasted over twenty hours, so why wake anyone? I tiptoed in the dark to the bathroom, took a long shower, and ate a quiet breakfast. Soon the house began to stir—first my toddler, my parents, and then my husband.

"I'm in labor by the way," I said casually. They shot me a look. "I'm fine," I chuckled. "We'll be here for a while."

But in less than an hour, my casualness took a sharp turn into panic.

"Okay, we have to go," I said, putting on my jacket. "We have to go right now!"

I felt a familiar pressure that made me certain I'd give birth in the cab. I breathed and yelled as our cabbie zipped through the streets.

Soon I was in a wheelchair going up the hospital elevator. My previous labor was long and painful, but I was medicated. This was a pain I'd never known.

"I can't do this!" I shouted. "I can't do this!"

The nurse took my hand and looked at me in the eyes. "But you *are* doing it."

One year later, as my husband left me a single mother, I uttered those words again. But even as they left my mouth, I knew I *was* doing it. I was being the best mom I could be every day. For over a decade now, I've often had the same internal conversation I had with that nurse so long ago.

"I can't do this!"

"But you are," I always remind myself. "You *are* doing it."

Father, thank You for seeing me through so many moments
I thought I wouldn't survive.
—Karen Valentin

Digging Deeper: 2 Chronicles 15:7; Philippians 4:13

Wednesday, May 31

HYMNS OF PRAISE: In the Garden

"Why are you crying?" he asked her. "Whom are you looking for?" She thought he was the gardener. "Sir," she said, "if you have taken him away, tell me where you have put him, and I will go and get him."
—John 20:15 (TLB)

I t's been more than forty years since I sat at Grandma Roma's kitchen table, number 2 pencil in hand, doing my homework. Grandma stood at the sink washing dishes. On the windowsill, a pale yellow transistor radio blared country and western tunes. When Loretta Lynn crooned "In the Garden," Grandma sang along.

And He walks with me
And He talks with me
And He tells me I am his own
And the joy we share as we tarry there
None other has ever known

Recorded by countless artists and appearing in most church hymnals, the lyrics to "In the Garden" were written by C. Austin Miles, a manager at a music publishing company, whose hobby was photography.

Miles often read the Bible as he waited for his film to develop. One March day in 1912, he read John 20. He imagined the scene at the garden tomb when Mary met the risen Lord. That passage inspired the song. Miles is quoted as saying, "This is not an experience limited to a happening 2,000 years ago. It is the daily companionship with the Lord that makes up the Christian's life."

Grandma Roma loved that hymn. She also loved Jesus. The morning she passed, I awakened in the wee hours with the lyrics of "In the Garden" singing through my mind. Grandma was walking with Jesus.

Thank You, Lord, that I can commune with You just like those You walked with on earth. In You, I'm never alone.
—Stephanie Thompson

Digging Deeper: Matthew 28:20; John 14:2–3; Revelation 3:20

LET US SING FOR JOY

1 _____

2 _____

3 _____

4 _____

5 _____

6 _____

7 _____

8 _____

9 _____

10 _____

11 _____

12 _____

13 _____

14 _____

15 _____

May

16 _____

17 _____

18 _____

19 _____

20 _____

21 _____

22 _____

23 _____

24 _____

25 _____

26 _____

27 _____

28 _____

29 _____

30 _____

31 _____

JUNE

. . . be filled with the Spirit, speaking
to one another in psalms and hymns and
spiritual songs, singing and making melody
in your heart to the Lord.

—Ephesians 5:18–19 (NKJV)

Thursday, June 1

Pray without ceasing. —1 Thessalonians 5:17 (NRSV)

I was sad when I read the obituary of Michelle's husband in the paper. Her daughter Kristen and my Emily had played together as youngsters.

My sympathy note read, "You and Kristen have been in our thoughts and prayers. Emily and I will continue to send warm thoughts your way—especially as we pass your street—in the weeks and months to come." *Why did I impulsively add that about her street?*

Driving home from the post office, I found myself looking for familiar streets and houses. I could picture the inside of that white ranch on the left. Mary Beth and I met at the YMCA, then homeschooled our kids together for several years. We co-led the 4-H group we called the T.G.I.F Club, until she moved away. I prayed right then for Mary Beth. And for the family who lives there now, whose young mother I met at our quilt guild.

The next street reminded me of the wonderful fourth-grade teacher of both of my girls. I don't know if Mrs. Roth still lives there, but a prayer for her brought her close again.

Although it's been decades since my friend Kathy moved away, and I've visited her in three new houses, I always think of her as I drive by her old neighborhood. This time I didn't just think of her; I prayed for her and her family.

I was almost home when I passed Michelle's street. I prayed. Then I smiled. Instead of feeling foolish about my impulsive promise to her, I felt God's nudge.

> *Dear Lord, thank You for showing me that my town is full*
> *of reminders to pray for loved ones, near and far.*
> —Leanne Jackson

Digging Deeper: Proverbs 17:17; 1 John 4:11

BUILDING CATHEDRALS: Roots and Wings

For the Spirit God gave us does not make us timid, but gives us power, love and self-discipline. —2 Timothy 1:7 (NIV)

Mom, I'm really going to miss you," Olivia said as she looked up at me, her bright blue eyes welling with tears. Olivia was going to a spend-the-night party full of cheese dip, movies, family games, and everything else that comes along with turning eight. I should also mention the party was five houses away from us.

"Sweetie, you know you don't have to go," I said. "But I think you'll have fun, and you can always come home. You can see our bedroom window from Alice's! I think you're going to get there and have a great time."

As much as I wanted to keep her safe and warm in our own house, I knew how important it was for her to learn to do hard things on her own when her parents were really only seconds away. It's my job to encourage her, build her confidence, and convince her that the world outside isn't scary; it's hers to explore.

I often think of how God might've liked to keep us all safe and tight in heaven, singing praises and crying no tears. But instead He chose to send us out into the world. I knew God didn't want me or Olivia to be stuck in fear. I would always give her a safe place to call home and also the encouragement she needed to soar.

Olivia ended up going to the sleepover; in fact, she didn't want to come home! She proved to herself what I already knew: It's okay to be scared of new things, but try them anyway, especially when your team is cheering you on.

> *Dear Lord, thank You for giving me a strong foundation so that I can spread my wings to soar.*
> —Ashley Kappel

Digging Deeper: 1 Chronicles 28:20; Isaiah 41:13

Saturday, June 3

Be still before the LORD and wait patiently for him . . . —Psalm 37:7 (NRSV)

We were on a family hike on the Appalachian Trail, two carloads. Glad to see each other and enjoying the prospect of some exercise in the great outdoors, we headed off, chatting all the while, taking turns to lead the way, following the blazes on the trees.

The weather was kind—not too hot, not too cold, a summer breeze fluttering through the trees. The conversations rambled; sometimes we'd be chatting in pairs, sometimes a topic would be more wide-ranging, taking us all in.

Then my nephew Kirk said, "Let's not talk for the next twenty minutes. Just walk."

"Good idea," we agreed. The leaves crunched under our feet. We could hear the crack of a twig, a squirrel scampering through the underbrush—or was it a hedgehog? Birds called out, the sunlight shimmered, a pebble rolled down the hill. I could hear my own thoughts, worries, gratitude, my breath, a quiet marveling that these kids leading the way, like Kirk, had just been babes in diapers—was it so long ago?

The hike changed. I wanted to grab hold of the sunlight, pick up a leaf, study a cloud, fly with a bird, linger on a rock. Were the copper-colored striations on that boulder always there or was I just noticing them for the first time? At once, creation felt immensely close.

We came to the turnoff where our hike began. Our conversations resumed. "Thanks, Kirk," we said. "That was a great idea." The silence had spoken volumes. We took off boots and shoes and shook off the dirt, ready to forage for something to eat. We got in our cars and drove off, feeling closer to each other and the Creator, too.

> *You are always present, inside and out, with others and when alone. Let me be still and listen.*
> —Rick Hamlin

Digging Deeper: Psalm 42:1–2, 84:1–2; Matthew 6:6

"I will bless those who bless you . . ." —Genesis 12:3 (NIV)

I have a dear older friend who broke his hip. He's described the experience to me as going from reasonably fit and strong to feeling frail and elderly almost overnight. Before, he'd always been able to do for himself. And he liked it that way—he despises admitting need. I understand.

Accepting help makes me uncomfortable, too. I hate the thought of inconveniencing others when I feel I should be able to accomplish things on my own.

Now, in my friend's case, his physical limitations sometimes leave him no choice but to ask for assistance. I know he feels awkward and reluctant about it. I've tried to convince him how happy I am to be able to lend a hand. It feels good to be useful!

Recently, though, one of the tasks needed was outside my skill set. I cringed at the idea of asking my husband, Jim, for help. His days are already so busy! But I was touched by how quickly he agreed. And now here he was high up on a ladder, wrestling with a recalcitrant motion-sensor light. Watching him, I thought about all the pressing things I knew were on his to-do list. Things he'd readily put aside to help my friend. As the broken light—fixed now—blinked back to life, my heart filled with gratitude. For Jim, and also for my friend, who—by admitting his need—allowed my husband this opportunity to demonstrate his love to me. What acts of generosity on both their parts.

Thank You, God, for the reminder that my human limitations are a blessing from You. For when I admit them to others, I'm allowing them the chance to shine Your love into the world.
—Erin Janoso

Digging Deeper: 1 Corinthians 1:27; 2 Corinthians 12:9

Monday, June 5

Take my yoke upon you and learn from me, for I am gentle and humble in heart, and you will find rest for your souls. —Matthew 11:29 (NIV)

Among friends and family, I have become the go-to person for automotive advice. This is ironic: If you saw me and my thirty-year-old pickup both wheezing up to a stoplight, you would probably seek someone else for mechanical wisdom. You'd seek anyone else.

But my sordid history of dead and dying vehicles has given me valuable experience. My friend Mike was in the market for a used car and handed me a list of possibilities. One choice was a lesser-known European model—the kind I had once owned. I pointed to that item and simply said, "No. Absolutely not."

"But Mark," Mike said, "I thought you said they were easy to fix."

"They are," I replied. "I fixed mine every weekend. *Every* weekend, plus some holidays."

"Easy to fix" sometimes translates to "easily broken." I should know: My relationship to the heavenly Chief Mechanic is easy to fix—He's always forgiving and receptive. But while He's hard at work doing repairs, I'm out breaking more things—breaking vows, breaking promises, breaking commandments. Again. And again. And again.

Mike ended up with a nice car that needs little maintenance. Meanwhile, his friend Mark (me!) has been plagued by continually poor performance and an inability to steer on the straight and narrow. Luckily he has a Chief Mechanic with endless patience and the ability to fix all that is broken . . . again. And again. And again.

Lord, much of me is in need of repair. Let Your loving kindness heal me as I travel in my sometimes-wayward journey to You.
—Mark Collins

Digging Deeper: 2 Chronicles 5:13; Psalm 136

The LORD is my shepherd, I lack nothing. He makes me lie down in green pastures, he leads me beside quiet waters, he refreshes my soul. He guides me along the right paths for his name's sake. —Psalm 23:1–3 (NIV)

My wife grew up a farm girl. And, except for a few years when we were first married, she has always lived in the country. As we do now. Ever since her stroke, afternoons regularly find us getting in our pickup truck and going for long rides along the back roads. On our meanderings, we've seen seedtime and harvest, summer and winter. We've been on roads we didn't know existed. When a car or truck approaches, we give a small wave, a nod, or tip of the seed cap in greeting, as is the Midwest custom. We go slow, maybe thirty miles an hour. If another car or truck appears behind me, I pull over and let it by. And we then continue our road roving. While we may not always know exactly where we are, we do exemplify the saying "Not all who wander are lost." Both of us find these trips renewing and restful.

Often, I've returned from one of our travels and thought about how closely they resemble my spiritual journey. When I am closest to God, listening to the nudges of the Holy Spirit, I find myself in places I need to be. Some familiar. Some strange and new. Some challenging. Some comforting. Regardless, my Guide is with me and knows what I need and what I need to see. Metaphorical deep forests crisscrossed by plunging ravines. Hills spotted with wildflowers and gentle green pastures. Waterfalls and raging rivers. Still pond waters. Each are things that have enriched my soul.

God knows they always will.

Oh, Great Love that always leads me, thank You for being an always True Guide and taking me to the places I need to go to grow my soul—even when they are hard. Amen.
—J. Brent Bill

Digging Deeper: Deuteronomy 8:1–3; Luke 8:22–25

Wednesday, June 7

HYMNS OF PRAISE: He Lives

But in your hearts revere Christ as Lord. Always be prepared to give an answer to everyone who asks you to give the reason for the hope that you have. But do this with gentleness and respect. —1 Peter 3:15 (NIV)

A missionary?" chided my father when I confided my vocational choice after high school graduation. "You've never even gone camping."

Dad wasn't a believer and had little use for spiritual things. I didn't know how to answer other than say that I felt the Lord had called me. He ridiculed me further about hearing voices. I was speechless. I knew what I believed, but I didn't know how to respond to his rebuff.

Alfred Ackley was also derided with a question from a skeptic. Born in 1887 in Pennsylvania, he played piano and cello and composed music. He later became a minister, but it was a conversation in 1934 that inspired a much-loved hymn.

Ackley shared the Gospel with someone who asked, "Why should I worship a dead Jew?" This blunt comment stayed on his mind. Preparing for Easter services, Ackley reread the resurrection account. Lyrics and a tune flowed easily. Within minutes, the hymn was completed.

He lives, He lives, Christ Jesus lives today!
He walks with me and talks with me along life's narrow way.
He lives, He lives, salvation to impart!
You ask me how I know He lives? He lives within my heart.

At eighteen, I abandoned my calling to missions. Two decades later, I went into ministry as a Christian communicator. Daddy still wasn't on board, but with Christ leading and guiding me, I took many opportunities to tell him about my Savior.

> *Lord, prepare me to give encouraging answers and to*
> *readily share my faith.*
> —Stephanie Thompson

Digging Deeper: Psalm 145:2; John 5:24; Philippians 1:21;
1 Peter 1:3–5

And he that sat upon the throne said, Behold, I make all things new.
—Revelation 21:5 (KJV)

An Airstream travel trailer is about as iconic Americana as it gets. Dreams of the open road, campfires, twinkle lights mixing with the stars . . . You can buy a trailer new—that's smart—or, if you're a self-deluded genius like me, you can talk yourself into the vintage DIY restoration route.

Which is exactly how I found myself standing on the rotting plywood floor of a 1971 Airstream Safari shaking my head and trying to imagine how any human without three master's degrees in engineering was supposed to build a curved wall (apparently those original Airstream elves had an aversion to anything resembling a straight line).

I feel a little vintage myself some days. This old chassis has seen some miles. I suspect I'm a constant project, packed full of rotting floors and crooked lines. I'm so glad God is in the business of restoration. If you're a project like me, it doesn't happen overnight. Lots of demo to do. Lots of tearing down to rebuild. But that's what the Great Restorer does. Unlike me, He's patient. And, unlike me, He knows exactly what He's doing. He's had a beautiful plan to rebuild this broken man from before He laid the foundations of the earth.

That trailer in my backyard is still a work in progress. So am I. And I will be. But God is faithful. One day I'll gleam. And, praise His name, I'll roll with perfected joy down a straight and glorious highway that cuts through that beautiful and eternal better country.

> *Dear God, I'm not perfect but You are. Thank You for*
> *seeing beauty in the broken.*
> —Buck Storm

Digging Deeper: 2 Corinthians 4:16–18; Revelation 21:4

Friday, June 9

"Blessed are the dead who die in the Lord . . . they will rest from their labor, for their deeds will follow them." —Revelation 14:13 (NIV)

Unable to travel to my husband's stepfather's funeral, I offered to edit his obituary a few weeks before the funeral service. Reading and editing Ray's obituary was a healing experience, as I poured my heart and mind into the project while miles away from extended family. I laughed and cried as I read Ray's obituary, while meticulously proofreading each word and punctuation mark. Ray had a gentle, kind spirit and a ready smile.

As I neared the end of the obituary, I smiled as I read my son Kalin's tribute to Ray. Kalin spoke of Ray's care for my mother-in-law, his excitement for Kalin's musical aspirations, and a recent opportunity he'd had to watch a movie with Ray in their home. He also gave thanks for a memorable gift he had received from Ray—a used car.

The cute compact car was Kalin's first car, and he drove it for two years. That little "green machine" transported him to college, work, and back and forth through town—until he saved up to purchase an upgrade.

For a while, Ray's old car sat outside our house, idle, until last month, when my youngest son, Christian, got his driver's license. For days Christian and my husband, Anthony, worked on the green machine—a new battery, some minor body work, and a few tweaks under the hood. Although Ray had passed away, he had blessed us with a tangible memory of his loving, generous spirit. And when Christian revved up and drove off for the first time, my heart warmed with the joy of Ray's memory and the precious gift of his life. And the gift of that little green car.

Lord, thank You for the legacies of our loved ones. May we also live with kindness, purpose, and generosity.
—Carla Hendricks

Digging Deeper: Acts 20:32–35; 1 Thessalonians 4:13–14

Set your minds on things above, not on earthly things.
—Colossians 3:2 (NIV)

I blew sawdust off solid wood, then placed the sanding block on my workbench.

Refinishing this end table had been relaxing. I had purchased the antique over a year ago. The table wasn't large, and I had planned to fix it up as a weekend project. However, in the busyness of life, the table had been pushed to the back of my garage and then the back of my mind. Until today.

I flipped the table and began to sand the next side.

This morning was a quiet one. Normally, I would listen to music or an audiobook while I worked. It was odd for me to work in silence.

Even stranger was the quiet inside my head. As I am a lawyer and writer, my mind is always busy. I'm constantly pulling ideas apart and putting them back together. But, today, there was stillness both outside and inside of me.

I continued sanding the table. Aged varnish peeled away. Dark stain made way to fresh wood.

When had my mind become so cluttered?

In simpler days, I had the luxury of more quiet moments. But busyness wasn't the only problem. In the past, I had used my moments of stillness differently. I had filled the quiet with prayer, not music. I had reflected on the Lord, not legal reasoning.

I needed to make a change. I needed to shift my focus.

I ran my hand across the newly smoothed wood. And, as I continued to work, I began to pray.

Lord, help me to remain focused on You in all that I do.
—Logan Eliasen

Digging Deeper: Ephesians 6:18; 1 Thessalonians 5:16–18

Sunday, June 11

. . . I will not fail you or forsake you. —Joshua 1:5 (NRSV)

I've spent the last couple of years reading everything I can about the human brain, researching a book on my family's history of Alzheimer's, especially my mother's. Not exactly bedtime reading.

I close my eyes to sleep, and I see my own brain, its cells surreptitiously compromised by amyloid plaques, tau tangles, and other neuronal detritus. Did I forget to turn on Gracie's collar light the other night when I let her out because I was tired or because my memory is slipping? Sometimes words I know maddeningly elude me for a few seconds or even minutes while I scramble around after them. Is this normal? Is this how my mother felt at my age? Her two older sisters and her father all died of Alzheimer's.

The more I think about what she went through, the more my heart breaks. When did she realize that she was going down the same path as her sisters?

"I think she fought it," my sister said the other day. "I don't think she ever forgot who she was even as everything else faded away."

Maybe it is that permanence of self, the person whom God ineluctably formed, that cannot be destroyed. There is nothing crueler than a disease that steals our memories. Yet memories are the past. For my mom, the present was only God. Even as a terrible tide swept away nearly all of who she was, she never forgot that she was a child of God. She was responsive to prayer and hymns, as if her soul were impervious to the ravages of the disease.

If there is a blessing to Alzheimer's, it is that. You are with God and God alone. As you lose everything to the affliction you are left with the only thing any of us need: We are children of God, unshakably merged with the divine.

God, whatever I lose to life, I know I will never lose You.
—Edward Grinnan

Digging Deeper: Psalm 139:14; Philippians 4:19

Forgetting what is behind and straining toward what is ahead, I press on . . . —Philippians 3:13–14 (NIV)

My twelve-month-old granddaughter, Charley, learning to walk, fell and hit her head on a bedpost. A bruise formed and swelled immediately. Charley hugged me, cried briefly, smiled as I held an ice pack to her forehead, then wiggled to get down, and was off again. This was one of her many falls as she learned to walk. Each time, she'd just get back up and try again, the hurt quickly forgotten. Soon she was nearly running around the house.

While I may not fall and hit my head literally, I've had my share of hurts. I wish I could say I'd forgotten them as readily as Charley did hers. A disagreement with a friend came to my mind. It wasn't the disagreement that hurt me. It was the fact that she'd hung up on me when I'd called to discuss it. "I don't want to hear your thoughts," she'd said. That had hurt.

But had I let it go? No, I'd rehashed it mentally and stubbornly decided never to call her back or answer her calls. *If she doesn't want to talk to me, I won't talk to her!*

I decided that maybe I should learn a lesson from a one-year-old. I took my hurt to God, listened to what He put on my heart, then picked up the phone and called my friend.

Lord, thank You for reminding me that when I get hurt, it's best to come to You for comfort and direction, then just get back up and try again, leaving my hurt behind.
—Kim Taylor Henry

Digging Deeper: Colossians 3:13; James 1:12; Revelation 2:3

Tuesday, June 13

Trust GOD from the bottom of your heart; don't try to figure out everything on your own. —Proverbs 3:5 (MSG)

I want to surprise Dad with a new TV," our son, Derek, texted me. "Wow!" I responded. "That's an extremely generous gift." Especially, I thought, for a son who's now the dad in his own family of six.

As Derek moved forward with his plan, I began to wonder how his dad would respond. For years, Derek encouraged us to get a new TV, and Lynn always defended our old one, saying, "It's just right for us."

Admittedly, it was outdated, but we knew how to use a single remote to change channels or record a show and even access movies. Our television felt like an old friend, and we were in a comfortable working relationship. In Derek's home, we can't even figure out how to turn on their television without the help of our grandchildren.

A few days later, Derek called. "I've got Dad's new TV. I'd like to surprise him and install it today."

"Sure," I said.

Then I began to worry again. What if Lynn's response showed that he's not excited about a new TV? How would Derek respond? How could I helpfully manage their responses?

Derek arrived while Lynn was doing errands. When he returned, the huge TV was leaning up against our old TV. Lynn stopped, stunned as he came in the room.

"Dad, I want to give you this gift, to thank you for all the sacrifices you made for me when I was growing up," Derek said.

Lynn paused. "I've never gotten a gift like this. Thank you, Derek."

"Thank *you*, Dad."

I said nothing.

Lord, thank You for the reminder that I'm not responsible for other people's responses. I can trust You to handle that responsibility.
—Carol Kuykendall

Digging Deeper: Matthew 6:34; Philippians 4:6–7

HYMNS OF PRAISE: Blessed Assurance

For it is by grace you have been saved, through faith—and this is not from yourselves, it is the gift of God—not by works, so that no one can boast. —Ephesians 2:8–9 (NIV)

I like to keep to-do lists. I have pages with daily duties, weekly goals, seasonal chores, and bucket-list items that are waiting to be crossed off with my black Sharpie. My lists are my scorecard of how well I'm doing in life. Am I accomplishing everything I want as the years pass?

In the same way, I sometimes keep score with God. Yes, I've given my heart to Jesus. I know my salvation is secure. But I feel the need to read the Bible, pray, serve in Bible study, and volunteer in my community to be worthy.

Blind at six months old, Fanny Crosby saw the work of salvation more clearly than I. Born in 1820, when middle-class women in the United States had little voice in worship, Crosby became one of the most prominent gospel songwriters of all time with a legacy of more than nine thousand hymns, gospel, and secular songs. In 1873, a friend played a composition on her piano. She asked Crosby what the tune said to her. After kneeling in prayer, she responded, "It says, blessed assurance, Jesus is mine!" Crosby proceeded to dictate the stanzas for the hymn on the spot.

Blessed assurance, Jesus is mine!
Oh, what a foretaste of glory divine!
Heir of salvation, purchase of God,
Born of his spirit, washed in his blood.

My blessed assurance is God's promise that salvation is enough. Nothing I do, or mark off a list, can improve on, or add to, what Christ did for me.

Dear Lord, help me to remember that You not only are enough
but all that I need to be made worthy.
—Stephanie Thompson

Digging Deeper: John 3:16; Galatians 4:4–7;
Philippians 1:21; Titus 2:12–13

Thursday, June 15

Through him all things were made; without him nothing was made that has been made. —John 1:3 (NIV)

This morning, even though it was drizzling, I walked into town for a cup of coffee. The bakery has the best blend, roasted locally and named after my town. On the return home with a chocolate brioche for Henry, chocolate-chip cookie for Solomon, quiche for Tony, and exquisite raspberry crumb cake for me, my spirit soars. A refreshing warm wind blows, and I think of all the things I love, starting with coffee.

I had an interesting dream years ago, where I was somewhere—I think right outside of heaven—and there was a man with a golden book. "Three things," he asked. "Your favorite three things." He spoke without sound, putting the words into my mind, and I knew he didn't mean the obvious living things, like my family and pets; he meant earthly things. Objects or experiences, things I experienced singularly. "A cup of coffee, the warmth of the sun through a window in winter, freezing cold ocean frothing on my toes," I said.

"Great answers," he said, writing it down with a felt-tip marker. "Always great answers!"

I remember waking up and thinking how wonderful it would be if maybe, just maybe, there actually is a golden book on the edge of heaven that carries every single person's favorite things.

Sometimes before I go to sleep, I lie in bed and think of answers. I edit and re-edit the list, adding pink sunsets, double rainbows, a clear summer night's sky. Almost always coffee makes the list. The Tivoli Blend, heaven-sent or so it seems.

> *Dear Lord, help me to see, know, and thank You for the countless beautiful, wonderful things in my life.*
> —Sabra Ciancanelli

Digging Deeper: Psalm 19:1, 96:11–12

As each has received a gift, use it to serve one another, as good stewards of God's varied grace. —1 Peter 4:10 (ESV)

My family sat on our back porch and listened to the night song. The serenade of frogs broke through twilight's haze.

"We could be at the old house," my husband said. "The sound takes me back."

"It's close," I said. "But there's a breeze. My wind chimes would be tingling."

There was only the melody of creation until fourteen-year-old Gabriel spoke. "What happened to the chimes, Mom? They were on the front porch of the old house my whole life."

I shared that the chimes had broken in a harsh wind and were put in the shed. In the stretched-long process of moving, who knew what happened to the pieces and parts.

"That's sad," he said.

A few weeks later, my family filled our plates and headed to the back porch to share breakfast. I heard the chimes as soon as I sat on our rusty glider. A smile that spoke a million words broke over my most quiet son's face. "I found the pieces, Mom," he said. "Mostly. I replaced the sail with wood. It's like our home now. Old mixed with new."

I could hardly breathe.

Gabriel is my fixer, working wonders with his hands. He mends the broken and builds things new. It's a talent the Lord gave him. But then there's his spiritual gift. Gabriel is a servant. He was intentional in weaving cord through metal and wood to create a balance that was just right.

He cared for my soul.

I hugged Gabriel tight as the breeze chimed a song of love.

> *Oh, Lord, may our gifts and talents be used to love others and honor You.*
> —Shawnelle Eliasen

Digging Deeper: Romans 12:6–8; 1 Corinthians 12:1–11

Saturday, June 17

The sun has one kind of splendor, the moon another and the stars another; and star differs from star in splendor. —1 Corinthians 15:41 (NIV)

I laughed out loud as I watched the screen in my daughter Lauren's FaceTime call.

The camera was on her two daughters. Her nearly four-year-old was seated quietly in a small chair, feet planted on the floor, engrossed in a book. Her eighteen-month-old had donned a basket, which had slipped over her eyes. She was laughing as she bumped into things.

"Book and basket—the perfect summary of their personalities," I said. Lauren agreed.

As I remembered that scene later, I thought about my two daughters. Lauren would have been the one reading; Rachel would have had the basket on her head.

As for my husband and me, he would definitely be the reader and I the baskethead. I realized that with nearly every couple I know, one would have the book, the other the basket. All my friends can readily be classified with either basket or book, or at least as leaning more in one of those directions than the other.

How dull life would be if we were all with books. How chaotic life would be if we were all with baskets. But God, in His wisdom, created us to be different, to complement, confirm, and balance each other's personalities. Another of his many wonders!

Thank You, God, that we are not all the same. Help us basketheads and book readers to appreciate and learn from each other.
—Kim Taylor Henry

Digging Deeper: 1 Corinthians 4:7, 12:4–6

". . . do that which ye have seen with your father." —John 8:38 (KJV)

People often asked what's it like growing up under the microscope where a minister's family lives. I think they expect common "preacher's kids" complaints, like unrealistic expectations, less money, more fault finding.

Well, ask me how I feel about the way I was raised, and I'll answer with one word: grateful.

My father, David Kidd, was the minister of the same Nashville church for the first thirty-something years of my life. When we reflect back on those years, both my younger sister, Keri, and I agree that we were fortunate beyond words.

My father, you see, brought a fledging church back from the edge of extinction and turned it into a loving community where no one was a stranger and everyone was welcome. Believing that God's Kingdom really could come on earth (Jesus's words), he set out to make that happen. He included all races, religions, and lifestyles, people with special needs and mental illness, refugees, the rich, the poor, the lonely—you name it. Our church was a sort of rainbow of God's creation.

We watched our father lead this extraordinary congregation by example, in the same way he and my mother led our family. Over and over, I have heard my mother say, "I never heard David preach a sermon and think, 'Why doesn't he practice what he preaches?' Because he does."

I know it couldn't have always been easy for him. How could he continue being kind to people who criticized him? How could he forgive those who spread untruths about him? The answer is simple. He tried his best to follow the teachings of Jesus and that made his path amazingly faithful and genuine. On Father's Day, I see his example. Shouldn't I follow?

Father in heaven, with great appreciation, I thank You for my earthly
father as I pray to follow his path.
—Brock Kidd

Digging Deeper: Exodus 20:12; 1 Samuel 16:7; Luke 12:32

Juneteenth, Monday, June 19

"For I know the plans I have for you," declares the LORD, "plans to prosper you and not to harm you, plans to give you hope and a future."
—Jeremiah 29:11 (NIV)

As the United States observes this 158th anniversary of Juneteenth—a holiday first celebrated in Texas to commemorate the end of slavery in the United States—I am reminded that although African Americans have borne a large share of challenges throughout the history of this nation, we are a resilient people.

As a preteen scouring the shelves of my local library, I discovered a children's book about Dr. Mary McLeod Bethune, the founder of what is now Bethune-Cookman University in Daytona Beach, Florida. Born in Mayesville, South Carolina, in 1875, Dr. Bethune was an educator, women's activist, and philanthropist. I was enthralled to read her biography, detailing her life as a daughter of slaves who progressed as a scholar, eventually landing as a member of President Franklin D. Roosevelt's Black Cabinet.

Dr. Bethune's path to success was not easy. Racism against African Americans remained rampant throughout the United States during her lifetime, yet, with a spirit fueled by faith, she persevered. She rose to serve others with a determination to not only lift herself but also raise up other young women as she climbed.

The freedoms provided to enslaved people were so necessary for our country to move forward as one nation, under God, and I praise Him for the successes that have been achieved so far. There is still much work to be done nationwide for equity and inclusion of all Americans, but on this day, we celebrate the successes that were initially achieved in 1865. What God has done, let no one undo.

Father, thank You for our ancestors, who toiled and worked
in Your name, in order to pave the way to freedom
for all enslaved African Americans.
—Gayle T. Williams

Digging Deeper: 2 Corinthians 13:11; 1 Thessalonians 5:11

"The kingdom of heaven is like a treasure hidden in a field."
—Matthew 13:44 (NIV)

Wayne has a television series that he faithfully watches each week—*The Curse of Oak Island*. It's about finding buried treasure. Two brothers have literally invested millions of dollars and several years searching for buried treasure, all based on a legend. They have no map to point the way. They are driven by the unshakable belief it must be there. It seems each episode they find some small encouragement that keeps them going. Honestly, I would have given up a long time ago, but not these two men. They are certain there is a huge treasure worth millions buried on this island. Despite the years and personal toll on their lives, they seem convinced they will find it.

Being cynical, I roll my eyes at the music and the drama when they find something as small as an iron button. But I have to admit, we're all looking for hidden treasure, aren't we? We're seeking that perfect life; you know, the one where your children make you proud and give you bragging rights.

We all seek success in our careers. Money. Appreciation. Acknowledgment. Those are treasures worth digging for . . . but do they really bring satisfaction? Paul David Tripp says, "The search for treasure is really a search for a Savior." That being the case, we have a map, our Bible, and we have a Savior. He is our greatest treasure, and with Him we have love, acceptance, acknowledgment, and all that satisfies. Now that's a treasure worth digging for.

Your Word is my map that leads me to You. In these pages, I find treasure
richer than gold and more precious than jewels.
—Debbie Macomber

Digging Deeper: Proverbs 2:4–5, 3:13–15; Matthew 13:45–46

Wednesday, June 21

HYMNS OF PRAISE: Amazing Grace

For by grace you have been saved through faith. And this is not your own doing; it is the gift of God, not a result of works, so that no one may boast. —Ephesians 2:8–9 (ESV)

I'd started my ministry three months earlier—a Christian talk show on a secular radio station—when an acquaintance called to say an anonymous donor wished to pay for my airtime. How could I ever repay such an extravagant gift from a stranger?

John Newton, the Anglican priest who wrote "Amazing Grace" in 1772, understood undeserved favor. His mother died when he was six, and he joined his father on board a ship as an apprentice at eleven. Newton grew to be insolent, disobedient, and lewd. Feeling miserable and seeking change, he went to church, gave his life to the Lord, and studied to become a minister. He often marveled to parishioners how God found him, opened his eyes, and bestowed amazing grace to him. No doubt, Newton penned the words to this beloved hymn as he marveled about God's graciousness despite his tumultuous past.

> *Amazing grace! How sweet the sound*
> *That saved a wretch like me.*
> *I once was lost, but now am found,*
> *Was blind, but now I see.*

When I asked my acquaintance how I would repay the anonymous donor, he answered, "No need. Consider it grace." Like God's grace, the unmerited favor of my generous benefactor wasn't bestowed because of who I was, but rather because of who this unidentified supporter was.

> *Thank you, God, that Your amazing grace is freely given*
> *and doesn't depend upon me.*
> —Stephanie Thompson

Digging Deeper: Romans 3:23–24; 1 Corinthians 15:10;
2 Corinthians 12:9

"How beautiful are the feet of those who bring good news of good things!"
—Romans 10:15 (NASB)

I perched on the grand old base of a silver maple that had grown in my yard as a teen. It had sheltered the parsonage for a hundred years before it was felled. Patting the weathered gray wood of the "Magnificent"—Mags for short—I felt grateful for my heritage raised in a pastor's family.

I recalled an unusual dream I'd had some weeks earlier about a high school classmate's daughter, whom I had not personally met, but we were Facebook friends. Her posts expressed deep personal distress. She did not seem to have a faith anchor.

I felt the Holy Spirit's urging to speak to her about opening a "seeking God" journey through exploring a relationship with Jesus. I didn't know how to begin the conversation.

Days later, filled with nervous determination, I called her. She lived cross-country in New Hampshire and was cautiously hopeful that her cancer, diagnosed when she was in her early thirties, would not return. She'd been thinking lately there might be "something bigger" beyond the human struggle.

She had begun taking calming nature drives. I shared the Bible's message of God making Himself known in His creation (Romans 1:20), promising to regularly text her some of my nature photography. I encouraged her to read about Jesus in the book of John.

"I'm introducing," I said, completely relaxed now. "I'm here if you choose, but the journey is yours."

I had done the first, best thing I could—bring Christ within reach.

> *The wonder is, Lord, that even as I begin seeking*
> *You, You are already seeking me.*
> —Carol Knapp

Digging Deeper: Isaiah 55:6; Romans 10:14; 1 Corinthians 3:5–9;
2 Corinthians 2:14

Friday, June 23

Rejoice with those who rejoice . . . —Romans 12:15 (NIV)

I was up in the laundry room when I heard the noise from next door. My friend and next-door neighbor, Heather, is mom to two athletic young men. High schooler Sam generally has a basketball game going in the driveway. Older brother Drew has always been more into soccer. Finally home for summer after his freshman year out of state, Drew and his friends had gotten up a backyard game. I looked out the window and watched them play for a moment as they shouted and laughed despite the oppressive Alabama heat and humidity. Their youthful exuberance made me smile.

A little while later, a sudden storm darkened the sky, and rain began to pour. Even so, the noise from next door continued. I looked out my window once more to see Drew and his friends still playing their game, not only undeterred by the rain but having even more fun because of it! This day of soaked socks and mud and grass stains would have Heather spending some time in her own laundry room soon enough, but I knew she'd be glad of it. The smile on Drew's face, the sound of his laughter . . . oh, how I wished I could bottle the joy he felt in that moment and give it to him when he grew old!

Someday Drew will have responsibilities that will keep him from a pickup game of soccer. He might even feel a coming rain in the joints that on this glorious day served him so effortlessly. But how precious it is that, today, these are things he cannot even fathom.

> *Father, thank You for the joy of youth, even for us who*
> *are now just witnesses to it.*
> —Ginger Rue

Digging Deeper: Ecclesiastes 3:1; 1 Timothy 4:12

It is to one's honor to avoid strife . . . —Proverbs 20:3 (NIV)

I yawned and stretched as I turned on the coffee pot. The last couple days had been heavenly. I'd had time off from work, and I hadn't checked my phone. I glanced at it, charging on the counter. *Maybe I should check my texts?* My tranquility shattered when I read the one from my neighbor. "Do you have a yellow cat? A cat was going after our chickens. I chased it and it ran into your barn."

Only a couple days ago, I'd adopted that tomcat. After I opened the crate to turn him loose in my barn, he earned the name "Stealth" as he disappeared like a stealth bomber to hunt mice. His personality was like a full-sized lion stuffed into a twelve-pound body. *Lord, You told me to get the yellow cat. What do You want me to do?* That still, small voice urged me to avoid strife at all costs.

When I returned the call, my neighbor briskly answered the phone. I shared that it was indeed my cat. To my horror, I discovered that Stealth had actually jumped one of the chickens to take it down! Fortunately, they ran him off and saved the chicken. I apologized and shared that I'd just gotten him from the humane society. "I am willing to take him back if you want me to. You tell me how you'd like me to go forward."

My neighbor paused, his voice softening, "No, you don't need to do that . . . maybe he's just learning his boundaries. Let's give him some time."

Stealth hasn't bothered their chickens since that day.

Lord, thank You for showing me that by being willing to give up something to avoid strife, I was able to keep it—and keep peace with my neighbors.
—Rebecca Ondov

Digging Deeper: Proverbs 26:21, 30:33

Sunday, June 25

A LIFETIME OF LOVE: Tears and Memories

Place me like a seal over your heart, like a seal on your arm; for love is as strong as death. . . . Many waters cannot quench love, rivers cannot sweep it away . . . —Song of Songs 8:6–7 (NIV)

I knew that my daughter Rebecca and grandson Mark talked often with my husband, Don, during his last days, but I didn't know they recorded an interview. Love was the main topic, and they shared Don's words with me shortly before Christmas. "Love is a big word," he'd said. "You can't define most of what love is. You just love." He paused, then added, "Love always ends in tears."

We've shed rivers of tears in the months since Don's passing. Each of us has taken comfort in a different way. My granddaughter Olivia grew cuttings from his plants in the windowsill of her apartment. Rebecca had one of Don's suit jackets cut down to fit her and wears it often. My grandson Caden learned how to weld using Don's farm welder. Sons and grandchildren called often to share favorite stories. I've kept Don's watch and glasses on the bedroom dresser, and his collection of farm caps still decorates the coat tree.

Love is indeed a big word, and Don was right: It always ends in tears. But I've come to understand that sorrow is a necessary and valuable part of love. And I cling to the promise in Revelation 21:4 (NIV): "He will wipe every tear from their eyes. There will be no more death or mourning or crying or pain, for the old order of things has passed away."

Eternal Savior, thank You for tears and memories, for actions that comfort, and especially for Your deep and abiding love that heals our hearts.
—Penney Schwab

Digging Deeper: Isaiah 25:8; John 11:25–26; 2 Timothy 1:9–10

"So be perfect, as your heavenly Father is perfect." —Matthew 5:48 (ISV)

Writing is a place of contemplation for me, and, although the internet is a valuable writing tool—supplying inspiration, answers, an elusive word shrouded in the folds of my brain—it's also my biggest writing hindrance, sucking me into its weird treasures and away from the writing itself. So it was that I sat down one morning to write and was soon reading a news article about changing your personality.

"Hey, ever heard of psychologists' 'big five' personality traits?" I called to my husband, Kris, who was at the breakfast table reading his own news articles. I listed them off: emotional stability, extroversion, openness, agreeableness, and conscientiousness.

"Sound more like moral traits to me," Kris commented.

Hours later, he's gone and I'm reading scientific studies proving you can change a trait simply by setting out to do so. Subjects were given trait-changing assignments—such as, for an introvert, attending a party—and months later they scored higher in the deficient area and stayed that way.

Wow, I thought. *I'll just practice agreeableness—my main personality deficiency, according to the personality tests I'd taken by then—and I'll improve.*

So, I planned assignments: send an appreciative email to someone I don't like, ask questions instead of disagreeing at the next department meeting, correct the judgmental voice in my head with more tolerant messages. Soon it was lunchtime, then time to grade papers before starting dinner. Another day of writing lost.

So it goes with all worthy enterprises, I thought. The agreeableness project would be no different, science or no science. Thank God my biggest self-improvement project, being worthy of God's love, is utterly independent of my own efforts.

Make me a better person, Lord: more introspective, more agreeable to those around me, more aware of Your unearned love.
—Patty Kirk

Digging Deeper: Romans 7:15–25

Tuesday, June 27

"I am the vine; you are the branches. If you remain in me and I in you, you will bear much fruit; apart from me you can do nothing." —John 15:5 (NIV)

I was living through a particularly hectic period, and the last thing I needed was the hassle of a power outage. Yet power outages have become a normal way of life in northern California.

Because our region is prone to wildfires, the electric utility shuts down the power grid during periods of high winds. This is to reduce the risk of a falling tree limb pulling down a power line and sparking a fire. These "planned outages," as they are called, can last for days.

So, like many homeowners in our semi-rural community, my son and I drag out a gas generator to power most of our home during these periods.

At the beginning of this past summer, we had an outage that was projected to last three days. Jonathan and I set up the generator, and our family went about business almost as usual. There were a few appliances we couldn't use, like our oven and, on some days, the air conditioner. We knew our limits and grew accustomed to living with less-than-optimal power.

On the second day of the three-day outage, I plugged in the shop vac to clean out my car. A minute later, the lights flickered and power went out. I'd overloaded the generator's circuit. Before restarting, I decided to throw a switch to test if our main power was back on. To my surprise it was. We had been limping along on generator power when we could have been using full power and didn't even know it!

God whispered to me in that moment that I'd been doing the same thing. I'd been limping along on my own power, disconnected from the power of Christ. It was time to flip the switch.

Precious Lord, remind me to stay close to You moment
by moment and day by day.
—Bill Giovannetti

Digging Deeper: Philippians 3:8–10

He has made everything beautiful in its time. . . . —Ecclesiastes 3:11 (ESV)

Mom, have you seen this?" My eyes widen as I open the curtains covering our living room window.

Vivid hues of orange and pink color the sky, cascading outward from the rising sun. Clouds form a horizontal column that seems to absorb the colors behind it, transforming from white into a brilliant purple. God, the Master Painter, created a spectacular work of art this morning. "It's perfect."

Then my gaze trips on a glaring flaw. Along the bottom edge of the cloud column, a renegade bit of cloud splits off, hanging loose like a ragged piece of torn cloth. "Why did God allow that?"

My mom has walked too far away into another room to reply, but that doesn't stop me from wondering why God was letting a blemish mar His work of art. Sure, God creates sunrises with the imperfect elements of our fallen world. But He still could smooth out that edge to make His painting perfect.

Wait a second. I blink at the sight again. The sunrise is still beautiful. And God created it using flawed materials.

Amazement warms me as I absorb the truth manifested in the sunrise. Most days, my imperfections make me feel like that jagged trail of cloud. I can't accomplish everything I'm supposed to, let alone perfectly. And some days, I'm an absolute mess, inside and out. But even then, I'm part of God's masterful, perfect plan.

I stare at the sunrise a little longer, tucking the memory into my heart so that when I feel too flawed to hold up my head, I'll remember God is using me, imperfections and all, to make something beautiful.

> *Father, thank You that even on my worst days, You are using*
> *me in Your beautiful and perfect plan.*
> —Jerusha Agen

Digging Deeper: Isaiah 62:3; 1 Corinthians 13:8–10

Thursday, June 29

Great is the LORD, and greatly to be praised; his greatness is unsearchable. One generation shall laud your works to another, and shall declare your mighty acts. —Psalm 145:3–4 (NRSV)

Despite the perfect summer day, I wasn't feeling very content. I'd spent the day trying, and failing, to do Gospel living. First, I brought chocolates to an older neighbor who'd been in the hospital, only to have her gaze yearningly at the box and tell me she'd been forbidden sugar. Then, trying to console a friend about a breakup, I made it worse by suggesting she join a church book group to get out, but she wasn't ready for that, and we ended the call with her more distressed. I struck out the third time by delivering a package left in the lobby for a woman who'd just moved into our building. After answering the door, she made it clear that she preferred to retrieve her own mail.

After hearing about my day, Charlie suggested we head to the beach, spread out our blanket, and nap. I agreed, deciding I was finished doing God's work for the day. We lay in the sun, Charlie's arm around me, my hand in his, our eyes closed. We heard the group of young couples near us packing up, laughing and teasing each other. They quieted as they passed us, lugging coolers and umbrellas. We heard their whispers.

"Hope that's us in forty years," said one boy softly to the girl beside him.

"I'm telling my husband about those two," said another young woman to her friend.

"Relationship goals!" answered the friend.

"They're like Gram and Gramps," one boy told an older girl, probably his sister.

I squeezed Charlie's hand. He whispered, "You never know when God might decide to go to work."

> *Lord, help me to remember that all good things happen in*
> *Your time, not necessarily mine.*
> —Marci Alborghetti

Digging Deeper: Proverbs 8:32–36; Luke 8:15–18

Friday, June 30

In peace I will lie down and sleep . . . —Psalm 4:8 (NIV)

A neighbor teen with special needs calls several times a day. Sometimes with a request for transportation. Sometimes with a school question: "How do you spell—?"

Most often she just wants to make a connection. In the morning, "What's your plan for the day?" Early afternoon, "What did you have for lunch?" On summer afternoons, "I'm bored." I might suggest an activity or commiserate. (I remember August doldrums.) Then, at about six, she often phones with a mail report. "I got a card today, from Ms. Julia"—in response to her recent enthusiasm for making and sending cards. Before saying our goodbyes, one of us asks, "Do you want to say Compline?"

I'm not sure she knows what the word means. A form of *complete*, it is the traditional name of the last liturgical evening prayer. Some years ago at vacation Bible school, we were introduced to a modified children's version: five minutes of invocation, confession, select Scripture verses, praises, the Lord's Prayer, amen. We brought home handouts. I still have mine. She has misplaced hers, though it doesn't seem to matter.

"Compline now?" Yes, she says, and then leads out. "Lord God, be with us and give us a peaceful night." She's memorized some lines. I prompt her on others, which I myself am learning to recite. "Guide us waking, O Lord, and guard us sleeping; that awake we may watch with Christ, and asleep we may rest in peace." We sign off with "thanks be to God." And an informal "good night."

I don't hear from her again until morning. Our evening connection is complete.

O Lord, support us all the day long, until the shadows lengthen and the evening comes . . . Then in your mercy, grant us a safe lodging, and a holy rest, and peace at the last. —The Book of Common Prayer
—Evelyn Bence

Digging Deeper: Psalm 16:5–11

LET US SING FOR JOY

1 _____

2 _____

3 _____

4 _____

5 _____

6 _____

7 _____

8 _____

9 _____

10 _____

11 _____

12 _____

13 _____

14 _____

15 _____

16 _____

17 _____

18 _____

19 _____

20 _____

21 _____

22 _____

23 _____

24 _____

25 _____

26 _____

27 _____

28 _____

29 _____

30 _____

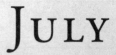

JULY

*Give thanks to G*OD*—he is
good and his love never quits.*

—1 Chronicles 16:34 (MSG)

Let each of you look not only to his own interests, but also to the interests of others. —Philippians 2:4 (ESV)

I wiped my forehead as the July sun beat down. It was not the best day to wear a suit outdoors. Still, I was honored to be a part of my friend Xuan's wedding.

The ceremony had been a small affair—just family and a few close friends. Now, we waited to share a picnic-style meal together.

"I can't wait for the pork to get off the grill," Xuan told us. "It's traditional Malaysian style."

I smiled to be polite. I was vegetarian, so I wouldn't be able to share the main course. I would stick to side dishes and a slice of cake. I could eat something more substantive when I got home.

"Food's ready!" somebody shouted. Everyone grabbed plates and headed toward the grill. I filled my plate with several salads. Then I took a seat at the table, waiting for the others.

Somebody set a hand on my shoulder.

"You didn't get your food off the grill," Xuan said.

"Thanks, Xuan," I said. "But I'd get really sick if I ate meat."

"I know," Xuan said. "I was worried you would be hungry, so I picked up some bean burgers yesterday."

I turned around. Xuan held out a plate with two burgers already on buns.

In the midst of planning a wedding, Xuan had been concerned about what I could eat. He had anticipated my needs, and he had met them.

I thanked Xuan as he handed me my plate. I was grateful for the food he provided for me. I was even more grateful to have a friend who cared so deeply for the needs of others.

> *Lord, help me to see the needs of others and to meet those needs.*
> —Logan Eliasen

Digging Deeper: John 13:34–35; Galatians 6:10

Sunday, July 2

Enter his gates with thanksgiving, and his courts with praise! Give thanks to him; bless his name! —Psalm 100:4 (ESV)

A few years ago, as I had breakfast with two sisters in Christ, the discussion turned to a familiar topic: "If you could do anything that you wanted to do in life, what would it be?" I had an answer immediately: I would learn to play the piano without practicing, or I would be a dancer.

While the first was impossible, the second was partially doable. My two friends were leaders in my church's liturgical dance ministry and immediately encouraged me to join them. But I resisted, offering a litany of reasons: I was too old to dance, didn't have the enduring fitness level, and didn't have as much time to devote to practice as they did.

One friend revealed that she had long wanted to incorporate flagging—dancing with flags—into the ministry. That sounded right up my alley! I could minister through dance without collapsing, as the flagging routines would be somewhat simpler than the dance moves. I was thrilled to be able to contribute to the service in this way.

I cajoled a few other church sisters to join me in flagging, and we practiced diligently for our first ministry opportunity, which was set to "He Turned It" by Tye Tribbett. We twirled, glided, and praised the Lord, all in front of the congregation, all things that I had never done before. It brought me such pure joy.

It also taught me that words of encouragement are never wasted. Without my church sisters' support, I never would have attempted to fulfill my childhood dream of dancing for others and especially for the Lord.

Heavenly Father, I am forever grateful for friends who encourage me to stretch my abilities to praise Your name.
—Gayle T. Williams

Digging Deeper: Proverbs 27:9; 1 Thessalonians 5:11; Hebrews 10:25

". . . the kingdom of heaven is like a merchant looking for fine pearls."
—Matthew 13:45 (NIV)

How am *I* supposed to know which months deer are most likely to run into the road?" sputtered my seventeen-year-old. "This is clearly an *upstate* New York question!"

I hid my grin. Stephen has decided to learn to drive before heading to college and is studying to get his permit. It's a challenge because—being city people—we've never owned a car. My husband, Andrew, grew up in New York City and has never even had a license. Thus my son is in the curious position of having logged more hours in a sailboat than in an automobile. He's got his work cut out for him.

Still, it's something he wants to know, and the information he needs is laid out neatly. I yearn to point out that most life lessons are not so tidy. Much of the important stuff—patience and self-restraint and humility and how to stand up for what is right—is learned the hard way.

But I keep my mouth shut. What *I've* learned the hard way: With teens, pearls of wisdom are only treasured when they are actively sought. It is better to be patient and wait for the right time to speak.

Father, help me bear witness to Your love at the times You
have prepared for me to do so.
—Julia Attaway

Digging Deeper: Proverbs 10:19; Ecclesiastes 3:7

Independence Day, Tuesday, July 4

All these people earned a good reputation because of their faith, yet none of them received all that God had promised. —Hebrews 11:39 (NLT)

When I was in grammar school, like so many children I learned the history of the American Revolution. But it wasn't until I moved to Carmel, New York, to be the interim pastor of the Gilead Presbyterian Church that the early history of our country became alive for me.

The church was founded in 1743, and for many years congregants worshipped in a building atop Seminary Hill, where the old Gilead burying ground is still located. One of those buried is a patriot spy name Enoch Crosby. His bravery wasn't without risk and near-death experiences. When he was uncovered, he was beaten and left to die, and another time he was shot. Many years after the war, he became a trustee of the church.

In the town, there is the bronze statue of Sybil Ludington. The statue depicts Sybil, a sixteen-year-old girl, on horseback, screaming and waving the stick that she used to knock on doors and whack highwaymen who got in the way. She called out the volunteer military by riding alone forty miles and alerting the countryside to the burning of Danbury, Connecticut, by the British.

The stories of Enoch and Sybil are vivid reminders of the valor and sacrifices it took for our country to become a nation. Their commitment for freedom gives us hope and inspires us on this Fourth of July: together, people from all walks of life can accomplish the impossible and keep on working to leave a better nation for future generations.

O Lord, unite us in hope to work together toward fulfilling the promise of our country for all people.
—Pablo Diaz

Digging Deeper: Nehemiah 4:9; Hebrews 11:13–16

THE PINK HOUSE: Pointing toward Home

In all thy ways acknowledge him, and he shall direct thy paths.
—Proverbs 3:6 (KJV)

My husband, David, and I are exploring a foreign city. We wander from street to street, until it's time to return to our hotel.

"Turn right at the corner," I say, "and another right here."

"I don't get it," David says. "How can you always find your way back?"

As we walk on, I consider his question.

"Hmmm," I think out loud. "Maybe it's the pink house. When I was a child, visitors often got lost looking for our street. Daddy's instructions were always the same, 'Look for the pink house . . . turn left there.'

"Thanks to the pink house, identifying landmarks became an early habit for me," I explain to David. "I just take mental photos as I move about. For, instance, see those red window boxes on that building ahead? They are my markers. We turn left there, and our hotel will be in sight."

David grins widely as we turn the corner, and there we are, just where we want to be.

Later in the evening, I think again of the pink house. After all these years, I'm pretty sure it's no longer there. But, there are, I think, other pink houses—intangible ones—that will always remain permanent signposts of Jesus's teaching. They can guide us home, too. They are put in place by God's promise that if we ask, He will lead us where we should go. To make good on that promise, He sent Jesus to make His guidelines clear: "love others," for instance, and "treat every person the way you want to be treated." If we want a steady journey through life, there are no better pink houses, no better markers, than His words.

Father, You promise in Proverbs that You will direct our path.
Instill in us the "pink houses" that point toward our one
true home where You long for us to be.
—Pam Kidd

Digging Deeper: Psalm 25:4; Isaiah 48:17; Matthew 7:12, 24

Thursday, July 6

BUILDING CATHEDRALS: Glory in the Ordinary

Lift up your eyes and look to the heavens: Who created all these? He who brings out the starry host one by one and calls forth each of them by name. —Isaiah 40:26 (NIV)

As we got closer to hitting the big 4-0, Brian and I got in a habit of taking daily walks right after school drop-off and before we headed into work. Our goal, taking better care of our bodies, quickly expanded as we reaped the rewards of the effort: clearer minds, bolstered spirits, and, yes, a few pounds shed. Forty minutes, nearly three miles, and a lot of conversation fed my soul and left me ready to face the coming day.

Every morning, I would look up into the sky; it seemed there wasn't room for a single cloud to interrupt the sea of brilliant blue. Day after day, I would comment on it, until I finally turned to Brian and said, "Has it always been this blue, and I've just never noticed it?"

As months rolled by, we certainly had a few rainy days that kept us inside. But most were sparklingly blue, which felt like a love letter straight from God to my heart.

I'm not a weather expert; I don't know if our year of walks featured more clear skies than others or not. What I do know is that God gave me the chance to see and truly notice them for the first time. Now, just as I always check to see if He's showing off with a spectacular sunset, I take a moment in the morning to look up and see the beauty He is creating. Doing so lets me refocus my thoughts on Him and energizes me for the day ahead, almost as much as my actual walk itself does.

Lord, thank You for taking my small changes and using them to open my eyes to the wonder of Your world. Allow me to always notice the beauty of Your works.
—Ashley Kappel

Digging Deeper: Psalm 19:1; 1 Corinthians 2:9

For he shall deliver the needy when he crieth; the poor also, and him that hath no helper. —Psalm 72:12 (KJV)

Ever since my hip replacement, I've become cautious about my movements. I take my time on stairs, use crampons and a walking stick in winter, and clamber gingerly over crumbling or slick rocks when hiking.

So how I managed to tumble—backward—out of my raised-bed garden, I'll never know. But I did know that I was in big trouble: I had smacked both my skull and tailbone on the pavement. Stunned with pain, I couldn't move.

And I live alone. And know few neighbors in nearby apartments.

But I believe in miracles. As I fell, two friends were just pulling out of my driveway after delivering my first air conditioner. Brad and Bob slammed the brakes, backed up, and came to my rescue. They eased me up, found a towel for my bloody head, and drove me to the hospital. Eight staples and two X-rays later, they drove me home and called frequently to check on me.

For the next few days, I recuperated in air-conditioned comfort and pondered the synchronicity of my rescue: No one had visited me for several weeks before or after my fall. Nor had Brad and Bob ever been to my house; I knew them from church. Even more astonishing, I broke no bones and suffered no concussion in the mishap.

To me, this qualifies as a miracle, not a coincidence. Sure, I probably could have managed to find medical care on my own, but I believe that God rescued me that day. With white goatees and white hair, Bob and Brad may not look like His angels. But I know better.

> *Merciful God, who marks the sparrow's fall, thank You for watching out for me, too.*
> —Gail Thorell Schilling

Digging Deeper: Psalm 18:19, 107:19–21; Daniel 6:27

Saturday, July 8

"Sing to the LORD a new song; sing to the LORD, all the earth."
—Psalm 96:1 (NIV)

As I pondered the *Walking in Grace* theme for 2023, "Filled with Praise," I reviewed the definition of praise. The primary meaning is "to offer grateful homages to God, as in words or song." Closing the dictionary, I suddenly recalled a memory from my teenage years and began to chuckle. I love to sing! Now as a senior adult, I still bellow forth!

My memory was of a blistering summer day when I was a college student driving down a busy city street in my rattletrap car. The air conditioner did not work, and I rolled down the windows. As a cool breeze blew across my face, the world became beautiful and wonderful again. I spontaneously began to sing the Swedish folk hymn, "How Great Thou Art!" Pulling up to a stoplight totally absorbed in song, I crescendoed dramatically and at full volume, forgetting my car windows were open. Suddenly I heard nearby pedestrians laughing and pointing at the crazy kid in his car entertaining downtown Atlanta. I quickly stopped my song and slid down in my car seat. However, for a brief moment, I was my "authentic best self" while singing praise and expressing joy to God!

Musical or not, God wants us to sometimes "let go" and express ourselves at full volume or quiet whisper, whether through music, speech, thought, laughter, or silent tears of joy glinting in our eyes. When we express true praise and gratitude, our peace is restored, our emotions find balance, and our perspective grows clear. Praise is one way to embrace and love God. And also to feel how much God loves us!

Dear God, may I praise You today in my most natural
and authentic way! Amen.
—Scott Walker

Digging Deeper: Psalm 34; Colossians 3:16

Each will be like a refuge from the wind And a shelter from the storm, Like streams of water in a dry country, Like the shade of a huge rock in an exhausted land. —Isaiah 32:2 (NASB)

Perhaps because I grew up in a home with a dug well, I learned as a kid to value and conserve water. Some summers the well grew perilously low, and Dad, who had measured it with a long stick, cautioned us to shut off the faucet during toothbrushing and face-washing.

We washed dishes in a dishpan and rinsed them with water from a saucepan, not under a running tap. Even laundry water from the first load was recycled with a "suds saver" to use for more heavily soiled items. Water the lawn? Never. We waited for rain.

After college, I moved to city apartments where water was readily available and wells not an issue. I forgot about water until I met New Americans and refugees at my community college. Their stories gave me pause. One young woman from Southern Sudan wrote about not being able to attend school because her family needed her to fetch water daily some miles away. She walked there. A young man, a school administrator, survived unjust imprisonment in part by drinking fetid water out of his shoe. He found only muddy river water for his baby's bottle when he and his wife ran for their lives in Rwanda during the civil war. Even in refugee camps, water was meted out in quantities so scant they had to choose between drinking it or washing baby's diaper.

My new friends from Rwanda have now settled here in New Hampshire. During my first visit, my friend turned on the faucet. "Look! Look!" he said, laughing as clear water splashed into the sink. "Plenty of water! God is good!"

May his gratitude remind me to be likewise.

Lord of All, bless those who remind us to be thankful.
—Gail Thorell Schilling

Digging Deeper: Exodus 23:25; Psalm 105:41; Isaiah 44:3, 55:1

Monday, July 10

As a father has compassion for his children, so the LORD *has compassion for those who fear him.* —Psalm 103:13 (NRSV)

I needed something to wear to the gym and grabbed a colorful old T-shirt from the bottom of a drawer. "Super Dad," it said in cartoon script, and "Man of the Hour," along with a list of all the qualities a Super Dad should have: "Faster than a speeding lawn mower, more powerful than the lid of a pickle jar, able to diet without losing a single pound . . . it's a repair man . . . it's a cash machine . . . it's Super Dad." A long-ago present from my boys. Must have been for my birthday or Father's Day.

"Looks just like you," some friend said, checking out the shirt. I'd already forgotten I had it on. I looked in the mirror while lifting some weights—not hugely heavy ones, mind you. I'm not that super. I could see the big "D" in reverse. How did I measure up as a dad?

I've never driven a lawn mower. I'm lousy at repair jobs. I couldn't open most tightly wound pickle lids without help from a jar opener, and heck, I've never been one to attempt any sort of diet. But as far as cash machine goes, well, I would take my own father as example. Even when we were grown—especially as we were launching out in our careers—he'd dip his hand into his pocket and pull out a couple of twenties and say, "You should take these. I'm sure you have a need for it." We did.

The thing is when any of us look in the mirror, or at a selfie for that matter, we don't really see ourselves. That picture can best be found in the eyes of those we love. We are as super as they think.

Clearly, I'd kept that funny old T-shirt for a reason.

> *May those I love see me with love as we mirror God's love.*
> —Rick Hamlin

Digging Deeper: Proverbs 3:11–12; Ephesians 6:4

"Whoever believes in me, as Scripture has said, rivers of living water will flow from within them." —John 7:38 (NIV)

I don't mind taking my car in for regular maintenance at the dealership because the waiting area is so pleasant with gourmet coffee, great spaces to work, and comfy chairs to read or just enjoy the artwork on the walls.

On this day, I brought my computer, but I didn't open it as I snuggled into one of the chairs. Today I needed some maintenance myself; time to reflect and ask God for strength to handle some difficult challenges ahead. That's when I noticed a painting that caught my attention because it reminded me of places where I always feel closest to God: sitting by a mountain stream and watching the water flow past me, pooling tranquilly in some spots and crashing into rocks in other spots. The stream in the painting seemed to hit more rocky places than tranquil ones. A metaphor for my life ahead?

I got up to get some coffee, choosing a chocolate mocha, a treat that I sipped slowly before returning to my chair, and that's when the most amazing thing happened. When I looked at the picture again, I saw something totally differently. Instead of the water flowing away from me, I saw the stream coming toward me, bringing the living water to flow through me and strengthen me for the journey over the rocks ahead. I was still staring at the picture, absorbing the powerful change in my perspective, when a serviceman found me. "Your maintenance work is done," he said. "You should be good to go."

> *Lord, surely You give Your children eyes to see what You transform for us, but when it happens like it did for me today, I'm especially aware of Your personal loving Presence.*
> —Carol Kuykendall

Digging Deeper: Deuteronomy 10:21; Psalm 42:1–2; Ephesians 1:17–18

Wednesday, July 12

". . . do justice . . ."—Psalm 82:3 (KJV)

Shortly after the killing of George Floyd, I heard a sermon on Jesus's focus on justice. "Love your neighbor as yourself," the pastor reminded us of the Bible's admonition.

Jesus's words in relation to Floyd's death instilled a desperation in me, and I left that Sunday wanting to act and not just talk. I knew I could no longer rest in my comfort zone, knowing that Jesus's words pointed me in a new direction.

But I needed help, and so I turned to my friend Shan Foster, sending a vulnerable text, asking for guidance. Shan is Black. He was raised by a single mom and had a talent for basketball. He rose to be the all-time leading scorer at Vanderbilt University, then moved on to play professionally.

He responded with searing honesty:

"Growing up in New Orleans, I would get into a lot of fights. Not because I wanted to, but because bigger, stronger bullies would beat me up. When I got bigger and had little brothers, I never let anyone pick on them. They always knew if they called, I'd run to their defense. Consequently, they never got bullied. Well, racism lives in the hearts of white bullies. We've been calling out to our white big brothers . . . still waiting for them to show up. This is a battle I can't fight. You have to fight it for me. I love you, big brother."

His words hit me hard. But, determined, I wiped my eyes and called a few like-minded friends. We started a racism awareness group. We struggle to learn more about what we don't know. We use this knowledge to create more equality in our community. We don't just talk. We act.

Father, we follow Your Son. His words point the way as we work for
equality and inclusion and show kindness to all Your children.
Thank You for allowing us this privilege.
—Brock Kidd

Digging Deeper: Micah 6:8; Matthew 7:12

We must pay the most careful attention, therefore, to what we have heard, so that we do not drift away. —Hebrews 2:1 (NIV)

Be very quiet," I whispered. "We can learn from the Potawatomi Indians who used to live on this land, how to walk through the forest without making a sound."

I was instructing my nine-year-old how to explore the woods near the cabin where we sometimes stay in rural Wisconsin. We had just embarked on a two-mile jaunt and were talking very little while practicing our quiet steps.

We saw long-legged cranes in shallow water and a dozen turtles sunning themselves on half-submerged logs. We were close to having come full circle around the lake. We knew that our cabin was just on the other side of a forest of trees.

Before stepping out of the forest, my daughter touched my arm lightly and put the index finger of her other hand to her lips. I turned and looked at her. She was pointing toward the glen that includes our cabin.

"There's that deer again," she whispered.

"Hmmm?" I muttered.

"The deer."

"What do you mean 'again'?"

At that moment, in a flash, a doe leaped three times and was gone into the forest, on the far side of the glen.

"She was there when we left, Dad. Didn't you notice her?" my daughter said.

I chuckled to myself as I realized my daughter hadn't needed my sage parenting advice about being quiet—but apparently, I did!

I will be quiet and pay attention to Your presence in my life today, Lord.
—Jon M. Sweeney

Digging Deeper: Proverbs 4:25

Friday, July 14

"Do not fear, for I have redeemed you; I have summoned you by name; you are mine." —Isaiah 43:1 (NIV)

Nine people mispronounced my first name yesterday. My name, Sabra, has been a problem my entire life. I remember the first day of school when I was in kindergarten, my very first day of meeting people by myself, the teacher said, "Oh, you're a girl. I wondered if you would be a boy or a girl. How do I say it?"

Not an easy start—and a difficult name to own—for a very shy little girl. Since then, meeting people has been problematic. Someone extends a hand and mispronounces my name, which leads to a back and forth of corrections. For years, I practiced how to introduce myself and how to subtly and kindly explain the right way to say it. At my college graduation, the speaker said, "I'm not even going to try this one"—and I knew it was me.

My name originates from the legend of Saint George and the Dragon. Saint George slays the dragon and saves Princess Sabra from a terrible fate. Over the years, I've been called Sabrina, Serena, Saber, Sabre, Zahra, Zorba, and even Zebra.

So last night, after decades of uncomfortable moments, graduations, bosses, and the nine people mispronouncing my name, it all came to a head, and I became angry. I went for a walk and stomped the pavement and complained. I asked, "Why, God, why is my name so hard? Why?"

You are my child, I heard in my heart. *Do not worry about your name. I know who you are.*

Heavenly Father, thank You for helping me shake my anger and calm my nerves by remembering what's most important.
—Sabra Ciancanelli (Say-brah Sink-can-nel-lee)

Digging Deeper: Proverbs 22:9; Jeremiah 1:5

"I will give you treasures concealed in the dark and secret hoards—so that you may know that it is I the Lord."—Isaiah 45:3 (JPS)

W hat does it mean," the visiting scholar asked us, "when this prayer says that 'God is overflowing' with blessings?" Our scholar in residence for the weekend had been taking us through some of the prayers we said in Hebrew in every service, often without thinking about them.

Earlier in the class, he had helped us explore some different translations of the standard prayers, the original reasons some of them had been included in the prayer book, and how they had been used in historical contexts. Now we were going beyond what we were saying when we prayed those prayers, into what was behind the words.

One of the other participants answered, "Maybe it means that God is so full of blessings for us that they just spill out." Another said, "Maybe it's saying that God's blessings are endless," and the scholar instantly responded, "But are you saying that the blessings are bigger than God can contain? That God has an end, but the blessings don't?" For a couple of minutes, there was silence.

Then I raised my hand. "We can't know God's essence," I said hesitantly. "Maybe the only way we can come to know God at all is to encounter God in the overflow."

The scholar kept the discussion going, but I was stalled in the new insight that had come to me. God would, it seemed to me, understand that I was too limited to grasp anything near the entirety of who and what He is. And God wanted me to seek, so He provided the place where we could meet. The prayer simply called that place "the overflow."

Lord of all that is hidden, I meet You in my heart. Thank You for showing me I can meet You in my mind, as well.
—Rhoda Blecker

Digging Deeper: Deuteronomy 29:28; Job 23:3; Micah 1:3

Sunday, July 16

But seek first his kingdom and his righteousness, and all these things will be given to you as well. —Matthew 6:33 (NIV)

It had taken us a year to reach our decision, but it still wasn't easy. My husband and I had decided it was time to change churches. Not because we were unhappy but because we'd been feeling a tug to make the move. We'd been attending the same church for twelve years and had made many lifelong friendships.

Moving to a new church was difficult, but within the first month, we knew we had made the right choice. We fit. Our friendships at the new church grew deeper, and we quickly felt like we'd been there for years.

But it didn't take me long to realize something profound. For over a year, my biggest concern had been will this church benefit my family? What I should have been asking was will my family benefit this church?

It humbled me to learn our family had been called to the church not just for our blessing but also to fill needs and answer prayers. My husband had been in worship ministry for years and was exactly what the floundering worship team needed to pull everyone together. My girls came alongside a young woman who was in need of friends and became an answer to her mother's prayers. And a strengthened friendship for me meant the opportunity to pursue a new writing-related ministry.

As I look back at that year, while we were wrestling with our decision, I'm convinced that if we had flipped the question around, we would have made the choice faster and with more confidence. When we're simply worried about how something will benefit us, we might miss the opportunity to be a blessing.

> *Lord, when I'm feeling a tug on my heart, help me to realize*
> *that it might not be for my benefit, alone, but to further*
> *Your kingdom purposes.*
> —Gabrielle Meyer

Digging Deeper: Romans 12:6–8; Ephesians 4:11–13

The LORD will keep you from all harm—he will watch over your life; the LORD will watch over your coming and going both now and forevermore.
—Psalm 121:7–8 (NIV)

A black cobra? On Tom's routine bike ride? In downtown Singapore? "I just rode around his tail, Mom. His head and hood were about six feet away . . ."

Just when I had convinced myself that his metropolitan cycling was safe, that I no longer needed to worry about my son, the professor: happily married with a child, a satisfying career, good health, many friends. Now a cobra. Of course, he was not harmed, and the snake's appearance was a rarity, but I must confront the chilling reality that life has its perils, no matter what.

Parenting four children, I must have dreamed that I could coast along, worry-free, once they could toddle without tumbling down stairs or flailing scissors. Childhood was fraught with bruises and bike wrecks—I bought antiseptic by the quart. Then we tackled driving safely and making good decisions about friends and parties. When they left home, I could stop worrying, right? Hardly.

My son Greg now works as a property manager, driving all over Los Angeles. He sends photos of himself seven stories high—outside—installing air-conditioning. And he's proud of his electrical installations of umpteen hundred volts. "It could fry me, Mom!" Even my daughters commute thirty to fifty minutes a day, often on ice or in blizzard conditions.

How I wish I could guard my adult children, but I cannot. Instead, I pray fervently, daily, that God will protect those I love. I know He does.

Father of all, thank You for holding us snug in Your almighty hands.
—Gail Thorell Schilling

Digging Deeper: Deuteronomy 31:6; Psalm 46:1–2, 138:7; Luke 4:10

Tuesday, July 18

*You, L*ORD*, are God! You have promised these good things to your servant.* —1 Chronicles 17:26 (NIV)

I'm walking through New York's Central Park on a flawless summer day, my dog, Gracie, in tow, no particular place to go.

A band is setting up at the Naumburg Bandshell for a concert. On the Great Lawn, a group is practicing tai chi. Further on, a man on a unicycle zips by blowing a kazoo (it is not for me to ask why). A woman pushes a twin stroller containing twin Yorkies. Gracie seems genuinely bemused.

On a bench in the shade of a voluptuous oak, a man reads his Bible. He looks up and smiles. I give him a little nod. Further down the mall, a young couple is selling used books spread out on a blanket. I hope they're doing it to make room in their apartment for more books.

We walk by the lake, the rippling breeze sending a toy sailboat scurrying across the water, its young captain running along the shore beside it. Further out, weekend sailors in rented rowboats try not to collide.

Gracie pulls me toward a hot-dog stand, and before I can change course, the vendor is smiling. He knows he has a customer. I give in and buy a hot dog, repairing to a bench where I share a bite with Gracie.

Here's the thing. I am not actually strolling in Central Park. It is a wet, sunless day when the rain won't stop, and the dampness goes right to your bones. Gracie is wet and, well, fragrant. Frankly, I can't wait for the day to end so I can crawl into bed. But all the things I described I have seen, and I will see again and more, for God is good and there are always brighter, warmer, drier, better days ahead. Until that next flawless summer day comes, I can live and dream God's blessings in my mind and praise him for the goodness that is sure to come.

> *Lord, I have good days and bad, but let me never forget*
> *the blessings that await.*
> —Edward Grinnan

Digging Deeper: Proverbs 16:9; James 1:17

When I am afraid, I put my trust in you. —Psalm 56:3 (NIV)

L ocal forecasters had warned of inclement weather, but into the early night the rolling clouds had only brought light rain showers. My family was tucked safely and snugly in bed and as was his usual request, our youngest son had convinced me and his dad to let him snuggle between us. After falling asleep, my husband dutifully scooped him up and returned him to his own room as he did most nights. The rain waned and I assumed we'd missed the brunt of it. However, I was awakened a few hours later when the storms intensified. Lightning lit up the entire house. Seconds later, the house shook with a rumble of thunder so strong that it felt like our king-sized bed also quivered in fright.

I heard the rapid thump of footsteps running down the upstairs hall-way and saw a shadowy figure through my open bedroom doors. I had no idea when my son had sprouted his wings, but it seemed he took flight before landing with a hard thud on our bed. "Mommy, I'm scared," he said, climbing under the comforter and scooting himself into my waiting arms. "It's just a storm. It will pass over soon." Unlike our teenagers, he hadn't lived long enough to brave the thunderstorms without fear.

Storms in life are inevitable. Matthew 5:45 tells us that it rains on the just and unjust. In those times, we have the privilege to run into the arms of our Lord, Who will assure us that even though we have days of trouble and what appears to be unrelenting rain, the sun will shine again.

> *Father, in the storms of life, I will trust in You.*
> *Thank You for being a safe place.*
> —Tia McCollors

Digging Deeper: Joshua 1:9; Psalm 91:1–6; Nahum 1:7

Thursday, July 20

". . . And surely I am with you always, to the very end of the age."
—Matthew 28:20 (NIV)

All I'd done was take an antique Bombay chest to a place that sells marble, and I'd had me a full-blown flashback. The estate-sale find had been an absolute steal because its marble top was jagged and crumbling in the broken places. I'd brought it along so they'd have a pattern for a replacement.

The guy ran his fingers through his scruffy, gray beard and grinned. "I believe I can almost fix this." My heart dropped to my feet. Twenty-two years before, I'd straddled the edge of a surgeon's cold exam table as he ran his fingers over my tumor-battered face. He'd uttered the same horrifying sentence.

I believe I can almost fix this.

Almost. Does Mr. Webster have a sadder, more hopeless word?

Now, the marble guy was suggesting he just glue the shards back together and cover the repairs with those doilies he'd heard about. Granted, doilies can be an art form. But my log cabin didn't need any more of them. Especially for this. And certainly not seven.

Finally, mercifully, he remembered a piece of marble in his workshop left over from another project. The price to cut and fit and bevel the edges was reasonable, with no need for doilies.

The finished product was lovely. Lovelier still is the message it sends to my spirit every time I look at it. I don't serve an *almost* Savior and Lord . . . one who comes through on occasion with repairs I need to camouflage. Mine is with me *always* with a plan that's *always* perfect.

In a world of almosts, Lord, I'm so glad You're my always!
—Roberta Messner

Digging Deeper: Deuteronomy 31:6; Isaiah 41:10

*. . . you cannot tolerate wrongdoing. . . . Why are you silent while
the wicked swallow up those more righteous than themselves?*
—Habakkuk 1:13 (NIV)

I once heard a man share his wisdom on how to maintain a solid
marriage. He and his wife had never had an argument, he boasted.
Young and full of my own untested wisdom, I blurted out, "If there's
never an argument in a marriage, someone is oppressed!"

Considering the prophet Habakkuk's complaint, I've come to see
that there was a bit of truth in my homespun conclusion. When it
seemed God's chosen people would suffocate under the thumb of their
bragging Babylonian captors, Habakkuk put his feelings before the
Lord. "Why are you silent?" he asks.

Though I flinch at his forthrightness when confronting the Creator
(and smile as he readies himself for the rebuke), Habakkuk's audacity to
say his piece before God models true friendship. Because Habakkuk knew
God to be a friend—knew He would listen and still love—he was secure
in stating respectfully what was in his heart. Fear shrinks the soul, but
open communication fosters relationship. God desires the latter. Even if
we sometimes stumble over our words and tremble in our boots, honesty
toward Him is always the best policy. In fact, it's the only policy that works.

One of my mother's favorite songs said, "Living below in this old
sinful world . . . where could I go but to the Lord?" Whether in thankfulness or striking lament—from Job to David to Habakkuk—in a
world that seemingly thrives on gossip, it provides comfort to know we
can always freely go to Jesus, who will give us His undivided attention
and never "go viral" with our complaints. What would we do without
His perpetually inclined ear?

> *Jesus, I am so grateful You are the one Friend I can talk
> to without restraint.*
> —Jacqueline F. Wheelock

Digging Deeper: 2 Chronicles 20:7; John 15:15

Saturday, July 22

*But those who hope in the L*ORD *will renew their strength. They will soar on wings like eagles; they will run and not grow weary, they will walk and not be faint.* —Isaiah 40:31 (NIV)

Our middle daughter, Hope, is married now. She and Griffin had met as sailors aboard a tall ship (the old-timey kind with canvas and rigging and wooden masts), so they used one of the ship's ropes to literally tie the knot at their wedding. It was a lovely and moving affair.

The reception, too, was wonderful. Then, suddenly, it was my turn to give the toast. As I looked out at my daughter and her shiny new husband, my well-prepared and oft-rehearsed speech drifted out of my mind, never to be seen again. I panicked and did the unthinkable: I told the unvarnished truth. (Despite what you hear, no one is completely honest at weddings or funerals. Imagine if they were—yikes!)

"Hope . . . wasn't like her sisters. She wasn't like anyone," I said. "I thought she was from a different planet. I waited for the Mother Ship to come and get her."

After a somewhat uncomfortable silence, I continued:

"Emily Dickinson once wrote that 'hope is the thing with feathers.' Griffin's name comes from gryphon, the mythical, protective beast that also has feathers. But Griffin isn't mythical. He's right here. Hope, I think the Mother Ship has finally found you."

After the toast, we sent Hope and Griffin—the things with feathers—on their journey together. I realized as I held Hope's hand that she wasn't from another planet, that she was part of me and always would be. Well-prepared and oft-rehearsed words wouldn't help me navigate this difficult moment—but the truth would. And so I set her free.

> *Lord, Your truth, too, is the thing with feathers, and the*
> *Truth will set us free.*
> —Mark Collins

Digging Deeper: Hosea 2:19; Hebrews 11:1

You rule the raging of the sea; When its waves arise, You still them.
—Psalm 89:9 (NKJV)

One week, I went through a tempest of insomnia. I would fall asleep just fine, but by midnight I was tossing and turning, like a ship on high seas. I was pulled down by waves of regret and threatened by dark clouds of doubt about my future.

I got up and went to my study, where I tried my usual ploy: playing soft music while reading boring encyclopedias. But this time it didn't work, so I decided to journal my troubles.

When I opened my desk drawer for a pencil, I gasped. "This drawer is a dumpster fire. How did it get like this?" I bore into the drawer, tossing out dried-up ballpoint pens, pencil stubs, stale Rolaids, empty tape rolls, and petrified chocolate candy. It felt good to work with my hands.

As I worked, my mind continued to rehearse its woes, but I found myself tossing out some old, dead-end issues. I did triage on the rest, organizing them in order of their seriousness. I punctuated my reverie with telegram prayers: "Forgive my past." "Give me courage." "Let me rest."

At last the drawer was clean, and suddenly I felt very sleepy.

Every night for a week, I cleaned out another drawer, and every night I slept a little longer. Just getting my mind cleaned out and organized seemed to bring my fears down to size. I now have a very clean desk and tranquil nights.

> *Thank You, Lord, for storms, which clear the air and*
> *ultimately bring peace.*
> —Daniel Schantz

Digging Deeper: Job 38:1–6; Psalm 107:28–31

Monday, July 24

My dear brothers and sisters, take note of this: Everyone should be quick to listen, slow to speak and slow to become angry. —James 1:19 (NIV)

Some people are natural when it comes to sharing their faith—they do it with an ease I envy. A friend told me about an airplane trip she recently took. Once in the air, she introduced herself to her seatmate. How she turned the conversation around to faith, I don't know. The woman beside her adamantly declared she was an atheist. Without missing a beat, my friend said, "How interesting; tell me about that." And from there she planted the seeds of faith and God's love in a dry and hungry heart.

Another friend has a lovely way of sharing her faith that I admire. We'd gone to lunch and when our order was delivered, my friend thanked our server and said, "I'm going to say a prayer. Is there anything on your heart you'd like me to pray about for you?" She's done this every time we're together, and I'm always amazed at how open people are to sharing their deepest concerns when they know someone is open to praying for them.

Both of these friends show genuine interest and care for others. As William J. Toms once said, "You may be the only Bible some people ever read." If people are reading me, I want to be sure they discover a woman who cares enough to listen, to hear, and to respond in love.

Father God, give me a caring heart for the concerns and pain of others. Open my eyes to see those in need of You. Open doors for me to share Your great love with the ease and sincerity of my friends.
—Debbie Macomber

Digging Deeper: Matthew 10:32–33; Acts 20:24; Romans 1:16

*. . . His radiance exceeds anything in earth and sky; he's built a monument—His very own people! —*Psalm 148:13 (MSG)

The comfortable waiting room projects an older style: stamped-tin ceiling tiles; 1950s-model floor lamps; picture window looking onto our village's gazebo at the intersection of Duncan, Hudson, and River roads; an expansive sill filled with succulent plants, Burgundy shamrock, and a potted miniature palm.

Yet, what really focuses my attention are the photos—a young sailor from Vietnam, wide-eyed shoeshine youth, brightly dressed Guatemalan pottery vendors. The office's atmosphere invites rest, serenity, and quiet.

Never mind that I was in Doc's dental office to begin the first of six visits. My aching upper left molar necessitated a root canal—the delicate removal of nerve and tissue, applying filling, and then final fitting of a new crown.

The winsome photos calmed my uneasy spirit. They bore visual testimony to Doc's medical mission trips. His humanitarian portable dentistry visits span from the mountain peoples of Vietnam and Bolivia to weekend Remote Area Medical clinics in Maryland to county fairgrounds along the Virginia/Kentucky state border. The good doctor's volunteer work inspires and uplifts me.

Sitting in the waiting room, I felt as if I were in a sacred space, a sanctuary made possible by the caring hands and kind heart of our dentist.

My internal celebrations applauded the global shared humanity of all God's children, and helped ease my "dental chair anxiety" and unrest. Thankfully, throughout the root canal process, I was at peace.

Ever-compassionate God, we give gratitude that You are excited to love and care for each one of us, the world over. We all bear Your image. We are thankful. Amen.
—Ken Sampson

Digging Deeper: Psalm 92:12; 1 Peter 5:7; 1 John 3:17

Wednesday, July 26

Submit yourselves, then, to God. Resist the devil, and he will flee from you. —James 4:7 (NIV)

The car parked below our window at 2 a.m., blasting music so loudly the vehicle's windows rattled. Startled out of sleep, I groaned and put a pillow over my head. It might be a five-minute problem. Then again, it could last hours.

Much as I wanted to yell out the window—blatantly inconsiderate people push my crazy button, even in the daytime—I'd only ever seen that strategy backfire. It would be more effective to pad downstairs to point out in a reasonable voice that schoolkids were sleeping. However, I lacked that much self-possession at the moment. Calling the precinct *might* work if it was a slow-crime night, but I'd probably wake up anyone in the family who wasn't already awake by talking on the phone. Since I can't wear earplugs due to an inner-ear condition, I clamped the pillow tighter over my head and fantasized about a yet-to-be-invented device that can disable a car stereo from afar.

Miraculously, after ten minutes the car drove away. Now came the task of getting back to sleep, never an easy one. I pulled out my phone and found a favorite song, which begins, "Jesus, I surrender myself to you . . ." by John Schreiner. The words washed over and through me. I let go of my frustration, my anger, my worries about staying awake in my 10 a.m. meeting. At some point just before I fell asleep, the boom car came back. I was too at peace to care.

Jesus, into your hands I entrust everything.
—Julia Attaway

Digging Deeper: Matthew 6:10, 26:42

Then you will find your joy in the LORD, and I will cause you to ride in triumph . . . —Isaiah 58:14 (NIV)

A re you up for a trail ride?" my neighbor Hannah asked. "I have a four-year-old that needs some miles put on her this summer."

In my head, pending projects and deadlines loomed up like a dark cloud poised to rain on any hope of fun. My mind wisely, but silently, screamed, "NO!" as my heart and my mouth both impulsively, and honestly, answered, "YES!"

I saddled my horse, Jack, and met Hannah and Liberty at the gate. Liberty was nervous at first and insisted Jack lead the way, but she soon settled into a terrific stride. Following trails made by wild horses in the forest behind our homes, we rode through towering pines, across flats of broken lava rock and scattered sagebrush, and through stream-fed meadows dotted with wildflowers. Peace bloomed within me the deeper we rode into God's creation.

Liberty was born for the trail. Nothing would faze her, even when we encountered the wild horse herd. We kept our horses collected until the wild bunch galloped away. Soon after, Hannah spotted shed antlers, which were almost too big to pack home on Jack, but, laughing all the way, I managed.

"Want to go again next week?" Hannah asked when we got back. It struck me that I had not fretted about my to-do list since we'd left. In fact, I felt completely rejuvenated and ready to tackle my projects.

"Are you kidding?" I grinned. "Wild horses couldn't keep me away."

Lord, I will never have time, I can only make time, so help me
make my time count. Joy in You is my strength!
—Erika Bentsen

Digging Deeper: Isaiah 61:10; Habakkuk 3:18

Friday, July 28

Finally, be strong in the Lord and in the strength of his might.
—Ephesians 6:10 (ESV)

My back feels like a tower of blocks," I said. "A tower that's going to tumble."

The physical therapist held the gait belt strapped around my waist. "Take it slowly," she said. "One step."

I'd had back surgery just hours before. My second surgery. I knew walking was important. But my top half was unsteady. Like I couldn't hold it up.

How I wished I'd built a stronger core! I wished I'd spent more time exercising so my back would be shored.

"Let's walk to the door and back," the therapist said. "Then you can rest."

Only after I'd done that, I couldn't rest. I began to fret about the next time I'd have to walk. What if I wobbled? What if I fell?

My spiritual strength seemed as weak as my back.

In the past, my back problems persisted for months before I needed surgery. This time it happened fast. A disk slipped and I was immobile. Right in the center of my busy life. My calendar-and-commitment life. My life that had recently been so full that I hadn't had time to spend with the Lord. My salvation wasn't at stake. But strength and confidence and peace? I was missing spiritual muscle because I'd neglected my true core.

I needed spiritual shoring for my soul.

Later that afternoon, the therapist returned. "You'll get stronger," she assured me. "Muscles will build in time."

"Yes," I said. In God's grace, they would.

Lord, my greatest strength comes from You.
—Shawnelle Eliasen

Digging Deeper: Matthew 6:33; Romans 10:17

I praise you because I am fearfully and wonderfully made; your works are wonderful, I know that full well. —Psalm 139:14 (NIV)

I looked out my hotel window at the pool below and saw her, a solitary mallard female, paddling around. It was early, before the sun replaced the shade and sunbathers gathered, and she paddled as if she didn't have a care in the world.

I smiled at her freedom and imagined the conversation she had with the rest of the flock before deciding to take a dip in the hotel pool.

"Where are you going? Don't you know you'll be the only duck there?" To which she replied, "The pool looks inviting, and I want to swim in it. You go ahead and I'll catch up later." The other ducks would shake their heads, think her foolish, and fly away.

So she paddled, seemingly unbothered by the fact that she was different, unlike the human sunbathers who arrived beside the pool. She was enjoying being a duck, stopping briefly on the side to preen, then resuming her swim before flying away.

I admired her and envied her. Here I was, trying to dredge up enough courage to go outside to the pool by myself. My insecurities told me I might not fit in, my body wasn't model-perfect, and I might draw unwanted attention to myself. But I also wanted to enjoy the cool water of the pool and swim without concern of others' opinions.

How odd that a lone mallard visited the pool that morning. How wonderful that I had witnessed it. Was God sending me a message? Was He telling me that I, too, could be myself without regard to what others thought? I accepted that encouragement, put on my bathing suit, and headed to the pool.

> *Lord, thank You for making me who I am. Give me courage to be the person You want me to be.*
> —Marilyn Turk

Digging Deeper: 1 Samuel 16:7; Psalm 139

Sunday, July 30

For we were all baptized by one Spirit so as to form one body—whether Jews or Gentiles, slave or free—and we were all given the one Spirit to drink. —1 Corinthians 12:13 (NIV)

As a Black girl in New York City during the racially turbulent 1960s and 1970s, I was blessed with a family that encouraged me to forge friendships with whomever was a friend, despite different skin tones and backgrounds.

Ilene was one such friend. A girl of Jewish faith, we were only children who bonded over Barbies, brownies, and our pets. And her parents happily included me in many of their weekend jaunts—including a trip one weekend to a local beach.

I had such a great time that I hounded my own mom and dad to take me again a few weeks later. We enjoyed the surf and sun, but the aftermath was less than perfect. We returned to our car in the parking lot to find that all four tires had been slashed. I quickly realized that while it was okay for me frolic at this beach with a White family, my Black family was not welcome. It was a life lesson that I have never forgotten.

But rather than holding on to that hurt, I chose to grasp on to the love. Ilene's parents, Emma and Rae, always made me feel welcome, respected, and safe. I wondered whether they saw any side glances or other signs of racism during our trip? If they did, I am confident that they deflected them to protect my feelings—that's how much they cared about me. I am forever grateful for their loving friendship. At Emma's funeral recently, I focused on how very blessed I was to have had her love as an example of God's grace in my life.

Father, You created all of us to be different in this world.
Help us remember that we are all Your people.
—Gayle T. Williams

Digging Deeper: John 7:24; Galatians 3:28; Ephesians 4:32

You are Christ's body—that's who you are! You must never forget this. Only as you accept your part of that body does your "part" mean anything. —1 Corinthians 12:27–28 (MSG)

My son Johnny told me about a book he's reading tonight. After I asked several questions, he said, "Mom will understand—she reads a lot."

His comment took me back to when he was in first grade. I often got home late from work. One evening, arriving just before Johnny went to bed, his mom suggested he stay up while I had dinner. Sitting across the table, Johnny said, "Mommy is the smart one."

"What makes Mom smart?" I asked.

"She knows everything; she's a teacher, Dad."

"If Mom is the smart one, then who am I?"

Johnny answered, "You're the funny one."

The next evening, my wife, Pat, and I were with friends. Kathy asked, "What's new with Johnny?" I shared his dinnertime observation and that I was not too thrilled to be seen by him as the family clown. "With as little time as you have with Johnny, would you really want to be anyone other than who he has fun with?" Kathy asked. Her question reassured me that I could be content with the role my young son had assigned me.

Paul tells us in 1 Corinthians 12:27–28 to accept the parts Jesus gives us. And that only when we accept His parts for us, will they have meaning. Do you ever wish you had the gifts or talents of someone else? The next time I want to be someone I'm not, I hope I will remember how much I enjoyed being the *funny one* once I accepted the part.

Dear God, help us to rejoice in the roles You give us and to honor You by using them to bless others. Amen.
—John Dilworth

Digging Deeper: Romans 12:6–8; 1 Corinthians 12:12–26

July

LET US SING FOR JOY

1 _____

2 _____

3 _____

4 _____

5 _____

6 _____

7 _____

8 _____

9 _____

10 _____

11 _____

12 _____

13 _____

14 _____

15 _____

July

16 _____

17 _____

18 _____

19 _____

20 _____

21 _____

22 _____

23 _____

24 _____

25 _____

26 _____

27 _____

28 _____

29 _____

30 _____

31 _____

AUGUST

Rejoice in the Lord always; again I will say,
rejoice! Let your gentle spirit be known to all
people. The Lord is near.

—Philippians 4:4–5 (NASB)

. . . and all the trees of the field shall clap their hands. —Isaiah 55:12 (KJV)

I am a dendrophile, a lover of trees. I study them, grow them, and sing their praises.

In the past, I felt sorry for trees because wherever they are planted is where they will spend their entire lives. Personally, I would go mad if I couldn't move around, but trees are clever at thriving wherever the acorn fell.

A tree that springs up in shade, for example, may simply produce more and larger leaves and send branches out far and wide, seeking stray sunbeams. In so doing, it becomes an unusually beautiful tree. A tree planted in poor, dry soil might send roots out a hundred feet in every direction, seeking moisture and nutrients, and good roots make a tree as strong as iron.

Mulberry trees grow everywhere around our town, in strange places. Along fences, where birds dropped seeds. In sidewalk cracks and peeking through sidewalk gratings. They grow out of drainpipes and junked cars. I've even seen them flourishing in roof gutters!

Doomed to be small, because of their poor location, they are nonetheless pretty trees, with glossy, lobed leaves and delicate caramel branches, loaded with dark purple berries that birds fight over.

There are times when I feel like a tree, trapped in an aging body, stuck in a small town, living on a modest pension, and I get to feeling sorry for myself. But from watching trees, I am learning to "clap my hands" in praise to God for the blessings I enjoy right here, where I am planted.

Help me to trust You, Lord, that where I am is right where
I should be, for now.
—Daniel Schantz

Digging Deeper: Psalm 1:1–3, 148:7–12

Wednesday, August 2

"I will give you a new heart and put a new spirit in you . . ."
—Ezekiel 36:26 (NIV)

The morning had finally arrived when I'd hear the results of my echocardiogram. My brother had recently been diagnosed with heart disease, and I was beyond nervous. The past year, nearly every system of my body had been affected by a medication mishap. Anemia, overwhelming weakness and fatigue, and shortness of breath had sent me to the cardiologist.

I looked up to see the man himself sauntering into the exam room. "Roberta!" he said. "A patient I get to give good news to today." To my astonishment, I had no evidence of permanent heart damage. All of my meds had been discontinued, and my physical assessment was perfect. "I feel like I have a new heart," I told him.

As I stood to leave, the nurse and I got to talking about the beautiful facility. "I used to cheer games here," she said. "This was the old Fairfield Stadium, you know." The years fell away, and I was back on those bleachers on May 29, 1963. Not for a ballgame but a Billy Graham crusade. A pig-tailed nine-year-old, I joined the crowd headed to the makeshift altar to give my heart to Jesus. It was—and is—the best decision I've ever made.

The cardiologist popped his head back in the door. "I needed to tell you something," I said. "This isn't the first time I've received a new heart on these grounds." His eyes twinkled as I recounted my best heart change of all.

> *How I praise You, dear Lord. Is there anything You can't make brand-new?*
> —Roberta Messner

Digging Deeper: 1 Samuel 10:9; Ezekiel 11:19, 18:31; 2 Corinthians 5:17

BUILDING CATHEDRALS: Holding onto Hope

If we endure, we will also reign with him. If we disown him, he will also disown us. —2 Timothy 2:12 (NIV)

It's totally gone!" my friend Haley texted us. The fort she had built for her kids by hand had fallen victim to a recent storm, which landed a tree square across its somehow still standing roof.

I felt terrible for Haley. Not only had she worked so hard to design and build the play structure, but she had also found great joy in watching her kids spend hours in the backyard becoming ship captains, mountain climbers, and tiny families all from the safety of their imagination, and their fort.

I wrote Haley back that night to ask how the day had gone. Had her children been upset? Was the mess too much for her to clean up without professional help?

"You won't believe it," she said. "I thought for sure they would be devastated, but they walked out to look at the debris, then came back in and said, 'Mom! Now it's a fairy house! Is it safe to play in? Can we?'"

The second round of pictures she sent us showed how she had removed the tree but left smaller branches for the kids to arrange, which they happily did, creating a woodland oasis in the middle of a neighborhood backyard. And her kids? Right in the middle, covered in ribbons and glitter from their upcycled crafting.

I learn a lot from children every day, and on this particular day, I learned that where I can see demise and destruction, they can see hope and opportunity. They remind me to always take a glance and consider the possibilities, even when all seems lost.

Dear God, please help my eyes to see and my heart to know that You can make all things beautiful, even when it seems hope is lost.
—Ashley Kappel

Digging Deeper: Psalm 37:24; Romans 5:3–4; James 1:12

Friday, August 4

As Jesus passed along the Sea of Galilee, he saw Simon and his brother Andrew casting a net into the sea—for they were fishermen. And Jesus said to them, "Follow me and I will make you fish for people."
—Mark 1:16–17 (NRSV)

Charlie and I have been discussing where to live during our "ancient" years, as we only half-jokingly refer to the near future. We've visited some fantastic places and enjoyed them all. But for me, it comes down to one thing: water.

I want to live near water—not a little pond or creek but moving, living water. From my childhood, I've associated Jesus with water. Our family Bible had glorious illustrations: His Baptism in the Jordan, calling the disciples from their fishing boats, preaching on the Sea of Galilee's shores, *walking* on its waves, stilling the storm. I've always felt that being near the water was being near Him, and it's no accident that we've always lived within view of moving water.

Here, in New London, Connecticut, our view of the Thames River, Long Island Sound, and an active shoreline offers me many opportunities to expand my too-often self-involved prayers and raise up others. When the Coast Guard ship *The Eagle* is docked at home, I pray for the young sailors and their teachers. When boats patrol the shore by submarine maker Electric Boat, I pray for the plant's workers and the naval guards. When the fishing fleet heads out, I pray for a safe, successful catch. As ferries steam to and from Long Island, I pray for the commuters and vacationers. When I glimpse a submarine slide under the surface, headed out to no-one-can-know-where, I pray for the families, a safe mission, and peace.

When we finally discern where God wills us to live out our ancient years, it may just be right here.

> *God, Who made the sea and land, thank You for daily reminders of our reliance on Your Will.*
> —Marci Alborghetti

Digging Deeper: Habakkuk 2:14; Luke 8:22–25

Does not the ear test words as the palate tastes food? Wisdom is with the aged, and understanding in length of days. —Job 12:11–12 (ESV)

My friend, whom I call Karla, and I go way back. I value our relationship and yet acknowledge that I've never worked so hard to maintain a friendship. She occasionally brings up past conversations, in tone or words misreading my motives or intentions. I'd slighted her; it was my fault. Over decades, I've grown afraid that I might misstep, and yet I persist.

One night, I called her. "The movie *Man for All Seasons* just started on PBS. Thought of you—that you might want to watch."

"Oh, thank you. But I have it on DVD—and, anyway, I'm streaming something else right now. I've put it on pause. How are you doing?"

"Well, fine, but I do want to watch this movie that's on, so we'll catch up later, okay?"

I phoned the next weekend and left a message. "Let's talk soon." When I didn't hear from her, I tried again a week later. I sensed a chill in her voice. She felt wounded. I tried to think back; where had I erred? "I called last Saturday and left a message. Did you get it?"

"Oh? No, I didn't," she answered before revealing my offense. "And the last time I called, you were busy and couldn't talk."

What? I spoke kindly but boldly: "No, I called you, to recommend a movie."

"Oh, yeah. That's right." Her warm acknowledgment settled like powdery sugar on my spirit. Fresh insights: Feelings of rejection can sour one's memory of events. Our misunderstandings aren't always my fault—though I'm likely responsible for my fair share. We all can reach out for grace.

Lord, give me wisdom and understanding to
maintain lifelong friendships.
—Evelyn Bence

Digging Deeper: Proverbs 2:1–11; 2 Timothy 2:7

Sunday, August 6

From him the whole body, joined and held together by every supporting ligament, grows and builds itself up in love, as each part does its work.
—Ephesians 4:16 (NIV)

I agree with the poster on that choir room wall, "To sing is to pray twice." I couldn't join the choir every week, but I always sang for our annual Gospel Sing Sunday. The entire service, including the sermon, was sung by the expanded choir.

One year, as we prepared for our first anthem, the minister read the morning announcements. I abruptly stopped arranging my music. He had announced the death, that morning, of a much-loved church member. I knew Vern had been ill with leukemia, but the news still came as a shock. I had seen him in church the previous Sunday!

The minister sat down, nodding to the choir. We slowly rose to our feet. I wondered where we would find the strength to do justice to "How Great Thou Art."

Through our tears, we began. Our individual voices were weak, they cracked, and at times they stopped altogether. But gradually I noticed a wondrous thing. When I faltered, my neighbor carried the tune. When she faltered, someone else sang out. Our voices held each other up, and gradually we grew stronger. We ended the hymn together, in pure resounding joy.

I'm convinced Vern was in that church, too, singing and praying with us. I could picture the heavenly choir surrounding him.

Dear Lord, thank You for my community of saints—friends and loved ones, here and in heaven—who support me every single day. Help me to support them as well.
—Leanne Jackson

Digging Deeper: Genesis 28:3; Exodus 32:18; Ephesians 6:7

Do not be conformed to this world, but be transformed by the renewing of your minds, so that you may discern what is the will of God—what is good and acceptable and perfect. —Romans 12:2 (NRSV)

I recently had my regular appointment with my dentist for a cleaning and checkup. As always, there was that pause in between the two, when the hygienist had finished her work, telling me, "The doctor will be in to see you shortly," and I sat in the chair, wondering: *What's he doing? Looking over my chart or finishing up with another patient?*

Okay, a dental appointment is something most people dread, but I really like my dentist. He's an interesting guy, passionate about his trade. We often talk about his kids, two of whom live in Israel. Truth to tell, he knows a lot about me. What could be more intimate than staring inside someone's mouth?

What was I going to do while I waited? I still had the bib around my neck. It would be awkward to get up and get something out of my bag on the floor. Then I thought about a Bible verse I'd read that morning. Could I still remember it? I closed my eyes for a minute. *Be transformed by the renewing of your minds . . .*

I concentrated, let go, imagined the renewing of my mind even as I could hear the dentist's drill in another room and the hygienist working on another patient. Renewing, cleaning, redoing. Giving up my own power for the divine power to do that. Something far beyond me.

Then I opened my eyes and looked down at an electrical cord plugged into a socket. *Plugged in,* I thought. Yes, that was exactly it. Being plugged in. Even here, even now.

Just then my dentist walked in. "How are you doing, Rick? So good to see you." It was good to see him.

> *Keep me plugged in to Your ways, Lord, no matter where*
> *I am and what I'm doing.*
> —Rick Hamlin

Digging Deeper: Psalm 23:1–2; John 3:5

Tuesday, August 8

You make known to me the path of life; you will fill me with joy in your presence, with eternal pleasures at your right hand. —Psalm 16:11 (NIV)

My friend, Wally, enjoys posting videos on Facebook of her cooking, walking on the beach, and dancing. A recent video she posted caught my attention: She is looking directly at the camera. I tapped my phone to watch and listen to the video. Wally shared that earlier in the day she went to the doctor for her annual cancer checkup. She is now cancer-free. I was elated for Wally and thanked the good Lord for the wonderful news.

Wally was filled with great joy but also shared her sadness in not being able to celebrate this moment with her mother. Several years ago, her mom, Elizabeth, was diagnosed with cancer. Elizabeth's diagnosis is what prompted Wally to check herself. When the report came back, cancer was detected. Wally began her treatments and over the years continued to go for her annual treatment. This was her fifth year of treatments, and she was now cancer-free. Elizabeth passed away a few years ago.

Wally shared her perspective on the situation. "I celebrate the goodness of God even if my mom died. Because the goodness of God is not in the outcome." Wally paused, and continued. "The goodness of God is in the awareness of His presence and what that does in our lives." She recalled how the presence of God brought comfort when her mother died and gave her strength and hope as she battled her own illness.

Friends on Facebook celebrated with her and shared their comments on the post. Many like me were touched by Wally's words, ". . . the goodness of God is not in the outcome . . . it's in the awareness of His presence and what that does in our lives."

Lord, thank You for Your presence that gives us hope and strength.
—Pablo Diaz

Digging Deeper: Psalm 30:11; Romans 8:28

"So I gave you a land on which you did not toil and cities you did not build; and you live in them and eat from vineyards and olive groves that you did not plant." —Joshua 24:13 (NIV)

It was our second summer in our new home when we realized the gift we'd been given. The move into this home had been difficult. Our previous house, the one we designed, built, and turned into a home—the place where we'd raised our children—was now occupied by another family. We hoped they would come to love it as we did.

We contemplated cutting down three small trees in our new backyard. Last summer, all they did was grow leaves. No blossoms, just leaves. Their shape was unappealing, and they were too small to provide shade. They had to go.

This spring, however, before I cranked up the chainsaw, something happened. Pretty pink blossoms told us we had more than we realized. The blossoms soon gave way to small, hard fruits. We had no idea what they were, so our family had fun watching them grow.

A few weeks later, we began harvesting the most delicious peaches any of us had ever tasted. A bumper crop. Day after day, we picked a dozen or more amazingly sweet, succulent peaches. More than we could eat. More than we could bake into pies and cobblers. Soon, we were giving them away.

"Well, I guess moving here wasn't all bad," Josie said. "God's grace came through again."

"Right," I said. "And we didn't work for it one bit."

> *Thank You, Lord, for blessings I didn't work for, never expected, and didn't earn.*
> —Bill Giovannetti

Digging Deeper: Deuteronomy 6:10–12

Thursday, August 10

A gentle tongue is a tree of life . . . —Proverbs 15:4 (ESV)

I've never attended an anger management workshop nor has anyone ever suggested it. But people have commented at times on my sharp tongue. And that when I am angry my nostrils flare, as in:

JULEE: Edward, are you mad about something?

ME: No!

JULEE: Your nostrils are flaring.

My nostrils and tongue aside, I'm as capable of losing it as the next person. The other day a delivery driver came roaring up our driveway in reverse. What if my beloved golden retriever, Gracie, had been out snoozing in the driveway as is her wont? I had some very sharp words for that driver as I snatched the package out of his hands. I didn't even say thank you. Just turned and stomped into the house. I guess I told him.

Right. Until I had trouble getting to sleep that night. I'd been kind of a jerk to that man, one of the regular drivers.

A few days later, he was back with another delivery. "I'm sorry I flew off the handle the other day," I said. "I was just worried about Gracie."

"Oh, I always keep an eye out for Gracie," he said, which makes sense because he delivers her food every month and has thereby attained superhero status in her eyes. "I backed in because of where your car was parked. I couldn't have turned around. Don't worry about it." With that, he gave Gracie a treat from behind his seat and was off.

Yes, sometimes it feels good to lose it. You know what feels better? Apologizing for it.

Lord, I try to keep my tongue civil and my nostrils unflared. When I fail, please bless me with the strength and wisdom to admit my wrong and make it right.

—Edward Grinnan

Digging Deeper: Proverbs 16:24; Ephesians 4:32

"And I will be a father to you, And you shall be sons and daughters to Me . . ."—2 Corinthians 6:18 (NASB)

Hey, Papa, let's start a band . . ."

As a longtime songwriter and musician, I've made friends around the world. Made records. Shared stages with my musical heroes. But I have to say I don't think I've ever had as much fun as I have playing music with my son.

Hey, I'm the old guy. I've (literally) been down this road a dozen times before. But I step on stage with him and his pals, and a few songs in, my face hurts from smiling. They're fantastic players; they really are. I watch my son there in the lights, tearing up some guitar part that literally boggles my mind and I have to scratch my head—man, what am I even doing here?

Later, I lie in the dark while the world sleeps. It's been a bit, I realize, since I talked to my own heavenly Father.

"You there?"

"*Have I ever not been?*"

"Did you see him play tonight?"

"*I did.*"

"The kid's left me in the dust. He definitely doesn't need me."

"*He always needs you.*"

"You know what I mean. Up there on stage."

We're quiet for a while. It's nice how we don't have to fill all the space, how simply *being* is enough.

After a bit I break the silence. "You know what? The only reason I can come up with is that he actually likes spending time with me."

There's no condemnation in the gentle laugh, just pure, overwhelming love. "*Imagine that—a child wanting to spend time . . . Yes, isn't that the best?*"

Thank You, God, for being an ever-present, faithful Father to this too-often wandering prodigal. Your arms are my home.
—Buck Storm

Digging Deeper: Proverbs 23:22; Luke 15:20

Saturday, August 12

Hot tempers start fights; a calm, cool spirit keeps the peace.
—Proverbs 15:18 (MSG)

I pulled on a pair of leather gloves and mumbled as I pitched chunks of firewood into the bucket on the tractor. I'd coordinated a gift exchange, and the volunteers who had promised me that they would help never showed up. *Once again* I ended up doing the whole thing by myself. Cutting thoughts of what I could say to the no-show volunteers swirled through my head with each toss.

I glanced up at Sunrise, my elderly, nearly blind and nearly deaf golden retriever, and lectured, "And you be nice to that cat." Recently I'd adopted Stealth, a tomcat from the humane society. Even though he was extremely affectionate toward me and shadowed me everywhere I went, his personality was of a full-sized lion stuffed into a twelve-pound body—vicious. He was perfect for a barn cat—except Sunrise hated cats. I wasn't sure how they'd get along, so I'd brought Sunrise outside while I worked so I could supervise.

Out of the corner of my eye, I watched Stealth sneak toward us with his eyes focused on the dog. When Sunrise looked toward Stealth, the cat would freeze mid-stride, just like in the game Simon Says. As soon as Sunrise looked away, the cat gained ground. He knew she was nearly blind! Soon he jumped up on the tall fence post by me and meowed, like he'd achieved a masterful feat.

I ruffled his fur and marveled. "Stealth, you're a pretty smart cat. Instead of confronting the dog, you worked through the situation." Throughout the rest of the afternoon, I pondered how I could do that. And came up with a solution.

Lord, when I'm tempted to get angry with someone, help me to remember to practice the "Stealth Approach." Amen.
—Rebecca Ondov

Digging Deeper: Proverbs 10:12, 26:21

I can do all things through Him who strengthens me.
—Philippians 4:13 (NASB)

I have a hard time knowing what to give my grandchildren for their birthdays. But this year, I knew exactly what to give Gracie for her twelfth birthday. She was about to start middle school, which can be a confusing time of fluctuating self-confidence. Yet I know she is remarkably bright and capable.

For instance, at our house recently she was playing with one of those plastic handheld puzzles with numbers 1 to 15 on little squares that you move around to get them in numerical order. When I try, I get frustrated and give up, calling it impossible. When Gracie picked it up, she kept fiddling until all the numbers were in place.

"You're amazing!" I told her. "I can't do that!" Then I hid the puzzle in a special place so no one could undo what she had just done.

As Gracie's birthday approached, I glued that perfectly completed handheld puzzle into a shadow box with the words, "Always remember, Gracie, you can do hard things!"

When she opened the gift, she seemed a little confused that I'd framed the puzzle, but I told her I wanted her to always remember that she could do hard things.

After school started, her mom took a video of Gracie sitting at her desk in her bedroom, struggling over some homework, but she looked up to see the shadow box on the wall and said, "I remember! I can do hard things!" Her mom sent me the obviously rehearsed message, which gave the gift of those words back to me. Now I often remind myself that "I can do hard things, too."

> *Lord, You give us strength and courage to do hard*
> *things; thank You for the reminders.*
> —Carol Kuykendall

Digging Deeper: Joshua 1:1–9; Isaiah 40:29–31

Monday, August 14

For every house is built by someone, but God is the builder of everything.
—Hebrews 3:4 (NIV)

When we first bought our house years ago, my sister, Maria, stood on the side porch and said, "This little porch would be brilliant screened-in. You could have your morning coffee here and watch the sun rise."

All these years later, her idea is finally unfolding. My husband begins work, slowly and methodically measuring and figuring out angles. The house is old and anything but level and square, so if you want to make things look right you have to work with the imperfections.

On the edge of the porch foundation is the cornerstone where someone over a century ago chiseled in the date 1867. I have researched the history of the house going back deed by deed. The property has only had five owners in its long existence. It was a fruit farm for a while, and some of the ancient apple trees are still in the yard, gnarled and old, bearing fruit that is hard and sour, but the deer eat it anyway.

When the last of the screen is nailed in place, the final white paint completed on the framework, and the new, fresh coat of paint on the floor no longer sticky, I bring out the wicker chairs inherited from a beloved friend.

The next morning, I wake up early before everyone else, go out on the porch, and sip my coffee just as first light peeks over the treetops in rays of glorious light.

"Brilliant!"

Dear Lord, thank You for my home—for my husband, who made this dream of mine come true; for my sister, who planted this seed of this perfect place long ago; and for the beauty of this morning.
—Sabra Ciancanelli

Digging Deeper: 2 Samuel 7:29; Proverbs 24:27

So teach us to number our days, That we may present to You a heart of wisdom. —Psalm 90:12 (NASB)

Here he comes," I said as I sat on the back porch watching a gray squirrel navigate the trees above my head, bounding from one branch to another as he traversed the leaf-covered highway. With a flick of his long, white-fringed tail, he grabbed a peanut from the bird feeder and whisked it away, returning to his home in a standing—but dead—ponderosa pine.

"That entire trunk must be filled with nuts by now," my husband, Kevin, commented. "He's been collecting peanuts all summer."

And not only peanuts. When we had torn down an old shed earlier that year, we had discovered the walls and insulation filled with acorns. As a scatter-hoarder, the gray squirrel had hidden his caches in several locations, so he had necessary food stored for the long winter. His powerful sense of smell would help him locate his food later, even under the snow.

But when was enough *enough*? The squirrel seemed to have no stop button, going and going, gathering and gathering.

"He's coming again," Kevin said.

I glanced up from the to-do list I was writing to watch the little fellow's antics as he scampered past a pair of stellar jays who also had eyes on the birdseed. They scolded each other as they each raced for the peanut prize.

"Relax. There's plenty to go around," I said as I stretched my stiff back. My gaze returned to my never-ending list of projects and tasks. When was enough *enough*?

"Want to go for a walk?"

"Good idea." I set aside my list just as the squirrel grabbed another peanut.

Jesus, there is time every day to do Your will. Help me know when to say, "Enough" and take a break.
                                    —Lynne Hartke

Digging Deeper: Psalm 39:4–5, 103:13–17

Wednesday, August 16

Cast all your anxiety on him because he cares for you. —1 Peter 5:7 (NIV)

My husband and I deliberated a while about getting rid of our landline, which I used only for calling friends abroad since it was cheaper than using my cell phone. Then I got a plan that let me call anywhere for the same price. Kris still wanted to keep the landline, though, for possible middle-of-the-night-emergency calls from our daughters, Charlotte and Lulu. We turn our cell phones off at night.

But, I argued, Lulu hates phoning. To chat, we use her gaming app, wearing headphones she gave Kris and me one Christmas that light up in bright colors, like we're wacky astronauts calling from outer space. And we may as well be. As Charlotte points out, she'd never call us in an emergency: "It's not like you could help from two thousand miles away!"

So, we got rid of the land line. Kris leaves his cell phone on all night, despite wrong numbers and clients so uncouth as to call after nine. I like having only one phone to manage, one number, one place where everything I need to know is located.

Then, coming home from birding one day, I dropped my iPhone in our cattleguard, a deep water-filled hole in our driveway covered with gridiron to keep cows from crossing. In my own minor emergency, voiceless and cut off from even Kris, I prayed an inane prayer—"Oh, Father, let it not be dead!"—and trudged home, hopeless.

Later, thinking even a dead phone might have trade-in value, I got Kris's grilling tongs, lay on the cattleguard, and fished it out. Amazingly, it was still on—a technological miracle, surely, that nevertheless reminded me God hears even my silliest pleas.

Father, what a delight it is that You're always nearby,
always eager to hear from me!
—Patty Kirk

Digging Deeper: Acts 17:26–28

Open my eyes to see wonderful things in your Word. —Psalm 119:18 (TLB)

When the small print in my Bible danced across the page in an unreadable blob, I knew a trip to the eye doctor ranked high on my list of activities this week. Sure enough, he confirmed what I suspected—I needed bifocals. My distance vision was fine, but anything within arm's length required magnification, unless my arms suddenly grew another two feet.

A week later, I sported the latest style in frameless glasses, but the optician warned me most people experienced a period of adjustment. She cautioned me to be careful on steps since my depth perception might be altered.

For several days, I held handrails like a vise grip as my eyes adapted to looking down through the lenses. A quick improvement was seeing the words in my Bible again, and I celebrated with reading all the scriptures referencing sight and eyes. In these verses, I found life instructions and cautions similar to those given by the eye specialists for wearing my new glasses.

Watch where I step, stay on solid ground, and don't hesitate to call if I had questions. Had I seen these words of wisdom before? Maybe. But now I better understood their meaning because I saw them through personal experience and clearer vision.

Lord, open my eyes to the treasures in Your Word and show me how to apply them in my life. Help me to live a life pleasing to You.
—Jenny Lynn Keller

Digging Deeper: Psalm 121:1–3; Proverbs 4:25–27; Hebrews 4:13

Friday, August 18

The earth was without form and void, and darkness was over the face of the deep. And the Spirit of God was hovering over the face of the waters.
—Genesis 1:2 (ESV)

I grabbed my children's telescope at sunset and headed out to the porch. With my unaided sight to the southwest, I could see what seemed like two stars very close together. I knew these were not stars but rather Jupiter and Saturn. They were as close to earth as they had been in eight hundred years! The sight filled me with wonder and awe even without the enhanced view through the telescope.

It turns out the telescope is not very intuitive to use, nor easy. It took lots of meticulous pointing, readjusting, and finding the right lens. Then, finally, as I looked into the lens, I saw a glimpse of a striated pattern. What was that? Was the telescope really so powerful that I could see the surface of the planet? I had lost it as easily as I had found it. I maneuvered again. This time instead of calling my family, who were annoyed I had lost it so easily, I just gazed at the planet's surface. This brightness shone in the vast darkness of space. All I could conjure was God. God, in His infinite presence, with no words, just awe.

I behold the work of God, in the vastness of space where wonder and awe fill me because I am aware of God's omnipotence. In this moment, I love God, because I know in His greatness and grandeur, He cares and loves me as Father. Wonder and awe fill my soul, because He loves little, old, and imperfect me.

Father, Creator of the universe, nurture in me the wonder and awe in all my eyes behold. I ask this in the name of Jesus. Amen.
—Jolynda Strandberg

Digging Deeper: Exodus 20:21; Job 11:16–18; John 4:46–48

Above all, love each other deeply, because love covers over a multitude of sins. —1 Peter 4:8 (NIV)

Six-year-old Shea was intensely focused on completing her art assignment: a self-portrait illustrating a real-life superpower that she possessed. As she sketched, my granddaughter explained that her "special gift" was her ability to eat a lot of sweets. I had to laugh, but on the inside, I cringed. I saw so many more admirable strengths in my granddaughter, such as creativity, musicality, and empathy. But this was her project, so I simply smiled and kept my mouth shut.

"Do you know what I think your superpower is, Mimsy?" Shea asked. I fully anticipated her saying, "Being able to eat even more sweets than me!" Instead, she responded, "I think your superpower is being kind!"

Surprised, flattered, and humbled, I rather sheepishly replied, "Well, thank you, Shea, but you know Mimsy isn't always kind. Sometimes I get angry or tired and say things that aren't very kind. Things I don't mean."

Shea stopped drawing, looked me straight in the eye, and said as seriously as a six-year-old can, "Mimsy, you're a lot kinder than you think you are."

I was taken aback. I wondered if the real me, the "Mimsy" God sees, more closely resembled Shea's version of me or my own. According to 1 Peter 4:8, perhaps both versions of me are true. Because I love my granddaughter, I see the best in her. Because she loves me, she sees me through eyes of love, just as my heavenly Father does when He looks at both my granddaughter and me.

Father, help me see others through Your eyes—the eyes of
love—and treat them accordingly.
—Vicki Kuyper

Digging Deeper: Romans 14:1; Colossians 3:12–14; Hebrews 10:24

Sunday, August 20

Jesus has been found worthy of greater honor than Moses, just as the builder of a house has greater honor than the house itself. —Hebrews 3:3 (NIV)

When I turned seventy-five, I wondered if I'd made my three-quarters-of-a-century life meaningful and worthwhile. Two months later, I was reorganizing my bookshelf and found two small hardback books published in 1893, 130 years ago. One, believe it or not, was titled *What Is Worthwhile* and it had my grandmother's name, Pearl Barclay, and the date, 1909, handwritten inside the cover. The other, titled *Love and Friendship,* had my grandfather's name, Porter Knapp, and the same date, 1909, written in his handwriting.

I can only assume they were gifts to each other three years before they got married in June 1912. In the *What Is Worthwhile* book, Grandma Pearl (who died when my mother was ten, so I never knew her) had underlined a few things that she thought important, including, "We may drop pretense. We may drop worry. We may let go discontent. We may let go of self-seeking."

When I finished reading that little book, I wondered if I was false or insincere, a worrywart, discontent with my life, or self-seeking. The answer was yes to all of those, at least on a number of occasions.

As a retired widow whose four children and nine grandchildren all live thousands of miles from me in five different states, I often give in to worry and discontent. But then I noticed that Grandma Pearl had also underlined, "Let us lay hold of faith. Faith, Christian faith, holds the key to the blessedness of the eternal life."

Heavenly Father, thank You for the nudges from my ancestors who no doubt struggled as I do and then moved on to eternity with You. Grant me the same deep faith they had.
—Patricia Lorenz

Digging Deeper: Matthew 10:37–38; Mark 1:7–8; Ephesians 4:1–3; Colossians 1:9–10

. . . But the LORD *was my support.* —2 Samuel 22:19 (NASB)

The phone call was unexpected and upsetting. "I didn't get the job." It was a dream position for a beloved family member. The rigorous application process successfully completed. The personal teaching video well received. Hours of work in each. There was the detailed internet interview. And later the new boss's encouraging words, "We knew after your interview we wanted to hire you first."

The former job was over—with the invitation, "Come back anytime." My family member had thought that wouldn't be necessary. Training for the dream position began in a week.

Then the crushing moment. Tripped up in the last requirement. A six-month hiring delay. Back to the previous less-fulfilling job. Thankful it was there—yet devastated over the loss, hopefully temporary, of the new one.

What encouragement could I bring? I thought of Jesus's disciple Peter. It was night. He and the others were rowing against the wind in the Sea of Galilee. Jesus came walking toward them on the water, which frightened them.

Peter wanted Jesus to call him to come to Him, if it was really Him. He did, and Peter started out on the waves just fine. But then he looked around at the storm and got scared and began to sink. He took his eyes off Jesus.

"This is a time to 'walk on water,'" I told my distraught family member. It was a time to keep Jesus front and center amid the waves of disappointment that threatened. A time for trusting Him to provide in the now and to bring about the best future outcome.

> *Lord, when the storm assails—with my eyes on You*
> *alone—make me a "wave walker."*
> —Carol Knapp

Digging Deeper: Matthew 14:22–32; Hebrews 12:1–2; James 1:2

Tuesday, August 22

And if your foot causes you to sin, cut it off. It is better for you to enter life lame than with two feet to be thrown into hell. —Mark 9:45 (ESV)

My puppy, Danny, cut his leg on some sharp metal.

I won't get into the gory details, but there was a lot of blood, a lot of screaming (by me), and eight hard-fought staples done by our skilled vet, who certainly earned her paycheck dealing with a wild, exuberant, wiggling puppy who wouldn't hold still.

A few weeks later, we went to the vet to get the staples out and she looked concerned. The actual cut had healed up fine, but the leg was really swollen and the puppy wasn't using it at all. She put him on a round of strong antibiotics and told me that we'd watch it for a few weeks and if it didn't heal, we'd talk about amputation.

I laughed. The good ol' we'll-just-cut-it-off joke.

"No, I'm serious," the vet said. "With injuries like this, oftentimes the dog is better off amputating the leg. Instead of enduring months of surgeries and pain, it's often better for the dog just to cut it off. And cheaper, too."

I was shocked. After asking a few more questions and consulting Doctor Google, I found out that my vet wasn't wrong. Most dogs are perfectly fine with just three legs, and extensive knee surgery costs upward of $10,000 and is painful and hard on dogs.

Fortunately, little Danny recovered in the end; today he has all four legs and just a bit of a limp. But I wonder what appendages in my own life I'd be better without. I'll keep my legs (thank you), but I wonder which habits, which relationships, which worldly things are dragging me down, costing me way more than they are worth.

> *Lord, show me the areas of my life that I need to cut out so that I can be closer to You.*
> —Erin MacPherson

Digging Deeper: 1 Kings 13:34; Jeremiah 51:62

Greater love has no one than this: to lay down one's life for one's friends.
—John 15:13 (NIV)

When I was in my twenties, I went to my father's hometown in Puerto Rico. I had a great interest in my roots and wanted to feel connected to my grandfather, who died when my father was just a child.

The stories my relatives from the island told were the same ones I already knew. He was a baker and built an outdoor stove made of heavy stones; he'd walk to town with bundles of goods to sell, but often came home with the bundles unsold. My father remembers him breaking down in tears after one of these trips.

I came back home to New York City not knowing much more about him than I already had.

Recently I had a renewed interest in researching my roots and found more than I could imagine. In one census, my grandfather's occupation is listed as "vendor of sweets." Seeing it in writing made it real, and now being a baker myself made the connection extra special.

But the one thing I found that helped me know my grandfather the most was his certificate of death. We never knew how he died at such a young age, and the words written in beautiful Spanish script spoke volumes: "pernicious anemia, nutritional deficiency." I could imagine my grandfather going without so his family could have more, sacrificing himself for their survival.

I had never felt so close to my grandfather as when reading those four heartbreaking words. That sacrifice was a gift for his family. It was his gift for me.

Father, thank You first of all for the sacrifice You made for me, and thank You for those in my life who followed Your example of sacrificial love. Help me to love others this way.
—Karen Valentin

Digging Deeper: Psalm 103:13; Luke 11:11

Thursday, August 24

THE PINK HOUSE: A Surprise Lily

Consider the lilies . . . —Matthew 6:28 (KJV)

Evening is falling across the lake as David and I arrive at the little cabin my father built. We, along with our children and grandchildren, love this place, but keeping it comes at a cost. We are here because there's work to be done: grass to mow, gutters to clean, leaks to fix, and more.

As morning breaks, I rise quickly and part the curtains for a first glimpse of the lake. But my eyes are diverted by a patch of surprise lilies that have popped up during the night. Long ago, in his playful way, Daddy planted the lilies, knowing they would appear, always quickly and unexpectedly.

After breakfast, David and I get busy.

Is it worth all this, not to mention the money it takes to keep this place going? I whine to myself while we work. *How long can we keep doing this?*

Then the lilies, as bright as the morning sun, catch my eye.

Like the long-ago pink house that served as a guide on my way home, they point me toward the place I want to be.

The cabin was a gift from Daddy, just as sure as each of our lives are a gift from our Father, God. Is it a never-ending effort to keep life sorted out and live on the bright side?

Yep.

But the lilies remind us that beyond the work, we'll find swimming, fishing, long night walks sprinkled with lightning bugs and singing frogs. Daddy planned the cabin for this, just as surely as God planned for our lives to be full. Our job is to heed His signposts, look for His lilies, and follow His path.

Father God, surprise us with Your lilies, make us mindful
of Your guideposts, guide us on.
—Pam Kidd

Digging Deeper: Psalm 34:4; Matthew 6:24–28

Let your eyes look directly forward, and your gaze be straight before you.
—Proverbs 4:25 (ESV)

We've left our son Samuel at college for the first time. When we said goodbye, he asked for one more hug. His arms went around me, and I felt the pounding of his heart. Now, as we drive away, I think of how it used to beat under my own.

My husband, Lonny, reaches over and takes my hand. It's warm and covering and familiar. I need this. I don't like this new terrain.

I want our car to be full again.

I remember when our old white Suburban was filled to the brim with boys. When I'd look back from the front seat, they'd fill the rows. In my mind, I see those blond boys, bangs too long, skin toasted brown by the sun. I don't even know why I twist in my seat now. I have to see the emptiness to believe it.

As I do, my phone rings.

"Hey, Mom," my oldest son says. "Have you dropped Sam off? How are you?"

Before I can respond, my phone pings. It's a text from my second-born son. "Just checking in, Mom," the text reads. "I love you. Holding up okay?"

And my heart breaks in my chest.

It's my boys who've reached out to me, but through them I feel the Lord's love. It was strong in Samuel's hug. It's in the spoken words of one son and in the typed words of another. His love is a voice, strong and calm, that speaks over the ache and chaos that's in my soul.

You don't have to look back. You can walk forward. I'm with you every step of the way.

> *Lord, You enable me to look and move forward rather*
> *than back. Oh, how I love You.*
> —Shawnelle Eliasen

Digging Deeper: Deuteronomy 31:8; 1 Kings 8:57; Hebrews 13:6

Saturday, August 26

"For the LORD sees not as man sees: man looks on the outward appearance, but the LORD looks on the heart." —1 Samuel 16:7 (ESV)

As I write this, there's a new trend on social media: creating avatars—computer artwork to represent what a person looks like. People have put a lot of time and effort into making their avatars appealing, with cute hairdos and outfits. Many have joked that the avatars represent not so much what people actually look like as what they wish they actually looked like.

At first, it amused me that anyone would take so much time on such a trivial pursuit, but I suppose it's not entirely different from what I do anytime I get ready to go somewhere. Don't I try to make my outward appearance as tidy as possible? Don't I try to look attractive for my husband? These aren't bad things in and of themselves, but I know I often worry far too much about my hair, my waistline, or whatever imperfection I happen to focus on that day.

All this attention to avatars makes me remember that our physical bodies are not who we really are. They're just outward representations people use to recognize us. Whether digital or flesh, these manifestations are just what people see, and if I'm honest with myself, who I am on the outside is fading away. I know that when my physical body perishes, my soul will live on, so I ought to spend a little more time cultivating that "gentle and quiet spirit, which is of great worth in God's sight" (1 Peter 3:4 [NIV]). I need to focus on how "the perishable must clothe itself with the imperishable" (1 Corinthians 15:53 [NIV]).

Nothing wrong with a cute avatar, but after all, it's just an avatar.

Father, I know someday You will transform us into bodies that will never die. Until then, help me focus on my soul.
—Ginger Rue

Digging Deeper: Matthew 16:26; 2 Corinthians 4:16

LETTING GO: Trusting God

Cast all your anxiety on him because he cares for you. —1 Peter 5:7 (NIV)

When Logan and I move next month, we're going to another state, probably out west. I'm thinking about Washington state, since my friend lives there," my son Cris said.

My breath caught, and I fumbled for a response. "That's a long way from Florida," I finally answered.

His announcement caught me off guard. Although my husband, Chuck, and I had prayed that one day our grandson Logan would live full time with his father, as the day drew near, I wasn't sure I was ready for Logan to move out, especially so far away.

Logan had been living with us for years—ever since he was three years old. After a mutual separation from Logan's mother, my son was granted custody of Logan. However, since Cris was a single man working two jobs, day and night, he asked us to be Logan's guardians for a while.

As a result, Chuck and I, newly retired and empty nesters, changed our schedules and rearranged our home and our lives to care for a young child. It was a big adjustment for us, but we loved Logan and wanted to provide the best possible home life for him.

For eight years, Logan only spent one day a week with his father while Chuck and I were the "parents" who cared for him 24/6.

I had thought I'd be happy when this day finally arrived—Chuck and I could get back to our empty-nest lives and spend more time with each other and our friends. Now that the time was here, my fears and doubts mounted about Logan's well-being. Would Cris take care of him as well as we had? I could only pray he would.

Lord, You are our heavenly Father, and You care for all Your children.
Please help me trust You to help Logan's father care for him.
—Marilyn Turk

Digging Deeper: Proverbs 3:5; Matthew 6:26–34

Monday, August 28

LETTING GO: Packing Memories
See, I am doing a new thing! —Isaiah 43:19 (NIV)

Mom, do you have more boxes?" my son Cris asked, holding an overflowing box.

"Chuck is checking the attic."

When Chuck came in with some boxes, I carried them to Logan's bedroom. I was shocked to see the room in shambles as he deconstructed it to move.

I swallowed the lump in my throat as Logan cleared his shelves of souvenirs from places we'd been, sports awards, and Lego creations, leaving only dust as he placed the items into a box.

Glancing at the other set of bookshelves, I asked, "Should I pack your books?"

"Yes, please. I'm taking everything that's mine." Everything we'd given him.

"Remember this one?" I said, holding up *One Fish Two Fish Red Fish Blue Fish*, his favorite Dr. Seuss book.

"Do you like my hat?" Logan said, repeating a familiar line from the book, one of the first he'd learned to read.

Logan talked excitedly about how he and Cris would set up their new home, looking forward to seeing his dream of living with his father come true.

Too soon, we were saying goodbye. "I'll talk to you later," Cris said. "Thanks for everything."

I hugged Logan one more time through the car window. And just like that, they were gone.

Thank You, Lord, for new beginnings, even though it's
hard to say goodbye to the past.
—Marilyn Turk

Digging Deeper: Jeremiah 29:11; Hebrews 13:8

LETTING GO: Resetting the Clock

This is the confidence we have in approaching God: that if we ask anything according to his will, he hears us. —1 John 5:14 (NIV)

It was that time again, time to buy school supplies.

Ever since my grandson Logan began kindergarten, I'd made trips to the store to purchase the necessary supplies. From crayons and washable markers in kindergarten all the way through notebooks and binders in the fifth grade, I had handled the task. I'd finally gotten the hang of it, buying early enough before the stores ran out.

But Logan didn't live with us anymore. He and his dad, my son Cris, moved into their own place two months ago. For the first time ever, Logan would start school from his dad's house, not ours. Did Cris know about school supplies? After all, he'd never had to buy them before.

"Should I go get Logan's school supplies?" I asked my husband, Chuck.

"That's not our job anymore," he said. "Cris can get them."

God, I sighed out a prayer, *give me wisdom. I don't want Logan to be unprepared for school.*

Just then my phone rang, and it was Cris.

"Mom, Logan's asking about school supplies. Shouldn't I wait until school starts to find out what he needs?"

"The stores might run out by then because most folks buy them early."

"But how do I know what to get?"

"Some stores have a list for each school. Or you can go to the school's website and find it."

"Okay, cool. Thanks, Mom."

I stared at the phone when the call ended. It was as if God had been listening to my conversation with Chuck. What a coincidence! I smiled. God had this.

Lord, Your timing is perfect because You're in control and I'm not.
—Marilyn Turk

Digging Deeper: Matthew 6:25–34; Luke 12:26–29

Wednesday, August 30

LETTING GO: Familiar Rituals
Jesus Christ is the same yesterday and today and forever.
—Hebrews 13:8 (NIV)

What are you looking for?' I asked my husband, Chuck, as he dug through the freezer.

He held up a box of frozen waffles. "These."

As he put two waffles in the toaster, I asked, "You're not eating cereal?"

"Not today. Somebody needs to eat these."

Chuck is set in his routines, especially when it comes to mealtimes. He eats cereal with orange juice every morning. So why was he eating waffles today? Because our grandson Logan wasn't there to eat them anymore. Logan was also a creature of habit and wanted waffles every day.

Now the fridge was full of the mandarin oranges Logan loved. And suddenly we had enough string cheese, another favorite of his, to last for months. We didn't have to buy those items anymore, much less plan our other meals around what Logan liked.

Other routines changed as well. We could go out for an evening without needing a babysitter. We could sleep later if we wanted to. In fact, we could go anywhere anytime we wanted without worrying about who was taking care of Logan.

We were free again, like empty nesters should be. So why was there an ache in my heart like a piece was missing? Sure, one more bird had left the nest, but the nest felt uncomfortably empty, and our new routine felt equally empty.

> *Lord, sometimes it's difficult to adjust to change, even if*
> *we know it's necessary. Comfort us in knowing that even*
> *when other things change, You do not.*
> —Marilyn Turk

Digging Deeper: Numbers 23:19; James 1:17

LETTING GO: God's Perfect Timing

There is a time for everything, and a season for every activity under the heavens. —Ecclesiastes 3:1 (NIV)

I headed to the adult pool the first day of our vacation to find a lounge chair, but they were all taken. However, there were other pools, so I went to one of those and claimed a chair. I sat down with my book, ready to zone out from the world around me. Then a voice called, "Grandma!" I instinctively looked up, thinking it was Logan's voice. But it wasn't. A pang of sadness bit my heart with the awareness.

I returned my attention to my book, determined to enjoy this vacation with my husband, Chuck, the first time in eight years it was just the two of us. When Chuck arrived at the pool and announced he was going down the giant slide on the beach, I grabbed my phone to video his adventure.

But standing at the bottom of the slide, guilt gripped me because Logan wasn't with us to enjoy the slide, too. Was it fair for us to take a vacation without him? Until now, he'd gone everywhere we went. And to think that at one time, we didn't see how we could travel *with* a young child.

"I guess we won't buy an RV," Chuck had said with resignation. He had looked forward to retiring and traveling. I hated to see him give up on his dream and prayed God would make things work out.

And God did. We bought a travel trailer comfortable for the three of us, planned our trips to coincide with school breaks, and made sure our destinations included children's activities.

God had surprised us by infusing our lives with the energy of a young child. We had adjusted then, and we'd adjust now.

Lord, thank You for our time with Logan. Show us how to enjoy being just a couple again.
—Marilyn Turk

Digging Deeper: Proverbs 16:9, 27:1; Ecclesiastes 3:11

LET US SING FOR JOY

1 _____

2 _____

3 _____

4 _____

5 _____

6 _____

7 _____

8 _____

9 _____

10 _____

11 _____

12 _____

13 _____

14 _____

15 _____

16 _____

17 _____

18 _____

19 _____

20 _____

21 _____

22 _____

23 _____

24 _____

25 _____

26 _____

27 _____

28 _____

29 _____

30 _____

31 _____

SEPTEMBER

*And they sang responsively, praising
and giving thanks to the LORD:
"For He is good, For His mercy
endures forever toward Israel."*

—Ezra 3:11 (NKJV)

LETTING GO: Perfect Peace

You will keep in perfect peace those whose minds are steadfast, because they trust in you. —Isaiah 26:3 (NIV)

I clicked through my computer photo file, looking at pictures of my grandson Logan through the years. I chuckled at the photo of him as a toddler climbing through the doggie door. The next picture showed him wearing his Superman cape, the next his Peter Pan costume, then one of him in his soccer uniform. One after another, the photos took me down memory lane as tears rolled down my cheeks.

How had the time gone by so quickly?

Another photo appeared. I stared at the picture of a sweet four-year-old's cherubic face sleeping on a white teddy bear as big as the child wearing Ninja Turtle pajamas.

I remember that night eight years ago, Logan's first Christmas with me and Chuck. How innocent he was—unaware of the problems that brought him to us in the first place.

He had been as guileless as the pure white teddy bear on which he lay. He slept without fear, he slept in peace, and he slept in our home.

When the authorities had asked us to keep him temporarily, we agreed. At the time, we had no idea how long "temporary" would be. Only the present was known, and Logan needed a home. So we provided that home until his father was able to provide one for him.

Logan started middle school this year, and this was the first Christmas he spent at his father's house instead of ours.

My heart wants to reach into that picture, hold that sleeping child close, and protect him forever. But my time for that is past. We gave Logan the peace of a loving home. Now I need to let God give me peace to let go of the past.

Lord, please let peace rule in our hearts to embrace a new future.
—Marilyn Turk

Digging Deeper: John 14:27; Romans 15:13

Saturday, September 2

Give thanks in all circumstances; for this is God's will for you in Christ Jesus. —1 Thessalonians 5:18 (NIV)

Recently I found myself complaining over the mounds of laundry I faced on a typical Saturday morning. My children range in age from thirteen to twenty-four, capable of managing their own laundry. *So why,* I wondered, *is there still so much laundry to do?* After more than a few minutes of griping, I flashed back to a conversation I'd had in Ghana, West Africa. My husband, Anthony, and I had spent a week there on a mission trip a decade ago.

In Ghana, I had enjoyed connecting with another mom who, like me, was raising young children. Even though she had grown up on the other side of the world, I marveled at the many similarities we shared. One day we were discussing the arduous task of laundry—how laundry appeared to multiply minutes after washing several loads. I commiserated with fervor, grateful for another mom who understood my laundry woes.

A few minutes into my tirade, she mentioned softly, in her beautiful Ghanaian accent, "I'm sure laundry is hard for you too, but you probably have a washing machine. Here, we wash our clothing by hand."

Stunned to silence, I paused for several moments, rightfully convicted. She was right. Although the laundry of a six-person household is no small task, as a middle-class American, I have the luxury of an appliance to do much of the work for me.

During my recent laundry ranting, I remembered the teachable moment with this wise, but gracious, mom. It reminds me that I am blessed and should live with a heart full of gratefulness. Even for my bottomless piles of laundry.

> *Lord, may I learn humbly from others, complain less, and thank You more.*
> —Carla Hendricks

Digging Deeper: Psalm 34:1, 118:29; Ephesians 5:20

BUILDING CATHEDRALS: Walking with Purpose

But those who hope in the LORD will renew their strength. They will soar on wings like eagles; they will run and not grow weary, they will walk and not be faint. —Isaiah 40:31 (NIV)

One of the best parts of where I live is that we can walk our kids to school. Each morning, for ten minutes, I get their undivided attention as we talk about anything and everything as they jump the shadows of passing cars.

As we walked one brisk morning, I noticed that while I walk in a relatively straight line down the sidewalk, the kids bound around me, running up the grassy bank toward an office building, hopping off a little cement bump-out, running up steps, then down again, twirling, hopping, and often actually walking in circles around me. For every ten steps I take, I'm confident they take one hundred.

At first, this drove me crazy. I would almost trip over one, get bumped in the back by another, or have my heels clipped by the toy ride-on car that sometimes joined us. Then I realized what a beautiful picture of parenthood it was: My job is to remain steadfast and steady, giving my kids a safe place around which to circle.

In my stage of life, I relate a lot of my care of my children to God's love for us. Now, when I roar into my day with intentions and actions swirling, hopping from one chore to the next, I can almost see God there, in the middle, moving smoothly through the day with me. The next time you feel unmoored in your daily doings, remember the Anchor who holds you steady.

Dear Heavenly Father, help my steps to remain straight and steady in a direct line to You as I lead these tiny feet to heaven.
—Ashley Kappel

Digging Deeper: Lamentations 3:22–23; 1 Corinthians 15:58; Hebrews 10:23

Labor Day, Monday, September 4

In the same way, let your light shine before others, that they may see your good deeds and glorify your Father in heaven. —Matthew 5:16 (NIV)

One of my first jobs was in the marketing department for a factory that made rubber gaskets. During my training, the boss took me into a storage room and showed me the many parts they made for other manufacturers, the seals around windshields and other rubber gaskets. Then he took a can of cheese from his windowsill, flipped it over, and showed me a little rubber nub on the bottom of the can. "We make these, too," he said proudly, "and without these, no cheese."

I had no idea how the little nub on a bottom of a can of cheese worked, but I was in awe of his presentation. There were so many little things I had never noticed or wondered about, and just like that, my perspective on the world shifted. I would go into a store and pick up a can of soup and before putting it in my grocery cart, I would think about all the work involved to get that can on the shelf—the manufacturing of the can, the soup itself (including the growing of the ingredients), the making of the label, the delivery of the can, and then the person who put it on the shelf. There were so many parts of the process I had never once considered.

For the first time in my life, common objects represented teamwork, hard work, passion, and determination. People putting their hearts and minds together so seamlessly and perfectly that their role is, for the most part, invisible to many, and yet the fruits of their labor benefit each one of us.

Dear Lord, today on Labor Day, thank You for the workers of the world, who do their jobs so well we often forget all that they do to make the world a better place.
—Sabra Ciancanelli

Digging Deeper: Psalm 128:2; Colossians 3:23

". . . And surely I am with you always, to the very end of the age."
—Matthew 28:20 (NIV)

I spent the first half of my boyhood in the Philadelphia area, specifically Havertown, sometimes called the thirty-third county of Ireland because of the names on most of the mailboxes. Philadelphians have a very distinct accent, as thick as the provolone cheese that properly goes on a Philly cheesesteak. "Hey, yo, give me a glass of wooter with that hoagie dere!" So, when my family moved to Michigan—I was around nine—I took my accent with me.

Of course, I was clueless to the fact I had an accent. I thought everyone drank *wooter,* which was why it was so disconcerting when Michiganders treated me like I was speaking a foreign language. I vowed to abolish my accent as fast as I could, which is why today I speak with a kind of neutral accent, a linguistic compromise. I can't voluntarily resurrect my Philly accent even if I try.

Except when I am upset or excited and raise my voice. Then, suddenly, I'm shouting *wooter* all over again.

Is that nine-year-old-boy from Havertown still somewhere inside me? Does this mean a person's immutable roots never run far beneath the surface and that much of who we are is formative? And maybe that's true about faith as well. I went to the St. Denis school and parish as a kid in Philly. I have not remained a strict Catholic. In fact, you could say I am denominationally agnostic. But in times of stress or excitement, the basic tenets of faith I learned in my formative years always move to the fore. Faith is always there, rooted within me.

We are raised by our families and our communities. But we are also raised by a God who gives us a faith accent we carry our whole lives.

Father, may I always raise my voice to You in times of need and in times of rejoicing because—forgive me—I trust that, yo, You will always be dere.
—Edward Grinnan

Digging Deeper: Psalm 139:7–10; Proverbs 16:9

Wednesday, September 6

Listen to me, my people, and give heed to me, my nation; for a
teaching will go out from me, and my justice for a light to the peoples.
—Isaiah 51:4 (NRSV)

As a child, I was mesmerized by the story of Helen Keller and her teacher, Anne Sullivan. Anne was just twenty years old when she met Helen—a furious little terror, by her own admission, frustrated and made wild by the loss of her senses from a childhood illness.

I think children reading Helen's autobiography were meant to identify with her and her progress under Anne's patient tutelage. But it was Anne who fascinated me. I yearned for a teacher who could calm my fears, redirect my anger, teach me how to live.

When I met Grace at church, I didn't know she would become that person. I admired her strength and commitment to ministry, but it wasn't until she had several strokes a few years ago that she became my teacher. I visited her in the hospital and then the convalescent home, witnessing her work inch-by-inch, step-by-step, to recover her life. I watched her learn to breathe and swallow, then to sit up, climb into a wheelchair, use a walker. I rejoiced with her when she learned of an apartment opening in an assisted-living facility. In everything, Grace became my teacher. She let me witness how daily, even hourly, she chose to turn things over to God. Big things, like whether she'd qualify for assisted living, and small things, like her disappointment when the first meal she'd been able to eat in months arrived cold. Through all of this, she taught me patience and, yes, grace.

Grace is, indeed, God's gift to me, my Anne Sullivan. And I pray my lessons have just begun.

Lord, God, You've given me Grace upon Grace; help me to share Your
gifts with others who need them as I do.
—Marci Alborghetti

Digging Deeper: Proverbs 7:1–4; Luke 6:47–48

*. . . the LORD your God will bless you in all your produce and in
all the work of your hands, and you will have abundant joy.*
—Deuteronomy 16:15 (CSB)

I'm discarding several boxes of good cotton fabric," a friend told me.
"Have any interest?"

Sure, I told my friend. I couldn't use all of it, though, so I gave half of it
to a seamstress I know. I had no specific plan for the rest, but I valued the
promise of colorful yardage. *Thank You, Lord, for this unexpected resource.*

I'd recently rediscovered my grandmother's portable Singer and the
joys of sewing. I'd found a dozen vintage wardrobe patterns tucked in
a closet. With so much material at hand, I let nostalgia influence my
vision. One pattern was for a muumuu, a loose, Hawaiian-style house-
dress popular in the 1970s. Yoke neckline, no zipper, no buttonholes—
it looked easy. I'd made one decades ago, though not this exact design.

I set out to make six, maybe more, as gifts. Let's say my skills were
rusty. On my first effort, I mismatched a critical seam, sewing front
left to back right. Ripped it out. Started over. Next were the unusual,
fully lined "lapped" sleeves—were the directions written by an intern?
When I stitched the shoulders to the yoke, one sleeve lapped—or
flapped—toward the front, the other toward the back. I struggled at
length to tug—taut, tauter—the threads that gathered fullness at the
bodice. Ugh. *Am I enjoying this?* No. Not yet.

But after I'd pressed the hem crease and inspected the finished piece,
my distress dissipated. *There's a charm in those skewed sleeves. Maybe
I'll keep this one for myself.* One success, even if imperfect, renewed my
vision. The next weekend, I cut out muumuu no. 2. I'm now choosing
fabric for no. 4.

> *Lord, though the making process may be difficult, help me
> to find joy in the finished work.*
> —Evelyn Bence

Digging Deeper: Proverbs 31:10–31

Friday, September 8

A woman giving birth to a child has pain because her time has come; but when her baby is born she forgets the anguish because of her joy that a child is born into the world. —John 16:21 (NIV)

Have you ever looked at your children, amazed at what God formed through you? My children are now older than I was when they were born. That God allowed me to bring them to birth wows me even now.

Similarly, I marvel at the way I struggle with the birth of fictional characters. In one of my unpublished works, a developing character "spoke" to me in despair: "Why is life so hard?" she asked. As crazy as it sounds, I felt her desperation. I knew things would get better for her, but right then I wanted her to understand that the agony involved in giving birth to gifts and callings—a failed sermon, the embarrassment of stage fright, a ruined meal prepared for a sick neighbor—is always worth the realized gift.

In John 16, Jesus prepares His beloved disciples for His death by likening their grief to childbirth. Later on the cross, mirroring the words of his ancestor David: "My God, my God, why hast thou forsaken me?" Jesus is in the throes of that delivery He had spoken of earlier. His trust might seem on trial, but at the end of an outcry, the Lord delivers new life. "It is finished," He says. And I picture the Father smiling, now that "whosoever will" may become children of the promise.

Whether experiencing pain while God ushers forth a gift through us or standing alongside someone else's struggle, life's pushes are often hard. But, as in natural childbirth, the sweet fruit snuffs out the memory of the labor, and, in Christ, "grief will turn to joy" (John 16:20 [NIV]).

Jesus, I thank You for the continuous yield of new births through You!
—Jacqueline F. Wheelock

Digging Deeper: Matthew 27:46; John 16; Romans 8:22–23

May the God of hope fill you with all joy and peace in believing, so that by the power of the Holy Spirit you may abound in hope. —Romans 15:13 (ESV)

I want to gather flower seeds on this hike," I said to my husband, Kevin, as we grabbed our backpacks and headed up Mormon Mountain in northern Arizona.

He nodded as we took our first steps on the tree-lined path on a warm September afternoon. Throughout the summer, I had seen the orange-flowering paintbrush, the trumpeting red penstemon, and the violet showy phlox and was hoping to gather their seeds. As we climbed in elevation, the plants seemed to have vanished from the landscape. Their time of blooming had ended.

I walked on, discouraged. The weeks leading to this day had been filled with tension and stress as important events on my calendar had been cancelled at the last minute after weeks of preparation. I stared at an uncertain future.

And today? All I wanted was a few seeds! And *not* those of the hardy thistle plants that grew next to the trail. Was that too much to ask?

"How about those flowers?" Kevin pointed at dozens of spiky clusters growing in a meadow up ahead. Bluebonnet lupine—exactly what I wanted. A few late bloomers clung to the stems, but the two-inch seed-pods were what interested me.

Back at our cabin, I laid out the gathered pods on the kitchen counter, figuring I would retrieve the inner seeds once they had dried. Checking on the pods the next morning, I was surprised to discover seeds all over the kitchen. The pods had spiraled open on their own, shooting seeds into an unknown future.

> *Jesus, plant seeds of beautiful hope in the places where*
> *I am discouraged and uncertain today.*
> —Lynne Hartke

Digging Deeper: Psalm 16:9; Lamentations 3:24–25;
1 Corinthians 2:9

Sunday, September 10

. . . for I have put my trust in you. Show me the way I should go, for to you I entrust my life. —Psalm 143:8 (NIV)

I recently came across an old photograph. I could still vividly recall taking it. I'd been sitting on a bench in the rear of a bright rehearsal room. In the center of the space sat the Fairbanks Community Band, their backs to me as they played through one of their pieces, their music echoing from the walls.

As I'd quietly slipped my phone out of my pocket to take the photo, I remembered the fear I'd been feeling. I hadn't played my trumpet in twenty years. That I was here, checking out a band rehearsal and thinking about joining, was plenty crazy enough. But way more significant was the fact that I was looking out at a room full of strangers. I didn't know a single person there. Not at all. I absolutely wasn't one to bravely walk up to someone I didn't know, let alone an entire group. It felt impossible.

Looking at the picture now, though—years later—I realized I was smiling, because it was no longer a snapshot of strangers, as it had been then. Instead, I was looking at the familiar backs of my friends. I didn't need to see their faces to know who they were. They were people who were about to become my teachers, my encouragers, my friends. We were going to play music together and also share meals, frozen pipes, broken cars, tools, stories, laughs, lessons, and more. I just didn't know any of that then. But God did. And now, I do, too. I'm so very glad.

Sometimes, God, the blessings You have planned for my life feel scary at first. But those that I can't imagine for myself often turn out to be the most beautiful of all. Thank You.
—Erin Janoso

Digging Deeper: Proverbs 3:5–6; Jeremiah 29:11

So do not fear, for I am with you; do not be dismayed, for I am your God. I will strengthen you and help you; I will uphold you with my righteous right hand. —Isaiah 41:10 (NIV)

A plane just crashed into the World Trade Center," my mother said, waking me up. She has a flare for dramatics, so I didn't take the announcement seriously.

"You woke me up," I grumbled. "I'll call you later."

Imagining a tiny plane sticking out from one of its windows, I tried to go back to sleep. I couldn't. I brushed my teeth, then turned on the television as the phone rang again.

"Oh, thank God," my aunt yelled. "You're home!"

We stayed on the phone together, crying as the towers crumbled, first one and then the other. That afternoon, I walked over forty blocks to my cousin's place—the view of the World Trade Center from her balcony was now a mountain of smoke.

For days, it felt like New Yorkers were lost in that fog. We were in shock and paralyzed with fear. I wanted to avoid crowds and the subway, but living and working in the city did not afford us that choice.

We had to get to work and live our lives, so we moved through our fears together, knowing we weren't doing it alone. I wasn't the only one trembling inside as I boarded my first crowded train after the attacks, and somehow that gave me strength. Each year, I'm reminded of the fear that threatened to paralyze me. But I'm also reminded of the strength and unity that helped me to overcome it.

Lord, no matter what I go through, there is solace knowing others have walked that same journey and overcome. But my greatest peace is knowing You are with me always.
—Karen Valentin

Digging Deeper: Joshua 1:9; Psalm 133:1

Tuesday, September 12

"Give heed to the laws and rules that I am instructing you to observe, so that you may live." —Deuteronomy 4:1 (JPS)

Unlike a number of the other instructors in the adult education program at our community college, I demand a lot of my students. I realized I was probably an exception when I heard some of my fellow writing teachers telling prospective students that they didn't ask for homework, so the class would not be that exacting.

When it was my turn to speak to the students, I said, "I'm going to warn you. I teach craft, and I do assign homework. My philosophy is that you don't have to do everything I ask of you, but the more you try to do well, the more you'll learn. The learning is the key."

One of the listeners raised his hand and asked, "What if a student keeps doing the stuff wrong?"

"There's no right and wrong," I answered him. "There's only more or less effective and more or less interesting. I teach fiction, not real life."

As I said it, I realized that there are a great many ways that writing fiction differs from everyday living. But one I had never thought about before is: We control the fiction we write, and that means it's acceptable not to have right and wrong; we do not control our real lives, and the One who does expects more from us than I do from my students. But the philosophy can be seen as the same: The more we try to do well, the more we'll learn, and our learning is the key.

Your teaching is life-giving, Lord of Learning.
—Rhoda Blecker

Digging Deeper: Deuteronomy 6:6; Proverbs 13:4

"Forget the former things; do not dwell on the past. See, I am doing a new thing!" —Isaiah 43:18–19 (NIV)

The broken teacup sat on my kitchen counter for several weeks. It had been my grandmother's, one of the few family heirlooms I possessed. Painted with dainty flowers and embellished with a gold rim, the porcelain was almost translucent. Its handle, as thin as a reed, was so petite that it really only fit my young granddaughters' tiny hands, which was why I'd chosen it for our tea party. But as I was washing up, I'd bumped the fragile cup into a sturdier mug. That's all it took for it to break in two. I could try to glue the fragile pieces together, but it would always look broken, and it certainly would no longer hold tea. Nevertheless, I couldn't seem to let it go.

Yes, it was lovely. Once. Yes, it held a tenuous tie to a family tree of which I was now the oldest living branch. But the relational roots of that tree didn't need a teacup to support them. Love was enough. The truth of the matter was this teacup was simply shards of shattered ceramic, cluttering up an otherwise useful countertop.

I picked up the teacup, finally ready to dispose of it. Then I heard God's subtle whisper: *What other useless things are you holding onto?* Grudges, hurt feelings, bad habits that had become a comfortable part of my routine, outdated dreams that had passed their expiration date . . . all of these and more immediately came to mind. With renewed determination, I tossed the teacup in the trash. Then I had a chat with God about what other areas I needed to attend to in my life.

Father, help me let go of anything that no longer serves Your purpose in my life, making room for whatever new things You send my way.
—Vicki Kuyper

Digging Deeper: 2 Corinthians 5:17; Ephesians 4:22–24; Philippians 3:13–14; Colossians 3:2

Thursday, September 14

*For the L*ORD *is great, and greatly to be praised . . .* —Psalm 96:4 (KJV)

I can't say I was a starving musician, but I sure skirted the edge. I'd often pick up grocery money busking on the Los Angeles boardwalks. People would stop, listen, ask for some classic rock song or current hit. I wasn't getting rich, but it kept me in ninety-nine-cent hamburgers.

One sunny day on the Santa Monica Pier, I noticed a woman standing on the edge of the crowd. Shabby clothes—more bedraggled than beach. She looked about as hungry as I felt. After a few minutes, she approached.

"Can you play 'How Great Thou Art'?"

Funny, the words of the hymn rose from some worn church pew in my memory. "I can try," I said.

The crowd wasn't in a hymn mood. By the time I finished, the woman was the only one left. She fished through her coin purse and dropped a few folded bills into my guitar case. Then, with a nod and smile, she drifted off.

I'm not sure what I played next, but I know this—only one refrain echoed my mind as I looked out over the endless Pacific. *Then sings my soul . . .* As I played, the Good Father put His arm around the shoulders of this wandering son.

Later, I stared as those folded bills turned out to be four twenties. A fortune. In the years since, I've silently thanked that good woman from a hundred stages, every time I've played that hymn.

I know there aren't enough twenties in the world to pay her back. But one day, at that great feast—no ninety-nine-cent burgers there!—I hope we can sing those beautiful words together.

> *Thank You, God, for Your beautiful, relentless pursuit.*
> *Your love surprises me at every turn.*
> —Buck Storm

Digging Deeper: Psalm 136:4; Isaiah 55:9; Ephesians 2:4

"Meanwhile, Jesus kept on growing wiser and more mature, and in favor with God and his fellow man." —Luke 2:52 (ISV)

A t my university, we increasingly use an online course management system called Blackboard that lets students submit assignments and faculty grade them remotely. No more lugging papers around, scribbling comments, feeding Scantrons one-by-one into the reader across campus.

Such a system makes grading sound better, but it's not. Even the simplest quiz takes hours to "build" such that a brainless-robot version of me can assess it. How do you phrase a question to let students give nuanced answers without true/falsing everything into meaninglessness? Then there's the quiz's administration. When should students take it? What about students who work? What if someone's internet fails mid-quiz? Should I proactively enable students to take it twice? Won't that tempt them to just look up the answers instead of knowing them?

Each of my questions requires an actual person to make a decision, then figure out how to translate that decision into Blackboard Speak, then deal with the inevitability that students will invent some unforeseen way of making the grading impossible or inequitable or pointless.

When colleagues complained that students were gaming the system, I started worrying along those lines—particularly after letting students resubmit assignments I'd already graded. *What about deadlines?* I stewed. *Won't they just use my feedback to fix what's wrong?*

Then I had a revelation. Isn't that what learning is: finding out you're wrong and replacing your thinking with something truer? By definition, learning is, I would argue, holy. Even Jesus, the embodiment of truth, grew in wisdom, according to the gospels. So what if my students don't meet my arbitrary deadline! Learning is the goal, and it's a process.

> *Grow me, Lord. Make me wiser, more mature,*
> *an ever-clearer reflection of You!*
> —Patty Kirk

Digging Deeper: Romans 12:1–3; 2 Corinthians 3:7–4:6

Saturday, September 16

But when he was still a long way off, his father saw him and felt compassion for him . . . —Luke 15:20 (NASB)

It had been awhile since Terry and I visited his sister on Grays Harbor, south of Seattle. Her A-frame home stood above the quiet water. On a misty autumn day, I decided to walk along a sheltered beach near her property with the tide still out.

Suddenly from behind a pile of driftwood came an eruption of wings; a large bird flopped onto the dark, rippled sand. A bedraggled loon, gray as the sky.

I was immediately in protective mode. Loons are my favorite birds. Here sat one stranded and exposed. I thought its wing might be broken.

I stood guard. The tide was coming closer. The loon tried awkwardly to push itself toward the water, but the water was too far. I watched its painful struggle.

Another person joined me. The tide was closer now. Again it tried to heave toward the water. This time, the loon had found its element. It began to swim and soon rose up, stretching healthy wings. Out on the water its mate had been waiting all along. Thankfully, I hadn't interfered.

Carrying home the image of the loon's battle to reach where it belonged, I thought of our "stranded" granddaughter—separated from family, rejecting her faith, striving in young adulthood toward her niche in life. Painful to watch.

I needed to allow the struggle—to stand guard through prayer—and believe God waited for her on the incoming tide.

> *God, You are the rescuer, You know the struggle,*
> *You never abandon Your own.*
> —Carol Knapp

Digging Deeper: Exodus 14:14; Jeremiah 23:23–24;
Luke 15:11–32, 22:31–32

Let everything that has breath praise the LORD. —Psalm 150:6 (NIV)

Early this morning, I sat on our back porch with our young golden retriever, Lexie, lying beside me. She is two years old and a beautiful creation of God.

I was in a reflective and prayerful mood as the sun slowly rose and I sipped good fresh coffee. Cardinals, sparrows, and doves visited our bird feeder, chirping loudly. It was a dawn that reflected Eden.

As Lexie slowly rolled over on her mat and sighed with delight for life, the last verse in the final Psalm in the Bible flowed through my memory: "Let everything that has breath praise the Lord!"

God delights when we enjoy, appreciate, and delight in His good Earth. Such joy is healthy and free yet is so easily squeezed from our awareness as the sun rises higher and our day becomes hectic and demanding. Our sense of praise and joy is transformed into worry, work, and frenetic energy. Our natural love and praise of God are stifled.

It is important to cultivate such moments of simple praise and wonder each day. For everything that has breath must praise and enjoy the vitalizing presence of God.

Dear Lord, let me praise You today with all the breath I have!
—Scott Walker

Digging Deeper: Psalm 104:33, 148; Romans 15:9

Monday, September 18

First of all, then, I urge that supplications, prayers, intercessions, and thanksgivings be made for everyone . . . —1 Timothy 2:1 (NRSV)

For as long as I've worked at Guideposts and many years before, we've gathered as a company on Monday mornings to pray. To pray for others, to pray for colleagues and their families, to respond to the countless requests that come to us online and by mail. Reading about what people are going through—the health emergencies, the financial setbacks, the relationship struggles—can be overwhelming. How could anyone begin to help them? Then I remind myself how God knows what those needs are better than I possibly could. Our job is simply to offer up the prayers and trust they are being heard.

One day I was attending prayer fellowship remotely from home, as were many of my colleagues, and we all logged on through Zoom. It was great to see everybody's faces in "gallery view" and hear a bit from them before we settled in to read prayer requests. The perfect way to start a week, focusing on the needs of others while counting my own blessings and giving thanks for the work we do.

I sat on the couch, stared into the screen, laptop in my lap, and felt a warming sensation come over me right where the computer sat. Must have been some spinoff from the machine's innards, the battery or something like that. But I could also imagine God's presence warming the hearts and hands of all those people who needed help. I closed my eyes, listened to my colleague Ty'Ann Brown, our director of ministries, pray aloud. As she covered all the bases—I don't know how she does it—I echoed her words and thoughts. Then said "Amen" and left the Zoom room.

I was ready to begin the day.

> *You know better than I do what people need, Lord. Let me be a conduit in any way I can.*
> —Rick Hamlin

Digging Deeper: Jeremiah 33:3; Ephesians 6:18

"For where two or three gather in my name, there am I with them."
—Matthew 18:20 (NIV)

K aris is on lockdown in her high school classroom! Rumor of shots fired! Please PRAY!"

Those desperate words were from my daughter Lindsay in a group text to family members about my granddaughter Karis, her daughter.

My heart pounded as I gripped my phone, waiting for more messages:

"Lots of sirens. They are locked in their classroom in the dark and told to be quiet."

"The school is surrounded by police and SWAT teams who are entering the school."

Responses from the family began appearing:

"Praying. Oh my word, PRAYING!"

"Oh no, a mother's WORST nightmare!"

More endless waiting and then sounds coming from a totally black screen. Karis had recorded what she heard in the darkness.

Loud pounding on the door. "Police! You all okay in there?" Door opening. "You can turn the lights on now. You are safe."

Finally a message from Karis's dad. "Police have swept the building and are calling this a false alarm."

What followed were many prayers of praise.

Later, as I looked back over the string of text messages, I clearly saw a story of fears and faith, blessed by cell phones that connected us and kept us informed; creation of a prayer team finding strength and trust in praying together; and the quick responses of law enforcement who were able to tell Karis and all the others: "You are safe."

> *Lord, You promise that You are with us always, regardless of the*
> *circumstances, and we are blessed when we form circles of*
> *prayers who remind each other of Your presence.*
> —Carol Kuykendall

Digging Deeper: Isaiah 41:10; John 14:27; 2 Timothy 1:7

"Therefore, as we have opportunity, let us do good to all people, especially to those who belong to the family of believers." —Galatians 6:10 (NIV)

We were surprised and honored when the vice president of my husband's seminary asked if we'd be willing to do him a favor on behalf of a student in need. When we immediately agreed, Mr. Trulock asked us to place $50 cash in an envelope with a short anonymous note: FOR NEW SHOES. I worked in the seminary mail room, so it was not difficult to slip the envelope containing the money into the student's mailbox. It was far more difficult coming up with the cash. We lived on a tight budget but willingly gave up pizza one weekend and trimmed our grocery list in order to keep our promise. We were happy to do so. The Lord loves a cheerful giver.

Still, we were puzzled. Mr. Trulock was independently wealthy. He could buy new shoes for every student on campus. Why had he asked us to do so? Was he demonstrating how to cultivate the Holy Spirit's fruits of kindness and goodness? Years later, we mentioned the incident to another seminary couple. Bob and Jenn laughed. They'd been asked to do something similar for a different student. "That was Mr. Trulock's way of teaching us to look out for one another's needs. Didn't *you* ever receive an anonymous gift?"

We had indeed. Bill's semester tuition had once been paid for by an unknown donor. We never learned who. That didn't matter. We'd learned an important lesson instead—a lesson in how to love one another.

> *Dear Lord, remind me often that if my love isn't in action,*
> *it isn't love at all.*
> —Shirley Raye Redmond

Digging Deeper: John 13:34–35; Galatians 5:22; Philippians 4:19

*Do not be anxious about anything, but in every situation, by prayer
and petition, with thanksgiving, present your requests to God.*
—Philippians 4:6 (NIV)

They hear me open the door from the house to the screen porch.
Before I even get to the bench where their dry food is or reach for
the door onto the deck, they are there in supplication. Ebony, Gracie,
and Bamboo—our farm cats, ranging in age from seven to fourteen.
This has been our routine for years. They look imploringly up at me. I
open the door and shuffle through the cool morning air, then stoop to
pour dry food into the old skillet that serves as their bowl. Bamboo has
learned to nudge my arm so more food gets poured. Then a can of wet
food. And then, I am out of their consciousness.

As I go back into the warmth of the house, I am reminded of Anne
Lamott's saying that there are three essential prayers—"help," "thanks,"
and "wow." My cats never seem to make it past "help." Actually, their
"prayer" is "help, we're starving," even though they've been out hunting
in the woods and prairie all night and are far from short of food. They
never get to the "thanks" or "wow" prayers.

I settle in to sip some more coffee and wonder how often I'm like the
cats. Too often, I'm afraid. So many times I stop at the "help" prayer
and after help comes, I forget to be thankful or awed. In those times
that I'm most spiritually aware, though, I am flooded with gratitude
and amazed by the goodness of the God who watches over me and
gives me the things I need. And some extra goodies besides.

*Giving God, teach me the spirit of gratitude and awe. Help me see Your
goodness all around me. Astound me with Your care for me. Amen.*
—J. Brent Bill

Digging Deeper: Colossians 3:16

Friday, September 22

"Therefore everyone who hears these words of mine and puts them into practice is like a wise man who built his house on the rock."
—Matthew 7:24 (NIV)

After several years of marriage, my wife and I bought our "starter home"—the first one you buy before moving on to a larger house to raise your family, have cookouts, and curse at the endless landscaping.

That was thirty-five years ago. We're still here. Our starter home may be our ending home.

Like many of our peers, Sandee and I are downsizing—but we did it the old-fashioned way: The kids grew up and left, so now we have some room.

Emphasis on *some*—it's still a mighty small house. Yet it's largely full of . . . um, quirks, some of which leak. We have more drafts than most breweries. The plumbing is held together by putty and prayer.

But it's home. We could use new pipes but still have old memories. The kids once hated the shared rooms and the bunk beds—now they remember everything through a joyful lens. Me? I still wrestle with the leaking quirks (there's a family of hair bunnies breeding in every drain), but I can't imagine leaving—there's too much history, too many family dinners, too much *us* here to start again elsewhere.

I'll bet the hair bunnies feel the same way.

Lord, when we leave this earthly home, take us to Your mansion with many rooms, hopefully one with updated plumbing and big, bright windows that look backward with gratitude and forward to forever.
—Mark Collins

Digging Deeper: Matthew 7:14; Acts 7:49

THE PINK HOUSE: The City on the Hill

A city that is set on an hill cannot be hid. —Matthew 5:14 (KJV)

David drives and I Google the news on my phone. We are on our way to a Metro Council meeting, where David is first on the agenda. He will be opening the meeting with prayer.

As I look out the window, I realize something's very wrong.

Alarmed, I blurt out, "David . . . where are we?"

My eyes dart down to our car's navigation system. Either David has mistakenly typed in "Metro Center" instead of "Music City Center" or the little guy who lives in our nav system has taken the first letter and jumped to the wrong conclusion. David, as usual, follows little guy's directions without question.

I feel terrible. My "Pink House habit" of spotting familiar landmarks would have prevented this if I hadn't been Googling. Now, we are miles from where we need to be and will be unacceptably late . . . unless . . . my eyes sweep the horizon, looking for the city.

David has pulled over to the road's shoulder. Envisioning the people waiting for his prayer, he is reentering an address into the nav.

"Stop," I say. "Turn around and drive toward the skyline."

Suddenly, Nashville, the city on the hill, has become our Pink House.

We fix our eyes on the city, and finally, with great relief, David turns into the Music City Center garage, hops out, and dashes for the door. By the time I park the car and make my way into the meeting, the prayer has been delivered.

Nav systems often serve a great purpose. But landmarks stay steady. Like the words of David's prayer, meant to turn the council meeting toward the ultimate Pink House of Jesus's teachings, landmarks point the way to where we need to be.

Father, fix our eyes on Your city, Your Pink House of Jesus's teachings.
—Pam Kidd

Digging Deeper: 2 Chronicles 20:12; Hebrews 12:2

Sunday, September 24

Peace I leave with you; my peace I give to you . . . —John 14:27 (ESV)

It had been a rough morning. I'd slept through my alarm and woken up in a panic. There wasn't enough time to get ready, but nobody seemed to share my sense of urgency. How many times did I have to ask my daughter to get changed? Then I couldn't find my phone. Or the car keys. To top it off, I'd forgotten my coffee on the counter as we'd finally rushed out the door—late for church. Again.

The mortification of traipsing into the sanctuary after Mass had begun hadn't helped. It felt like every eye followed us as we filed, shame-faced, to an empty pew—all the way up front, of course. All throughout the service, my frame of mind teetered, threatening to tip over into a full-fledged bad mood. But then:

"Let us offer each other a sign of peace," the priest said.

I didn't want to. I didn't feel even remotely peaceful. I would much rather have been left alone to stew. But, going through the motions, I pasted a smile on my face and turned to the woman behind me. Our eyes met as she caught my hand in hers. "Peace be with you," she said, sincerely.

"And with you," I answered, reflexively. But I felt my heart lift just a little. By the time I'd repeated this familiar exchange with a half-dozen fellow parishioners, I was surprised to notice that my pasted-on smile had become real. And it remained as I settled back into my seat, restored, my sour temper vanquished by God's peace—and some heaven-sent human connection.

Sometimes, God, my thoughts are petty and small-minded. Despite this,
You offer me Your perfect peace. Thank You.
—Erin Janoso

Digging Deeper: Romans 8:26; Philippians 4:7

This is the day which the LORD hath made; we will rejoice and be glad in it. —Psalm 118:24 (KJV)

I am fortunate to have had loving and caring godparents. They were fellow missionaries and teachers with my parents in the Philippine Islands during my childhood. After my father died when I was fourteen, I grew especially close to my godparents. I felt welcomed and loved in their home and learned many important things through them.

I particularly enjoyed the experience of eating delicious meals with their family. We sat at a large round table, and before we ate, we all held hands and my godfather would offer a "blessing." The blessing that I most remember is when he would look at each of us and recite in his resonant voice, "This is the day that the Lord hath made; we will rejoice and be glad in it!"

My godparents' positive perspective on life has nourished my attitude and my spirit long after their generation has passed away. Every time I face an anxious day, I sense my godfather kindly looking at me, winking and intoning, "Scott, this is the day that the Lord hath made; you must rejoice and be glad in it."

Father, thank You for people in our lives who have taught us to be positive and filled with praise. Amen.
—Scott Walker

Digging Deeper: Proverbs 17:22; Philippians 4:8; 1 Thessalonians 5:16–19

Tuesday, September 26

. . . walk worthy of God . . . —1 Thessalonians 2:12 (KJV)

When my son Harrison was young, I looked for ways to inspire him to be the best he could be. Bedtime stories often centered on heroes like King David and Sampson.

Now, with two young daughters, I find myself reading tuck-in stories of women like Ruth and Esther, which lead me back to my own childhood. It's then, I realize, that Bible stories actually open the way to real-life lessons that show us how to be strong and good.

My parents, you see, had this way of including people in our lives that no one else thought to include. I never questioned the unusual jumble of people who sat around the table at my birthday dinners. That's just how it was in the Kidd house. Most of our guests had no families. An old missionary from China, a lonely viola player from the symphony, a never-married loner who had worked for the city of Nashville for fifty years, the custodian from our church, a man with a lifelong history of mental illness . . . the list goes on.

My parents highlighted the heroism of these everyday people, their kindness, their generosity, their victories over adversity. For me, they became nothing less than real-life heroes, and because of my parents' inclusion, they came with the added bonus of being heroes who adored me until their dying days.

And so, in my history I found a perfect example of moving my children toward good. Invite good into our lives. Show good in how we treat others.

"Hey, Ella Grace," I say as I finish our bedtime read, "let's talk about your birthday dinner."

Father, show me how to show good, so that my children follow.
—Brock Kidd

Digging Deeper: Leviticus 19:34; Galatians 6:1

But for you who fear my name, the sun of righteousness shall rise with healing in its wings. You shall go out leaping like calves from the stall.
—Malachi 4:2 (ESV)

My husband, Kevin, and I slogged among the tall grass in a waterless lake bed in northern Arizona, a dried-up reminder of the delayed summer rains and a visual image of my own weary heart. I thought of a sign next to my desk at home. *Laugh out loud,* it declared. I could not remember the last time I had done so.

A few wildflowers still lingered: a stand of sunflowers, a cluster of evening primroses, and a few stems of goldenrod. Our rust-colored mutt, Mollie, rolled around in the trampled grass, leftover evidence of where the elk had bedded down on previous evenings.

"There's the herd," Kevin whispered as the evening sky shifted to tangerine. He pulled out a pair of binoculars. "About 120. Cows and calves." Handing me the binocs, I easily identified the elks' darker brown bodies in the golden grass, with their buff-colored rumps and long legs. Using a series of mews and bleats, the mothers kept track of their lighter-colored calves, some with spots.

As we stood motionless with Mollie at our feet, the herd moved closer until they stood less than thirty yards from us. With the wind in our favor, we watched the nightly migration, until the final cow moved across our range of vision, along with two calves.

"Twins!" I whispered as the calves frolicked in the tall grass. I laughed at their spindly legs, causing several sentries to turn in our direction. With a barklike call of warning, the herd began to run, faster and faster, kicking up dry mud. They moved to the far end of the lake, as mothers called to their young, making sure none were left behind.

Surrounded by Your protecting presence, let me frolic with joy and laughter today.
—Lynne Hartke

Digging Deeper: Isaiah 49:13, 55:12–13

Thursday, September 28

The LORD is close to the brokenhearted and saves those who are crushed in spirit. —Psalm 34:18 (NIV)

When our daughter was four years old, she received a Little Red Riding Hood bell as a gift. When rung, it made a pleasant tinkling sound. Bethany treasured it. She kept the bell on her small desk next to her coloring books and crayons. Throughout the day, we would occasionally hear the happy tinkling of the bell coming from her bedroom.

But one morning, she carelessly knocked it over. It fell to the floor, shattering into several pieces. Bethany was devastated. In tears, she carried the broken ceramic bits to my husband, crying, "Daddy, fix it. Please fix it."

Despite Bill's best efforts, he could not adequately repair the bell. We ached for our daughter as we watched her cope with other, deeper losses in life, too: the death of a close college friend, being passed over for a dream job, grieving over her broken marriage.

Sometimes life is hard—really hard. As a result of mistakes and sinfulness, all of us are broken in some way or another. Sometimes, we're the victims of others' sins against us. We may carry scars for the rest of our lives. But God understands our pain. He cares. Healing begins when we bring the broken pieces of our lives to Him, saying, "Heavenly Father, please fix it."

> *Lord Jesus, thank You for healing our brokenness.*
> *Thank You for easing our pain.*
> —Shirley Raye Redmond

Digging Deeper: Matthew 5:3; Ephesians 2:10

. . . let us strip off every weight that slows us down . . . We do this by keeping our eyes on Jesus, the champion who initiates and perfects our faith. —Hebrews 12:1–2 (NLT)

I nearly choked on my coffee when my husband suggested we cancel our television subscription. *Randy going without constant sports and news?* This was monumental! Within the hour, the deed was done, in spite of the condescending prediction from the satellite provider: "You'll be back. What will you do without television?"

The first few weeks we watched every DVD in our collection, and I ordered more Christian movies and Westerns. As the selection of new material thinned out again, I wondered if our resolve would weaken. But then, God stepped in.

Released from the constant barrage of negative news, it freed us up for a closer relationship with each other. Evenings revolved around card games, talking about our day, our dreams and goals. We reconnected with distant family and friends over the phone. We hosted impromptu dinners with neighbors. Books we'd been "too busy" to read were read. The Christian films inspired deeper discussions about our faith, where we are now and where we'd like to be. Hungry to grow in Christ, we joined a church and met an entirely new family of friends and fellow believers.

Eight months later, I asked Randy if he ever missed TV. "Every time I see it on at a restaurant I'm reminded why we don't have it," he said. "It makes me really mad. Do you miss it?"

"Nope," I say, laughing. "When would we ever have time to watch it?"

Lord, it is so easy to lose sight of You in all of life's distractions.
You are who we hear when we turn down the noise.
Keep us always tuned in to You.
—Erika Bentsen

Digging Deeper: Psalm 141:8; Hebrews 3:1

Saturday, September 30

For as he thinks in his heart, so is he. —Proverbs 23:7 (NKJV)

I wanted to give up. I felt like everywhere I turned I got negative feedback. Within only two days, I'd learned one of my books had not been chosen as a finalist in a contest, an editor had rejected an idea I pitched, and I was having difficulty on a project whose deadline loomed. Why did I bother? Negative thoughts filled my head. *Your writing isn't good. No one wants to read it. You're not as good a writer as . . .*

I knew I needed to quit thinking those thoughts, but they continued to multiply, each one adding more weight like stones piling up on my shoulders. Stinking thinking, it is called. The more these negative thoughts assaulted me, the less motivated I was to keep writing and the more I wanted to give in to depression.

Then my husband, Chuck, called me to the kitchen.

"Look at that bluebird."

One of the beautiful azure birds was flying into our glass sliding doors.

"He's going to hurt himself," I said.

"He probably thinks his reflection is a rival and he must fight it," Chuck responded. "He's his own worst enemy."

His own worst enemy. The phrase reverberated with me.

I opened the door so the bird's reflection disappeared. Satisfied he had dispatched his rival, the bird returned home, where his mate patiently waited while he defended his honor.

The threat was gone. In fact, it had never been there. Just like my negative thoughts, I was attacking myself and being my own worst enemy. I had allowed fear, failure, doubt, and lack of confidence to defeat me. It was time to change my thoughts and make that enemy go away.

> *Father, forgive me for slandering Your creation, me.*
> —Marilyn Turk

Digging Deeper: Ephesians 2:10; Philippians 4:8

LET US SING FOR JOY

1 _____

2 _____

3 _____

4 _____

5 _____

6 _____

7 _____

8 _____

9 _____

10 _____

11 _____

12 _____

13 _____

14 _____

15 _____

September

16 _____

17 _____

18 _____

19 _____

20 _____

21 _____

22 _____

23 _____

24 _____

25 _____

26 _____

27 _____

28 _____

29 _____

30 _____

OCTOBER

I will bless the LORD at all times: his praise shall

continually be in my mouth.

—Psalm 34:1 (KJV)

Sunday, October 1

Then one of them, when he saw that he was healed, turned back, praising God with a loud voice . . . —Luke 17:15 (ESV)

Then what do you think happened?" I scan the children seated around me for Sunday school. One child raises her hand. "Yes, Fiona?"

"They didn't thank Him."

I nod. "You're right. Nine of the ten lepers didn't thank Jesus after He healed them. But one came back and thanked Him."

Another student raises his hand. "Why didn't they all thank Jesus?"

The question hit too close to home. The last time I felt my vertigo coming on, I prayed that the Lord would heal my symptoms and keep me from getting vertigo again. I went to bed and the following morning proceeded with my usual routine.

"How do you feel?" my mom asked.

I paused. Why was she asking me that?

The memory rushed back—the headache and dizziness of the night before that had led me to fear I'd awake with vertigo. The symptoms had disappeared. The Lord had healed me and spared me from vertigo. But I had forgotten to thank Him.

I smile at the kids. "It's easy to forget to thank God for the good things He gives us. He does so much for us all the time, but we often only remember to ask Him for things, not to thank Him. Do you know why we should thank God?"

The kids listen as I explain the surprising answer echoing in my heart. God doesn't need my gratitude. But I need the benefits that come from having a thankful heart and praising the God who gives me more blessings than I can count.

Lord, give me a thankful heart that daily seeks to praise You.
—Jerusha Agen

Digging Deeper: Psalm 92:1–5; Luke 17:16–19; 1 Thessalonians 5:18

Then Jesus answered and said to them, "Most assuredly, I say to you,
the Son can do nothing of Himself, but what He sees the Father do; for
whatever He does, the Son also does in like manner." —John 5:19 (NKJV)

As I was reading my Bible, the words in John 5:19 lifted from the
page. Jesus didn't happen into His miracles or sit down the night
before and decide what to teach the next day or make a list of who He
wanted to meet with. He watched what His Father who sent Him into
the world was doing—and He was right there doing "in like manner."

Jesus was flexible with His time—willing to detour when asked to
come help or linger when people wanted to listen.

Could watching for where and how my heavenly Father is working
change my way of being?

I had a chance to find out one morning when walking past a rural
neighbor's gate. This person had become increasingly incensed over
what he considered an unsightly structure new owners had hauled in
on prime land bordering his.

He was so upset by this daily dose of "ugly" that he blocked his view
of it by constructing his own "ugly"—a tall, rusted corrugated tin bar-
rier with a flapping stained paint tarp alongside.

Offer a caring word to him and his wife, an inner voice nudged. Would
I make a volatile situation between two neighbors worse? Not if the
Father was working.

Obeying the prompting, I sent a compassionate text message straight
from my heart. The next morning, I received a return note that
exceeded my hopes. "Thank you for reaching out to us," it read.

More reconciliation work lay ahead, but this was a beginning. Respond-
ing to the Father's invitation, I had found a way through that angry wall
of tin. I couldn't wait to see where His next invitation would lead.

Where You are working, Father, is where I want to be.
—Carol Knapp

Digging Deeper: Luke 2:41–52; John 5:30, 14:8–14; Acts 4:13–20

Tuesday, October 3

You are altogether beautiful, my darling; there is no flaw in you.
—Song of Songs 4:7 (NIV)

I finally got around to purchasing a replacement floor trim that smoothly connects the kitchen floor to the hallway.

I measured the space, then cut the piece with my handsaw. Yet when I went to fit it in, I realized I'd purchased the wrong piece. It was expensive and there was no way I could return it now after I'd cut it in half.

I threw my hands up in frustration. "I'm such an idiot!" I shouted.

My son who was nearby scolded me. "Mami, don't call yourself that word! You're not an idiot!"

I mumbled, "Okay," but I still felt like an idiot. I'd wasted time, energy, and money, and now I'd have to go back to the store.

"Why did I think this would be easy?" I mumbled quietly, getting ready to head back out. "Nothing is ever easy for me."

My self-pity was louder than I thought, and my son sweetly said, "Things may not always be easy, Mami, but you always find a way."

The love of this wise old soul has seen me through some of the hardest moments in my life, and it was at that moment I realized how closely he'd been watching my journey.

I need to be more mindful of my negativity, not just for myself but for my children, who are clearly learning from my example. I held him close, thanking him for recognizing my strength and worth, even when I could not.

> *Lord, in those moments when I'm unkind to myself, help me to remember Your infinite love for me.*
> —Karen Valentin

Digging Deeper: Proverbs 19:8; 1 Timothy 4:12

BUILDING CATHEDRALS: Noticing Beauty

. . . What no eye has seen, what no ear has heard, and what no human mind has conceived—the things God has prepared for those who love him. —1 Corinthians 2:9 (NIV)

My kids have a love/hate relationship with sunsets. "Quick!" they hear me yell. "It's golden hour!" That's the moment when the sun is hitting the houses and trees of our neighborhood just right, when we all rush to a window or into the front yard to revel in the beauty of our Creator. I do it mostly for myself—taking a hot minute during the evening to breathe in beauty is most welcome when I'm knee-deep in finishing homework, prepping dinner, refereeing fights, or trying to fold a basket of laundry—but also for my kids. I want them to see all that God has done for us.

One morning, while we were walking to school, James cried for a halt. "Look!" he called out. He leaned over the curb to the tiny strip of grass between our sidewalk and a CVS parking lot and plucked a dandelion from the shadow of the concrete. "James, I am so glad you take time to find the beauty everywhere," I told him, as he happily watched the "blow flower," as we call it, fly on the morning breeze.

That night, as I tucked James into bed, I asked him what he was thankful for from his day. "I'm thankful that you notice the little things, Mom," he said. I almost slid off his bed. In noticing God's efforts to bring beauty to our lives, I'd taught my kindergartener to see beauty, both in tiny strips of grass and in one another. "Me too, buddy," I told him.

Lord, allow me to always notice the beauty in the world that You created for us. When the world gets crazy, help me see the little things and find joy.
—Ashley Kappel

Digging Deeper: Ecclesiastes 3:11; John 1:3; Colossians 1:16–17

Thursday, October 5

. . . I am the resurrection and the life. Whoever believes in me, though he die, yet shall he live. —John 11:25 (ESV)

Gray skies hovered, appropriately gloomy and dark. Dear friends were burying their twenty-one-year-old son, and an army of supporters had filled the burlap blankets and wooden benches lined up in the massive field they had chosen for his memorial service.

I sat on a red and beige blanket, feeling the earth's hardness beneath me. We waited in reverent quiet, the cool October air moving us to huddle together, hold hands, and link arms. The family began their march onto the field, a sea of blackness pouring in slowly, deliberately. Young men bore the exquisite, but simple, handcrafted casket. As if all of heaven and earth had stopped, there was silence among us. As the first speaker approached the podium, it seemed we collectively exhaled.

The service was the most beautiful I have ever attended—honest and raw, captivating. His friends told funny stories of their good friend's antics and his heart for the marginalized. His siblings wept through stories of their hero. His parents shared stories about the kid who broke bones climbing the tallest of trees. The boy who spent his life thrill-seeking. The young man who lost his way at times but loved Jesus passionately.

There was beautiful music and poetry. We sang along, laughed along, cried along, and near the end of the service, witnessed a miracle. Gray skies that mirrored our sadness gave way to a glorious sun. I looked upward, feeling the warmth on my face, and praised God for showing up.

Through the sunshine, the Son reminded us that He was still present, still in control, and still in love with this young man, this family, and us all.

Lord, help us trust You with the loved ones who precede us in death, knowing that You love them and You love us.
—Carla Hendricks

Digging Deeper: Psalm 34:18; 1 Thessalonians 4:13; Revelation 21:4

I run in the path of your commands . . . —Psalm 119:32 (NIV)

There were twelve jumps in the course. They weren't in a neat row, one after the other, but set out with twists and turns in an order I wouldn't be able to remember no matter how many times I tried, let alone stay on the horse jumping over them.

I was watching my adult daughter, Rachel, in her jumper riding competition. If she were to go off course, miss a jump, jump the wrong one, or fall off, she would be out of that competition, period. No do-overs. No second chances.

I'm happy to say that my daughter stayed on course and on her horse. (In fact, she won Grand Champion.) Others were not so fortunate. Out of sixteen, two went off course and one fell off. All three were out.

It set me to thinking how gracious our God is. My life is full of twists, turns, and jumps of sorts. I always try to follow God and stay on the path He has set before me. But I do go off course. I'm not consistently loving, patient, self-controlled, or kind. I fall down in my efforts to be the person I want to be for God. But I am not out. I thank God that He does allow do-overs. When I make mistakes, I can turn to Him. He will forgive me and gently set me back on the right path.

I will never win Grand Champion in my life's course. But thankfully, God will let me continue to ride.

Thank You, God, that with You there are do-overs. Thank You for Your grace, Your mercy, and Your loving kindness, which pick me up when I stumble or fall and set me back on course.
—Kim Taylor Henry

Digging Deeper: Psalm 119:73, 104; Hebrews 8:12

Saturday, October 7

. . . this one thing I do: forgetting what lies behind and straining forward to what lies ahead. —Philippians 3:13 (NRSV)

It was the middle of the day, and I was rummaging around in the refrigerator, looking for something to eat. I reached for some yogurt, but as I pulled it out, it bumped a half cup of cold coffee that my wife, Carol, had left there to go with her lunch. At once, coffee spilled down through the layers of food and into the produce drawer. I grabbed the cup. Too late. What a disaster.

I knelt there on the kitchen floor, with a sponge and a roll of paper towels, taking out one jar after another, wiping them off, and putting them on a dish towel on the floor before taking out the rack and the drawers.

Who knew that we had five water bottles all lined up, not to mention a jar of mayonnaise way past its expiration date (along with one that was more recent) plus some hot sauce—yes, past its expiration date— that we never used? What bounty. What excess. No wonder shelf space seemed so limited.

After some scrubbing and consulting with the inventory expert— Carol—I put everything back. Well, not everything. Just the stuff we needed, the stuff we used, the stuff that was still good. The produce, in fact, looked fine after a bit of cleaning, and the refrigerator itself had never looked better.

I wiped the sides and the front and then closed the door. Opened it one more time just to check and, frankly, to admire my handiwork. The twenty-year-old fridge gleamed like we'd just bought it and filled it—half-filled it—up.

Sometimes disasters can be blessings in disguise. Depends on what you do with them.

May I treat the challenges that fill my days with ingenuity, courage, and patience, qualities that are all God-sent.
—Rick Hamlin

Digging Deeper: Matthew 6:19; 2 Corinthians 12:10

. . . His powerful Word is sharp as a surgeon's scalpel, cutting through everything, whether doubt or defense, laying us open to listen and obey.
—Hebrews 4:12–13 (MSG)

I pray for God to reveal to me the offensive or sinful things I do and don't recognize. The words from Proverbs 18:13 (MSG) stung like a bee today: "Answering before listening is both stupid and rude." I like to think I am a good listener, but too often I catch myself trying to move a conversation forward when I already know what someone is telling me.

I thought about the best listeners I've known. Jim, a manager I once reported to, came immediately to mind. I remember telling him about a problematic situation. Jim listened intently, never interjecting a thought or question before I finished. Before leaving his office, a colleague came to tell him about the same issue. Jim listened to him with the same patient focus he had given me. Later, I asked Jim why he spent time listening to the same story twice. He said, "I was listening for what he told me that you didn't and what he didn't tell me that you did. Several others will tell me about the same thing today, and each will offer something different. Only then will I be closer to having the full story."

Jim listened to everyone that way—his leadership team, union representatives, and all employees. And he never had to ask anyone to tell him about the "pulse" of the organization. I don't remember Jim ever interrupting me even when my explanations were long. I wish others could say that about me. I want to listen to others the way that Jim listened to me—the way I imagine God listening to our prayers: intently, patiently, without interrupting, but always with an eye toward leading events toward the best outcome.

Dear God, thank You for showing me things I need to fix. Fill me with discipline, grace, and patience to extend the same listening courtesy to others as Jim did to me. Amen.
—John Dilworth

Digging Deeper: Matthew 22:29; Luke 24:45; James 2:8

Monday, October 9

Be strong, and let your heart take courage, all you who wait for the Lord. —Psalm 31:24 (NRSV)

We're hiking Monument Mountain, my golden Gracie's favorite place in all creation. This was where she experienced life off leash in the wild for the first time. I still let her off at certain points, though not too close to the famous quartzite cliffs.

Gracie is obedient off leash. But every so often she goes crashing off into the trees chasing some scent or sound or just exulting in her freedom.

Today she disappeared into the woods. I found a nice rock to sit on and wait. Five minutes. Ten. I fingered the whistle in my pocket. Waited. Finally, I deployed the whistle. Still no Gracie. Just the empty silence of the trees.

I've learned that the best thing to do when Gracie is off on a frolic is to wait at the spot where she last saw me. Not charge into the woods and down a ravine after her. Just wait. It always works.

But it is so hard when I want to act. When I am anxious. As I sat on that rock worrying, I was reminded of the Bible's charge to wait on the Lord. I have trouble there, too. A lot. I pray, then a minute later I'm checking my watch. I ask God for help, but then try to do it all myself. I'm impatient with the Lord. Still, I am admonished to wait on the Lord. And when I finally do, the answer I get is usually better than what I asked for. *Lord,* I prayed now, *teach me to wait on You. Teach me patience and trust.*

It wasn't long before Gracie came bounding down the trail. She seemed a little frazzled, as if she might have lost her bearings for a bit. It was okay, though. I'd found mine.

Lord, You use my beloved dog, Gracie, to teach me lessons I am often unable to learn on my own. Today I will remember to wait on You.
—Edward Grinnan

Digging Deeper: Proverbs 3:5–6; Philippians 4:6

But I tell you, everyone who is angry with his brother or sister will be subject to judgment. Whoever insults his brother or sister, will be subject to the court. Whoever says, 'You fool!' will be subject to hellfire.
—Matthew 5:22 (CSB)

My daughter, Charlotte, and her husband, Reuben, both not yet thirty and working for the first time, plan to retire at forty-five. To get there, they're investing half their yearly income and otherwise living frugally. During their three-month stay with my husband and me—so Reuben could train for more lucrative, less demanding work than he'd been doing since he got his PhD—we constantly debated their plan. It's popular among millennials. It's even got a name: Financially Independent, Retire Early, or FIRE.

I hate the FIRE plan. To me, it's lazy, elitist, and irresponsible. I've worked most of my sixty-two years and love my current job, teaching writing and thereby empowering my students as thinkers and citizens. Every job I had before that—from cleaning houses, selling books, altering clothes, and cooking in my youth to working on our farm and writing books—has given me not only skills but also life knowledge, friendships, and stories that make me who I am.

In retirement, Charlotte and Reuben hope to have an alpaca farm, a yarn store, and maybe a food truck—interest-driven jobs similar to the jobs of my own youth. I hate that plan too, though. To me, it seems more about having fun than contributing something of value to the world.

But isn't diversity of opinion—like the diversity of creation, so many different trees, grasses, birds—part of God's plan? Surely others' opinions are as valuable as my own, equally worthy of my respect! I need to remember that and live it, daily.

> *Father God, help me to love all Your children, especially*
> *those different from me.*
> —Patty Kirk

Digging Deeper: Matthew 7:1–5; Ephesians 4:1–13

Wednesday, October 11

". . . do not do as they do, for they do not practice what they teach."
—Matthew 23:3 (NRSV)

I used to work beside Rick. His office was two offices down from mine. We sat in meetings together every week. He invited my family to his Fourth of July barbecue a few years ago.

But Rick left the company last year, and we lost touch. Until I saw him recently on a street corner on the other side of town singing Christmas carols, with a hat on the ground for loose change.

Rick?! I thought to myself, walking quickly away. I didn't want him to see me. I'm not sure why I felt that way. I gave a five-dollar bill to my daughter and said, "Go, throw that in that man's hat."

I'm a disciple of Christ, or so I think. I know about being slow to anger. I know about turning the other cheek. In fact, I sometimes think I'm doing those things when I refrain from impatiently honking at the car in front of me that is taking too long in the lane. Is that my discipleship? Jesus never said, "Blessed are the nice." I need to do more than be nice.

Dorothy Day once said, "If you have two coats, one of them belongs to the poor." I have several coats. I need to do more.

I imagine Jesus saying the verse above to me—"they do not practice what they teach"—when I'm sitting in church feeling good about myself just for being there.

I can't stop thinking about Rick. I want to give him a coat, and then some. Most of all, next time I will not be embarrassed. I will be there for a friend, a neighbor.

Lord, make me a better disciple today.
—Jon M. Sweeney

Digging Deeper: Matthew 23:27

. . . His understanding is infinite. —Psalm 147:5 (NKJV)

I do my own car repairs, but I was stumped by an engine that wouldn't start. Tired and frustrated, I actually laid hands on the engine and prayed for it.

In the afternoon, I was in the home improvement store when I noticed that vacuum cleaners were on sale. I knew my wife, Sharon, was looking for a new one.

The clerk was knowledgeable, but he was pushing the expensive models. I listened, patiently, but he was crowding me. "You know," I broke in, "I think I just need some time to look over these machines for myself."

He didn't get the hint, so I added, "Thanks for your help. Now I can take it from here. If I find something I like, I'll look for you." Reluctantly, he drifted away.

That night in bed, I thought about how God helps me with cars. He gave me a good mind and skilled hands. I have a heated garage and many tools. I find a lot of help online, and often I have "lucky breaks," which I prefer to call "answered prayers."

But above all, God is a gentleman. He doesn't crowd me. He lets me struggle, and most of what I know about cars—and life—came from struggling to understand.

When I finally got the engine running, I was exultant, and I gave praise to God, because He deserves it. God's knowledge is infinite. He knows everything there is to know about cars, but he also knows better than to hand the answers to me on a platter.

Thank You, Lord, for giving me the freedom to learn things for myself and not crowding me when doing so.
—Daniel Schantz

Digging Deeper: Job 28:12–24; Daniel 2:20–22

Friday, October 13

Peace I leave with you; my peace I give you. I do not give to you as the world gives. Do not let your hearts be troubled and do not be afraid.
—John 14:27 (NIV)

I had been on tour for one of my books and was so grateful to arrive home. Wayne had spent the time at our second home, which is in the country on a long, dark road. I met him there and knew almost right away something was wrong. When I quizzed him, Wayne said he'd been having "funny pains" in his chest. Alarm bells rang like Big Ben, and I insisted he go to the emergency room right away. Wayne, being Wayne, refused and claimed I was overreacting. We sat down to eat, and I pleaded with Wayne until he agreed to go to urgent care.

We weren't there more than ten minutes when the doctor called for an aid car (ambulance) to take Wayne immediately to the hospital with a heart center. I followed behind. Wayne was quickly admitted, and it was determined that he would need two stents put in the veins leading to his heart.

Exhausted from my travels, I waited until Wayne was settled and resting before I left the hospital, which was several miles from our home. The rain and windstorm were mild compared to the one taking place in my mind as I drove and silently prayed.

Driving down the dark, twisting roads without streetlights, I could barely manage to see more than two feet in front of me. I couldn't see what was ahead for Wayne, either. Although alone and fearful, I had the headlights to guide me. And I knew I had God's light, too, to guide me no matter what the future held for my husband.

We don't know the future, Lord, but we have the assurance that no matter what happens Your light will guide us through.
—Debbie Macomber

Digging Deeper: Isaiah 26:3; John 8:12, 16:33

We humans keep brainstorming options and plans, but GOD's purpose prevails. —Proverbs 19:21 (MSG)

My eight-year-old granddaughter was melting down like an ice cream cone in a Saharan summer. Lula was adamant—she was NOT going to Vail! Her reasons for not wanting to leave the timeshare where we were staying went on and on . . . *It's going to take forever to get there! It's not going to be fun! I like it HERE!*

What Lula didn't understand was that Vail was only a ten-minute drive from where we were staying. Also, we were headed in that direction because we knew Lula would love it there—if we could just get her into the car. So, Lula's parents and I chose not to heed Lula's pleas to stay where she was. That's because we have her best interest at heart, even when she doesn't realize it. In the end, Lula loved Vail. The following day, she pleaded to head right back to Vail Village to play on the pirate playground, walk over the bridge, say "hi" to all the dogs, and devour the (gulp) $15 hot dogs.

When Lula was throwing a fit that morning, I rolled my eyes at her "childish" behavior—until it dawned on me how often I act the very same way. When God wants me to head in a new direction, leaving behind what I know, enjoy, and feel safe and comfortable with, more times than not, I throw a fit. I refuse to trust that Father knows best. But time and time again, I see God's plan turn out to be far superior to whatever I had in mind. Someday, I hope I'll grow up, instead of just growing old.

Father, You know me better than I know myself. Teach me to trust
You more each day and faithfully follow wherever You
lead—without hesitation.
—Vicki Kuyper

Digging Deeper: Proverbs 3:5–6; Jeremiah 19:11–13;
1 Corinthians 13:11

Sunday, October 15

My grace is sufficient for you, for my power is made perfect in weakness.
—2 Corinthians 12:9 (NIV)

I whisper in my dog's ear, "God took everything I didn't know I wanted in a dog and perfectly made you!" So, when the twinkle in Soda's eyes seemed dull, I made an urgent vet appointment. But by the next day, it was too late. Soda had become completely blind.

"There's nothing you could have done," the veterinarian said. "Happens like this sometimes. Don't worry. He'll adapt. Sight isn't so important to them. You'll see."

For the first few nights, I slept with Soda in the living room on the floor, for fear he would fall off the couch. There were mishaps, like walking into walls, tripping over the cats. I joined groups on social media for support and tried their many tips. I prayed Soda would be okay. I tried not to let guilt that I could have prevented his blindness cloud my heart. I cried.

I hated that our eyes would never connect again. I worried he wouldn't be able to map out the house or jump on the couch. And then—just like that, he figured it all out: the couch, the stairs, the bed, the loop we walk around our house. Even the cats recognized that something was very different about Soda and grew kind to him.

I worried about him, though; deep inside I agonized over his happiness. Was he really okay? And then it happened: Soda had just eaten and I was watching the news when he found a scrap of sun on the floor and for the first time since his blindness, he rolled on his back and did his silly roly-poly, whole-body-wagging, goofy dance of sheer joy. My eyes filled with tears and I clapped my hands.

Dear Lord, thank You for my dog. I love him with all my heart.
—Sabra Ciancanelli

Digging Deeper: Joshua 1:9; Psalm 16:8

When I am afraid, I put my trust in you. —Psalm 56:3 (NIV)

In the days leading up to a recent medical procedure, I faced many growing what-if fears about cancer . . . again. I've dealt with these fears before, and I've gotten pretty good at knowing what to do with them.

First, I picture myself gathering all my fears and putting them in an imaginary dark room. Then I stand at the door and ask Jesus to go into that room with me and, of course, He agrees. We enter together and I'm immediately aware that His presence brings light into the darkness.

Slowly He walks beside me as one by one, I look my worst possible fears right in the face. Jesus watches, silent and patient. I'm thankful He doesn't try to talk me out of my fears or remind me how many times "fear not" is repeated in the Bible. I sense that He understands, and His presence validates the reality of my fears. He simply stands quietly beside me and that is enough.

Finally, when I am ready, we walk out of the room because I don't have to stay there. I faced my fears with Jesus and now I know, even if one of those fears becomes a reality in my future, Jesus will be right beside me.

I carried that trust with me as I was wheeled down the hospital hall for the procedure and afterward, as I waited in recovery for the doctor to come tell me the results.

Suddenly he appeared, and with a smile, he said, "You're clean."

> *Fears feel less fearful when I know You are with me, Jesus,*
> *and You are always enough.*
> —Carol Kuykendall

Digging Deeper: Psalm 23; 1 Corinthians 2:14

Tuesday, October 17

So do not fear, for I am with you; do not be dismayed, for I am your
God. I will strengthen you and help you; I will uphold you with my
righteous right hand. —Isaiah 41:10 (NIV)

Once when I was on my way home after a visit to my son Andrew
in California, he broke off two chunks of his healthy jade plant
and stuck them in my suitcase. Back in Florida, I babied that plant and
it quadrupled in size in two years.

One day I noticed that some of the leaves were dropping off and
there was white fuzz all over the bottoms of the succulent leaves. My
sister Catherine, who is a certified master gardener, came to the rescue.
She can grow anything and knows exactly how to care for all plants
native to our state of Florida.

Catherine told me to look at the fuzz with a magnifying glass. I saw
that it was actually fuzzy bugs destroying my plant. So she said, "Spray
it with 70 percent isopropyl alcohol, then rinse it off in the shower." I
did and that jade plant continues to thrive.

During that same time, Andrew's health began to fail, and with him
in California and me in Florida, I felt so helpless. But just as I had
to depend on Catherine's expertise to save my jade plant, I understand that I have to depend on Jesus to take care of Andrew. I can't do
anything to make him well except pray. But Jesus knows exactly how
to take care of Andrew. And I just know that my faith in God and in
Andrew's doctors will get both of us through the scary times.

Jesus, You know how much I depend on You to get Andrew through the
tough days of his illness. Thanks for the peace of knowing
You will never leave his side.
—Patricia Lorenz

Digging Deeper: Psalm 22:19, 28:7–8, 33:20–22

. . . they shall feed every one in his place. —Jeremiah 6:3 (KJV)

Ever since I received my *Betty Crocker Cookbook for Boys and Girls* at age eleven, I have loved to cook. By the time I was twelve, I could produce an entire supper for my family. When I fed my four children for umpteen years, I consistently enjoyed the meal planning, purchasing, preparation, and serving. I daydreamed that once my brood grew up, I'd continue cooking for them. I even envisioned a trestle table to seat ten to twelve to accommodate my kids, their spouses, and grandkids.

Alas, my reality is quite different. I now live in a modest apartment with a table that seats four, max. My two sons and their families live thousands of miles away. My local daughter now hosts holiday gatherings because her husband is allergic to my cat. Though I may serve one or two dinner guests from time to time, my delight in feeding others has been stymied. Cut short. I'm no longer needed.

Or so I thought until I joined the Comfort Food Team at my church. Now I'm invited to help feed families recuperating from medical procedures ranging from tonsillectomies to knee replacements. Some have been displaced by fire; others hindered by immobility and living alone. Once again, I rise to the challenge of creating a tasty meal, whether it be for a family of eight (with picky teens), for someone adhering to a low-fat, gluten- and dairy-free menu, or for the person recovering from the tonsillectomy who needs everything pureed. When I deliver the meals, I often visit with the recipients, nourishing old friendships or starting new ones.

I may not be able to feed my relatives much anymore, but God has convinced me that my culinary skills are, indeed, needed.

> *Dear Lord, in my apron-wrapped ministry, help me*
> *dish up plenty of love with my meals!*
> —Gail Thorell Schilling

Digging Deeper: Isaiah 58:10; Matthew 25:35; Romans 12:13

Thursday, October 19

Hear my prayer, O LORD, And let my cry come to You.
—Psalm 102:1 (NKJV)

Fall break was upon us, and while I was content with relaxing at home for the next few days, my children were eager to get outside. Frankly, I was trying to avoid the allergy flare-ups of itchy eyes and throats. They finally convinced me to venture out to a local family farm known for celebrating the harvest with a pumpkin patch, hayrides, four acres of corn maze, old-fashioned ciders, and entertainment you can only find in the South—like pig races.

Since work responsibilities kept my husband from joining us, my mother agreed to come along. I packed up my crew of three along with my two-year-old nephew for a day of fun. We headed straight for the corn maze, and the attendant assured us that we'd work our way through the high stalks in twenty minutes or less, so my mother took a seat at a nearby bench to wait.

Twenty minutes . . . thirty minutes . . . forty-five minutes passed, and unbelievably we were still attempting to find our way out. We'd tried to follow others who themselves were confused. As the dry stalks towered like tall men above our heads, I yelled out jokingly but with all sincerity, "God, help us get out of here."

Soon after, we stumbled upon a family whom we followed to the exit. We emerged tired and ravenous, and I vowed that day never to enter a corn maze again. But it also reminded me that when I cry out to God, He hears me. No problem is too complicated and no request too trivial. I would be lost without him.

God, thank You for hearing my cries and coming to my rescue.
You've also sent the Holy Spirit to lead and guide me, and
for that I'm forever grateful.
—Tia McCollors

Digging Deeper: Psalm 4:1, 5:1; John 10:27

Whoever is slow to anger has great understanding, but he who has a hasty temper exalts folly. —Proverbs 14:29 (ESV)

Passing slower vehicles is a dedicated effort when my town trip involves mountainous, two-lane roads with few opportunities for passing. Recently I was behind a particularly cautious driver. When my chance came to pass, I signaled and eased into the other lane. Glancing in my mirror, my heart skittered when I saw a green car behind me suddenly dart into the lane to pass, accelerating hard. I swerved back behind the slow driver and stomped on my brakes to avoid a collision with either vehicle.

Even though the green car blinked "sorry" with its taillights, it didn't stop me from muttering about the driver's intellect. "Thank You, Lord, for keeping me safe," I prayed. But I felt no forgiveness, only mounting frustration. "What's in town that's worth dying for?" I eventually got around the slow car, still grumbling. "Are there no courteous drivers anymore?"

Around the next bend, I saw the green car again, and my self-righteous anger immediately turned to fervent prayer. I was waved past the scene but slowly enough that I could see why the driver of the green car had driven recklessly to get here.

A white car had wrecked sometime before. An obviously shaken, bruised teenager was leaning against the mangled car, being treated by medics. From the green car, which had pulled off the road next to the wreck, a distraught dad was running toward the teenager with his arms outstretched.

> *Please bless that family, Lord. And forgive me when I'm not courteous. Teach me patience with impatient drivers, who may have reason for racing.*
> —Erika Bentsen

Digging Deeper: Exodus 14:14; Psalm 37:7; Ephesians 4:2; Philippians 4:6

Saturday, October 21

For he satisfies the longing soul, and the hungry soul he fills with good things. —Psalm 107:9 (ESV)

"Who knew that owning a hundred-year-old cabin would mean so much work!" I exclaimed as I scraped flaking paint from the exterior walls.

"Looks like the sills need scraping, too," my husband, Kevin, said as he removed a framed window screen.

Staining. Painting. Scraping. Raking. Our free time at the cabin was not quite the relaxing getaway we had imagined or dreamed, yet in between work projects, we managed to explore the nearby area. We were surprised to discover black walnut trees on an abandoned road, the green fruit of early summer hidden in the branches.

"Wait until the outer husks dry before collecting," a local friend advised.

By October, dried walnut husks covered the ground around the trees. Under the watchful eyes of circling ravens and red-tailed hawks, we harvested over twenty-five pounds.

"Put the nuts in an old pillowcase and run over them with a truck," our friend suggested when the husks refused to release their inner prize. After this unconventional method, many husks still needed to be removed individually, covering our hands with black walnut stain. After rinsing multiple times, we had a cardboard box filled with one-inch nuts.

While our daughter Katelyn stirred up a bread recipe, Kevin wielded a hammer and vice grips to crack the walnuts after a regular nutcracker proved useless. After months of waiting, we enjoyed the nutty goodness found in the warm bread while seated at the table of our work-in-progress cabin.

Jesus, black walnuts and old cabins are best enjoyed by those who persevere. Help me in the gathering, scraping, and cracking of other dreams today.
—Lynne Hartke

Digging Deeper: Philippians 3:13–14; Hebrews 10:23; James 1:12

We love because he first loved us. —1 John 4:19 (NIV)

After two-and-a-half years, we're working through an offer on our Victorian. We've already moved, but this is truly letting go. Until now, I've gone back home to prune bushes. To pull weeds. Any sale would hurt, but this one has been exhausting.

First, things fell through two days before closing. Now, even still, this new offer reflects that Lonny and I are in a bind. We've negotiated for days. Every interaction stings.

I'm angry, grief-stricken, and I just want to go back home. I want to walk where I know every nick in the floorboards. But our reasons for moving remain. My husband is exhausted from years of owning a home that owns us, and we need to live closer to our boys' high school.

This road has been long.

I hide in the laundry room of our new home because I need to be alone. I shove the washer full of towels, but my soul can't come clean. I want to shout. *Lord, this move was best for everyone else! But what about me?*

Right then, my husband comes in from the garage. Lonny stands in the hall, a rotisserie chicken tucked under his arm like a football. He's tired. Tired of old-house repairs. Tired from having two homes. Tired from the tangles of this sale. There are new lines around his eyes. His shoulders curl under his jacket. This ordeal has been tough on him, too.

And a dam inside me breaks.

Suddenly I'm so filled with love for this man that I can't even speak. It's always been the two of us, leaning into the Lord together. He anchors me when tethering is tough. He needs this release, and I want it for him more than I want it for myself. The answer to my question falls like fresh rain.

Sometimes love is an offering.

Jesus, I thank You because Yours was a sacrifice that saved me. Amen.
—Shawnelle Eliasen

Digging Deeper: John 15:12; Colossians 3:14

Monday, October 23

"I am the good shepherd; I know my sheep and my sheep know me . . ."
—John 10:14 (NIV)

Last night, I received a phone call from a former student whom I taught at Mercer University. She was in one of my first classes, and we became close friends over her four years of college. Now, several years after her graduation, she is an excellent elementary-school teacher, and we often talk about decisions that she is making in her career and personal life.

As we talked, she thanked me for "helping her along the way" and I was instantly filled with gratitude and joy for our friendship. To help someone "find their way" along life's journey is the greatest joy I have experienced.

Jesus's favorite teaching model was often the Galilean shepherd. Though his family trade was carpentry, he also wanted to love others by being a shepherding presence in their life. He told his followers to "shepherd my sheep." My former student is now a shepherd of first-grade students. She teaches children the basic tools of survival—reading, writing, arithmetic, social skills, and fun at recess! No matter what our vocation or age, we can all be teachers and shepherds. In this process, we will discover the greatest joy and positive challenge in our lives.

> *Dear God, help me to shepherd Your sheep and to know the*
> *joy of friendship and commitment. Amen.*
> —Scott Walker

Digging Deeper: Psalm 78:52, 79:13; John 10:11–15; 1 Peter 2:25

THE PINK HOUSE: A Friend Leads the Way

Take heed that ye do not your alms before men, to be seen of them . . .
—Matthew 6:1 (KJV)

It's not unusual for Jesus to place "pink houses" before us in the actions of our friends. What better way can He make His directions clear?

My friend Mike has dropped by for a visit. With a pure heart for the AIDS orphans we serve in Zimbabwe, he has been a faithful contributor to our cause. "I have a question," he says. "How much would it cost to add a library to our Village Hope School?"

"I don't know, but I can find out," I answer.

This is an astounding new chapter in our Zimbabwe story, one that will enhance the lives of many, many people. Soon, the gift comes, but with a condition: "I don't want anyone to know my name," Mike says.

"Mike, this is big. I want to name the library after you."

"You know my condition," he answers.

As the library becomes a reality that includes adult literacy classes, tutoring programs, and other services, I try a different approach. "What inspired you to do this?" I ask. "My grandmother, Annie Sue," was all he said.

Of course, Mike's way reflects some mighty fine advice from Jesus. He gets it. Happiness comes when we give freely, asking nothing in return. Mike has become a "pink house" pointing the way.

Still, our Zimbabwe children needed to know.

I didn't tell Mike about the plaque until we attached it to a wall in faraway Zimbabwe. It's in a place visible to every child who passes by:

Say Her Name
Annie Sue Totty Shelby
Her love brought these books to you

Father, You show us how to live, contented, through friends like Mike. Thank You.
—Pam Kidd

Digging Deeper: Proverbs 11:24; Matthew 10:8

Wednesday, October 25

Devote yourselves to prayer, being watchful and thankful.
—Colossians 4:2 (NIV)

My walk to work takes me up a hill in Fort Tryon Park behind the Cloisters Museum. It's the same steep incline (now paved) the Hessians scaled in 1776 during the battle of Fort Washington. I climb and use various landmarks to remind me to pray for particular people.

At the curve where the Hudson River first comes into view, I pray for the marriage of some friends who are having friction. A little farther on, I pray for a mom undergoing difficult times. At the top, where the path widens into an overlook, I pause to gaze at the sparkling river and the Palisades. This is where I say, every day, "Thank You, Lord. I love You."

Some days there is fog, and I can see nothing. I say thank You, anyway, because the beauty is there even if I can't see it.

Some days it is raining, and I want to keep moving so my feet don't get too wet. But I say thank You even though I'm not feeling grateful, because thankfulness is more than a feeling.

Some days I am preoccupied with problems and barely notice where I am. Habit helps: Even if my thank-you doesn't emerge until a hundred yards farther down the path, I remember there are things to be thankful for in spite of the darkest times. From there I can move forward.

Thank You, Lord, for Your goodness and mercy.
—Julia Attaway

Digging Deeper: 1 Corinthians 11:23–24; Philippians 4:6

"Ask, and it will be given you; search, and you will find; knock, and the door will be opened for you. For everyone who asks receives, and everyone who searches finds, and for everyone who knocks, the door will be open."
—Matthew 7:7–8 (NRSV)

I banged down the phone, groaned, and threw my hands up in frustration. I'd just wasted another hour, one of many, trying to convince a friend to take the necessary steps to change a dangerous situation in her life. I felt angry and righteously so. I, with other friends and family members, had done just about everything we could think of to convince her to end a toxic relationship that was becoming abusive. We'd confronted her, helped pay for therapy, and one of us had even intervened when it looked like her job might be on the line. She'd already lost the chance for a promotion because of her partner's behavior.

"That's it! I've had it!" I told a mutual friend over coffee later that afternoon, flinging one hand in a gesture of release. A few people in the coffee shop glanced over, and I lowered my voice, but it made me even angrier. Here I was, so exasperated I was acting like a fool in public.

That evening when I settled down for my prayer time, I felt calmer but still justified in my anger. I breathed deeply in the silence, raising my hands to the Lord, as I always do when starting my prayers. I noticed my hands and remembered how I'd raised them in anger that morning and waved them in rejection that afternoon. Suddenly I felt ashamed, all my rationalizations crumbling into dust. When it came to my friend, really to any difficult situation, this—prayer—was the only way I should be using my hands. And my heart.

Merciful Father, thank You for teaching me prayer-full humility.
—Marci Alborghetti

Digging Deeper: Psalm 121:1–2; Luke 6:37–42

Friday, October 27

The earth was empty and had no form. Darkness covered the ocean, and God's Spirit was moving over the water. Then God said, "Let there be light," and there was light. God saw that the light was good, so he divided the light from the darkness. God named the light "day" and the darkness "night." Evening passed, and morning came. This was the first day.
—Genesis 1:2–5 (NCV)

I'm not an early riser. But being the first person to see the sunrise in the United States motivated me to roll out of bed at 4 a.m. on a cold October morning while visiting Bar Harbor, Maine. My destination was the top of Cadillac Mountain, the highest point along the North Atlantic seaboard and located in Acadia National Park. Would trading a warm bed for freezing wind be worth the trip?

At about 6:15, a faint yellow light eased above the Gulf of Maine horizon and spread across the water like waves rolling to shore. Minutes later, a red flash shot along the golden glow like fireworks piercing the night sky. Over the next half-hour, a dome of orange brilliance breached the edge of darkness and sparkled like a fire opal rising from the deep. In speechless awe of the beauty and grandeur of night turning into day, I glimpsed a tiny portion of God's power witnessed by the universe during Creation when He said, "Let there be light."

At that moment, I felt God's presence surround me with the same warmth and strength. And I realized His love and mercy are available to me new each day. Would rising early and climbing a mountain be required? No, a simple whispered prayer brings me just as close.

Lord, thank You for rescuing me from deep water and turning my darkness into light. Remind me daily You are the light of the world and help me to walk in Your light.
—Jenny Lynn Keller

Digging Deeper: Psalm 18:28; Lamentations 3:19–23; John 8:12

Weeping may endure for a night, but joy comes in the morning.
—Psalm 30:5 (NKJV)

The wind pressed against my Jeep, rattling the soft top. Normally, I would listen to music on my way to work. Today, I had a lot to think about. A recent breakup. The end of a friendship. The sale of my childhood home. Lately, I had been experiencing a season of letting go. In the wake of that loss, I felt empty.

I stopped at an intersection and flipped my left-turn signal. I knew that the next block would be lined with small maples blazing red in the October sun. I had appreciated them each morning this week.

The light changed to green, and I turned. For a moment, I thought I was on the wrong street. This block was dull and colorless. Then I saw the skeletal outline of the trees. Several red leaves still clung to their branches. In just a day, the wind had stripped the trees bare. They had been drained of their color.

My chest hurt. I identified with them.

As I drove by the trees, I looked at their isolated trunks. Despite their loss, the trunks stayed strong and firm. I knew that, deep within, life still pulsed.

A season of cold and snow lay ahead of the trees. But then, the sun would shine, the ground would thaw, and buds would break forth. And with the spring would come restoration.

As I turned off the street, I knew that God would bring the same to me.

> *Lord, lead me through seasons of loss, and bring me the*
> *blessing of Your renewal.*
> —Logan Eliasen

Digging Deeper: Isaiah 44:24–26; Joel 2:25

Sunday, October 29

A friend loves at all times, and a brother is born for a time of adversity.
—Proverbs 17:17 (NIV)

Depression affects people from all walks of life no matter their background. Sometimes people we least expect find themselves battling depression. When I learned a good friend of mine was in a dark place, I wanted to be present for him. I wasn't sure how to help him in his time of need, and I didn't want to make things worse by trying to remind him of better days. Yet I decided to err in caring rather than worrying about what I might say or do wrong.

When I called him, he was delighted to hear from me. We talked for a long time. I could hear the pain and struggle in his voice. He was having a hard time running his business, managing staff, and serving his customers due to his depression. It was also affecting his ability to do the simple things of life. Some days he was afraid to drive his car to do errands. The worst for him was getting up in the morning to face another day. He had been through divorce, losing his parents, and tough economic times. But never through depression.

The more we talked, the more I sensed his faith and hope even in the midst of this dark time in his life. Sessions with a therapist and anti-depressant medications were helping him to feel better. Daily prayers and reminding himself of all the good things in his life offered spiritual strength. At the end of our talk on the phone, we prayed together and every call thereafter. These days he is in a much better place and our friendship is stronger.

> *Lord, teach us how to care for our friends in their darkest days.*
> —Pablo Diaz

Digging Deeper: Ecclesiastes 4:9–10; Lamentations 3:19–24

. . . for the happy heart, life is a continual feast. —Proverbs 15:15 (NLT)

When I was growing up in the '70s, Halloween night always saw our neighborhood filled with trick-or-treaters. On one such Halloween night, my mom took my brother and me trick-or-treating with her friend Peggy and Peggy's children, leaving my dad to man the door at our house. We weren't gone more than a couple of hours, but when we returned, Daddy was handing out unwrapped cookies from a package. Mother was aghast. "You can't give unwrapped cookies to trick-or-treaters!" she insisted.

My dad, always quick with a witty reply, responded, "What choice did I have? I was this close to frying eggs and giving them steaks out of the freezer!"

Mother and her friend nearly fell down laughing . . . then quickly ran to the grocery store to stock up on more candy.

That was more than forty years ago. Recently, my parents and I went to a funeral for one of Peggy's family members. As we visited and caught up, Peggy reminded us of Daddy's punch line from all those years ago. We laughed so hard we cried—even Peggy, who was mourning her loved one.

I'm sure Daddy had no idea that we'd be laughing about his joke decades later, even under sad circumstances. What a beautiful gift, reminding me of the Proverb that for the happy heart, life is a feast. Sometimes, a feast of fried eggs and steaks out of the freezer!

Lord, thank You for the gift of laughter and for those
who share it so generously.
—Ginger Rue

Digging Deeper: Proverbs 15:13, 17:22

Tuesday, October 31

The entrance of thy words giveth light . . . —Psalms 119:130 (KJV)

"Come on, Dad," my eight-year-old son Harrison complained. "Do I have to spend my trick-or-treat time going to Kate's house?"

He was at that "me" age. He wasn't thinking of Kate, one of the older folks my parents had "adopted" over the years. Unmarried, Kate lived alone. In her eighties, we were the closest thing she had to a real family. She attended all of my birthdays and later Harrison's major events.

"Now, Harrison, Kate loves you with all her heart. Without us she would be a lonely person without any family at all."

In truth, Kate lived in an old neighborhood where I doubted any children would be. She probably wasn't prepared for trick-or-treaters, and I had dragged Harrison away from his friends.

Still, here we were, at Kate's little house. Harrison stood at the door in his mummy costume and knocked . . . once . . . twice. Then, the door opened. And there stood Kate wearing an old gypsy costume, smiling from ear to ear. "I was hoping you would come," she said, in answer to Harrison's "trick or treat?!"

She held out an old plate flecked with fake jewels that circled around an amazing caramel apple. "I rode the bus down to Candyland to get you a special treat just in case you came. Harrison . . . oh, you are a gift from my Heavenly Father."

Kate's there now, at home with her Heavenly Father, and Harrison, well, he's a college student now, no doubt making Kate very proud. And there's one thing for sure. A Halloween never passes without Harrison remembering his knock on that door and the light of love that waited within.

Father, continue pointing my son Harrison, and all of us,
toward the light that spills out from Your words.
—Brock Kidd

Digging Deeper: John 8:12, 12:36

LET US SING FOR JOY

1 _____

2 _____

3 _____

4 _____

5 _____

6 _____

7 _____

8 _____

9 _____

10 _____

11 _____

12 _____

13 _____

14 _____

15 _____

October

16 _____

17 _____

18 _____

19 _____

20 _____

21 _____

22 _____

23 _____

24 _____

25 _____

26 _____

27 _____

28 _____

29 _____

30 _____

31 _____

November

Through Jesus, therefore, let us continually offer to
God a sacrifice of praise—the fruit of lips that
openly profess his name.

—Hebrews 13:15 (NIV)

Wednesday, November 1

I will praise the LORD all my life; I will sing praise to my God as long as I live. —Psalm 146:2 (NIV)

I am sometimes perplexed by what it means to "praise God." Often, praising God is perceived as singing, thanksgiving, and the emotive expression of our love for God through worship or personal devotional time. However, perhaps the most important way to praise God is through loving and caring for another person.

This afternoon, I noticed a college freshman in my class who looked lonely and depressed. After class, I asked him if he would like to walk with me to the student center and have a cup of coffee. He looked a little startled, but he smiled and accepted the invitation. An hour later, I had a new friend and he had discovered someone to talk with on a new college campus.

Centuries ago in Israel, many people thought that what pleased God the most was attending temple services and presenting an offering. But the prophet Micah proclaimed that God is most pleased when we try "to do justice, to love kindness, and to walk humbly with your God" (Micah 6:8 [NASB]).

> *Father, may I praise You by loving my neighbor as much*
> *as I love myself. Amen.*
> —Scott Walker

Digging Deeper: Psalm 150; Micah 6:8;
Matthew 22:3–4; Luke 10:25–37

The Spirit of God has made me, and the breath of the Almighty gives me life. —Job 33:4 (ESV)

Sixty feet doesn't sound like much. If you had to stop a car at speed in that distance, it would be nearly impossible. But, when you're on the seabed and the nearest breathable air is sixty feet above you, it sure seems like a long, long way.

Which is exactly the predicament I found myself in.

Commercial divers generally work tethered to a ship, dock, or some other structure. Your air comes through a long hose. Which means your life is literally in someone else's hands. When the air stops, there's not a lot of choice and not a lot of time to think about it. Where there *is* a lot of time is during that eternal-seeming ascent.

I broke the surface about the same time as the two other divers working from the same boat. The compressor that supplied us wasn't running, the tender responsible for keeping it gassed up and working nowhere in sight. I'm convinced God was looking out for us that day. If we'd been working much deeper, the story would have had a very different ending.

I think of my relationship with Jesus in much the same way as a diver on a tether. He alone is my lifeline, and I know this without a doubt. In the diving world, there's always the nagging thought of *what if.* But with our God, there's never a question. He is *Faith* even when I'm faithless. He is *Love* even when I am unlovely.

He is my safety.

He is my watchman.

He is my very breath.

Jesus, Your arms are our safe harbor. Guide us and guard us, Lord,
as we make our way through this shadowy deep until that day
we see You face-to-face in the eternal sunlight.
—Buck Storm

Digging Deeper: Psalm 139; Isaiah 41:10; Hebrews 6:19

Friday, November 3

When anxiety was great within me, your consolation brought me joy.
—Psalm 94:19 (NIV)

No matter how many times I hit a key, my laptop refused to power on. It had crashed. While I was normally great at backing up documents and files, I'd gotten a little lazy in doing it on a regular basis. Would my notes be lost? Worse, would I remember what all was open in my infinite browser tabs?

When I finally got it to reboot, a little box popped up: Start from where you left off, or start fresh?

Instead of clicking the option that would immediately launch seven programs, open no fewer than forty tabs, and likely cause my computer to crash all over again, I took a breath, said a prayer, and opted to start fresh instead.

When the screen came to life, it was bright and clean. From there, I could choose what to tackle first, then next. Doing only the next thing, without the other ninety-nine things looming in my vision, allowed me to be terrifically productive and, well, calm. At the end of my workday, I turned to the rest of my house and immediately felt like crashing myself: toys scattered, dishes piled, laundry heaped, and floors cluttered. Instead of crashing, I picked one thing to start with and then moved on to the next.

I know God doesn't speak out loud in burning bushes anymore, but it turns out He can use just about anything to speak to us when we need Him and His grace most, even overloaded laptops.

Lord, help me to clear my mental cookies so that I may be able to focus on You and Your plans for my life. Help me in my work today—and every day.
—Ashley Kappel

Digging Deeper: Psalm 9:10; Jeremiah 17:7–8;
Matthew 11:28–30; John 14:1

Why do you see the speck in your neighbor's eye, but do not notice the log in your own eye? —Matthew 7:3 (NRSV)

My daughter, Charlotte, and her husband, Reuben, moved to Seattle and immediately started looking for a house to rent. ~~Miraculously, within days,~~ they found the perfect house—all for $700 less than they'd paid for a much-less-than-perfect house in the San Francisco Bay area.

When Charlotte called, she gushed about nearby parks, one an off-leash dog park with "over 200 species of birds" and "gigantic ferns everywhere!" Another plus was the "family-friendly" neighborhood. She and Reuben hope to start a family soon. "All the neighbors look like they have kids, and there are no homeless people anywhere!"

Our conversation soured then into me pontificating about her heart-lessness toward those less fortunate than she is and her sounding embar-rassed but nevertheless defending the desire to "just live somewhere nice."

After the call, I felt bad about sullying Charlotte's excitement with my self-righteousness. Who doesn't want to live somewhere nice? And what do I do for the rare homeless person I encounter in rural Okla-homa beyond passing a twenty out my car window and feeling briefly sad in some benevolent annex of my consciousness?

My childhood best friend's family took in a woman and her children, a commitment that lasted decades. Another friend shared her apart-ment with a family camping out on her street. My friends' compas-sion for the homeless has impressed me my whole life, speaking more persuasively than words ever could have. I resolved to exchange my sermons on compassion for a legacy of compassionate action for the instruction of those around me.

> *Father, empower me to actually love those less fortunate than*
> *I am, rather than merely talk about how we all should.*
> —Patty Kirk

Digging Deeper: Isaiah 58:7; Matthew 25:31–46

Sunday, November 5

My comfort in my suffering is this: Your promise preserves my life.
—Psalm 119:50 (NIV)

It must be really hard for you to be around alcohol," a person commented to me the other day.

I get that a lot.

After more than twenty-five years of sobriety, I rarely experience the urge to drink, and it has nothing to do with the proximity of alcohol. But I am not cured. I will never be cured.

I first got that news from an old-timer at an AA meeting early in my sobriety. I had shared something with the group the old-timer had apparently taken exception to. I have no recollection of what I said. The old-timer sidled up to me after the meeting.

"You're never cured, you know," he said. "You strike me as someone who thinks he's going to get cured here. That doesn't happen."

The conversation ended there, but those words have stayed with me. He was right. I was looking for a cure so perhaps, just maybe, I could someday drink again. It may not have been conscious, but it was lurking within my character flaws. That, my sponsor said, is why we work the twelve steps. To address the thinking that leads to the drinking.

One of the things I am most grateful for in sobriety is the fact that I have come to accept that I have an incurable, fatal disease. Accepting that my alcoholism was incurable liberated me from the self-delusion that I could ever go back to drinking "normally."

Without that acceptance, I would never have experienced the gifts of sobriety. I would never have found a relationship with a God of my understanding and the peace that flows from it. It is that peace, that serenity, that I now want to feel all the time.

A day at a time, Lord, I am grateful for my sobriety. May I grow closer
to You the further I get from my last drink.
—Edward Grinnan

Digging Deeper: Psalm 34:18; Proverbs 3:5–6

Yet you, LORD, are our Father. We are the clay, you are the potter; we are all the work of your hand. —Isaiah 64:8 (NIV)

I thought my daughter's picky eating habits were a stage she'd outgrow and even wondered at one time if it was my cooking that she didn't prefer. From a very young age, she'd push away her plate for some meals, scrunching her nose up at the smell, taste, or texture of the food on the plate. While the rest of us would scoff down family favorites of spaghetti, chicken and broccoli casserole, or baked fish with seasoned vegetables, she'd spend the time to meticulously pick out the specks of seasoning, diced green peppers, and all the miniscule items she set her eyes on. Truth be told, it was—and still is—a bit frustrating.

I'd resolved to allow her to experiment with cooking and preparing her favorite foods in a way that suited her taste. I could never understand how she'd choose the bland over savory and hearty dishes that delight the palate.

God's creativity isn't only used to paint the skies with amber sunrises and purple sunsets. He doesn't just form every snowflake with its own design or carve every mountain with its own set of ridges and cliffs. He purposely fashioned my daughter—the tone of her skin, the way her eyes squint into small slits when she smiles, her artistic ability and mathematical mind, and the way she eats her hot dogs with no fixins at all. If God accepts her for the way she is, then certainly I can, too. And when all else fails, we spend time together over a food that we both love and enjoy—ice cream sundaes.

Lord, I embrace my uniqueness. You've given me my personality, preferences, and purpose for use in Your kingdom.
—Tia McCollors

Digging Deeper: Psalm 119:73–74; Ephesians 2:10

Tuesday, November 7

Be joyful in hope, patient in affliction, faithful in prayer.
—Romans 12:12 (NIV)

"Oh no! I lost an earring," I said out loud as I looked in the bathroom mirror late one night. This wasn't just any earring. It was my most favorite, go-to one.

"Please, Lord, help me find my earring!" I immediately prayed.

I knew this prayer about lost things was sometimes answered and sometimes not. Recently I found a special necklace that went missing for weeks, and we're still looking for my husband Lynn's glasses that we're sure are somewhere in the house. Now my favorite earring.

I mentally retraced our steps that evening. From the house to the car to a movie theater. I checked around the house and car with a flashlight. No earring. The next day, I called the theater. No earring in lost and found. I described exactly where we sat in the theater and held on to hope while the nice movie-man went to search.

I heard his footsteps as he came back to the phone. "I found it!" he told me.

"Oh, thank you! Thank you! I'll be right there to pick it up."

I grabbed the car keys and told Lynn I was off to retrieve my lost earring.

"Maybe there's hope we'll find my glasses," he said.

I thought about his words while driving. I'd just received an answer to a prayer while he held on to an unanswered prayer with hope. God obviously blesses answered prayers. But I never thought how unanswered prayers make space for hope.

I came out of the theater clutching my earring and thanking God, but I had a new desire to go home and once again search for Lynn's glasses. Holding on to hope.

Lord, finding hope in an unanswered prayer is a blessing. Thank You.
—Carol Kuykendall

Digging Deeper: John 15:7; Philippians 4:6–7; 1 Thessalonians 5:16–18

Whatever happens, give thanks . . . —1 Thessalonians 5:18 (GW)

A flat tire was not on my agenda. I'd just enjoyed a lovely lunch with friends and was in high spirits as I headed home to work on a writing project. Now, here I sat, parked by the side of the road, thankful to have made it safely across six lanes of traffic as a loud *clunk, clunk, clunk* had resounded from the back of my little red Jetta. My tire wasn't just flat—it was shredded. The strips of tread looked like I'd run over an ink-black jellyfish that had somehow ended up in the middle of a road in the Rockies.

As I waited for roadside assistance, I was overwhelmed with thanks. Thanks for the driver who'd alerted me to the problem. Thanks for a convenient place to pull off the road. Thanks for the unseasonably warm November day. Thanks that I didn't have to change a tire by myself. Thanks for being able to salvage a scrap of paper from the bag of potatoes my friend had given me so I could write while I waited. And once the spare was in place, I thanked God the entire way home for every little thing that had gone *right.*

The next morning, as I left a local tire shop with my new set of all-weather tires (paid for thanks to a check that had arrived just that week), the temperature was in the 20s, the wind was howling, and the first flakes of an impending blizzard had begun to fly. I couldn't help but sing all the way home. Never had a flat tire felt more like an honest-to-goodness gift from God.

Lord, please help me continue to focus on what goes right in my life, all those little ways You care for me each and every day.
—Vicki Kuyper

Digging Deeper: Psalm 31:19; Colossians 3:15; Hebrews 13:15

Thursday, November 9

Let all the earth fear the LORD; let all the inhabitants of the world stand in awe of him! —Psalm 33:8 (ESV)

I was walking in the woods late one evening, long after dark. The birds had long gone quiet. It was November, so the crickets were gone, and the frogs were somewhere in hibernation deep in the lake. It was very quiet, which is why I was out walking.

It had been a difficult day. My wife and I got into an argument about something; I've long since forgotten what it was. And work was dispiriting. Problems at work can feel intractable, and at those times, I feel like the kid I once was who fell behind in French and so wanted to drop the class and run.

I needed this dark, silent night.

I didn't expect to be gifted with anything in particular beyond the darkness and the silence. Space to breathe and think.

Then, I saw a flashing light in the sky. A tiny one—just a streak. I looked more closely.

Then, I saw another streak and then another.

It was a meteor shower. This went on for nearly a full minute. Some minutes are more glorious and memorable than other minutes. This was one of those times.

> *You are my world, O God. My faith shakes and rattles,*
> *but my hope in You is forever.*
> —Jon M. Sweeney

Digging Deeper: Hebrews 12:28

The thief comes only to steal and kill and destroy. I came that they may have life, and have it abundantly. —John 10:10 (NRSV)

Lying open on my kitchen table is a college-level music theory textbook. A friend lent it to me, with the suggestion that I work my way through it if I wanted to. Just on my own time. There's no professor, class, or syllabus pushing me along. No time pressure. It's just me and the book. And this ever-present, self-talking voice in my head, doing its level best to convince me I'll never learn any of it. "It's too hard," it tells me. "You're not the type of person who can understand this stuff. You'll give up. You'll fail." And on and on. Gosh, it's believable. Its authority doesn't quaver. It doesn't ask questions. It just says, "You can't," as if it knows exactly what it's talking about.

But the thing is, I really, really want to know what's in this book's pages. And so, despite the inner critic, I've kept at it. In the process, I've discovered something startling: That voice? It's wrong. Music theory is hard, yes. But not *too* hard. With work, I *do* understand. I *am* learning. I haven't given up. Therefore, this voice's declarations do not bear up. Its authority is false.

It would be nice if that realization silenced it. But, of course, it's still there, saying its same old, terrible things. Thankfully though, this theory textbook is long. And as I keep plugging my way through it, I'm becoming practiced at recognizing my inner critic for what it is: a liar that would have my life remain small, less full, and less abundant than God wants it to be.

> *Thank You, Lord, for helping me learn to discern the voice of the deceiver so that I might turn from it toward You and the purpose and blessings You have planned for my life.*
> —Erin Janoso

Digging Deeper: Romans 12:2; 1 John 4:1

Veterans Day, Saturday, November 11

I will surely bless you, and I will surely multiply your offspring as the stars of heaven and as the sand that is on the seashore. And your offspring shall possess the gate of his enemies. —Genesis 22:17 (ESV)

With hundreds of channels for my viewing pleasure, there was nothing I wanted to watch on television one lazy afternoon. *Saving Private Ryan* scrolled on the menu. *Why not? It is Veterans Day,* I thought. I was glad it popped up in my menu because while it is a weighty movie, I had the opportunity to reflect upon hope, sacrifice, and love as I intently watched.

Fittingly, *Saving Private Ryan* stirred within my soul gratitude and reverence for all those who have sacrificed their lives, their family, and their stability in service of our country. I was most struck by the scene when Captain Miller, whose mission it was to save Private Ryan as the only remaining son in his family, said, dying, "James, earn this. Earn this." Captain Miller's words whispered to my heart and reminded me that in order to honor all veterans, I must be a good steward of life and liberty. Blood has been spilt and sacrifice has been made so that I have the opportunity for prosperity and freedom. Our veterans' sacrifices weren't the only sacrifice my heart drifted toward.

Saving Private Ryan also stirred within my soul gratitude for the Lord. I am blessed to love a Lord who does not require me to earn His sacrifice. My life was paid in full, free and clear, with love. I am blessed when I can pause and remember the great sacrifices borne for my own life, sacrifices that allow me to love more deeply, appreciate more clearly, and honor more reverently.

God of peace, grant me a heart of gratitude and reverence for those who place honor, duty, and love above self. Amen.
—Jolynda Strandberg

Digging Deeper: Leviticus 3:5–7; Romans 12:1–3

Give, and it will be given to you. —Luke 6:38 (NRSV)

I always keep a few one-dollar bills in my front right pocket to give to any beggars who come my way. Of course, I know all the arguments about why not to give: that the person might use the money for drugs or drink, that it would be better to give them something to eat or a card with a list of soup kitchens and food pantries.

I understand all that. I give out of a prayerful desire not to dehumanize some needy individual. That I will, at least for a moment, acknowledge how much pain and suffering is out there. I'm always surprised, too, how, in this most secular city, that the response from the recipient is invariably, "God bless."

One Sunday I was walking out of church with some friends to get some coffee and hot chocolate. We'd barely left the building when an ill-dressed woman harangued us for a handout. Impatiently, I dug into my right pocket, pulled out a bill, and handed it to her. (Okay, I don't always feel generous, even after church.) "God bless" came the routine response. And then another "God bless!" hollered after us.

It was only later, when we were at the coffee joint that I realized it wasn't a one-dollar bill I'd relinquished. It was a twenty! "I thought I had that twenty in my other pocket," I said to my friends. No wonder the woman seemed so enthusiastic.

"Your hot chocolate is on us," my friends said. And the bill must have been more than twenty after they insisted on giving me a bag of fresh-baked treats to take home.

"God bless you," I said to them, adding a silent prayer for the woman in need.

Thank You, Lord, for the reminders that my true self is my giving self.
—Rick Hamlin

Digging Deeper: Proverbs 28:27; Acts 20:35

Keep yourselves in the love of God . . . —Jude 1:21 (KJV)

My wife's birthday was near and I wanted to give her something special.

Before we met, Corinne was a nurse practitioner who took care of many patients, some of whom were very ill. When we started dating, I began hearing stories from grateful folks who had a parent or grandparent whom she watched over in the hospital. She also led Bible studies for young women and sometimes used her nursing skills to go on mission trips to other countries.

She had given all that up to be my wife, a challenge at best, and to mother our three young children as well as my son, Harrison.

Now, with her birthday fast approaching, I had an idea. I asked her friends to email me one word that best described Corinne. As the responses came in, I reviewed them with great pride. "Kind." "Compassionate." "Caring." "Giving."

My plan was to have a birthday gathering for her and read the words aloud. But I wanted to have something to say, too, and all the best words had been taken. I searched for a romantic poem or apt scripture. Nothing.

There's no doubt that God helped Corinne and me find each other at a time when both of us were down. We longed for the same things: home, family, useful things to do in our community, living full and meaningful lives. Corinne lived alone and I was alone, too, except for my time with Harrison.

And then, everything came together just right and here we were. Happy home, great family. My perfect word for Corrine's birthday celebration hit me like a ton of bricks. Of course. It was simple and true. My word is "love."

Father, Your love surely brought Corinne and me together. I pray that You keep us always living in Your love.
—Brock Kidd

Digging Deeper: Song of Songs 8:7; John 13:35

Show yourself in all respects to be a model of good works, and in your teaching show integrity, dignity. —Titus 2:7 (ESV)

I came across one of my son's drawings on the living room floor and laughed, putting it all together. The night before, Henry had asked me how he should answer one of the questions on his science homework.

"I'm supposed to diagram a flower," he said. "Should I draw it on paper and then upload it to the computer to hand it in?" I nodded. Later, I had seen Henry on the couch, bent over his drawing pad with his colored pencils spread out on the table, but Henry draws all the time so I didn't think anything of it.

The drawing in my hands was a detailed, exquisitely colored, painstakingly shaded diagram of a flower that looked like a vintage print from a botanical text. It must have taken hours. "Henry, this was your homework?"

He nodded.

"You scanned it and handed it in?"

"Yeah, why?"

"It's beautiful! Can I have it? I want to frame it."

"You want to frame my science homework? You're weird, Mom."

I hung it up in my office. Proof of answered prayer. From prayers in elementary school for Henry to talk more in class, to finding his voice, to hoping he put his heart and passion into everything he did—to all the prayers that every mom has for her kids to always do their best.

> *Thank You, Lord, for my son who teaches me so, so much about this world and Your love.*
> —Sabra Ciancanelli

Digging Deeper: Proverbs 22:6; 2 Timothy 2:25

Wednesday, November 15

But he [Thomas] said unto them, Except I shall see in his hands the print of the nails, and put my finger into the print of the nails, and thrust my hand into his side, I will not believe. —John 20:25 (KJV)

Someday, you'll wear this experience like a badge." My sister spoke of my fight with cancer.

Recoiling from the idea of ever broadcasting my experience, I quietly appropriated her well-intentioned words to another place in my mind: a place with no memory of surgical scars or treatment schedules or even a pink badge of survivorship. Simply put, I hoped for a day when it was as though the diagnosis never happened. So when my doctor said he thought I'd be just the person to speak with a few of his struggling patients, I balked. *Me, Lord?*

But then my thankfulness to have the choice to answer yes or no as a cancer-free woman yielded a shaky "yes." Friendships forged over time with women who needed to talk with someone who had been in their shoes slowly gave me confidence in a badge of empathy I'd once shunned. Numerous years and testimonies later, my deceased sister's words hold not only purpose for me but also an abiding humility that God chose me to provide an "I've been there" to his children in despair.

When the disciple Thomas refused to affirm the Resurrection, Jesus—understanding that scars of victory can increase faith and hope—didn't hesitate to show the proof of His completed mission, a critical turning point in Thomas's faith walk.

Blessedly, God sometimes uses us to display His ability to change painful wounds into demonstrations of deliverance. And even when we feel reluctant, He empowers us through His Son, who readily shared His badge of sacrifice to encourage others.

> *I'm so thankful, Lord, that a testimony of Your power*
> *brings peace to the soul.*
> —Jacqueline F. Wheelock

Digging Deeper: John 20:19–28; Acts 1:8

I press on toward the goal for the prize of the upward call of God in Christ Jesus. —Philippians 3:14 (NASB)

Colorado leads the fifty states in mountain peaks with an elevation over 14,000 feet. The 14er Fan Club in Boulder is made up of people who want to "bag a 14er." I'm not one of them; the fear of heights makes me dizzy. I once climbed too high on a hike, scrambling up rocks. I froze and had to be helped down.

But I have summitted many of the peaks in my life challenges.

I was always afraid of losing my mother. Then, at nearly ninety-two, we traveled her end-of-life journey. I had the strength, the tenderness, and the joy those final weeks because I threw myself on God. We played an old hymn, "I Need Thee Every Hour"—but I called on Him every moment.

The move to Alaska in my early thirties overwhelmed me. The place was too far, too big, too wild. Again I cried to the Lord, "Help me!" He sent the tiniest thing—a raindrop, sparkling like a diamond, left over from the storm that pounded us on our arrival. He spoke to my spirit that His "diamonds" awaited in my years there—and I believed Him. I embraced my new home.

After thirty years of marriage, in a pall of discouragement, I came close to letting go. I read the story of the poor widow dropping her two small copper coins into the treasury. Jesus said she gave from her lack and so gave more than all the rest. I began to carry two pennies with me—a reminder to give to our marriage. Terry and I are now past fifty.

These personal "summits" are a record of my faith journey. I may not successfully scale every peak, but the ones I do remind me of God's unchanging faithfulness—and, ultimately, my faithfulness to Him.

> *Jesus, climb with me. With You I can reach the summit.*
> —Carol Knapp

Digging Deeper: Psalm 59:10; Isaiah 2:2–3, 40:9;
2 Corinthians 1:8–10

Friday, November 17

*In their hearts humans plan their course, but the L*ORD *establishes their steps.* —Proverbs 16:9 (NIV)

If the saying that you're old when you buy apparel in multiples is true, then I've officially and unabashedly arrived. It all started with a foot problem resolved by wearing a certain brand and style of soft leather flats. Then, of course, they were being discontinued. I remedied that by purchasing every closeout color they had. After a cobbler stretched them in just-the-right spots, I stored them all in a large shopping bag.

When the morning of my podiatry appointment arrived, I reached for the cheery red pair on top. But the more I walked in them, the odder they felt. When my podiatrist assessed my progress, he noticed my struggle. Then he burst out laughing. "Why, you're wearing two left shoes, Roberta!"

The more I tried to explain, the more hysterical we got. At the checkout counter, they all wanted to know what was so funny. "You want the condensed version?" I asked. A man in the waiting room hollered, "Show-and-tell!" I took a load off my feet and admitted I could hardly put one foot in front of the other without a lot of help from the Divine. Before I knew it, testimonies flowed of walking in His steps.

My heart overflowed at that impromptu gathering of believers. "There's no place like home for comfortable footgear," I said, clicking my ruby slippers together three times as I wobbled to leave.

"Or any place we can't celebrate God," a lady added. I was certain the sky split right open with praise.

> *I asked for a chance to tell folks about You, Lord. But*
> *I sure didn't expect this one.*
> —Roberta Messner

Digging Deeper: Psalm 37:23, 119:133; 1 Peter 2:21

The grace of the Lord Jesus be with you. —1 Corinthians 16:23 (NIV)

L ast July, heat bore down on me as I dragged the hose across the yard toward a tray of wilting plants. I'd purchased them from a nursery way back in May. It had been a dream of mine to have a vegetable garden, but life had thrown so many curveballs at me that I never even had a chance to make a bed in which to put them.

There they sat, months later. The spindly squash had wrapped its tentacles around the leggy tomato plants. *Maybe I should just give up on them. That would be a whole lot easier. Besides, they're half-dead anyway.* But when I picked up the tray to toss it in the trash, I questioned myself. *How can I toss them away? After the neglect of the last couple months, they're still half-alive.* In a way, those plants reminded me—of me. So often I'd experienced rough times, yet God always had extended His grace and His kindness. *Okay, God, I won't give up if You don't.*

I pulled the tractor out of the barn, scooped a few buckets out of the dirt pile, and heaped them into a temporary bed. After topping the dirt with a sheet of black plastic, I cut circles in the plastic, tucked the plants in the holes, and watered them well throughout the summer, knowing that with the short growing season in Montana, it would be a miracle if I got a harvest.

In September and October, when most folks' gardens got nipped by frost, mine didn't. Now, a month later, I'd harvested enough to freeze, can, dry, and most importantly, to generously give away.

God, thank You for demonstrating how important it is that I never,
ever give up because Your grace and kindness encompass
every area of my life. Amen.
—Rebecca Ondov

Digging Deeper: 2 Corinthians 1:2–7, 13:14

Sunday, November 19

Jesus went throughout Galilee, teaching in their synagogues, proclaiming the good news of the kingdom, and healing every disease and sickness among the people. —Matthew 4:23 (NIV)

When I visited the Holy Land, being where Jesus was born, taught, performed miraculous healings, and was crucified was enormously impactful. My favorite part was the region of Galilee. I loved walking along the shore of the Sea of Galilee, imagining Jesus calling His disciples, walking on water, sleeping in a fishing boat during a storm, and cooking breakfast for the disciples after His resurrection.

While our tour group visited a nearby church, I enjoyed lingering along the seashore in the area commemorating Jesus's reinstatement of Peter and thought about my own denials. When I went to the Church of the Beatitudes, standing by the hillside where Jesus delivered the Sermon on the Mount, I listened as a fellow traveler read aloud the beatitudes.

No trip I've taken remains etched in my mind like the Holy Land. *Why is this?* Just being where Jesus lived made His presence profoundly real to me. I experienced a peace beyond peace, perhaps *shalom*, that Eugene Peterson describes as "life in all its abundance, which we have brimming over from Christ living inside us."*

Dear Jesus, thank You for being a Lord we don't have to travel to find and who comes to us where we are so that we can experience shalom from Your presence always within us. Amen.
—John Dilworth

Digging Deeper: Matthew 4:18–20, 15:29–30; John 21:4–17

---

*Peterson, Eugene H., *Conversations: The Message with Its Translator* (Colorado Springs, CO: NavPress Publishing Group, 2007), 201.

Dear friend, I hope all is well with you and that you are as healthy in body as you are strong in spirit. —3 John 1:2 (NLT)

I've occasionally sent greeting cards to a neighbor teen who stops by often and now attends church with me. Like young and old for generations before her, she quickly learned to anticipate personal greetings delivered by the mailman or "mail ma'am" as she likes to joke. Sensing the warm welcome of my congregation, last spring she announced her plans: "I'm going to make cards for our church friends."

I supported her endeavor, providing cardstock, envelopes, and twenty stamps. I peeked at a few of her messages and smiled at her closing: "Please write back." And many did. A few told me how happy they were to receive a personal note. She's mailed more, every two months or so, and now is making and addressing Christmas cards.

This morning, I went to the post office to mail early Christmas gifts and replenish "our" supply of stamps, this time with a Madonna and child picture. When I got home, I saw a friend's social media post: her latest entry on a November challenge, each day naming something she was grateful for. Today, on the Monday of Thanksgiving week, she wrote, "I'm thankful for the U.S. Postal Service." *What a quirky choice,* I thought.

But only until I heard the telltale *clink-clank* of the mail ma'am at the door. What did she bring? A colorful card from afar—"Thanksgiving wishes" that here and now I pass along to you.

Lord, thank You for the systems and channels—whether newfangled devices or old-fashioned pen and ink—that allow us to reach out to one another.
—Evelyn Bence

Digging Deeper: 3 John 1:1–8, 13–15

Tuesday, November 21

But God chose the foolish things of the world to shame the wise; God chose the weak things of the world to shame the strong. —1 Corinthians 1:27 (NIV)

They're gone. All my credit cards, my driver's license, employee badge, all my wedding gift cards. Gone." My daughter Rachel's fiancé, thinking he was being helpful, had put her recycling in a paper bag, then out for collection, not knowing her wallet was at the bottom of that bag. By the time they realized his mistake, the recycling had been picked up.

I called the recycling service. "There's nothing we can do, absolutely no way to locate her wallet," they said.

I remembered an email from a reader, offering to pray if I ever needed anything. I sent him a short note explaining what had happened and asked for prayer for Rachel to have peace. His quick response included his prayer: "Father God, I thank you for Kim and her family. I lift them up to You and ask You to perform a miracle for them and give them peace. In Jesus's name, Amen." I was grateful but silently did not see why or how God would perform a miracle in this situation.

A few hours later, my daughter called again. "Mom, a homeless man just rang my doorbell."

"Oh, dear," I said. "I hope you didn't open the door."

"I did, Mom, and he handed me my cards. Over twenty of them—they're all here, everything! I got every single one back!" The man had found them strewn over a street, about an hour's walk from her home. He'd found her address on her driver's license and come all the way there to deliver them.

God had indeed sent a miracle, one that not only returned Rachel's lost cards but also, more importantly, taught me a lesson in both faith and humility.

Dear Lord, thank You for Your beautiful answer to prayer and for opening my eyes to goodness where I had not expected it.
—Kim Taylor Henry

Digging Deeper: Luke 1:37; James 5:16

When they heard the report, all the believers lifted their voices together in prayer to God . . . —Acts 4:24 (NLT)

Our church has an amazing prayer chain ministry with dedicated volunteers. The prayer requests are prayed for and passed along to others, increasing the number of people praying. Serving on the team is filled with jubilation and sadness. Our hearts are uplifted with updates about someone who has been healed or found a job. But not every prayer is answered in the way we expect or want. Couples get divorced. Sick people die. A person is unemployed and stays that way for months and months. It's an emotional and spiritual roller coaster. But we keep on praying.

On our prayer list is the brother of a member of our church. He is battling serious physical and emotional issues. The sister who traveled to be with the family sends emails with updates on his progress. One week the brother is talking over the phone from the hospital with family, feeling hopeful. Then we received an urgent request for prayers. The brother was weak, unable to get out of bed, and refused to eat or drink much of anything.

No matter the situation, praying folks never give up. They keep on believing when others don't; they keep on hoping against hope. Trusting God for a miracle. A few days later, we got word: "Just to give you an update on my brother, he really was miraculously pulled from the depths of despair the day after I asked everyone to pray for him." He is now on his way to a full recovery.

Although we don't know how God will answer our prayers, we keep praying and believing because God is able.

Lord, encourage our hearts to keep on praying and hoping against hope, believing You can perform miracles.
—Pablo Diaz

Digging Deeper: Job 42:7–10; Acts 12:12

Thanksgiving, Thursday, November 23

Give thanks in all circumstances; for this is God's will for you in Christ Jesus. —1 Thessalonians 5:18 (NIV)

Six of the seven of us were at the table, one young adult absent because he had to work. I looked from one end of the raucous dining room table to the other and counted my blessings.

I counted the things I needed and had been given this year: mostly healthy kids, a safe space to live in, food on the table (some of which someone else cooked!), and a job I love. Then I flipped things around to give thanks for the things I *didn't* want and *didn't* have to deal with. After a decade of hardship, the absence of difficulty is as real a blessing to me as the presence of joy. I was grateful not to struggle with financial instability, for the lack of major mental health crises, for an interlude with no parents in the hospital.

A burst of laughter from my children startled me from my reverie. I noted a flicker of sadness in one kid's face. That reminded me there are still things my family needs but lacks. There are problems we don't want but are stuck with.

But there is a blessing in that, too. Difficulty forces me to reach for God more frequently, listen more carefully, and surrender my will and accept His instead. Perhaps in the long run it is the hardships for which I will be the most thankful of all.

Thank You, Father, for the blessings I see and don't see and for every cross that has helped me seek You more fervently.
—Julia Attaway

Digging Deeper: Ephesians 5:20; Colossians 2:6–7

THE PINK HOUSE: Born in a Kitchen

Therefore all things whatsoever ye would that men should do to you, do ye even so to them . . . —Matthew 7:12 (KJV)

It's important to realize that a single person, a simple act, can also be a "pink house."

"I just had the best visit with this lady in T.J. Maxx," Mary Ev says, when she arrives at our home for dinner. "She was from Venezuela, I think . . . well, I'm not sure. She didn't speak English."

I suppress a giggle. "How do you have a conversation when you don't speak each other's language?"

"Well, you know how so many people treat anyone different from them like they're invisible. It's terrible. Not exactly what Jesus expects from us. Sooo, I looked into her eyes and acknowledged her humanity, and I talked and she talked and we both laughed. It was a good conversation."

Later, cleaning up the kitchen, I realized that Mary Ev had planted a pink house right there in my kitchen to show me where to turn. Loading the dishwasher, I vowed that I would never let an opportunity pass to look someone in the eyes and acknowledge their humanity.

I began the next morning when David handed me my coffee. "Hold on," I said. "Let me see your eyes."

I had forgotten how blue they were.

And so it goes, even until today. I try never to miss a chance to let a person know that I really do see them. That I care.

All because a friend placed a pink house signpost in my daily path, one I intend to keep following.

Father, Mary Ev lives with You now, but her directions
stand strong. Thank You.
—Pam Kidd

Digging Deeper: Leviticus 19:18; Luke 10:27

Saturday, November 25

Bear with each other and forgive one another if any of you has a grievance against someone. Forgive as the Lord forgave you.
—Colossians 3:13 (NIV)

I sipped my drink as I watched the door to the coffee shop. I felt tense waiting for John.

Not long ago, John had been my best friend. I had relied on him. I had trusted him. Then, John had suddenly changed. He stopped showing up to events we had scheduled. He stopped answering text messages. He evaporated from my life.

Months of silence went by. Then I received a single text message: "Want to grab coffee?"

Now I waited for John as I would wait for an opponent. Guard up. Jaw tight.

The bell above the door jingled, and John entered. He took the seat across from me. "Thanks for meeting," he said. He adjusted his ball cap up, then down. He was nervous. He was right to be.

Today, I would not be ignored or blown off. I had chosen my words and crafted my sentences. I was ready to call John out.

John adjusted his cap one more time, then looked me in the eye.

"I messed up, Logan," he said. "I am so sorry."

My head reeled. Part of me wanted to unload the verbal artillery I had prepared. For months, John had disrespected me. Now I felt like he was robbing me of my vindication. But I also saw how afraid John was. He had come to offer an apology he knew might not be accepted. That took character. And it reminded me why we had become friends in the first place.

I breathed deeply, letting go of my rehearsed lines. "John," I said, "I've missed you."

Lord, help me to forgive others as You have forgiven me.
—Logan Eliasen

Digging Deeper: Matthew 18:21–22; Ephesians 4:32

For we all stumble in many things. —James 3:2 (NKJV)

It was a foggy Sunday a few weeks before Christmas, and the church sanctuary was dimly lit with candles. We worshippers sat in gloomy silence, waiting for the service to begin.

Lacking a pianist, the sound technician was using recorded music, but he was struggling with old equipment. At last, the words to "Silent Night" appeared on the projection screen, and we waited for the music to begin.

Suddenly the loudspeakers blasted out: "Chestnuts roasting on an open fire . . . Jack Frost nipping at your nose . . ."

The congregation exploded in laughter. Confused, I tried to sing both songs at once: "Silent night, roasting on an open fire . . . holy night, nipping at your nose . . ."

The technical snafu was just what we needed to lift our spirits, and it reminded me of tech troubles I had as a beginning college teacher. I tried to be the perfect professor, but I soon learned that my students were not interested in perfection; they were looking for someone "real." They could hardly wait for class to be over so they could come up and tell me about my bloopers. "Schantzy, do you realize that you told that same animal story in class yesterday? Also, you really butchered the name of that movie star."

I wish I had known back then that perfectionism is not a virtue, that it is actually classified as a psychological disorder.

Sure, I need to shoot for perfection, especially in moral matters. But I also need to remember that I will often fail, and that's okay. To expect flawless performance from myself is a formula for a breakdown.

I am relieved to know, Lord, that even my blunders can be used for good.
—Daniel Schantz

Digging Deeper: 1 Corinthians 2:1–4; 2 Corinthians 12:9–10

Monday, November 27

Above all, keep loving one another earnestly, since love covers a multitude of sins. —1 Peter 4:8 (ESV)

I've reached that "certain age" where I can't see small things without a pair of reading glasses. It's annoying at times: Why do they print those recipes so small? Does that say 1/2 cup or 1/3 cup? What's the dosage on this medication? Oh, where did I put my glasses? (Probably on top of my head, but that won't stop me from frantically searching the house for them, even though I have five or six pairs . . . somewhere!)

But I've also reached that "certain age" where each passing year (or day!) seems to bring a new imperfection: another wrinkle or spider vein or who knows what else.

It occurred to me today that it was awfully thoughtful of God to make my vision loss coincide with my deterioration!

Seriously. Without my glasses, I can't see every little thing about my youth fading away. And not only do I not see my own flaws so starkly, but I don't see other people's so well, either. And if they're around my age, neither do they see mine clearly.

What a lovely gift that God takes away the harshness of age by giving us soft focus! I have to think this is a physical manifestation of the wisdom that comes with age. As our eyes become more forgiving, perhaps so do our hearts. We can have better perspective about what really matters. We can be gentler and have the love that "covers a multitude of sins."

Lord, You really did think of everything. Please filter my vision so that I can be kinder to others and to myself.
—Ginger Rue

Digging Deeper: Ephesians 4:32; Colossians 3:13

Happy is he who has the God of Jacob for his help. —Psalm 146:5 (JPS)

I've always been pretty bad at asking God for anything. I can sail right into gratitude or awe, and I can shoehorn my way into guilt and contrition. But asking for stuff in a humble manner somehow does not go with being Jewish. True to the name "Israel," we struggle with God. I am more likely than not to think that God isn't paying attention and should step up and butt in where needed.

But then, irresistibly, I was drawn to studying to become a spiritual director, which meant I would be able to accompany people on their paths to bring an awareness of the divine much more solidly into their everyday lives. After three years of study, I received my certification, yet I worried that some of my directees might not be Jewish (I was right), and I would have to keep from imposing my own spirituality into their unique, personal relationship with God. Sometimes I wondered if I was succeeding. But I reminded myself that the nuns who had trained me told me they were confident I would be a good director, so I told myself to take their word for it.

Recently, one of my directees was really struggling with genuine pain and longing. I recognized that I was feeling more helpless than usual. Slowly I found myself constructing an unfamiliar kind of prayer and saying it before every meeting with a directee, even those who seemed to be moving well on their individual spiritual paths.

Now it comes easily to me, and it's helping me understand my own relationship with God a little better. I have learned to say, "Please help me to help them."

I always suspected that You were my spiritual director, Lord of My People, so thank You for Your forbearance and for Your sustaining love.
—Rhoda Blecker

Digging Deeper: Psalm 20:3, 33:20

Wednesday, November 29

But exhort one another every day, as long as it is called "today," that none of you may be hardened by the deceitfulness of sin. —Hebrews 3:13 (ESV)

Lonny and I ran into our friends Chris and Maryanne. It had been a while since we'd seen them, but we're drawn in, so we chatted about our families, who's doing what and where, and then Chris suggested that we gather one evening to study and pray.

"Hey," he said. "We should even think about getting together regularly."

A few days later, I'm fluffing throw pillows and getting the tall glasses out for iced tea. But the day has been long and the week is commitment-tight. I love the idea of gathering, but now panic pings in my chest. I'm not sure that our schedule can handle one more thing.

The bell rings at seven, and we usher our friends in.

Chris and Maryanne have a way about them, and as we take chairs in the living room, I understand why Lonny and I are drawn. This couple's love for the Lord is powerful, and they know how to live in the grace and glory of who He is. Gratitude stirs their hearts and overflows into ours. Their relationship with Jesus is intimate. It spurs us on.

Words become worship and our home becomes holy ground.

We share from secret spaces. We trust one another, and guard gates open wide. We read from the Word as we encourage. We pray and these prayers hold power. We're gathered for His glory. We're gathered in His name.

At the end of the evening, we're lifted. We're lighter. The calendar on the wall is still crowded. But when our friends wave goodbye, I shout from the porch, "See you soon!"

Two weeks from tonight, this is where I need to be.

Lord, thank You for relationships that move us closer to You.
—Shawnelle Eliasen

Digging Deeper: Proverbs 27:17; Hebrews 10:25

Each of you should use whatever gift you have received to serve others, as faithful stewards of God's grace in its various forms. —1 Peter 4:10 (NIV)

From the time my friend Liz first discerned her calling to the Episcopal ministry, I had eagerly followed her journey: selling her home, moving to seminary, discussing her classes, and writing exegesis papers. For a while, I wanted to follow her path to ordained ministry, too, but finally realized it was not for me. Instead, I continued my modest lay ministries of singing and cooking for parish events.

As Liz's ordination drew closer, I delighted in knowing that I'd have a front-row seat in the choir loft behind the altar. I'd see Liz's face as she took her vows and slipped on the red stole that signified her new role. After the liturgy, guests would lunch on my treats. Would I make finger sandwiches? A pretty fruit display? Maybe baklava, the honey-drenched pastry she loved? Such were my plans.

God had others.

A few months before the ordination, Liz stunned me: "I'd like you to be my sponsor for ordination. You'll process with me, sign my Oath of Obedience, and help me put on my stole."

"What! How do I deserve this honor? I'm just a friend."

"Gail, I couldn't have done this without you."

I reflected. Sure, I'd sent cards and silly notes while she was slogging through Ancient Greek and systemic theology in seminary. I had initiated chatty phone calls before those first anxious sermons. I had read Christian history aloud to her when she had a mild concussion and double vision. We had prayed each other's children through crises.

By being "just a friend," by using my ordinary, everyday gifts, I had given Liz more than I could have imagined. Perhaps friendship is the most precious ministry of all.

Lord, let me be a blessing to someone today.
—Gail Thorell Schilling

Digging Deeper: 1 Thessalonians 5:11; 1 Peter 2:21

November

LET US SING FOR JOY

1 _____

2 _____

3 _____

4 _____

5 _____

6 _____

7 _____

8 _____

9 _____

10 _____

11 _____

12 _____

13 _____

14 _____

15 _____

16 _____

17 _____

18 _____

19 _____

20 _____

21 _____

22 _____

23 _____

24 _____

25 _____

26 _____

27 _____

28 _____

29 _____

30 _____

DECEMBER

Because your love is better than life, my lips

will glorify you. I will praise you as long as

I live, and in your name I will lift up my hands.

—Psalm 63:3–4 (NIV)

You saw me before I was born. Every day of my life was recorded
in your book. Every moment was laid out before a single day had passed.
—Psalm 139:16 (NLT)

I parked my car in front of the hearse and walked over to the burial site to officiate the interment service for Merilyn, a longtime member of our church. The light breeze and the abundance of trees in the cemetery offered comfort from the sun as we gathered for worship and celebration of life. I went over the service with the daughter overseeing the arrangements. We agreed to ask attendees to offer words and share memories about her mother toward the end of the service.

After the celebration of life prayer, I invited people to say something about Merilyn. A young woman in her thirties wasted no time. "Merilyn was an amazing person." I waited for the next person, but no one volunteered to say anything. I quickly changed the approach and asked people to describe Merilyn in one word.

Slowly they began to shout out words. "Caring!" "Loved shoes." "A good water-skier." Like a flowing river, beautiful words kept on coming. "Wonderful sister." "Best mother-in-law." "Great bridge player." "A loving grandma." Love, laughter, joy, and happiness turned the sad moment into a celebration. It was one of the most beautiful tributes I have ever experienced at a graveside service.

I knew very little about Merilyn other than what her daughter shared with me. By the end of the service, I had learned so much about her through her friends and family. She lived her life with a sense of adventure and impacted others in her own special way.

> *Lord, give us the courage and wisdom to live our life*
> *and who we are to the fullest.*
> —Pablo Diaz

Digging Deeper: Psalm 139:1–16

Saturday, December 2

To this day I have had the help that comes from God . . . —Acts 26:22 (ESV)

Several decades ago, wise, wizened Fr. Bill served as my pastor. He and his wife, Carol, eventually retired and left my close circle. But then, last Thursday, Bill showed up as a helper in a dream.

Earlier that day—in real life—I'd been sorely stressed by a neighbor girl's talk of "moving far away." What? I had been informally mentoring her on a daily basis for ten years. I wondered: *How would we handle the separation?* I worried: *Would she thrive in a strange environment?*

My dream started well: I lived at a hotel and traveled by city bus to serve as her job coach. But one day, unannounced, the bus rerouted, so I searched tirelessly for a taxi until I awoke, panicked. Unusual though it was for me, I soon fell back asleep and reentered the dream. I was back at the hotel. Even there, I couldn't find a cab, until Bill unexpectedly stepped onto the curb. "Right here," he said, hailing a driver.

On Saturday, I called Bill and Carol to tell my story. Carol shared her greater grief: that Bill was dying, in hospice. We talked at length. "Your encouraging dream was Thursday?" she asked. "That's the evening Bill rallied—a 'life surge'—that's common before someone slips away." We wept, tears that strengthened our resolve to face our tomorrows. When I asked for her email address, she said, "I've never worked with computers. But a friend here *is* helping me."

I sent an email that included a photo of the neighbor teen. Carol's surprising Sunday response? "This is my first email ever . . ."

By God's grace and the help of friends, Carol could embrace a new challenge. Newly inspired, I can, too.

Lord, "to this day" You have provided help and hope in difficult seasons.
I entrust our tomorrows to You.
—Evelyn Bence

Digging Deeper: Psalm 100, 121

A SIMPLE CHRISTMAS: Keep My Eyes on You

And the peace of God, which surpasses all understanding, will guard your hearts and your minds in Christ Jesus. —Philippians 4:7 (ESV)

My mom must have had much better time-management skills than I do.

When I was little, the first Sunday of Advent was a family celebration. Plates of homemade cookies were brought into the living room alongside steaming mugs of cocoa; songbooks were handed out, and my siblings and I snuggled under plaid blankets on the couch as my mom opened the lid to her beloved antique piano and played Christmas carols.

Oh, how I want to pass on those same sticky-fingered, peace-that-surpasses-all-understanding Advent memories to my kids.

But I'll be honest: the first Sunday evening in December is hard.

Last year, I almost just said no. To be fair, it had been a tough few days. First Thanksgiving, then Black Friday, then setting up the Christmas tree. It should have felt like idyllic family time but instead turned into me screaming, "Ornaments are not soccer balls" 243 times, and by the time the first Sunday of Advent came along, I was ready to tap out.

Instead, I simplified.

I bought cookies. I used powdered packets of cocoa. I found an awesome Christmas playlist on iTunes. I downloaded "a parents' simple guide to Advent" online.

And we gathered.

Turns out those sticky-fingered, peace-and-joy memories don't come from me being the perfect Christmas mom. They don't come from homemade cookies and my learning how to play "Silver Bells" on the piano. They don't come from my time and effort.

They come from Him.

Lord, help me to keep my eyes on You this Christmas season.
—Erin MacPherson

Digging Deeper: John 16:33; 2 Thessalonians 3:16

Monday, December 4

And I will not be a burden, because I do not want what is yours but you; for children ought not to lay up for their parents, but parents for their children. —2 Corinthians 12:14 (NRSV)

We talked about the book of Genesis. We talked about Ezekiel. We talked about Jesus. We discussed a church in the South Bronx where he'll do some work. We shared notes about praying the Psalms every day.

Some minister I happened to meet? Some holy soul I would interview for a potential article? Some transformative author? No, just a long, satisfying chat with our younger son, Tim, newly enrolled in seminary, studying to become a pastor.

Ten years ago, who would have guessed? The kid who played in a rock band in high school, who saved up after he graduated college to traverse on the cheap around the world, who hung out in India, whose long hair at one point looked like it *did* belong to a rock star felt called to the ministry and was pursuing it with all his heart.

We also discussed fatherhood because he would soon be a dad. He wanted to know what it was like. Would he be up to it?

"The thing about being a parent," I said, "is that you never know what your kid will become. You try to do all the right things, but how they turn out and who they become is entirely out of your hands. There is an element of grace."

Look at you, I wanted to add. *Exhibit A.*

Yes, we took our boys to church, and yes, I taught them in Sunday school, but how they were called to serve in life was God's doing. And that I did manage to say.

Father God, thanks for being a co-parent in all we do.
—Rick Hamlin

Digging Deeper: Psalm 127:3; Proverbs 1:8

And you will seek Me and find Me when you search for Me with all your heart. —Jeremiah 29:13 (NASB)

Anyone who knows me understands that I'm a Christmas fanatic. It's my absolute favorite time of the year. For years, my home was filled with fifty or more Nativity scenes and six fully decorated Christmas trees. I took joy in baking cookies and candies, sorting through hundreds of recipes. I plan social gatherings, hold an open house. I have a number of traditions with the children and grandchildren.

Since I'm easing into retirement and often writing from home, Wayne and I have transitioned to living in our weekend home on Hood Canal. With the change in residences and slower pace of life, we decided to cut back on some of the hoopla around Christmas. I mean, really, who needs six Christmas trees? One thing I couldn't downscale was my Nativity scenes. I carted the majority of them from our Port Orchard home to the canal and set them up. Once I finished getting everything in place, I noticed the most important piece of the largest set was missing. Knowing I'd need to return to the house, I put a note on the kitchen counter to remind myself: FIND JESUS.

Wayne happened by, saw my note, and chuckled until I could explain what the note meant. In thinking about it, I was struck by the deeper truth: Isn't this what Christmas is all about—finding Jesus? For years I'd been so caught up in creating the perfect Christmas for our family and friends that I fear I'd missed the most important aspect of the holiday. Jesus. I don't ever want to lose Him.

I was able to locate the lost Jesus figurine and put Him in place. In the Nativity scene and in my heart.

> *Dear Jesus, my prayer is that You will find a place in every*
> *heart this holiday season and that those who have lost*
> *You will find their way back.*
> —Debbie Macomber

Digging Deeper: 1 Chronicles 16:10–11; Psalm 105:4

Wednesday, December 6

But Mary treasured up all these things, pondering them in her heart.
—Luke 2:19 (ESV)

I am a collector of things—I think it runs in my blood. My grandma by today's standards would most likely be described as a hoarder. Her closed-in back porch was jam-packed with items stacked against walls. She would be in the living room telling a story and a flash of recognition would come to her eyes. She would disappear to the back porch and return holding proof—a ticket to the play, my mother's report card from kindergarten, a letter from the president of the United States. You never knew exactly what might be among Grandma's possessions, but as a child, and even now as an adult, the objects confirmed what we hoped—Grandma's fantastic stories were true.

They're real, I remember thinking. *Grandma has had an amazing life and she keeps magical proof.* And so it seems my sentimental nature began to form and with it a desire to keep mementos.

Just this morning, I opened a white jewelry box that held a keepsake from my oldest son's first haircut. The fragile little blond curl was soft in my fingers. *Was his hair really this blond?* I am glad, so very glad to remember that day, to remember the milestone, and to hold that lock of hair that unlocks so much in my heart.

> *Dear Lord, I know that my life here isn't permanent, but how*
> *I love to hold these delightful reminders that connect me*
> *to the deepest and dearest moments.*
> —Sabra Ciancanelli

Digging Deeper: Ecclesiastes 3:6; 2 Corinthians 4:16

You have changed my sadness into a joyful dance . . . —Psalm 30:11 (GNT)

The match seemed like an unlikely romance. Here I was, a mid-sixties woman enamored with my son's virtual reality video game. What makes it even more unlikely is that I've always shied away from anything 3D or VR (virtual reality) because I'm prone to extreme motion sickness. I need antinausea meds just to use a treadmill—or the massage feature on my recliner. But here I was slicing virtual flying boxes with a lightsaber to the beat of the music. Joy-filled and nausea-free. Yup, it was love at first swoosh.

But why? As a cerebral type, I couldn't just let my deep connection with an electronic device go unexamined. Was this a positive pastime or time-wasting escape? Posing this question to God opened a door I'd long kept closed. And bolted. A scene from several years earlier bubbled to the surface. I was enjoying a cruise with three delightful single women. We were together on the top floor of a lofty atrium, watching couples dancing below. A deep ache of loss overwhelmed me. I'd always loved to dance. Not just praise songs, but rock, jazz, classical, blues . . . all kinds of music made me want to lift my arms and move my feet, praising God for the joy of simply being alive. But when I found myself unexpectedly single, I felt my dancing days were over—and along with them, this joyful expression of praise.

Until now. So, my quiet time is no longer always quiet. Sometimes, I slip on my VR headset, use lightsabers to destroy flying boxes to the beat, and praise God for the joy of life with every move I make.

> *God, thank You for the gift of music, dance, and life itself.*
> *Every moment, You are worthy of praise.*
> —Vicki Kuyper

Digging Deeper: Psalm 57:7, 149:3, 150:1–5; Ecclesiastes 3:4

Friday, December 8

Out of Zion, the perfection of beauty, God shines forth. —Psalm 50:2 (ESV)

Around 5 o'clock last evening, Deery came to dinner. That's the name we've given to the young doe who shows up almost every day at this time. Earlier, I had put a fresh mineral block out for her to lick. Then our daughter Lisa dropped off some old pumpkins, squash, and apples. Just as the predicted heavy snow started falling, Deery came out of the prairie, sauntered across the yard, and enjoyed the mineral block. Then she took a small pumpkin in her mouth and threw it up in the air so it would fall on the ground and break open. She feasted. All while the snow fell in the soft evening light.

I sat and looked out the tall great-room window, blessed to be surrounded by so much beauty. It drew me in. The deep brown of the trees contrasted with the fluffy white snow. The colorful pumpkins, squash, and apples atop the white. The gray clouds. The lighter brown and white of Deery and her silhouette when she stood stock-still, startled by any slight sound.

A sublime slice of life. Yet I am surrounded by beauty at all times. As Gerard Manley Hopkins reminds me:
for Christ plays in ten thousand places,
Lovely in limbs, and lovely in eyes not his.

Lovely in deer limbs and eyes. Lovely in my family and friends. Lovely in the grocery store clerk, the waiter who serves me, the doctor who cares for me, the man who picks up my trash . . .

Divine beauty all around me. If I only use the eyes God gave me to behold it.

Open my spirit, beautiful God, that I witness and bear witness to the great loveliness You've surrounded me with. And in witnessing that loveliness, teach me to love as You have loved me. Amen.
—J. Brent Bill

Digging Deeper: Ecclesiastes 3:11–13; Ephesians 2:10

*And whatever you do, whether in word or deed, do it all in the name
of the Lord Jesus, giving thanks to God the Father through him.*
—Colossians 3:17 (NIV)

I have a love-hate relationship with social media. I love the way it easily connects me with people and offers helpful information and humor, but I don't like messages that state an opinion and then criticize anyone who doesn't agree with that opinion. Often what follows is an online argument about who is right and who is not. The tone of those conversations is contagious. Though I don't comment, I often take sides and create defensive messages in my head.

However, a few days ago, I was surprised to see an unusual message on social media from a friend who sometimes shares her opinions. She wrote:

"I have been so convicted about my crass, snarky, and negative comments here over the past few months! I know that my God is not pleased with that attitude! I have asked HIS forgiveness and I now ask the same from the people I love and cherish."

I read it over several times as I saw responses beginning to show up on my screen:

Several emoji hearts and praying hands.

"Virtual hugs."

"Forgiven!"

"Me too."

"Love you!"

I immediately added my response.

"A brave message that I needed to hear. Thank you, my gracious friend."

*Jesus, please help me to pause and ask You whether my words—written
or in my thoughts—are helpful or hurtful, especially on social media,
where the tone of the messages are contagious.*
—Carol Kuykendall

Digging Deeper: Philippians 4:8–9; Colossians 3:12–17

A SIMPLE CHRISTMAS: Treasuring Each Moment

For you have need of endurance, so that when you have done the will of God you may receive what is promised. —Hebrews 10:36 (ESV)

My great-grandmother Frieda saved wrapping paper. She would slowly unwrap gifts using an envelope cutter to make sure she didn't tear the paper. Then, before she opened the box, she would carefully fold the paper into a neat square, making sure that not a wrinkle could be found.

This was likely annoying to anyone watching, but to me, a creative and exuberant tear-the-paper-off-as-quickly-as-humanly-possible type, it was pure torture.

And on Christmas, well, I could hardly stand it. One year, I blurted out, "Could you just hurry up and fold your paper later?"

My mom glared at me and my dad squeezed my arm in a death grip. But Grandma Frieda, she smiled kindly.

"Be patient and enjoy the moment, child. Your gifts will be there even if I take hours to open mine."

What treasured wisdom for this Advent season: Our gift of Christ is there. For us. Waiting, welcoming. So we can savor this season. We can treasure every moment, unwrap every gift, fold every piece of holly-clad paper if we want to.

There's no need to hustle and bustle. There's no need to frantically figure out the right parties to go to, the right presents to wrap, the right songs to sing, the right words to read.

Our ultimate present will be there. For us. With all of the magic and hope and peace that He promises.

> *Lord, help me to be patient and enjoy these moments during*
> *this special season. Amen.*
> —Erin MacPherson

Digging Deeper: Romans 8:25, 12:12

"For I know the plans I have for you," declares the LORD, *"plans to prosper you and not to harm you, plans to give you hope and a future."*
—Jeremiah 29:11 (NIV)

I treaded down the sidewalk with my Labrador pup, Sport. Snow fell gently to the ground. Sport held his tail high as he dipped his nose into a drift of snow. His world was full of new, wonderful things.

The street was quiet. No cars. No people. We were alone.

Sadness crept into my chest. Loneliness had been a familiar feeling lately. Several months before, my girlfriend and I had broken up. It was the right decision—our lives had been headed in different directions. But it was also a painful decision.

As we rounded the block, Sport's ears shifted forward. He pounced on a flattened soda can. I pulled on his leash. "That's not for you, Sport."

As we continued walking, I remembered how hopeful I had been about dating Erika. I had believed I found my person. But I had been wrong.

"Lord," I prayed. "I don't understand this. I'm twenty-eight. I want to be married. Why are you withholding this from me?"

I heard crunching. Sport was chewing on something. I stooped, opened Sport's jaws, and pulled out a rock. Sport's head drooped as I tossed the rock away.

"I'm sorry, Sport," I said. "It wasn't good for you. Trust me."

And as the words left my mouth, I began to understand. God loves me. I don't know why I'm still single, but I do know God wants His best for me. I need to trust His judgment. I need to submit to His wisdom.

Sport and I turned toward home. And on the way back, a little bit of my sadness drifted away.

Father, help me to trust You with every aspect of my life.
—Logan Eliasen

Digging Deeper: Isaiah 26:3; Philippians 4:19

Tuesday, December 12

But Jesus said, "Let the little children come to Me, and do not forbid them; for of such is the kingdom of heaven." —Matthew 19:14 (NKJV)

It was a typical school night during a nippy December and per usual I was perched on the side of the tub while my then five-year-old son was using a cup to scoop and pour water through his soapy fingers. He loved bath time and would soak until the water grew tepid and his fingertips were like wrinkly raisins.

"Mama," he said, calmly, pulling me out of my thoughts. "I want to be baptized." I told him I'd make plans immediately to get him scheduled for the next baptismal date at our church. "Right now," he said.

He stopped scooping water and looked at me with bright, wide eyes. It was a simple but powerful request. My husband is a minister, so I figured there was no time like the present. I called him into the bathroom, and we led my son through a confession of faith that he could understand. Even though my son wanted to be completely submerged in the cloud of soapy water, I turned on the faucet to refill his cup with fresh water, then poured it over his head. It was a private moment I'll never forget. And I'll never forget God's promises as it pertains to all of my children. Promises to give them hope and a future.

Parenting our teenage son hasn't been without its growing pains. He cultivated a heart for God at a young age, but that didn't mean we'd escape the middle school mishaps and roller-coaster ride that sometimes comes with parenting teenagers.

During those times, I drew strength from my memories of my son's childlike faith and the moments that God revealed Himself in our daily lives. There will never be a time when I won't need His help.

> *God, give me a childlike faith and a heart to follow You.*
> —Tia McCollors

Digging Deeper: Psalm 8:2; 2 Timothy 3:15

"I am making everything new!" —Revelation 21:5 (NIV)

That December evening, I sipped coffee in the McDonald's parking lot with my window rolled down. Everything seemed brand-new this Christmas season. I'd been delivered from a lifetime of horrible pain and two decades of dependence on prescription OxyContin. When the haunting melody of the modern classic "Mary, Did You Know?" came on the radio, I sang along with the fullest heart I'd ever known:

Did you know that your baby boy has come to make you new?

Just then a male voice cut through my reverie. "Opioid OD at the motel. Girl didn't make it. Died alone." My eyes found the flashing lights in front of the adjoining Red Roof Inn. Two EMS attendants rolled a gurney with a shrouded figure from one of the rooms. Then three police vehicles and the EMS truck formed a silent procession that circled onto Route 60. There was no family car, no friends who followed. Not one person mourning the loss of a fellow human being. Just a neon sign advertising rooms for $77 a night, a guy delivering a pizza on the top tier of the motel, oblivious to it all.

I was never so heartsick in my life. "Was the motel clerk kind at check-in?" I wondered aloud. "Did anyone reach out to her? Did she call out to God in those final, fleeting moments?"

Here in the opioid capital of America, the memory stirs me still. *Oh, God, that could have been me. If not for Your extravagant grace and mercy, the welcoming place where I withdrew from opioids. The caring people who prayed and believed that the old Roberta could be made new.*

> *So many in my town are still enslaved, Lord. Help them believe You already see them new.*
> —Roberta Messner

Digging Deeper: Isaiah 43:19; 2 Corinthians 5:17; Colossians 3:9–11

Thursday, December 14

Pay attention, come close now, listen carefully to my life-giving, life-nourishing words. —Isaiah 55:3 (MSG)

First thing each morning, I brew a cup of coffee, sit in my favorite chair, and begin my prayers. Then, I read the Bible and *Walking in Grace* and get going with my day.

Nicky Gumbel, vicar of Holy Trinity Brompton Church in London, England, said, "Nearly always, I start by reading the Bible, as I believe it's more important that Jesus speaks to me than I speak to him."*

As New Year's approached, I looked for something different to grow spiritually. I became focused on how I essentially pray the same prayer every day. My words of praise and thanksgiving to God are for the same things, my confessions vary but seem rooted in the same sins, and my prayers for others are for the same loved ones. The part that changes most is the special prayers for those in difficult circumstances. There is nothing wrong with repetitive prayers—Jesus gave us the Lord's Prayer to pray. But I wondered: *Had my prayers of familiar words become a mindless routine?*

Like Nicky Gumbel, I started reading the Bible first, then praying. I am praising God now for different blessings that the Scripture awakens in me. And my prayers are more energized and conversational as I respond prayerfully to verses that I read moments before from the Bible.

Dear God, we know You are glad to hear from us whether we pray
before, after, or as we read Your Word. Help us to be open to
new ways that can enrich our time with You. Amen.
—John Dilworth

Digging Deeper: Luke 8:21; 2 Peter 3:5

---

*Gumbel, Nicky, *Bible in One Year,* Audio Comments, February 20, 2020; London, England.

O my soul, bless GOD. From head to toe, I'll bless His holy name!
—Psalm 103:1 (MSG)

The text message arrived from a friend I've known since first grade: "I would like to send you a book I read . . . Love to hear your comments, Kenny."

I recalled our grade-school times, memorizing the 103rd Psalm in the fourth grade, experiencing growth and friendship during the nearly twelve years we spent together at our Christian school.

Then, over the years, we've exchanged Christmas greetings. They've been free and unfettered, often exuberant times of encouragement. But, in recent times, our friendship has become a little strained, perhaps reflecting unfortunate societal divisions.

Now, here was this text message. While I was not familiar with the spiritual book mentioned, the title struck me as ominous, threatening, and confrontational.

I answered that I would accept a copy, hoping I could exercise love-in-community, respectful friendship. Just before Christmas, a US Post Office mailer came with the hardback book enclosed.

Some weeks later, I maneuvered seven pages of carefully worded feedback into a letter. In the response, while I listed some topics of agreement, there were many areas of concern.

In time, I received a letter in response, ending with "I've been praying for you my friend, and will continue to do so. You are precious to God and me." Gifted with this unifying blessing, I celebrate God's grace.

Reconciling God, we praise You for lasting friendships. When strained, enable us to bear through differences. Amen.
—Ken Sampson

Digging Deeper: 1 Corinthians 13:4; Ephesians 4:2, 32; Colossians 3:13

Saturday, December 16

Finally, all of you be of one mind, having compassion for one another; love as brothers, be tenderhearted, be courteous. —1 Peter 3:8 (NKJV)

Have you ever moved a woodstove? You'd know if you had. If there's a word to describe the thing, it's *heavy*. And I don't mean heavy in the normal sense. It's like the manufacturer builds them with as much cast iron as possible and then—out of what I imagine to be gleeful malice—adds in a healthy dose of the heaviest element in the universe.

At least these were the thoughts depressing my mind as my neighbor and I stood in the living room staring at one such beast. We had blocks of wood, a floor jack, and a pocketful of not-very-well-thought-out ideas.

Yup, it wasn't gonna be pretty.

We were all set up and seconds away from sending ourselves to the emergency room when my son and two of his young and very strong friends walked in. Let me tell you, my praises echoed heaven's halls.

We can plan, and we can scheme, but sometimes it simply takes community to get us through this life journey. I'm convinced this is why God gave us each other. How many times have I faced some seemingly immovable obstacle in life and had the beautiful experience of a brother or sister (or several of them) in the Lord step in and link arms with me?

Our God supplies all our needs, sometimes in the most unexpected ways.

I think I'll sit by the fire for a while now.

Hey, maybe I'll even invite a few friends over.

Dear God, thank You for providing faithful friends. And help me to be the same when the need arises.
—Buck Storm

Digging Deeper: Romans 15:5; Galatians 3:28–29; 1 John 4:11

A SIMPLE CHRISTMAS: Extravagant Blessings

*And I will make them and the places all around my hill a blessing, and
I will send down the showers in their season; they shall be showers of
blessing.* —Ezekiel 34:26 (ESV)

My friend Becky invited my family over for Advent dinner.
When we arrived, Christmas music was playing in the background, her tree was lavishly decorated with sparkling lights and ornaments, and there was a lovely tray of cheese and olives waiting on the counter.

Thirty minutes later, Becky called us in to pray before the meal. Then Becky explained that she had made lasagna soup, homemade chicken noodle soup, a white chicken chili, and crab bisque. She set a stack of paper bowls on the counter and invited us to take as many bowls as we wanted and to try all four if we wished.

"Four kinds of soup?" My always-hungry teenage son was amazed as he quickly filled several bowls.

I laughed and asked Becky why she had made so many kinds of soup and she smiled. "It just felt like an extravagant kind of celebration."

A few minutes later, we all sat down, baskets of warm bread on the table, and enjoyed what was one of the most delicious and memorable meals of my life.

Extravagant, lavish, and a bit over the top. Just like Jesus at Christmas.

His extravagant, lavish, and a bit over-the-top love is something to be celebrated.

> *Jesus, this season is extravagant but so are You.*
> *Thank You for showering us with blessings. Amen.*
> —Erin MacPherson

Digging Deeper: Jeremiah 14:22; Zechariah 10:1

Monday, December 18

Therefore, if anyone is in Christ, he is a new creation; old things have passed away; behold, all things have become new. —2 Corinthians 5:17 (NKJV)

I'd lived in my new home for a couple of years, but I hadn't stopped missing my old place. My wife and I built it as owner-builders. We raised our kids there.

With our kids up and out, it made all the sense in the world to sell that place. Our downsized home was lovely, and my wife's keen designer eye made it nicer all the time. My mind knew, but my heart struggled to catch up.

In time for Christmas, I ordered a special coffee mug for Margi with a picture of our whole family riding horses in Hawaii. I knew she would love it.

Weeks later, the mug was delivered—to my old address.

I found the owners' phone number, called, and left a message. That afternoon, the new owner called back. We got talking. He and his wife had two young kids. They absolutely loved everything about our home. They appreciated Margi's design touches. They couldn't get over the postcard view of Mt. Shasta. Their kids enjoyed running around six wooded acres. They were excited to use their new metal detectors and to pan for gold on what had actually been an old gold mine.

He said, "Bill, you and your wife have created something remarkable here. We want you to know how much we appreciate what you've done. Come and get your mug."

A newfound peace settled into my heart. I've been able to quit lamenting my loss and to start appreciating my memories, confident we've blessed another family for years to come.

Thank You, Father, for Your invitation to live in light of Your blessings,
which are new every morning.
—Bill Giovannetti

Digging Deeper: Lamentations 3:22–24

. . . the joy of the LORD is your strength. —Nehemiah 8:10 (KJV)

Christmas was near, but it wouldn't be the same this year. Harrison, in Ireland for special studies, was unable to travel home, and sister Keri's kids couldn't be with us for our traditional celebrations.

As we approached the holidays, there would be no family gatherings with everyone there, no late-night talks with Harrison, no elaborate Christmas dinner when I looked around the table and saw my mom and dad smiling in the candlelight, with all their family circled round. I was deep in the throes of doom and gloom when the call came.

"Hello."

I immediately knew it was Wanda, my ninety-six-year-old friend. Her sweet Southern accent could not be mistaken.

"Honey," she said. "Have you heard about the Christmas star?"

"Well, no," I answered.

"It hasn't been seen on earth for eight hundred years," she said in that drawl of wonderment. "I am promising you this, honey . . . in the middle of a difficult year, it is God Himself, sending us a message . . . just like the rainbow with Noah . . . God is sooo good, Darlin'."

We all have memories of not-so-perfect Christmases, but Wanda's phone call relayed a powerful message, much bigger than our temporary disappointments.

Standing in the backyard with my family on a cold, crisp night, we set our eyes on the Christmas Star and considered Jesus's birth. There would be lonely times and empty seats ahead, but Wanda's words won out over all: "God is soooo good, Darlin'."

Father, Your signs sustain us. Your Messengers, like Wanda, make us strong.
—Brock Kidd

Digging Deeper: John 15:11; 1 John 1:5

Wednesday, December 20

I will hasten and not delay to obey your commands. —Psalm 119:60 (NIV)

I sat on the sofa, surrounded by boxes stacked like a stone wall. Our Victorian, after two-and-a-half years on the market, had sold. During that time we'd lived in our new home, but because it's smaller, we'd left boxes behind.

Now it was time to sort what we'd stored.

"What are you finding?" my husband, Lonny, asked as he sat down beside me.

"The boys' artwork," I said.

One of the creations was by our son, Samuel, the painter. This work of art was a decade old. In the center of blizzard white was a Christmas tree with a gold star. The rest of the canvas was peppered with brown squares.

"Presents?" Lonny asked.

"No, trunks," I said. "Samuel never painted the trees."

Lonny and I continued to sort, but my thoughts returned to those trunks. One night, long ago, I must've called a boy to dinner. Or maybe we went to a brother's basketball game. Maybe it was bedtime. For whatever reason, Samuel never returned to the trees. They were unfinished. Like a few things in my life.

There was a friend I needed to make peace with. The neighbor I said I'd look in on. Had I prayed for those who'd asked me to? Had I forgiven offenses or asked for forgiveness? Oh, the things I'd left undone.

Lonny put his hand on my knee. "What are you thinking?" he asked.

We've been married a long time. He didn't even look puzzled when I said, "It's time to paint trees."

Father, help me be obedient to finish good things that bring You glory.
—Shawnelle Eliasen

Digging Deeper: Nehemiah 6:15–16; Galatians 6:9; Colossians 3:23

Thursday, December 21

Bring a gift of laughter, sing yourselves into his presence.
—Psalm 100:2 (MSG)

I sighed as I fluffed the tissue paper inside the Christmas gift baskets that lined my kitchen counters. This past week, I'd been making goodies to give; some of them were the chunks of cheese that I cold-smoked to a mouthwatering flavor. Normally I loved Christmastime, but this year it seemed like something was missing.

My thoughts drifted as I tucked a couple chunks of cheese and packages of crackers in each basket. Although the baskets looked festive, it seemed as if normal everyday life had gotten to be so serious that the cheer-meter in my heart read "empty."

Next, I cut pieces of plastic wrap to package the bars of homemade goat-milk soap. On each caramel-colored bar, I stuck on a label that read "Goat Milk," then dropped one in each basket. Even after delivering them, which normally would have given me a lot of happiness, I trudged through the rest of the day rather downcast.

A couple days later, I received a call from one of my friends to whom I'd given a basket. We chatted a few minutes and then the tone of Mary's voice changed. "What was that caramel-colored bar in the basket?"

"Oh, that's goat-milk soap."

Mary laughed. "I thought it was goat-milk cheese, and I took a bite out of it. Everything else in the basket was edible." The two of us laughed so long that my cheer-meter became full.

Mary had given me the gift of laughter—it's what had been missing.

> *Lord, help me to remember to laugh while facing the*
> *seriousness of life. Amen.*
> —Rebecca Ondov

Digging Deeper: Job 8:21; Psalm 126:2–3

Friday, December 22

In his hand is the life of every creature and the breath of all mankind.
—Job 12:10 (NIV)

Heavy, slow-moving traffic, slushy roads. Not a parking space to be had. My shoulders clenched with tension. Two days before Christmas. There seemed be as much stress in the air as holiday cheer.

I was doing my last-minute shopping. I stopped first at a pet store so my golden, Gracie, could pick out a Christmas present for herself.

It's a small store that was made smaller by several other shoppers. The manager has a dog named Soma who's sometimes allowed to roam about. Now, there's a little history between Soma and Gracie. When Gracie was a puppy, Soma intimidated her a bit. Nothing serious. We'd been in there many times since and there was never a problem.

Until today. In the blink of an eye, they were fighting with all the attendant growling and snapping and flying drool. The manager and I finally got them separated.

Gracie added insult to injury by shoplifting her present as I dragged her outside. I had to toss it back in through the door and then get Gracie safely in the Jeep.

What got into my precious, peace-loving golden? Maybe it was me. My tension. My impatience. My stress. Dogs can feel their owner's feelings.

Now she was sleeping peacefully in back. I'd find her another present. She'd already given me mine. A reminder that Christmas isn't about last-minute stress and rushing around. It's about peace on earth. In our hearts, the only gift that matters.

> *Jesus, You lay as an infant in that manger in Bethlehem ready*
> *to give peace to all who would receive it. Let all hearts find*
> *peace, starting with mine.*
> —Edward Grinnan

Digging Deeper: Psalm 4:8; John 14:27

THE PINK HOUSE: Generous Gifts

And if any man . . . take away thy coat, let him have thy cloak also.
—Matthew 5:40 (KJV)

How many times has the pink house metaphor pointed me in the direction Jesus would have me go? It's impossible to say. I'll bet your life is no different, for don't we all have those signposts in the form of Bible verses or lessons taught to us in Sunday school or examples that a loved one has set, all guides that we have chosen to follow?

It's Christmas Eve and Brock has a big smile on his face as he hands me his special gift. As I open it, I'm a bit confused. "It's my coat, Mom. The best one I've ever had. I'm giving it to you, so you can have the pleasure of giving it to someone who needs a good, warm coat."

Happiness engulfs me, as my thoughts fly to Doug, this wonderful man who cooks for the homeless. I know he walks miles to work in the cold.

"Wow," I say, thinking to Brock's childhood, when he gave up a new coat as a gift to a friend without one, and how Keri has worked the last few weeks to deliver warm coats to over fifty children in need.

My children have become my pink houses.

And so, here's another truth for us to tuck in our travel bag as we make our way through life. Our pink houses, our markers that point to Jesus's ways, are contagious.

"What's in the bag?" I ask David, as he returns from an errand.

"Oh, I knew you were planning to deliver the coat to Doug today," he says, "so I picked up a hat, some gloves, a scarf, and a few more things."

Life is good in the Jesus lane, where pink houses keep popping up in unexpected places.

> *Father, thank You for those who show us the happiness*
> *that comes with Your way.*
> —Pam Kidd

Digging Deeper: Matthew 5:42; Acts 20:35

Fourth Sunday in Advent/Christmas Eve, December 24

A SIMPLE CHRISTMAS: Jesus's Free Gift

For if many died through one man's trespass, much more have the grace of God and the free gift by the grace of that one man Jesus Christ abounded for many. —Romans 5:15 (ESV)

Oyster stew. Gelatinous canned whole oysters floating around in a thick, fishy broth. This decadent meal (note: sarcasm most definitely intended) was the Christmas Eve tradition of my dad's family going back for generations.

When I was growing up, my mom always made it for my dad on Christmas Eve, along with a much tastier alternative of clam chowder. For some reason, I decided that my dad would be so impressed with me if I joined him in his oyster stew tradition.

And so I forced it down. Year after year, one blobby glob of oyster after another glugging down my throat as my face turned red in my effort not to gag. One year, as I watched my brother happily dipping his sourdough bread into his clam chowder, I started to cry.

"I want you to be impressed that I'm keeping your family tradition, but the oyster stew is just . . . gross!"

My dad hugged me. And then he said, "Erin, I love that you're trying to make me happy, but there is nothing you can do to make me love you more."

I felt visceral relief. My dad loved me just the same regardless of whether I ate clam chowder or gluggy oysters.

And Jesus is the same. Nothing I can do will make Him love me more. What a relief! What a blessing.

Jesus, thank You for loving me enough to give me the perfect gift. Today, on Christmas Eve, and every day.

—Erin MacPherson

Digging Deeper: Psalm 37:4; John 14:27

A SIMPLE CHRISTMAS: The Promise of God's Love

"The grass withers, and the flower falls, but the word of the Lord remains forever."—1 Peter 1:24–25 (ESV)

Something strange was going on.

The Christmas sweet rolls were already baking in the oven, Christmas carols were already playing on the Jambox, the coffee pot was already half empty . . . and the house was . . . silent.

I sat down on the couch and propped my feet up on the coffee table and stared at the twinkling Christmas lights, savoring both my coffee and the peaceful quiet.

For so many Christmases, I had been awakened before dawn to tiny feet racing down the stairs, to screams and giggles, to impatient moaning when I asked for just five minutes to make a cup of coffee.

But it turns out that teenagers don't like to wake up before dawn, even on Christmas. And so that morning, I savored a new season, a quiet morning, a bit of time to rest and revel in it all.

The kids did eventually get up (after 8 a.m., thank you very much) and the chaos eventually did ensue, but that quiet start to Christmas Day just set a tone for the day. A tone of peace, of gratitude, of hope.

A few hours later, my mom was quick to remind me that quiet Christmas mornings won't last long because before I know it there will be the pitter-patter of grandkids running down those stairs.

Seasons change, kids grow up, life changes, but the love of the Lord and the promise of Christmas is steadfast.

Always there, always waiting for us.

Regardless of whether we get up at 5 a.m. or 8 a.m. on Christmas morning.

Lord, thank You for Christmas, for Your love, and for the wonderful gift of Your son. I will treasure today, and every chaotic, joyful, peaceful moment that comes with it.
—Erin MacPherson

Digging Deeper: John 3:36; James 1:12

Tuesday, December 26

And the scroll of Isaiah the prophet was handed to Him. And He opened the scroll . . . —Luke 4:17 (NASB)

Our nineteen-year-old grandson was home for Christmas from his study and work commitment with a mission organization in Florida—a long way from our Pacific Northwest area. I knew he could use some cash when he returned in January. After purchasing a book I thought he'd like, I taped an assortment of ten-dollar bills among its pages. Wouldn't he be surprised!

Terry and I drove the seventy miles to drop off our packages ahead of Christmas. On Christmas morning, after Caleb's mom texted they had opened gifts, I heard nothing from him. When I finally phoned, I learned he'd gone back to sleep, having been awakened early by his younger siblings.

I wondered if he'd found his surprise. "Where?" she asked. I left instructions for him to take a second look at his book when he woke up. This time, it was a different story. When he first unwrapped the book, he'd only glanced at its cover, flipping it over to read the synopsis on the back. He hadn't delved inside to discover what was there.

He and I laughed over his near miss. I thought about it later in connection with another book—the Bible. I need to open my Bible—search inside—to find its treasure.

One of my favorite passages is Jeremiah 15:16 (NASB)—"Your words were found and I ate them, And Your words became for me a joy and the delight of my heart . . ." The Bible holds the words of eternal life. The good news of a Savior who offers love and forgiveness and comfort and courage.

Every page is filled with riches!

> *Lord God, keep me eagerly seeking the treasure in Your Book.*
> —Carol Knapp

Digging Deeper: Psalm 119:105; Romans 15:4; 2 Timothy 3:15–17

And when he [Herod] had gathered all the chief priests and scribes of the people together, he demanded of them where Christ should be born.
—Matthew 2:4 (KJV)

After the loss of my niece at Christmastime, a friend from my childhood chose not to send the standard sympathy card. Instead, Lillie baked a cake and mailed it to me. I've been known to linger over a colorful, well-crafted commercial greeting, but as much as I cherish receiving cards on special days, something about the effort and aroma of Lillie's mailed cake surpassed poetic words, reaching another level. Words matter, but the expression of Lillie's soul meant so much more.

Likely, some of the scribes of Matthew 2:4 were men whose aim was more to spew impressive words than to extol prophecy from the living God. Summoned by King Herod, they were relying upon a reservoir of knowledge to prove the expected circumstances of the Messiah's birth. Their goal was to satisfy the king. But the determined wise men, obviously not schooled in Jewish Scripture, were searching for Jesus. They sensed His unparalleled authority and sought to please *Him*. Without preaching to the king, they pointed him toward the end of all the scribes' knowledge-filled sayings, and had Herod's heart been open, he could have received the Living Word. Simply put, the Magi's quest was ultimately for worship, not a show of verbiage. Like Lillie, they offered a quiet door into joy not dependent upon lofty speech.

While many of us on earth are blessed with recorded Scripture, it is what's written on the tables of our hearts that helps us to help others. Whether with a well-chosen card or a luscious baked cake, when we're focused on God's assignment, we can speak from the wellsprings of caring concern.

> *Help me remember, Lord, that it is not pretty words but the condition of the heart that brings true comfort.*
> —Jacqueline F. Wheelock

Digging Deeper: Psalm 19:14, 119:11; Matthew 5:20, 6:7

Thursday, December 28

A LIFETIME OF LOVE: Journey toward Healing

Direct my footsteps according to your word . . . —Psalm 119:133 (NIV)

The 'firsts' are hard," my friend Joan said after my husband, Don, died, "but step back into your normal activities as soon as you feel ready." I'd admired her ability to move forward following her husband's death in a tragic accident, and I took her words to heart.

My first Sunday in church, I sat in the pew with tears running down my face. But I was surrounded by friends, many who cried with me, and it was comforting to be back. Next, I attended an outdoor birthday party for a friend celebrating her 103rd year. Five weeks after Don died, I traveled to Oklahoma for a wedding, followed by a birthday celebration for my sister-in-law Connie. I drove home on what would have been Don's eighty-second birthday. It was a lonely drive, but the evening was filled with phone calls and messages. The first funeral, the first time back teaching children's Sunday school, the first time to attend a play . . . each activity gave me confidence to move forward to the next one.

At Thanksgiving, I hosted our annual family dinner. I cried a bit when I sat in Don's place at the table and my oldest son offered the blessing, but the fellowship and fun outweighed the sadness. I played hymns for Christmas Eve service, just as I'd done for many years. The old year rang out in the home of dear friends—the same couples Don and I almost always spent New Year's Eve with. There were tears, but lots of happy memories as well. I was ready for the New Year to begin.

Heavenly Father, thank You for walking with me on my journey toward healing. I'm never alone because I have Your promise (Matthew 28:20 [NIV]): "And surely I am with you always, to the very end of the age."
—Penney Schwab

Digging Deeper: Proverbs 3:5–6; John 11:21–27

Be devoted to one another in love. Honor one another above yourselves.
—Romans 12:10 (NIV)

I love Christmas cards. I love to design them, send them, receive them, and even save my own in a scrapbook as a tiny diary of our family's years going by. When the Christmas season ends, I always find myself eager to remove the wilting tree and garland but find that I dally in pulling down the cards from our friends.

In years past, I would pick a day, pull them down, and, well, toss them in the recycling bin. It was sad, but there was no way for me to save nearly a hundred cards every year! Then, one of my kiddos suggested we keep them up for a little while longer.

"Momma," he said, "we can look at them while we're brushing our teeth and say a prayer for the people in the picture." Well, of course, we could! So now, what was once a few weeks-long decoration in our home has stretched into almost three months of nightly family fellowship. Those two minutes never fail to bring up old family stories that get us giggling as we remind them who the people in the cards are and how much they love them. Mostly, it gets us all in the right mindset before bedtime, a time we encourage our kids to use to dwell on Jesus, His love for them, and how we can share His love in the world.

Now, when cards arrive, I hang them up with a big smile because I know we'll enjoy them during the season, then use them as inspiration to pray for friends near and far after the holiday hustle and bustle has subsided.

Lord, thank You for the blessing of friends and family in my life. Call them to my mind often so that I may pray for them daily.
—Ashley Kappel

Digging Deeper: John 15:13; 1 Timothy 2:1, 5:8

Saturday, December 30

Fear not, for I am with you . . . —Isaiah 41:10 (ESV)

"Ten, nine, eight . . ." We counted aloud from the deck one brisk evening during New Year's Eve weekend, watching silhouettes of my husband and my brother against the moonlit snow in the back pasture. ". . . Three, two, one!" The fuse twinkled. A glowing dot thumped aloft . . . *boom!*

But that *boom* was far bigger than I'd anticipated. Innocently labeled "for backyard use," the fireworks proved to be professional-grade pyrotechnics! As the snow radiated the brilliant explosions of color, horses squealed and cattle bellowed around the valley. Hooves pounded in the semi-darkness as my horse, Jack, quit the country at full gallop. The dazzling and thunderous display went on for another twenty minutes to the whoops of delight from my family, but I was nearly sick with worry. *Please be okay,* I prayed for all the animals. My stomach knotted to think one of them had been injured in the stampede.

I sought out Jack, but he shied and bolted. My heart wrenched. Although unhurt, he didn't trust me. Hours later, I found him, a shadow merged among the pine trees in the snow. Still frothy and eyes rolling, he finally let me put a hand on his shoulder. I whispered, "It's okay. I'm here. There's no need to fear." Minutes went by. Slowly I felt the heat go out of him. His neck softened.

How often do I need that same reassurance that God is here, that I have no need to fear? Why did I let fear ruin the fireworks? I put my forehead against Jack's, and we stood together for the longest time. *Everything is okay.* "Praise God," I breathed aloud. Together, Jack and I left our fears in the shadows and stepped out into the moonlight.

Father God, You have never left my side. Of whom should I ever fear?
—Erika Bentsen

Digging Deeper: Deuteronomy 31:6; Jeremiah 1:8; Matthew 14:27

Blessed are those servants, whom the Lord when he cometh shall find watching . . . —Luke 12:37 (KJV)

I t's New Year's Eve. The phone is ringing. I am asleep.

I grab the phone. "Are you watching?" my mother asks as she did every year. "The ball is about to drop."

Somewhere along the way, I had lost my enthusiasm for New Year's celebrations.

We had some very about-town friends who, for some reason, adored David and me. Their yearly party was big news in Nashville, with lavish food and great entertainment. They always wanted us there, smiling for the photographer.

But as parents, we began finding excuses to stay home with Brock and Keri. A few bars of "Auld Lang Syne," party hats, sparkling cider, and then off to bed.

Our kids left home, and occasionally we accepted invitations for parties, but mostly we stayed home, where my mother's five-minutes-till-midnight calls became ritual: "Are you watching?"

And then she was gone.

How could she have known that she was creating a spiritual tradition? New Year's falls and I hear her voice: "Are you watching?" And I remember to pay attention.

The ball falls on Times Square. We have a brand-new year.

Are you watching? Are you embracing each day? Cherishing each moment with those you love? Finding new ways to make things better for others?

The year is new. Are you watching?

Father, help us remember on this day and every day to pay attention, to watch for every opportunity to do Your work and follow Your way.
—Pam Kidd

Digging Deeper: Isaiah 21:5; Colossians 4:2

December

LET US SING FOR JOY

1 _____

2 _____

3 _____

4 _____

5 _____

6 _____

7 _____

8 _____

9 _____

10 _____

11 _____

12 _____

13 _____

14 _____

15 _____

16 _____

17 _____

18 _____

19 _____

20 _____

21 _____

22 _____

23 _____

24 _____

25 _____

26 _____

27 _____

28 _____

29 _____

30 _____

31 _____

Fellowship Corner

As a teacher and student of God's Word, **Jerusha Agen** is awed by the letters of love the Father writes into every moment of our lives. Writing devotions is a special opportunity to sit down and focus her attention on these evidences of God at work. Jerusha loves to interweave such displays of God's providence into her suspense novels, too. Her stories are infused with the hope of salvation in Jesus Christ. When Jerusha isn't writing, you'll often find her sharing irresistibly adorable photos of her big furry dogs and little furry cats in her newsletter and on social media. Get a free suspense story from Jerusha and find more of her writing at jerushaagen.com.

This past year has been a time for discovering God's gifts closer to home for **Marci Alborghetti** and her husband, Charlie. Marci says, "The view of the seasons changing and Long Island Sound from our seventh-floor apartment is a constant prompt for us to be thankful and to realize how blessed we are to live near the water and on an active waterfront." They've taken many long drives and walks in southeastern Connecticut, visiting beaches, forts, a nearby naval base, and gardens. "We've been consciously and deliberately grateful for what God has put right in our backyard!"

"It was a good year for our family in many ways," writes **Julia Attaway** of New York City. "I took a new job last May that I absolutely love, and the kids are almost all grown." Stephen graduates from high school this spring, while Maggie is in nursing school, and Mary is in her last year of college. John and Elizabeth are both working. Her husband, Andrew, continues to audit college classes and walk the dog. "When I look back on the years of difficulties we faced," Julia says, "I still don't know how we got through it. But I strongly suspect the prayers of *Daily Guideposts/Walking in Grace* readers had a key role in helping us survive."

Evelyn Bence of Arlington, Virginia, writes, "In an odd way, I'm rather proud of my twenty-five-year-old car with its eighty-one thousand miles. It still serves me well, thanks to the temperate climate and my trusty mechanic, one among many supportive people in my community. A neighbor girl with special needs who befriended me a decade ago, now a teen, remains an energetic presence in my world. (She didn't move away after all.) She attends church with me, comes by after school, and is always asking keen questions. When we were reading a Narnia tale that introduced the phrase, she asked, 'Am I a Daughter of Eve?' Yes, you are! We both love music, I as a listener, she as a participant. Her favorite song, any season of the year? 'O Come All Ye Faithful.' A joyful praise."

Erika Bentsen is filled with praise this year as she and her husband, Randy, have found their church home. "I've worshipped on my own most of my adult life," she says, "especially when I ranched full time. We both felt God's call to join." Her greatest joy has been discovering a Bible study group with whom she connected right away. "I fell in love with these wonderful ladies the first day. I love the insight from every walk of life. I've learned so much because we all approach the same verse from a different perspective. I find it so refreshing and fulfilling. I already know what I think; I want to know what they think." Erika continues to illustrate children's books, writes for several agriculture publications, pastures cattle, and trail rides every chance she gets. "This year we took the horses and found the perfect Christmas tree. I brought it home across the horn on my saddle. I'm truly blessed to have a horse that will put up with just about anything!"

J. Brent Bill is a photographer, retreat leader, and Quaker minister. He's also the author of numerous books, including *Holy Silence: The Gift of Quaker Spirituality*; *Beauty, Truth, Life, and Love: Four Essentials of the Abundant Life*; and *Life Lessons from a Bad Quaker*.

Fellowship Corner

Bill is a graduate of Wilmington College and the Earlham School of Religion. He is recognized as one of the most important communicators of the spirituality of the Quaker tradition today. He is a member of *Spirituality & Practice*'s "Living Spiritual Teachers Project." Of Bill's writing, one reviewer said that he's ". . . a substantial spiritual guide, but never in a flashy way. Think of—oh, perhaps something like Mister Rogers meets the Dalai Lama."

He has been a local church pastor, a denominational executive, and a seminary faculty member. He lives on Ploughshares Farm, about fifty acres of former Indiana farmland being converted into tall grass prairie and native hardwood forests.

"I must have been in a state of heightened awareness this past year," says **Rhoda Blecker** of Bellingham, Washington. "I kept getting God messages at the most unexpected times. Like when I had a flat tire and encountered three good Samaritans who offered to change the tire for me— and it turned out that they had been on the pit crew for a NASCAR/Formula One championship driver. They did a great job, by the way. Or the time I was looking for a prayer to suggest to one of my directees, found one that I hoped would do—only to have the directee pose a question for which the prayer, which I had not yet offered, was a perfect answer. Stuff like that happened all the time, and it always took me by surprise with a jolt of recognition. I knew I had better be on my best behavior, because it was very clear that God was watching closely!"

Sabra Ciancanelli of Tivoli, New York, writes, "This year my oldest began college, my role at work shifted, and we weathered a few storms here and there—all leading me to reflect on the power of surrendering to the present moment. Something miraculous happens when I stop trying to force what I want and accept the present—letting go of my investment in the outcome and truly experiencing the grace of now. My sister, Maria, used to say that she was comfortable in her harness, and it took me a long time to really embrace her attitude as my own, to find comfort in my life's work and peace on the journey."

"I'm scheduled for another knee surgery," muses **Mark Collins** of Pittsburgh, Pennsylvania, "but I'm starting to run out of knees. The surgeon asked if I 'had any faith' left in my joints. I told him, 'No. And it doesn't stop there.'" Fortunately, Mark's rickety pins are buttressed by his blessedly grounded wife, Sandee, and three grown daughters. "My kids may be a bit unsteady themselves as they navigate the roiling waters of young adulthood, but luckily Hope floats—and so do her sisters, Faith and Grace. And it doesn't stop there."

"One of the great benefits of living in the Sunshine State is that family and friends love visiting us," says **Pablo Diaz**. "And my wife, Elba, and I enjoy hosting and spending quality time with our guests. There is no rush and lots of opportunities for meaningful conversations. We catch up on the past, learn what is new, and talk about the future. These moments allow for deepening our friendships and relationships. It's also fun taking friends to our favorite restaurants, beaches, and towns. We are creating lifetime memories filled with meaning, love, and laughter. When our guests leave, we stay connected via FaceTime and Zoom. As time passes, we have a greater appreciation for every minute we can get with loved ones and friends."

"My wife, Pat, and I didn't travel this year other than to spend weekends at a lake place we have about an hour's drive away," says **John Dilworth**. "We started a new family tradition of weekly FaceTime dinners with our son, Johnny, who lives in Virginia. It all began one night when we shared a pizza supper together. Soon Pat and Johnny were busy planning something for the next week. He would pick the menu one week; she would choose for the next week. Each week's menu got more elaborate. I enjoyed whatever they chose. We all had a lot of fun, and we've had more family meals together this year than since Johnny graduated from college. In the evenings, we've enjoyed watching all the past seasons of several of our favorite TV shows like *Blue Bloods* and *Chicago Fire* beginning with the pilot episode. Nice walks with our dog, Skipper, beautiful days, gorgeous sunrises, and spectacular sunsets have made living *simply* this year special! All is well. And for that we are richly blessed!"

"This year has been full of plot twists," says **Logan Eliasen** of Port Byron, Illinois. "Some were exciting. Others were frustrating. Through it all, I've come to better appreciate God's constant and consistent love. I'm grateful that His provision is not dependent on my expectations. And I'm thankful that He is a firm foundation in a world of uncertainties."

"The past couple of years have brought many changes for our family," says **Shawnelle Eliasen** of LeClaire, Iowa. "This year kept us on that path. The house we raised our boys in finally sold. One son went to public high school after a childhood of home learning. Another boy went to college. Many things about our home have changed. But the Lord is right in the center of those changes. He's brought courage and strength and peace and joy! It's during these times of letting go that I'm learning to lean into Him more and more. I'm walking new terrain, but the Lord never leaves me to walk alone." Shawnelle has found delight in new things the Lord has brought. A new puppy for one son. A new garden. New friendships. New ways to serve others. And a back porch that almost breaks at the seams when everyone is home and gathered. "Lonny and I are growing closer during these changes, too," Shawnelle says. "God is good."

"I'm still privileged to be the senior pastor at Pathway Church in Redding, California," says **Bill Giovannetti** of Santa Rosa, California. In addition, Bill has started an online graduate school for everyday Bible scholars called Veritas School of Biblical Ministry at veritasschool.life. Bill's wife, Margi, continues to serve with him at church, and both of their kids are in Christian colleges. Life with God is blessed.

"Every few years, I remind you good readers that these back-of-book bios are written well in advance of publication," says **Edward Grinnan** of New York, New York. "Certainly, I could tell you about the challenges and blessings of my life as I write this today, but maybe a better exercise would be to share the prayers I hope have been answered by the time you read this, a kind of future prayer list: that Gracie, our beloved golden retriever, is still well and active and acts more like a puppy than an elder dog (she's six now); that Julee's health—and back—remains strong and her spirit uplifted; that my book on Alzheimer's is ready—or almost ready—to help people in their own struggles; that the world is more healed and peaceful than it is today; and that all of you find the love and peace of God everywhere you seek it. Oh, and the Yankees win one more World Series in my lifetime." Edward is Editor-in-Chief of *Guideposts* magazine and Vice President of Strategic Content Development.

What a fine year it's been for **Rick Hamlin** and his wife, Carol, of New York, New York. This year, they've experienced the birth of not just one but two grandsons. The first to arrive, baby Silas, is the offspring of their son Tim and his wife, Henley. Tim is a full-time student at Union Seminary, and he and Henley live only half a block away, giving Rick and Carol plenty of babysitting opportunities. On the other coast, Will and his wife, Karen, will give birth to their son in December. "We look forward to meeting that baby for Christmas. The name they've chosen? Same as me—what an honor," says Rick. Carol's newest novel, *Our Kind of People*, will be released in January. Rick's new book, *Even Silence Is Praise*, on the power of meditative prayer, will be published in February.

Lynne Hartke often hears the Sonoran Desert, where she lives, described as a desolate, godforsaken place. At one time, Lynne would have agreed with that statement. But after three decades of exploring desert trails with her husband, Kevin, and rust-colored mutt named Mollie, Lynne has encountered the beauty found in barren places, a beauty enjoyed by the couple's four grown children and four grandchildren. A pastor's wife and breast cancer survivor, Lynne receives inspiration from other survivors at the cancer organizations where she volunteers. She is looking forward to more adventures near the hundred-year-old cabin they purchased in an old-growth forest in northern Arizona. She is the author of *Under a Desert Sky: Redefining Hope, Beauty, and Faith in the Hardest Places.* Connect with her at lynnehartke.com.

"The one thing that remains constant in the Hendricks household is change," says **Carla Hendricks** of Franklin, Tennessee. "When God wants me to grow spiritually, I think He just throws in a major life transition or two." Her most recent transition took place a few months ago when she began a new role at CASA, a national organization that advocates for abused and neglected children. She spends her days using her voice to speak for foster youth in juvenile court with judges, attorneys, and state social workers. She spends her evenings and weekends pursuing her lifelong love of writing and enjoying movie nights and Costco meals with her husband, Anthony, and their four children, who seemingly change with the days. One constant in Carla's ever-evolving life is the much-appreciated opportunity to share her God moments and life lessons with *Daily Guideposts/Walking in Grace* readers each year.

"With so much turmoil in the world, I try to focus on simple daily joys," says **Kim Taylor Henry**. "There are so many—like watching the sunrise, my morning coffee and quiet time, working through my to-do list, taking a walk, playing foosball and ping-pong with my husband, watching hummingbirds whir at our feeders, eating dark-chocolate chips, picking out pillows for our deck chairs, and even going to the grocery store. A huge blessing was added to our lives with the birth of our seventh grandchild—Emersyn Taylor Jones, 'Emma,' born to our daughter Lauren and son-in-law Chris. She and all our grandchildren bring me abundant joy. Though we spend quite a bit of time together, I can never get enough of them. I'm trying to become more like they are—full of enthusiasm, wonder, eagerness, adventure, and energy. (The energy part is becoming more difficult, but I try!) A big thank you to every reader who has reached out to me by email. I love hearing from you and getting to know you. If you haven't already, please visit my website at kimtaylorhenry.com and/or send me a note at kim@kimtaylorhenry.com.

Leanne Jackson of Fishers, Indiana, praises God for a year without major changes or crises. "We're thankful that my husband Dave's tumors are stable. They cause unpredictable abdominal pain, which makes him grateful to be retired. He takes pain meds and rests, then resumes biking, golfing, or playing violin. I get to write, quilt, and garden. Another passion is tackling food waste and hunger; every week I pick up unsold bagels and deliver them to a food pantry." She looks forward to meeting you at leannejacksonwrites.com.

"This summer, we welcomed my husband Jim's parents to Montana," says **Erin Janoso**. "They'd lived in the same house in Allentown, Pennsylvania, for fifty-plus years, but—with all of their children and grandchildren living west of the Mississippi, they decided it was time to finally make a move. They bought a house neighboring our property in Roundup and have stayed busy unpacking and settling into their new community. It has been decades since we've had the privilege of living close to family, and we are so excited for the blessing of more time together. As for our little family of three, Jim, Aurora, and I continue to split our time between two states: Montana in the summer and Alaska in the winter. Aurora's enjoying homeschool second grade. Jim's microscope sales and service business is thriving. And I continue to love spending time on music and my writing. Life is good, and I am so very grateful."

Ashley Kappel is a big believer that you get out what you put in. This year, she's been focused on filling herself, her work, and her family with praise for Jesus, praying on the way to school, putting on praise music while calling out homework, and being verbally thankful for every blessing of God's she can see, from sunsets to fireflies. Ashley lives in Birmingham, Alabama, with her three kids, her amazing husband, Brian, and her lovable golden retriever rescue, Colby. When not writing for *Daily Guideposts/Walking*

in Grace, she works in food media, loves taking walks with Brian, and is desperate to teach her kids to play tennis so they can enjoy the neighborhood court. She asks for your prayers that her days be filled with joy and praise, even amidst hardships. She prays the same for you and your families.

Jenny Lynn Keller is an award-winning author who transforms her family's rowdy adventures into stories filled with hope, humor, love, and plenty of Southern charm. On her website jennylynnkeller.com, she highlights Southern folklore and places of interest through her weekly blog. Follow her on facebook.com/jennylynnkeller. Her animal stories appear in Callie Smith Grant's *The Horse of My Dreams, The Dog Who Came to Christmas,* and *The Cat in the Christmas Tree.*

"When I think over this past year, much of it was summed up by a comment made by my younger daughter, Ella Grace," reports **Brock Kidd** from Nashville, Tennessee. "My family was all together on Weiss Lake, and a glorious sunset unfolded right in front of us. Ella Grace shouted with pure joy, 'Daddy, look what God made for us!' I smiled at my wife, Corinne, and in that moment, we all realized how blessed we were." Brock continues to enjoy his career in wealth management and remains very proud of their sons, Harrison and little David, as well as their oldest daughter, Mary Katherine.

"When our children were young, my mother sent me a poignant poem about a mother who lived in regret of not stopping to watch her children when they called," says **Pam Kidd**. "I no longer have the poem, but the message seared itself into my days. 'Watch, Momma,' Brock or Keri would call, and I would remember. Stop. Watch. Today, I hold on to my mother's message. There is so much to see in the world. When I wake up each morning, there's a sunrise . . . and trees outside my window, in some season of growth. Later, over coffee with my husband, David, there are birds flocking to the feeder, then the beauty of grains and nuts and berries as I prepare breakfast. 'Watch,' don't miss the morning. Don't miss noon, with people who come and go, falling rain, sunshine, sunset and dusk, the velvet night. Stop. Watch. I watch with pride as our children go through their days, and our grandchildren, well, watching them is a constant delight. I've found that the more I watch, the more I see and the more I want to see. Here's the truth: The world is full of wonder if we just remember to 'Watch.'"

Patty Kirk taught remote summer courses for the first time ever in addition to her regular course load, resulting in a year of uninterrupted teaching. She also worked on writing a book. Ankle injuries curtailed her running. To avoid sitting at her computer constantly, she helped research an Oklahoma bird breeding atlas by biking regularly through two assigned segments of her county, counting every bird she encountered. Her husband, Kris, raised the beds in her garden an additional foot and added a third raised bed, so now it's in the best shape it's ever been in. Her daughter, Charlotte, moved home for several months with her husband, Reuben, and their beagle, Milo. Reuben taught Patty and Kris how to cook smash burgers, birria tacos, and several Indian dishes, as well as how to play disc golf. To everyone's relief, Milo, a well-behaved and docile indoor dog, got on splendidly with Patty and Kris's rowdier farm dogs, Sawyer and Karl. In matters spiritual, Patty consciously practiced obedience as a spiritual discipline that she had previously preferred to avoid, and it has blessed her in many ways. It has been, in all, a taxing but rewarding year.

"I have a favorite proverb," says **Carol Knapp** of Priest River, Idaho. "The cheerful heart has a continual feast" (Proverbs 15:15). A heart filled with praise brings joy to Carol and others . . . and serves Christ. This year has been the summer of family, amid record-setting heat for north Idaho. Carol and family gathered for her husband Terry's surprise seventieth birthday—their four children and many of their twenty grandchildren were in attendance. Two Alaska grandkids spent five weeks with Carol and Terry— fourteen-year-old David even contributed to Carol's weekly newspaper column.

Fellowship Corner

Carol and Terry drove to Ocean Shores, Washington, with their Minneapolis grandkids and their mother for time on the beach with Terry's sister. Carol and Terry's new-to-them travel trailer took them camping to their favorite spot—where Carol praised God for His stunning rainbow that seemed to rise from the lake—and the cloud of swallowtail butterflies on the beach. And, yes, for their eleven-year-old granddaughter, Natalia, winning twelve in a row in their dice games! Carol loves finding praise in family, in nature, in writing, and in all the myriad ways God appears for His good in her life.

Carol Kuykendall says, "'Filled with Praise' is the theme of this book, which nudges me to think about some praises that currently fill me: ten grandkids (and their parents), who live close enough for spontaneous family gatherings; Zeke, a puppy who's become a two-year-old dog that mostly comes when called; the beauty of the Rocky Mountains that we see from our windows every day. I especially like watching how the storm clouds come and go, yet the rock-solid mountains never budge, which makes me praise God for His creation. Praise for stable health for both my husband, Lynn, and me. A new praise is for the prayer class I agreed to teach this year at our church, which forced me to practice praying and learn how to be still and listen to God. That made me realize I'm used to doing all the talking in my prayers. I also praise God for the ministry of MOPS, where I'm a mentor, encouraging young moms, like my recent talk on 'How Mothering Grows Us Up.' I also praise God for all the faithful *Daily Guideposts/Walking in Grace* readers who connect with us."

"For more than thirty years, when people asked me 'What do you do?' I'd reply that I was a writer," says **Vicki Kuyper**. "Writing over fifty books, including *Wonderlust: A Spiritual Travelogue for the Adventurous Soul* and *A Tale of Two Biddies (A New Wrinkle on Aging with Grace)*, has been a true joy in my life. But seasons change, and so has my job title! With the birth of my fifth grandchild, I became an official Granny Nanny. I now spend several days a week caring for baby Taylor, as well as for her elementary-school-age sisters, Lula and Shea. I spend less time writing and more time snuggling, which is a pretty good trade-off. Of course, writing for *Daily Guideposts/Walking in Grace* continues to be part of my abbreviated freelance schedule. I so enjoy putting into words the ways I see God working in my life throughout the year. It's like keeping a very public journal. Having the opportunity to share my firsthand experiences with other members of the Guideposts family serves as a daily reminder to keep my eyes and heart open, expectantly ready to catch a glimpse of God's presence."

"As I navigate my way through the last half of my seventies, I am astounded at how the struggles of life affect everyone so differently," says **Patricia Lorenz**. "A few years ago, my youngest son, Andrew, who was suffering with physical and emotional problems, accused me of having an unrealistic Pollyanna attitude about life. Perhaps I do, but I honestly believe the sun is always shining above the clouds. I've seen it! When I fly to visit my children or to see the world, the sun does shine brightly above the clouds when flying at 35,000 feet. I've seen it when things go wonky in my life, and I've made lemonade out of turnips by holding tightly onto my faith with both hands. I also believe that all the struggles that come with aging or the problems my four children face in their forties and fifties are one of two things: blessings in disguise or lessons to be learned. So here in Florida, I continue to swim daily, volunteer at the airport, and rely on the kindness of good friends and neighbors to keep me entertained and interested in all that life offers. Most of all, I love my struggles, because they bring me so many good life lessons."

Debbie Macomber is a #1 *New York Times* bestselling author and one of today's most popular writers, with more than 200 million copies of her books in print worldwide. In addition to fiction, Macomber has also published three bestselling cookbooks, an adult coloring book, numerous inspirational and nonfiction works, and two acclaimed children's books.

Celebrated as "the official storyteller of Christmas," Macomber's annual Christmas books are beloved and five have been crafted into original Hallmark Channel movies.

She serves on the Guideposts National Advisory Cabinet, is a YFC National Ambassador, and is World Vision's international spokesperson for their Knit for

Kids charity initiative. A devoted grandmother, Debbie and her husband, Wayne, live in Port Orchard, Washington, the town that inspired the Cedar Cove series.

Erin MacPherson is a multi-published author (with ten books in print), a wife, an artist, an amateur chef, and mom to three kids, including one newly licensed driver. With teenagers in the house (not to mention on the road!), she has learned that pressing toward God every day and every hour is the one and only way to find peace and contentment. Erin lives in Austin, Texas, where the sun (and the salsa) are always hot. Connect with her online at christianmamasguide.com.

Tia McCollors is a simple woman. It doesn't take much to make her happy—Mexican food, fresh flowers for the kitchen table, a rainy day watching movies, and the chance to escape into the world of a new novel she's writing top the list. "It's hard to believe this is my fourth year as a *Daily Guideposts/Walking in Grace* contributor. I wasn't sure how long I was invited to be on the ride, but I'm so incredibly blessed that each year I enter into your home to share a little slice of my life. Guideposts has now become a permanent part of my home. I place them in several rooms so my family can enjoy the devotions any time of day or so guests can thumb through them and get hooked." Tia expresses her creative side through writing, speaking, and trying new recipes and DIY projects that she finds on Pinterest. You can connect with Tia online at tiamccollors.com, through her "Fans of Tia" Facebook page, or follow her on Instagram @TMcCollors.

Psalm 95:2 (NIV), "Let us come before him with thanksgiving and extol him with music and song," was especially meaningful for **Roberta Messner** this past year when she gave her beloved baby grand piano away. "My hands had long been weak from a medication side effect," she says. "Despite rehab, I never regained strength or fine motor coordination." Roberta was delivered from a lifetime of chronic pain and dependence on prescription opioids during Easter week 2018 at her friend Sue's home (*Daily*

Guideposts/Walking in Grace series, 2021). "Sue was downstairs playing the age-old hymn, 'He Arose,' when from my bed I heard a weak voice singing along. That someone was totally pain-free . . . me!" The piano was meant for Sue, "who played better than I ever did anyway," says Roberta. She recalls that the day it changed residences was one of the best days of her life. "When neighbors wondered what the moving truck was all about, I got to share about the miracle and the music one more time." A story and song of praise that will never end.

Gabrielle Meyer grew up above a carriage house on a historic estate near the banks of the Mississippi River. Her father was the caretaker and her mother homeschooled her and her siblings. Her parents instilled in her a deep faith and appreciation for family. Gabrielle went on to work for the Minnesota Historical Society, where she fell in love with the rich history of her state and began writing fiction and nonfiction inspired by real people, places, and events. She currently resides in central Minnesota on the banks of the upper Mississippi River, not far from where she grew up, with her husband and four children, including teenage daughters and ten-year-old twin boys. By day, she's a homeschool mom and a small business owner, and by night, she pens fiction and nonfiction filled with hope. Her work currently includes historical and contemporary romances, cozy mysteries, and home and family articles. You can learn more about Gabrielle and her writing by visiting gabriellemeyer.com.

"Celebrate is my word for this year," says **Rebecca Ondov** of Hamilton, Montana. "As the difficulties of the past few years have increased, I've found a need to focus on the faithfulness of God and the beauty He created around me. By doing this, God becomes so big and so real that He overshadows everything I'm facing. Living in praise to Him creates peace in me." Rebecca's life is filled to the brim between her menagerie of a cat, chickens, dogs, a horse, and a mule; her job; and farming her little hayfield, as well as finishing the landscaping around her house. On evenings and weekends, you can find her basking in His presence in her rose garden, kayaking a high mountain lake, or horseback riding in the Rocky

Fellowship Corner

Mountains with Willow, her German shepherd, trotting by her side. Rebecca invites you to connect with her by going to her website, rebeccaondov.com, to learn where to find her on social media.

Shirley Raye Redmond has sold articles to such publications as *Focus on the Family Magazine, Home Life, The Christian Standard,* and *Chicken Soup for the Soul's Touched by an Angel* edition. Her devotions have appeared in multiple volumes of Guideposts' *All God's Creatures* and *Daily Guideposts/Walking in Grace.* Her children's book, *Courageous World Changers: 50 True Stories of Daring Women of God* (Harvest House) won the 2021 Christianity Today Book Award in the Children & Youth category. The companion title, *Brave Heroes and Bold Defenders: 50 True Stories of Daring Men of God,* was released in October 2020. She has been married for forty-seven years to her college sweetheart. They live in the lovely mountains of northern New Mexico and are blessed with two children and several grandchildren, who all live nearby, which makes for festive Sunday dinners after church services!

Ginger Rue is trying really hard not to nag her kids. "They are all eighteen and over now, and of course, I am positive I know what is best for all three of them," she says. "It's so hard to let them make their own mistakes. I have to remind myself that God is in control, not me. Thankfully, my husband, Dwight, is such a calming presence, and he reminds me to step back and let our children figure things out for themselves. And I'm lucky to have my dog, Cookie. She's become my outlet for my need to be a caregiver!"

"This has been a year of gratitude, renewal, spiritual deepening, and risk," says **Kenneth Sampson**. "My wife Kate's six-month cardiologist visits, to monitor effects of open-heart surgery two years ago, continue to bring good results. This time of restricted travel is calming. Kate and I enjoy a sense of renewed appreciation and tenderness not unlike our first years of marriage while at Southern Normal School, Brewton, Alabama. A real gift. I've taken up piano practice after a hiatus of sixty years and enjoy playing hymns, spirituals, and Taizé songs. Especially enriching has been facilitating weekly Cornwall Presbyterian Church Zoom book studies on *Paul: A Biography* and *Jesus: A Pilgrimage*. Lastly, I'm participating for the first time in spiritual direction with Brother Randy of nearby Holy Cross Monastery. In the times of direction, and reflection after, I feel tethered to the community of monks who pray following the Rule of St. Benedict. In all, I'm exceptionally blessed and grateful—all praise to our loving God."

Dan Schantz and his wife, Sharon, continue to enjoy their retirement, taking many day trips, which cost little, require no packing, and enable them to sleep in their own bed at night. Because of a series of surgeries, Dan has not been able to ride his bicycle all summer, and that is the "unkindest cut of all." Daughters Teresa and Natalie are doing legal work now that their children are grown. Natalie works for a prosecuting attorney. Teresa is courtroom deputy for a U.S. magistrate in Kansas City. Dan's granddaughters are married but have no children yet. His grandsons are still schooling and working. Dan is trying some new trees: Stanley plums, sassafras, and purple robe locusts. Working out in nature, he sees the glories of God up close and often pauses to give praise to the Creator.

"My morning devotions begin by praising God, often wordlessly, as I admire dawn and the splendor of the skies," writes **Gail Thorell Schilling** of Concord, New Hampshire. "Other times, I praise in song." Gail continues to serve on her church's hospitality team to bring comfort food to those unwell or unable to cook for themselves. "Even though I live alone, I can still cook for a crowd—and feel very appreciated." Her mulligatawny (chicken curry) soup and lemon tartlets are big hits. Recently, Gail rediscovered the joys of sewing when she created porch pillows for her daughter's family. She continues to knit for her grandchildren and learned a new color technique on a Windjammer knitting cruise. Her popular memoir-writing courses help women of a *certain age* to find their voices and to honor their stories. Prompts on her website gailthorellschilling.com help jump-start first drafts. She would love to hear about your writing projects.

Fellowship Corner

"My journey as a single person continues," writes **Penney Schwab** of Copeland, Kansas. "God, family, and friends have provided practical help, comfort, and company to ease my transition into a new way of life. I still live on the farm and have learned to handle many chores my husband, Don, did prior to his death. My son Patrick, his wife, Patricia, grandson Mark, and daughter Rebecca all live less than an hour away, so we visit often. My grandson David and wife, Robyn, are in San Diego, and the rest of my children and grandchildren live in Colorado. My grandson Caden graduated from high school, leaving Naomee the only grandchild still at home. I'm part of an active church and assist with our children's after-school program; serve as a substitute Sunday school teacher; and occasionally play the organ for worship. Blessings flow, and I can wholeheartedly come before the Lord 'with thanksgiving and extol him with music and song' (Psalm 95:2 [NIV])."

"It's no secret the world as we know it has been turned on its head over the last couple of years," says **Buck Storm**. "But I have to say: Life at the Storm compound, as challenging as it can be, is pretty wonderful. Surrounded by the laughter of new grandchildren and constant music, my wife, Michelle, and I count our blessings every hour. This year, the days have been spent working on the third book in my *Ballads of Paradise* series for Kregel Publications. If I close my eyes, I most likely couldn't tell you what I'm wearing, and if you want to know what month or day of the week it is, you'd probably have to ask someone else. Yes, life is good. Thank you, Jesus . . ." Buck Storm is a critically acclaimed literary fiction author, musician, and traveler. His books and songs have made friends around the world.

Jolynda Strandberg serves as a director of religious education who has spent twenty-four years as a civilian with the military. She and her family currently reside in Clarksville, Tennessee. She is also a proud wife and mom to three children, ages twenty-eight, eleven, and seven. This past year, the Lord has blessed the family with the opportunity to start homeschooling their two youngest children.

Jon M. Sweeney is a writer and book editor who lives with his wife, daughters, and cats in Milwaukee, Wisconsin. In the past year, Jon had a short biography of Thomas Merton published, as well as another installment in his series of books for children about a fictional pope and his cat, Margaret. Jon has worked remotely for almost twenty years, but this past year he was delighted to have his wife working from home, too. They were able to spend a lot more time together.

Our 2023 *Daily Guideposts/Walking in Grace* theme, "Filled with Praise," inspired **Stephanie Thompson** to write about a few of her best-loved hymns. "The churches I grew up in during the '60s and '70s predominately used hymns in their services. Our family attended Sunday mornings, Sunday evenings, and Wednesday evenings, so sacred songs became etched in my memory. Twenty years ago, I married and formed a family of my own. Our church used an overhead projector instead of hymnals and a praise band instead of an organist. I didn't realize how much I missed the hymns I sang in my youth until I joined BSF (Bible Study Fellowship). We opened our hymnals before weekly lectures, in leaders' meetings, and in the children's program. I might have hidden those hymns in my heart decades earlier, but their meaning is so much richer for me today." Stephanie; husband, Michael; and daughter, Micah, live in an Oklahoma City suburb with Missy, a schweenie (shih tzu/dachshund mix), and a tuxedo cat named Mr. Whiskers. They recently added an orange tabby, Ron (Ronald Weasley Swanson, named by Micah), so Micah could have a kitten to raise and love after their beloved twelve-year-old pug, Princess, passed over the rainbow bridge a year earlier.

"My husband, Chuck, and I praise God for the long-awaited move of our grandson, Logan, from our home into his father's," says **Marilyn Turk** of Niceville, Florida. "Although the transition has been one of adjustments, Logan is very happy, having looked forward to this move for years. Chuck and I are still adapting to our empty-again nest, learning how to be real grandparents to Logan instead of surrogate parents. And Chuck has finally agreed to have a golden retriever! Now, we're raising our puppy, Dolly, and looking forward to her traveling with us in our RV as we visit our other grandchildren in Connecticut, seeing lighthouses along the way." Marilyn stays busy writing from their home in Florida. Her first split-time novel, *Abigail's Secret,* was recently published, along with more novellas. *Not My Party* is her first contemporary novella, loosely based on the story of how she and Chuck found each other later in life.

"I've been in denial for years," says **Karen Valentin** of New York, New York. "My parents are not that old, my father's dementia is not that bad, they're not leaving me any time soon. As I spend a few weeks with my parents this time around, I know the years of denial are over. Facing it is incredibly painful but surprisingly beautiful as well. I soak in each moment like never before as I nestle my head on my father's shoulder or sing with my mother in the car. I savor the laughter and conversation as my mother and I prepare dinner and treasure each Spanish word my father says as he prays over our meal. Those long prayers before dinner used to frustrate me, but now I wish they were just a little bit longer. As this season nears its end, I'm incredibly thankful for the many years I've been blessed to be their daughter and equally thankful for every second together we have left."

"This year the moment finally came," says **Scott Walker** of Macon, Georgia. "I officially entered retirement. I look back on thirty-five years of being a pastor, twelve years a university professor, and amidst those years the joy of being a writer, a husband, a father, and a grandfather. Now I face a new chapter and experience the feelings of anticipation and thanksgiving mixed with some grief and anxiety. Life never stands still. But God is always with us, opening doors as we close doors, ushering us to new beginnings as we bring chapters to conclusion. We hear God's voice exclaim, 'The best is yet to be!' Along these years, the Guideposts family has been very important to me. I am delighted that we will continue to walk life's pathway together. Most of us have never met, but we will meet in the 'time beyond time' and realize that God has always been in our midst. I rejoice and take courage in our continuing journey together!"

Fellowship Corner

Jacqueline F. Wheelock writes, "Having grown up in a tiny community in coastal Mississippi, I recall the numerous summer nights spent staring at bits of the moon through the leaves of live oak trees. Though I was always a dreamer, the possibility of becoming a published author never entered my thoughts. Yet, through what could appear to the human eye as a maze of circumstances, in 2014 I published my first novel. Now, years later, I cannot help but remember with humility that God's thoughts are not mine; neither are His ways, evidenced in the sweet memories He forged for me last Christmas as the family gathered in Tybee Island, Georgia—another reminder that, with Him, possibilities are limitless." The mother of two adult children and the grandmother of two granddaughters, Jacqueline treasures her years spent in the company of her husband.

Gayle T. Williams is a native New Yorker, now living in the city's suburbs with her husband, Terry, and rescue cat, Solomon. She has two adult sons and is a faithful member of New York Covenant Church in New Rochelle, New York. While she has covered a variety of exciting and interesting news topics as a reporter, writer, and editor for magazines and newspapers for the past thirty years, it's her work for Guideposts that truly feeds her soul. Still a news junkie, she enjoys a good crossword puzzle, all kinds of games that expand her vocabulary, and public radio programming. She and Terry initially bonded over a variety of music thirty-five years ago, and it still fuels their marriage. She is honored to be able to share God's blessing upon her life with the dedicated readers of *Walking in Grace*.

SCRIPTURE REFERENCE INDEX

AUTHORS, TITLES, AND SUBJECTS INDEX

Authors, Titles, and Subjects Index

Authors, Titles, and Subjects Index